Mary J. McCormick

Herod's Temple

PATTERN DIVINE

or

Our Lord's Hidden Life

BY

Patrick J. Temple, S.T.D.

B. HERDER BOOK CO.
15 & 17 SOUTH BROADWAY, ST. LOUIS 2, MO.
AND
33 QUEEN SQUARE, LONDON, W. C.
1950

Vail-Ballou Press, Inc., Binghamton and New York

Foreword

By Very Reverend Jacques M. Vosté, O.P.
Secretary of the Pontifical Biblical Commission

NEVER does God appear so lovable and so great as when He abases Himself. In His condescending lowering of self He gives us more abundant proofs of His infinite mercy; and nothing draws us to Him as much as this manifestation of His merciful love. Here is to be found the supreme teaching of the hidden life of the incarnate Word. The Word, the Son of God, becomes man: He becomes little in order to raise us up to His divinity, to bestow sonship on us by adoption, and to teach us by His example how to realize in ourselves the perfection of our Father who is in heaven.

This revelation of the hidden life of Jesus is not proclaimed in mighty words of wisdom nor in arresting displays of omnipotence nor even in the heroism of suffering, but in silence, humility, labor, and obedience. Are not these precisely the virtues that make for true greatness of character and for real Christian holiness? But alas! are not these the very virtues that are so conspicuously missing in our modern civilization, in which the atmosphere rather is that of overweening pride of intellect, luxury, sensual indulgence, and the abuse of liberty even unto license? Every real Christian and every sensible man should desire a return to the hidden life of the Son of God made man, who brought about at Nazareth in His humble labor and patient submission the perfection and glory of His heavenly Father. For St. Augustine has expressed this Christian ideal in a saying that is as profound as it is concise: "Quia ipse Christus Verbum Dei est, etiam factum Verbi verbum nobis est" ("Because Christ Himself is the Word of God, the work of the Word is also a word to us," that is a lesson and an example).[1]

That is what impelled Father Patrick J. Temple to make a specialized study of the hidden life of our Lord, and now induced him after twenty-five years of study and experience in the ministry to produce this present work entitled, *Pattern Divine, or Our Lord's Hidden Life*. In 1922 he presented to the Faculty of Theology at the Catholic University in Washington a thesis on *The Boyhood Consciousness of Christ*, for which he received the degree of Doctor of Theology. Since then he has continued to examine the life of Jesus at Nazareth in all its aspects. His modesty does not permit me to say how much that study has inspired, directed, and molded him, but he would readily acknowledge that the contemplation of Jesus, the Child and the Worker, has been the heart and the soul of his whole ministry.

For the past fifty years the accounts of the hidden life of Jesus in St. Matthew and St. Luke have been subjected to many critical studies which assume, rather than prove, their legendary character. Catholic authors generally write to refute the objections of the critics in their treatment of the Gospel of the Infancy, as Father Donato Baldi, O.F.M.,[2] and Father Alfred Durand, S.J.,[3] have done in two of the best books on the subject. Father Durand is especially preoccupied with the defense of the perpetual virginity of Mary. That is also the object of my study on the virgin conception of Jesus Christ.[4] In America the most complete and most learned work on the subject is by J. Gresham Machen.[5] Unfortu-

---

[1] *In Ioan.* tract., 24, 2; initio, Patr. lat., 35 (1902), 1593.

[2] *L'infanzia del Salvatore*, studio esegetico e storico sui primi due capitoli dei Vangeli di S. Matteo e di S. Luca (Rome, 1925).

[3] *L'Enfance de Jésus-Christ d'après les évangiles canoniques*, suivie d'une étude sur "Les freres du Seigneur" (Paris, 1908).

[4] *De conceptione virginali Iesu Christi*. Accedunt excursus I. De duplici genealogia; II. De fratribus Domini (Rome, 1933).

[5] *The Virgin Birth of Christ* (New York, 1930). Note that this title is not entirely exact, for the discussion is about the virgin conception and not the virgin birth.

nately, after having defended with great learning and praiseworthy zeal the doctrine of the virgin birth—which honors Mary as much as her Son—this author, who is Professor of the New Testament at Westminster Theological Seminary, Philadelphia, sacrifices the perpetual virginity of the Mother of God to the phrase "brethren of the Lord"; even though the wide meaning of that expression has been handed down to us by Hegesippus (second century), and proved exactly and defended by St. Jerome in the fourth century against Helvidius and Jovinian.

Father Temple's study does not assume that critical character, nor yet is it apologetical and consequently relative. His work rather is more positive and constructive: it is exegetical and historical, theological and ascetical. These elements are all perfectly blended and go to make this work, unique in its kind, a standard work, a monument in honor of the hidden life of our Lord. As good a priest as he is an exegete, the author treats the Gospel as a source of life, not failing when the occasion arises to draw the moral lessons that flow from the divine word and the example of Jesus. He does this judiciously and with deep conviction so that his work will serve not only as a stimulus to study but also as a source of edification. I recommend it therefore to theologians and exegetes and as well to all those souls who desire to make their life conform more and more to our divine Model, Jesus, "in whom are hid all the treasures of wisdom and knowledge" (Col. 2: 3).

Jacques M. Vosté, O.P.

Author's Preface

SINCE student days at the Catholic University, I have been specially interested in the Gospel records of the early part of our divine Lord's life. I have already written on some of the texts of the holy childhood Gospels. Thinking it would be worth while to try to give a survey or general account of the whole hidden life of Christ, in the present work I have put together chapters on the various Gospel events connected with the first thirty years of our Savior. The purpose is to present in a summary way all the reliable information that would help us in our endeavors to form a picture of the early and longer part of the divine life.

This first part of Christ's life is known as the hidden life because here He concealed to a great extent His divine character by not manifesting Himself by public preaching and miracles. Yet in His early years the Savior did not hide Himself in a desert or live apart from men. Rather He chose to lead a life as a carpenter with daily social contacts and family associations. Hence there are lessons from the many years at Nazareth that are of special importance for us today. There by deeds rather than by words God's holy will was made known to us on questions that are of vital concern to us in our confused world.

The Gospel records for the hidden life are meager in comparison with those for the public one. Indeed the silence of the inspired writer on so many questions creates for us here our chief difficulty, as Lagrange remarks (*The Gospel of Jesus Christ*, I, 53); yet we are fortunate in having the two early chapters of both St. Matthew and St. Luke, and other scriptural references to the hidden life.

These I have carefully examined and besides have tried to sift historical evidence that would throw light on them. The curious works known as the Apocryphal Gospels have been used only to illustrate the views of the second and following centuries in which they were written. Thus from all the reliable historical sources we have tried to gather facts and figures so as to present in a somewhat popular form a running commentary on the Gospel records of the hidden life.

I wish to express sincerest thanks to those who helped in the typing and correcting of the manuscript. I am most grateful to His Excellency, Most Reverend Henry J. Grimmelsman, D.D., to Reverend John J. Collins, S.J., to Reverend Thomas A. Becker, S.J., and to Reverend James E. Risk, S.J., for the time they devoted to the reading of the work and for their valuable suggestions. I must mention that Mrs. William F. Albright gave me the benefit of her many years' experience in the Holy Land, especially for the writing of chapter sixteen. My debt of gratitude must be expressed to Very Reverend Father Vosté, O.P., Secretary of the Pontifical Commission for Biblical Studies, not only for giving his valuable time to the reading of the manuscript and to the sending of constructive criticisms that were most helpful, but most especially for his great kindness in writing the Foreword with personal remarks that are far above my deserving. I may mention that Monsignor Dollard's poem was written specially for the chapter on the Annunciation and that of Mr. McDonough for the chapter on St. Gabriel. To all my friends who have helped and encouraged me, I render due thanks. My Archbishop, Cardinal Spellman, has kindly given me permission to dedicate this work to His Eminence as the patron of studies. Lastly, I gladly submit my writings to the decisions of the Holy See, and hereby retract any statement that may be at variance with Catholic doctrine.

The following abbreviations are used throughout:
PG for Migne's Patrologia graeca;

PL for Migne's *Patrologia latina;*
ANF for *Ante-Nicene Fathers;*
NPN for *Nicene and Post-Nicene Fathers;*
Loeb for *Loeb Classical Library.*

PATRICK J. TEMPLE

Contents

CHAPTER I

The Days of the Herods

HOW Herod the Great happened to rule as king of the Holy Land at the time of Our Lord's birth was brought about by a series of events that began three centuries before. The conquest of Alexander the Great had put an end to the Persian province of Judea and had ushered in the age of Greek influence known as Hellenism. In the division of territory made by Alexander's generals the land of Israel at first came under the protection of Egypt, but it was soon wrested from Ptolemaic rule by the Seleucid rival at Antioch. Then when the Syrian Antiochus Epiphanes tried to make one political unit out of most of Asia Minor, the Jews under Judas Machabeus rose to defend their nationality and religion. Here they had on their side Rome, which was making its early strides to world expansion with its policy of doing everything to weaken other great powers. But the Jews soon found they had to pay the usual price, namely, to permit those to rule who had been called in to help.

Under the Machabees the boundaries of Palestine were extended to those of King David's time, and also autonomy and independence, or what was little short of it, were secured. Then at the end of eighty years Rome found its opportunity to interfere when a civil war of succession was being waged by two Machabean brothers. One of the contenders, Hyrcanus II, had come under the influence of a clever Idumean named Antipater, whose followers opened the gates of Jerusalem to Pompey in 63 B.C. Hyrcanus II was left as a figurehead under the rule of Antipater as procurator. On the death of the latter, Rome appointed his son, Herod, to succeed as king. Conditions were so turbulent that three years elapsed, until 37 B.C., before he could come into possession of his kingdom.

Thus Herod's kingdom, into which Our Lord was born, was a Roman protectorate under a shrewd politician who was able to retain his rule until his death in 4 B.C., chiefly because he was found so serviceable to his Roman masters. He pacified the border states, kept down the turbulent elements of his own territory, and seems to have been responsible for the collection of taxes. Herod was of an uncertain race,[1] a circumcised Jew by profession, but a pagan by practice. He pleased the Jews by marrying a Machabean princess, Mariamne, and especially by beginning the construction of a new temple in 20 B.C. On the other hand, he was hated by the Jews for his Hellenizing efforts in building Greek cities and public buildings for Greek plays and games. The Jews called him "half-Jew" and "Edomite slave." The delegation sent to Augustus to complain against his son, Archelaus, said that Herod had been the most barbarous of all tyrants,[2] as cruel to the Jews as if he had been a wild beast,[3] and that he had brought more evils on

[1] His mother was an Arabian princess, and his father, Antipater, was from Idumea. At one time this was part of the Holy Land. When John Hyrcanus subdued it, he compelled the inhabitants to submit to circumcision and the laws of Moses (Josephus, *Antiquities of the Jews*, XIII, ix, 1). Accordingly some writers call Herod a Jew; others, such as Herford (*Judaism in the New Testament Period*, p. 61), say he was not a Jew. When Josephus (*op. cit.*, XIV, xv, 2) calls him a half-Jew, it is an overstatement.

[2] Josephus, *Jewish War*, II, 84 (vii, 2). Josephus lived in Palestine in the middle of the first Christian century and his works are a primary source of information for the background of Our Lord's life. In making use of this information caution has to be used because of the author's tendency to boast and exaggerate. As he wrote in Rome in the latter part of the century with the intention of glorifying his nation and magnifying himself in the eyes of the Romans, especially the figures he supplies are greatly exaggerated. The accounts he gives of Herod's acts of cruelty are likewise under suspicion as being too severe; on the other hand, his words of high praise are often attributable to a friend of Herod's, Nicholas of Damascus.

[3] *Antiquities*, XVII, xi, 2. They declared that under Herod their nation had sunk to poverty and to the last degree of iniquity.

them than all those endured by their forefathers since the return from Babylon.

Herod was an opportunist who in the name of law and order stopped at nothing in currying favor with the Roman officials. Pride, ambition, jealousy ruled this bloodthirsty tyrant whose own family plotted against him and in turn was not spared. After he put to death his favorite wife, Mariamne, he became subject to long fits of melancholy. Only five days before his death, he had his eldest son, Antipater, executed. During his long reign of thirty years, the people, groaning under cruelty and oppression, stormed Heaven with their prayers that the Anointed One would come to lead them out of the trough of misery and woe, on to the crest of hope and cheer. As an answer to these prayers and to the prayers and hopes of preceding generations, our divine Lord was born toward the end of this reign, one of the worst in all history. This king's cruelty in seeking the life of the divine Child constitutes the dark, sinister background for the coming of the Brightness of Eternal Light; just as the world-wide peace and security obtained under Augustus foreshadowed at least in a vague way, the spiritual peace and the eternal security of Christianity.

Probably the same year in which the King of kings was born in a stable,[4] to teach detachment from worldly power and possession, witnessed Herod's slaughter of his own two sons, Alexander and Aristobulus, on suspicion that they were plotting to seize his rule and authority. Already he had been led to kill their great-grandfather, Hyrcanus, and their mother, his favorite wife, Mariamne, through his lust for power; and now in his old age, this ruling passion of his had so much become his master[5] that it deadened in him the first instinct of nature, so that he descended

---

[4] This was 8 b.c. See Appendix 3, p. 335.

[5] Herod's physical condition was such that he could bring down forty wild beasts a day (Josephus, *Jewish War*, I, 429 (xxi, 13), and his ability to rule was such that Augustus made the comment that Herod's kingdom was not large enough for his great talents (*Antiquities*, XVI, v, 1). On the other hand, Herod was a prey to covetousness, vanity, and ambition, and these vices led him to bring havoc on his own family and on his own people.

to the barbarous, impious act of the murder of his own progeny.
At the trial [6] of the unfortunate young men which took place at
Beyruth before a large company of provincial officials and friends,
Herod's unhealthy character revealed itself in his impassionately
bellowing out his accusations as proven facts; so that only one
decision could be reached, that of condemnation. An old faithful
soldier who afterwards spoke candidly to the king was, with his
son, tortured and stoned to death, so incapable of perceiving who
were his friends had the aging king become through his passion
for power.

In Herod's last illness, that is, in his seventieth year, about the
time the infant Savior was a refugee in Egypt, a political disturbance occurred in Jerusalem. Two celebrated rabbis of the time,
Judas and Matthias, incited the people to pull down the large
golden eagle which Herod had dedicated to the Temple, placing
it over its "great gate." [7] In punishment, the two rabbis were burned
to death and forty of the young men who took part were executed.
When on the death of King Herod, in the spring of 4 B.C., the
holy family returned from Egypt, they found Herod's cruel, tyrannical son, Archelaus, ruling Judea. His rule was later confirmed as
ethnarch and not as king. From the start he displayed the savage
propensities of his father without having the latter's energy or
assertiveness. Trouble began early, and conditions quickly became
so dreadful [8] that St. Joseph was afraid to bring back the holy
family to Bethlehem because of its proximity to Jerusalem; but
rather, after receiving a warning, he sought a safe, secluded town
in distant Galilee (Matt. 2:21–23). What began as a group mourning patriotic dead grew into a threatening crowd that assumed large
dimensions during the Passover. After some of his soldiers, sent
to overawe the rioters, were stoned to death, Archelaus' men slaugh-

[6] The whole account of the murder of the sons through the intrigues of the preferred
son Antipater is a classic (*Jewish War*, I, 445–551 [xxiii–xxvii]; *Antiquities*, XVI, xi–xii).
[7] *Jewish War*, I, 648–55 (xxxiii, 2–4); *Antiquities*, XVII, vi, 2.
[8] They are described by Josephus, *Jewish War*, II, 3–14 (i, 2 f.); *Antiquities*, XVII,
vi, 2–4.

tered three thousand of the festive pilgrims; as if he wished to offer them as sacrifices for his throne, as may be read in the accusation afterwards made against him.[9] Then at the following feast of Pentecost an agitated multitude made up principally of Galileans, Idumeans, and citizens of Jericho besieged Sabinus, who with one legion had been left in Jerusalem. In this riot the beautiful cloisters of the outer Temple were burned and the Temple treasury was seized by Sabinus. These disorders were only the beginning, for they multiplied until they were so many that Josephus could say in his exaggerated way that there were "myriads of other troubles"; [10] and indeed after the nine years of Archelaus, when he finally left for Rome, the whole nation was in a tumult. Striving to prevent his appointment as ethnarch, the Pharisees had sent fifty prominent men to Rome, where in presenting their accusations they were joined by eight thousand from the Jewish colony. This delegation of its own accord requested as a solution of the problems of Palestine that Judea be incorporated in the Roman province of Syria.[11]

Among the many riots that occurred after the death of Herod the Great, there was that of Judas, son of Ezechias, who attacked Sephoris and seized its money and weapons. The procurator Varus with two legions that had come with him from Syria took the city, burned it to the ground, and reduced its inhabitants to slavery. Of the insurgents of the whole country, he captured two thousand, whom he crucified.[12] Ten years later, after the banishment of Archelaus when Judea was joined to the Roman province of Syria, the registration and taxation under the legate Quirinius occasioned the revolt of Judas the Galilean. This could not be a small affair; for it merited the mention in the Acts (5: 57), which states that Judas was killed and his followers dispersed. According to Josephus, it was "a bold attempt" that reached "a great height," and it filled

---

[9] *Jewish War*, II, 89 (vi, 2).
[10] *Antiquities*, XVII, x, 4.
[11] *Jewish War*, II, 91 (vi, 2).
[12] *Jewish War*, II, 56, 66–75 (iv, 1; v, 1 f.); *Antiquities*, XVII, x, 5, 9 f.

the state with tumults.[13] We are told that this Judas the Galilean
with his associate, Sadduc, the Pharisee, scolded their countrymen
for accepting the Romans and preached that it was wrong to submit to taxation by a foreigner or to acknowledge anyone but God
as ruler or lord. They found many disciples who enthusiastically
devoted themselves to the attaining of national freedom with an
utter disregard of the sacrifices or sufferings to be endured.[14] Here
Judas the Galilean had a lasting influence as the founder of the
party known as "Zealots," or extreme patriots.[15]

The conditions that developed after King Herod's death, described by Josephus as "great disturbances" that were "in many
places" and as political troubles that lasted "for a long time," induced a great many "to aspire to sovereignty." [16] In another place
he states the matter this way: Judea was "full of bands of robbers,"
and wherever the different seditious bands found a leader they
immediately made him a king.[17] The careers of some of these are
described. They wore the diadem, hoping to represent the traditional theocratic king of the past and perhaps to be chosen by
God as the long-looked-for Messiah.

Accordingly, we may say that the whole period of the hidden
life of Our Lord was beset by political troubles. The first half was
especially agitated. Dangers brought about the refuge in Egypt

---

[13] *Jewish War*, II, 118 (viii, 1); *Antiquities*, XVIII, i, 1.

[14] *Jewish War*, loc. cit.; *Antiquities*, XVIII, i, 6.

[15] It is referred to as the league of freedom. If Judas the Galilean is the same person
as Judas, son of Ezechias, then the date of its founding is to be placed shortly after
the death of Herod the Great. Because Josephus is not clear in his accounts, there is
diversity of view among scholars, about the date of origin of the "Zealots." Thackeray
(*Josephus' Works*, Loeb Classical Library, II, 367, note) seems to be following more
closely the Josephus text when he disassociates Judas the Galilean from Judas, son of
Ezechias. The latter had ambitions for royal rank (*Antiquities*, XVII, x, 5). Once out
of the four times mentioned, Judas the Galilean is also called "a Gaulanite" of the city
of Gamala (*Antiquities*, XVIII, i, 1). This reference adds to the difficulty of the problem for there were two cities named Gamala, one of which was in Galilee.

[16] *Jewish War*, II, 55 (iv, 1). He attributes "the wild fury" that spread itself all
over the nation to the fact that they had no king of their own to keep the multitude in
virtue. *Antiquities*, XVII, x, 6.

[17] *Antiquities*, XVII, x, 8. Josephus was writing for the Romans, with whom of course
all seizures of arms or food by rebels were branded as robberies, and deaths inflicted on
Roman soldiers or traitorous Jews were labeled murders.

and the seclusion of Nazareth. The middle of the hidden life, when Jesus was about fourteen years old, witnessed the revolt of Judas the Galilean; that of Judas, son of Ezechias, occurred ten years before. This latter disturbance and that of the subsequent capture and burning of Sephoris by Varus must have been felt in Nazareth that was only three miles away. In the last half of the hidden life political discontent continued to manifest itself in the numerous separate bands of Zealots that attracted so many young enthusiasts especially in Galilee; yet these men did not break forth into any organized revolutionary effort, and there was no disturbance of the peace on a national scale. Thus it is to be observed that in the second half of the hidden life, Herod Antipas was able to rebuild Sephoris with a wall that made it "the ornament of all Galilee," [18] and that on the shore of Lake Genesareth, he could erect a new city, Tiberias, that soon grew to be the rival of Sephoris. We should also note that the holy family made the annual Passover pilgrimage to Jerusalem despite the terrors of the reign of Archelaus and despite the continual political tumults in both Galilee and Judea.

In Galilee during the long years of the hidden life our blessed Savior lived under the rule of Herod Antipas, who was made tetrarch of Galilee and Transjordania at the death of his father, Herod the Great. Indeed He resided not far from the seat of government of this crafty ruler, Nazareth being three miles from Sephoris, where Herod Antipas held forth until he moved to Tiberias after A.D. 18. During the public life Our Lord referred to him as "fox" (Luke 13: 32), a word which sums up Herod's cunning and craftiness. The sickening weakness of this voluptuous king in contrast with the magnificent strength of his ascetic prisoner, St. John the Baptist, was as "a reed shaken by the wind" in comparison with the sturdy oak of the forest. Cowardly yielding to human respect made him the murderer of the last and greatest of the prophets, who had denounced him for his incestuous liv-

[18] *Antiquities*, XVIII, ii, 1.

ing. Herod the Great, under whom the God of might was born a helpless Babe, drove his God into exile. Herod Antipas, under whom Wisdom incarnate led the perfect life and preached the perfect way, treated his God as a fool. Father and son were both highly successful in helping to establish the law and order of the Roman Empire; but what miserable failures in promoting the kingdom of heaven! That our divine Lord lived under these two evil rulers should teach us that man can be a spiritual success under any form of government. That He was born under the most efficient of administrators, Augustus, shows that there is a need of the divine Savior under every governmental system.

The greater part of the hidden life was passed under Emperor Caesar Augustus who died A.D. 14. Since this man was not only ruler of his vast realm but as well was manager and steward of its property, his reign is known as the Principate.[19] Indeed he was so successful in collecting wealth and bringing lasting security to Rome that people began to call him a new Apollo and there arose the cult of his genius or his divine creative power. It was this emperor who incorporated Judea in the Roman province of Syria and appointed as procurators Coponius, Marcus Ambibulus, and Annius Rufus. The two other procurators of Judea during Our Lord's life, Valerius Gratus and Pontius Pilate, were appointed by Tiberius Caesar. The latter failed in his endeavor to be as popular as Augustus because, for one thing, he lacked the creative energy of his predecessor.

It may be summarily said that the Roman Empire of Our Lord's time was a world state in which Roman citizens were the masters and the provincials the servants. The center of business exchange and of the one-man rule was Rome, with an elaborate bureaucratic machine extending over the conquered lands. These latter were ruled by members of the senatorial class but they retained local

[19] M. Rostovtzeff, *A History of the Ancient World*, II, pp. 175–97; E. Homo, *Roman Political Institutions from City to State*, pp. 299 ff.; Buchan, *Augustus*, 166 ff.; Baker, *Augustus, the Golden Age of Rome*, pp. 266 ff.

self-government. With the triumph of law and order, the chief benefits of this "commonwealth of self-governing states" [20] were a flourishing trade and widespread opportunity for freedom of ideas. Its evils consisted largely of the herd of tenants who were serfs and of the vast army of slaves who were mere chattels. These unstable elements kept morality at a low ebb. Neither was morality helped by religion; rather religion was often in conflict with morality. The major philosophical and religious ideas may be classified under three headings: [21] Stoicism, which strove after individual discipline; Neo-Pythagoreanism, which sought refuge in Greek mysteries and astrology; and Epicureanism, which led to dissipation in the hectic enjoyment of the senses. These poor substitutes, however, could not satisfy the masses; and hence the prevailing temper was one of despondency and pessimism, which could not be suppressed by efforts at trivial materialism.

It is estimated that the Jews in the time of Christ were about seven per cent of the population of the Empire and numbered between four and a half and seven million. Between a tenth and a quarter of this number lived in Palestine.[22] Besides the Samaritans there, the Gentile population consisted of Syrians, Greeks, and Romans. For civil administration, villages depended on the nearest towns, and they in turn on the nearest cities. Thus all of Galilee for a while came under Sophoria and then under Tiberias,

[20] Rostovtzeff, *The Social and Economic History of the Roman Empire*, p. 50.

[21] Rostovtzeff, *A History of the Ancient World*, II, 198–211; also Glover, *The World of the New Testament*, pp. 227–31.

[22] Scholars are not agreed about the population of Palestine in Our Lord's time for the reason that there is no available evidence on which even an approximately accurate estimate can be based. See McCown, "The Density of Population in Ancient Palestine," *Journal of Biblical Literature*, LXVI (1947), 429. Here is to be found a summary of opinions and an attempt at an estimate based on the resources of Palestine and on its present population. He estimates the total population of western Palestine without Transjordania to be far less than one million; this is counting Jews and Gentiles there. As to the number of Jews in the homeland, he is of the opinion that these were less than half a million. He gives one hundred thousand for Jewish Galilee, and twice that figure for Judea with Jerusalem having a population of a hundred thousand. Albright warns us that the population of ancient Palestine has usually been overestimated. He gives the population of Palestine at the time of the Hebrew conquest, as about a quarter of a million. (*Journal of the Palestine Oriental Soc.*, V (1925), 20–25; *Biblical Archaeologist*, IX (1946), 4, 5, 8.

while the eleven districts of Judea were all subordinate to Jerusalem. Among the concessions that Rome had granted the Jews
was the leaving of a great deal of civil jurisdiction in the hands
of the Sanhedrin. The high priest was supposed to be supreme
in religious matters but in reality he was appointed and removed
at will by the Herods and by the Romans. He presided at the
deliberations of the Sanhedrin, which was made up of seventy-
one members taken from the three groups: priests, scribes, and
elders. The Sanhedrin had supreme authority in religious matters
for the Jews of the world, and to it was subordinated the local
tribunate established in towns and cities of the homeland and of
foreign countries.

The Jews living abroad in the time of the Empire would especially come under the influence of the prevailing culture of the
time, Hellenism. In the Holy Land itself there were Greek cities
with theaters for Greek plays, and amphitheaters for Greek games.
It was because of differences of view in regard to the means to be
selected to counteract the evils flowing from Hellenism as well as
from political disturbances that there were to be found two of the
sects among the Jews of Palestine in Our Lord's day. Those who
were not too ardently opposed to compromise with Greek culture,
chiefly from the wealthy materialistic class, especially from the
influential priests, banded themselves into the class known as
Sadducees. Those who kept apart from anything suggestive of
Hellenism and who placed their hopes in pacific means, namely,
adherence to the revelation contained in the Pentateuch and as
well to the regulations of unwritten tradition,[23] were known as
Pharisees, a sect about six thousand in number. Besides there was
a distinctively Jewish sect called Essenes, numbering about four
thousand,[24] who led ascetic lives in semi-monastic form, most of
them making their abode on the western shore of the Dead Sea.

[23] *Antiquities,* XVII, ii, 4.
[24] *Ibid.,* XVIII, i, 5; Philo, Quod omnis probus liber est, 75 (xi), Loeb, IX, 55. The
Zealots of this time were about the same number as the Pharisees (Herford, *op. cit.,*
p. 69).

The bitter uncompromising opponents of the Roman government who sought religious and national independence in armed revolt were known as Zealots. The latter, a religious sect at this time, were mostly in Galilee whereas the Sadducees lived in Judea. The mass of the people, mostly small farmers, day laborers, artisans, and tradesmen who lived from hand to mouth and had little secular education, did not openly join any of these sects.

Professing belief in the one all-powerful, all-knowing God who rules all things, the Jews had an immense advantage over all the other peoples of that time in their optimistic outlook on life and in their reliance on divine Providence. Another incstimable advantage was that the "oracles of God were entrusted to them" (Rom. 3:2), the Holy Writings inspired by the Holy Ghost. Most Jews of Our Lord's time believed that an eternal life of happiness with God after death was destined for the friends of God, while punishment awaited the wicked in the next world. It is true that under the influence of Greek philosophy the Sadducees doubted or denied the existence of angels and the resurrection of the body; however, in so doing they fell away from the genuine tradition of their race.

The other great doctrine of the Jewish religion was belief in, and hope for, a Messiah. The Anointed One, according to their Scriptures, was to be the liberator and special agent promised by God to do God's work; He was to be of the family of David and born of a Virgin; a real man yet He was to come from the bosom of God. He was to be the Servant of God, yet God-with-us. He was to be the ideal King to reign in peace; yet He was to be a priest after the order of Melchisedech. He was to govern the world in God's name and with God's power and majesty. The divine Messiah was to be "like the son of man" (Dan. 7:13) as well as son of David, and His reign was to last forever.

Because of these doctrines, the Jewish religion had an essential unity. This unity was strengthened by the Sacred Scriptures, which all Jews read or had read to them, and by the common prayers in the synagogues, which already for some time, perhaps generations, were established not only in the Holy Land but anywhere Israelites were sufficiently numerous to support one. Especially a unifying effect was produced by the frequent attendance of so many Jewish pilgrims at the Temple of Jerusalem during the great feasts of the year. The localization of God's presence, consecrating the sacred edifice and hallowing the Holy City, made a deep impression on young and old.[25] The Temple never had so magnificent a grandeur and splendor, the synagogues were never so widespread and so well attended, and the prayers and supplications were never more fervent, the sacrifices and services never more numerous, than in the time of Our Lord.[26] The religious dangers that lurked in Hellenism, and the dreadful political oppression that all felt, chastened many and brought forth a rich harvest of virtuous, prayerful lives.

The great hopes placed in the Machabees had been dissipated when a century before Christ a nephew of Judas Machabeus waged a civil and religious war against his own people, and when forty years before the Christian era the quarreling of two Machabean brothers occasioned the rise to power of Herod's father and the intervention of Rome. In a century about 200,000 Jews had perished in wars and rebellions. Under the long cruel reign of Herod the Great, the masses must have been pleading with, and crying to Heaven for a Messiah. As was already said, the delegation that went before Augustus to complain against Archelaus officially asked that their land be taken away from Jewish rule. When their request was granted and Judea was incorporated into the Roman Empire, then the scepter had passed from Juda and it was time for Him to be sent who was the expectation of nations. Thus it was felt on all sides that "the fullness of time" had come when God would intervene in a most special way with the heavenly Messiah. As God,

---

[25] Herford writes: "The services in the Temple brought to a focus the collective purpose of Israel to adore God and gave a local meaning to the thought of approach to Him" (*Judaism in the New Testament Period*, p. 19).

[26] Cf. M. J. Lagrange, *Le Judaisme avant Jésus-Christ*, p. 342.

"who is able to accomplish all things in a measure far beyond what we ask or conceive" (Eph. 3:20), in answering our prayers does so in His own way beyond all our expectations; so He fulfilled Jewish prophecies and the prayers and hopes of mankind, using the most effective means to draw the human heart to Himself. He sent His Son, the Second Person of the Holy Trinity, to be the Savior and Teacher of mankind. The God-man came in God's way. His two or three years of public teaching were preceded by an obscure life of a little more than thirty years.

PRIMARY SOURCES

1. Josephus ben Matthias. He was born A.D. 37, probably in Jerusalem and died about A.D. 110, probably at Rome. When he was twenty-nine years of age, he was in charge of Jewish troops in Galilee during the first six months of A.D. 67 in the Jewish War. He was captured and afterwards released and honored by Vespasian. This emperor prompted and "inspired" the first work of Josephus, *The Jewish War*, written sometime between 75 and 79. Originally written in Aramaic to impress certain nations in the near East and the Jews of Mesopotamia with the might of Rome, the work was afterwards rewritten in Greek for the Graeco-Roman world by the author himself. In 93–94, Josephus wrote his longest work, *The Antiquities*; and in the beginning of the second century, the *Life*, and *Against Apion*; the first being hastily written in answer to an attack by Justus of Tiberias, the second being a carefully written and planned defense of his own nation, religion, and culture.

In the writing of his works, Josephus tells us he relied on his own notes and memoirs, on the imperial commentaries of Vespasian and Titus, and on information sent him by King Agrippa II (*Against Apion*, I, 50–52 [9]). For the life of Herod the Great, Josephus would have before him the works of Nicholas of Damascus. This intimate friend of Herod, could furnish most reliable information about Herod and his household; but would be disposed to take Herod's side on questions and to give him undue credit and praise.

Because as a young priest he had been in Jerusalem and in its Temple and because he was an eyewitness of conditions in several parts of Palestine, especially in Galilee around the middle of the first Christian century, Josephus' works are valuable primary sources for the background of the New Testament. In making use of Josephus' writings, we should bear in mind that, although this historian boasts about his own qualifications and protests his purpose to write nothing but the truth, he is preoccupied with the intention of flattering the Romans and of glorifying himself and his own Jewish people. This political aim led him to give fantastic figures for Jewish populations, and in his own behalf to advance claims that border on the ridiculous.

See the Introductions and notes given to the *Works of Josephus* by H. St. J. Thackerey in The Loeb Classical Library. We give the reference to this edition whenever available. See also A. Momigliano, "Josephus as a Source for the History of Judaea," *Cambridge Ancient History*, X, 884–87; also L. de Grandmaison, *Jésus-Christ*, I, 189–94.

2. *Res gestae divi Augusti*. Ex monumentis ancyrano et appoloniensi interum edidit. Th. Mommsen, Berolini, 1833. Text and translation by F. W. Shipley is to be found in the Loeb Classical Library series, 1924.

BIBLIOGRAPHY

Arnold, W. T. The Roman System of Provincial Administration to the Accession of Constantine (Oxford, 1914).

Bailey, A., and Kent, C. History of the Hebrew Commonwealth.

Baker, G. P. Augustus, the Golden Age of Rome (London, 1937).

Chapot, Victor. The Roman World. Translated by E. A. Parker (New York, 1928).

Holmes, Thomas. The Architect of the Roman Empire (Oxford, 1928–31).

Homo, L. Roman Political Institutions from City to State (New York, 1929).

Jones, H. "The Princeps," Cambridge Ancient History, X, 127–57.

Matthews, S. A. A History of New Testament Times in Palestine (New York, 1914).

Marsh, Burr. The Founding of the Roman Empire (Texas, 1922).

————. Augustus Caesar and the Organization of the Empire of Rome (London, 1925).

Momigliano, A. "Herod of Judaea," Cambridge Ancient History, X, 316–39.

Mommusen, Theodor. The Provinces of the Roman Empire from Caesar to Diocletian, 2 vols. (London, 1909).

Oesterley, W. A History of Israel, Vol. II.

Rostovtzeff, M. A History of the Ancient World, Vol. II, Rome (Oxford, 1928).

Schürer, E. A History of the Jewish People in the Time of Jesus Christ, Vols. I and II.

For an extensive bibliography of the Augustan Age, see B. Allen, *Augustus Caesar* (London, 1937), pp. 253–56; *Cambridge Ancient History*, X, 954–69; A. D. Winspear, *Augustus and the Reconstruction of the Roman Empire* (University of Wisconsin, 1935), pp. 281–89.

CHAPTER II

Mary of Nazareth

THE Sacred Scriptures pass over in silence the early life of the Mother of Jesus. But a number of details concerning the parents and youth of the Virgin Mary are presented in a work that claims to be a Gospel written by St. James. This unreliable, spurious writing is classified as apocryphal and has not only been rejected by the Church but also has been condemned.[1] Its historic value is limited to the extent to which it reflects the view of the early date at which it was written, about the middle of the second century. When it tells us that the names of the parents of the Virgin Mary were Joachim and Anna, we may accept this information as it is also found in the Fathers who have handed down the names to us. On the question of the birthplace of the Mother of God, the most probable opinion is that it was near the Probatic Pool, a little outside the walls of Jerusalem, north of the Temple. Here over the site of the house in which she is said to have been born, a church was built in the fifth century, which formed the crypt of the one built later by the crusaders to the memory of St. Ann.[2]

The spurious works known as apocryphal Gospels were wit-

[1] For instance, they were enumerated and condemned under Pope Gelasius; see *Ad opera Gelasii Papae appendices*; PL, 59, 175. This does not mean that everything found in them is false. St. Jerome, who, like the other Fathers, is severe in his condemnation of these Apocrypha, admits that occasionally there are to be found grains of gold in the clay material. (Letter 107, *to Laeta*; NPN, 2nd ser., VI, 194.) Corroboration by Church Fathers, is required as the test for genuine tradition.

[2] Cf. Meistermann, *Guide to the Holy Land*, pp. 215–18. Two other places lay claim to the privilege of being the birthplace of the Blessed Virgin, namely, Sephoris and Nazareth. See Maas, "Virgin Mary," *Catholic Encyclopedia*, XV, 464.

nessing the view current in the early centuries when they tell us that the Virgin Mother, like Samuel of old, was born as a result of prayer; for this tradition is repeated by St. Gregory of Nyssa [3] and by St. John Damascene.[4]

Of all the events related in these apocryphal writings, the only one that has found a place in our liturgy is the presentation of Mary in the Temple. The purpose of the feast, as Scheeben [5] well points out, is not so much in its outward ceremony as in its significance. It is commemorative of the youthful Mary's complete dedication to God, and this fact is deducible from the Sacred Scriptures. In regard to the details of the early life of the Blessed Virgin, the truth is that the Fathers of the first three centuries followed the lead of the inspired writers of the Gospels in preserving a silence. Accordingly it seems idle for us now to speculate on the reason why her parents moved from Jerusalem to Nazareth, on the supposition that Mary was born in the Holy City. Whatever the cause, we know for certain from the Gospel that at the time of the Annunciation she was living in Nazareth and after the return from Egypt she lived in this town for thirty years. Rightly we call her Mary of Nazareth.

The name Mary was a common one in the Holy Land at the time of Our Lord. Contrary to popular belief, it does not mean "Star of the Sea." Although scholars are not agreed on its precise etymology, in the Aramaic language spoken in Palestine at that time, "Mary" would suggest "princess" or "lady." Certainly the name recalled the famous Miriam, sister of Moses, the prophetess who sang of God's wonderful intervention in the liberation of the people of Israel from the hands of Pharaoh. It was a most appropriate name, therefore, for her whom we love to call "Our Lady," who cooperated with the divine Redeemer in the spiritual liberation of man.

[3] *Oratio in diem natalem Christi,* PG, 46, 1137–40. The evidence for the names of Mary's parents is called a "respectable tradition," by Prat, *Jésus-Christ,* I, 42.

[4] Homily, *In nativitatem B.V.M.,* PG, 96, 661–97.

[5] *Mariology,* I, 44.

Just as all our graces come to us through the sacred humanity of Jesus, so all of Mary's unique privileges and graces come to her because she was chosen to be nearest this sacred humanity of the Son of God.[6] Words are most inadequate to express the sublime character of Mary's exalted motherhood. To borrow the brief laudatory remark from Scripture, she was "blessed among women," in being chosen from among all the daughters of Eve to give flesh and blood to the God-man while He was tabernacled within her, and then after His birth to tend to His infant body and to be associated with Him, as only a mother is with her child, for thirty years. As Jesus was a most loving Son, He endowed His mother with gifts of nature and grace beyond the realms of our experience. With the choicest graces and blessings the heavenly Father prepared her for her sublime vocation, spouse of the Holy Ghost and mother of His well-beloved Son.

Because of the foreseen merits of her divine Son, Mary was exempted from original sin.[7] Here was a great, unique privilege preeminently distinguishing her from all the other children of Eve, that from the first moment of her existence she was free from all stain of the sin which all others inherit because of the fall of our first parent. Then besides her Immaculate Conception, Mary enjoyed another privilege in being entirely free from actual sin throughout her life.[8] Since God especially prepares those whom He selects for particular offices, He preserved free from sin her who alone was to approach the confines of divinity.

Furthermore, Mary was unique in her mental faculties,[9] which were not obscured by the clouds of ignorance that darken our understanding as a consequence of original sin. Here exception was made for her because of her exalted position, as the mother

---

[6] The distinguishing mark of Mary's person and the source of her dignity was of course the fact that she was the mother of the God-man. See Scheeben, *Mariology*, I, 187–240.

[7] Cf. *ibid.*, I, 32–111.

[8] Cf. *ibid.*, I, 112–93.

[9] Scheeben (*ibid.*, II, 19–22) warns that no purely human standard may be set for her who is the "seat of wisdom" and the "new and better Eve"; yet here her resemblance to Christ was not the same as in the case of her fullness of sanctity.

and the intimate associate of the divine Redeemer. For her sublime office, God, who arranges everything so sublimely well, endowed Mary with exceptional, indeed supernatural, gifts of mind. Accordingly we are to expect that, in regard to religious ideas, she penetrated beyond the understanding of her time and that, in reading the Holy Writ, she was endowed by the Holy Ghost with spiritual wisdom and supernatural knowledge. We know from the Magnificat that the Blessed Virgin was steeped in the knowledge of the Sacred Scriptures and that through her meditation upon them they had become part and parcel of her habitual thought so that apt passages from the sacred text readily came to her lips. As she read Holy Writ to learn the will of God, and thereby to come closer to Him, she became thoroughly instructed by God (John 6:45). Contemplation of things divine became a habit with her; for twice in St. Luke's second chapter he mentions Mary's pondering over sayings and events. She maintained unbroken union with God through continuous prayer.

In a most special manner was Mary unique in regard to grace. The title "full of grace" [10] was accorded her by the archangel, with a far different meaning from the scriptural use of the expression "full of grace" used of St. Stephen (Acts 6:8) or from that of "filled with the Holy Ghost" (Acts 2:4) said of the apostles.[11] As fitting her most exalted office of Mother of God, Mary was adorned with such a rich largess of grace that St. Peter Chrysologus could well say: "Grace is bestowed on other individuals in portions. To Mary, however, the fullness of grace was given in all its entirety." [12] With the immense ocean of sanctifying grace that she possessed, she surpassed and excelled not only all human beings, but the angels in heaven.[13] Her initial grace placed her immeas-

[10] The term in Luke 1:28 is to be understood in the sense used in Eph. 1:6. In the angelic salutation, it holds the place of Mary's name as eminently suiting her. The perfect tense is used in the Greek text to convey the meaning of completeness.

[11] Cf. St. Bernard, Homily super "Missus est," III, 2; PL, 183, 72. Origen wrote that "full of grace" was not said of anyone else. Homily 6 in Lucam; PG, 13, 1816.

[12] Sermon 143; PL, 53, 583.

[13] Cf. Scheeben, Mariology, II, 4.

urably above every mere creature, and with her lavish store of the most precious gift from the bountiful heavenly King she ranks in sanctity somewhere between the holiest creature and the sacred humanity of Christ.[14] The Fathers of the Church make a distinction between Mary's sanctification before her sublime motherhood and that sublime perfection of her second sanctification when she was united with the very principle of grace and clothed with celestial glory as the Godhead dwelt bodily within her.[15] The Fathers also assert that she increased in sanctifying grace in a measure unequaled by any created nature except that of Christ and that for actual graces her mind and will were unceasingly endowed with the full supply from God's rich treasury.[16]

The effect of the fullness of grace that Mary received from her Son was to preserve her in an entirely sinless state. St. Augustine [17] writes: "We know what abundance of grace for overcoming sin in every particular was conferred upon her." Of course the Bishop of Hippo insists that Mary's exemption from all sin, being the great "exception" of all men and women, was owing to the merits of Christ. Speaking about the maid of Nazareth, St. Ambrose declared that she never stained the sincerity of her disposition by guile, and he asks: "What is more chaste than she?" [18] This doctor of the

[14] Cf. McGarry, "A Fundamental Principle in Mariology," *Theological Studies*, II (1941), 47.

[15] Cf. Scheeben, *Mariology*, II, 13.

[16] Cf. McGarry, *loc. cit.* After pointing out that it was due the Blessed Virgin to receive a greater fullness of grace than anyone else, and after explaining that there was a threefold perfection of grace in her, St. Thomas declares that without any doubt Mary was endowed in a high degree with "the gift of wisdom, and the grace of miracles and even of prophecy"; but he adds that they were to be used in accordance with God's providential design in her regard. For instance, she did not make use of her miraculous power while she was living on earth. (*Summa theol.*, IIIa, q. 27, a. 5.)

[17] *On Nature and Grace*, 42; NPN, 1st ser., V., 135. The following reasons are given by St. Thomas for Mary's being preserved from sin through fullness of grace. In choosing her to be the Mother of God, the Almighty made her worthy of that office, as we see clearly from the words of the angel: "Thou hast found grace with God" (Luke 1:30). Then Mary's sinlessness and grace come from the singular affinity between the Son and the Mother and from the singular manner in which Jesus dwelt within Mary, taking flesh from her. (*Summa theol.*, IIIa, q. 27, a. 4.)

[18] *Concerning Virgins*, II, 2; NPN, 2nd ser., X, 374.

Church goes on to the following rhetorical questions: "What is greater than the Mother of God? What more glorious than she whom Glory itself chose?" And St. Athanasius is not afraid to call Mary "Godlike," being amazed at "how much her glory is to be estimated." [19]

Having no experience of sin whatever, Mary of Nazareth detested every kind of evil. Being utterly free from the least inclination toward worldliness, she sensed the pride of the self-satisfied rich and the arrogance of those who exercised tyrannical power. As she grew up she realized more and more the havoc which sin wrought in the souls of others. For her, worldly pride was empty and hollow and was offensive in God's sight. On the one hand, she was conscious of her own nothingness and weakness without God; on the other, she appreciated God's all-availing grace. She called Him her Savior (Luke 1:46), because she felt the need of His grace to save her and the world from the slavery of sin and Satan. If holy Simeon and holy Anna so earnestly longed for the Redeemer and the salvation He was to bring, how much more did Mary under the inspiration of God desire Him to come and heal mankind! If the devout people of the time offered their daily prayers, their fastings, and their penances that God might hasten the coming of the Promised One, surely Mary outstripped them all in this regard, as the fervent outpourings of her spotless soul went before the throne of God for Him to intervene in favor of the poor and the downtrodden.

Because of her great humility, Mary would be the last person to think the Messiah would be born of her. From one of the families of Davidic descent that had standing and influence in Palestine, she would look for the Expected One to come. Perhaps it was her great sense of unworthiness that led her under the inspiration of the Holy Ghost to dedicate her virginity to God. In this regard her extraordinary spiritual knowledge would enable her

[19] *Ex Commentariis in Lucam; PG*, XXVII, 1394.

to rise above her generation and time. From the question that Mary put to the archangel, "How shall this be done, since I know not man?" (Luke 1:34), we are led to believe that she had consecrated her virginity to God—she need not have taken a vow as not considering it necessary.[20] Was she not here proceeding contrary to the established customs of her time?

It is certain that the Jews of old were accustomed to make vows. There is an example in the Book of Judges (11:30–40), where we are told of the vow of Jephte as the result of which his only daughter was offered in sacrifice to the Lord. In the time of our divine Lord we know that the members of the sect of the Essenes took vows of celibacy, and that holy widows, like Anna (Luke 2:36), who lived in chastity, were held in high repute.

Deuteronomy (22:13–21) is witness that from early times a Jewish maiden when becoming a bride was required to have preserved her virginal honor. That she be a *virgo intacta* was considered her strongest qualification for marriage and the most important element in the binding force of the contract. A purchase price (*Mohar*) was given her on the occasion of the betrothal as a compensation to her father for the loss of her services, and as a payment for the *pretium pudicitiae*. If the girl lost her virginity before the marriage, she was returned to her father's house, and the purchase price was almost certainly refunded.[21] The cares and worries that devolved on the father during the supervision of the chaste upbringing of his daughter as long as she remained at home are mentioned by Ecclesiasticus (42:9–11).[22] The father was re-

---

[20] See note 38 *infra*.

[21] Cf. Neufeld, *Ancient Hebrew Marriage Laws*, pp. 94–110.

[22] That there was no relaxation of the requirement of virginity for centuries after Christ, we have plenty of evidence. See Gaechter, "The Chronology from Mary's Betrothal to the Birth of Christ," *Theological Studies*, II (1941), 150 f. Luke 2:36 is witness that an unmarried woman was synonymous with virgin. The first Mishnic regulation of the tràctate on Marriage Deeds, orders that marriages of young maidens be held on Wednesdays so that if the *signa virginitatis* were not present, the suit of dismissal could be lodged on the following day, the regular court day. *Mishnah*, Ketuboth (Marriage Deeds), I, 1; Danby, p. 245.

sponsible for the betrothal of his daughter, which as a rule took place when she was between twelve and twelve and one-half years old, the days [23] of her girlhood. His responsibility did not cease then, but continued until she was officially taken to the home of the bridegroom.[24] At an early age, even as a minor, a girl could be betrothed.[25] But the general practice was to wait until the maiden had reached her full maturity, namely, at twelve and a half; [26] and then she was given one year after her betrothal in which to prepare her trousseau.[27] By the formal betrothal, the mutual presentation of gifts, and the paying of this "purchase price" by the groom, a mutual obligation of marriage was incurred and the parties were considered husband and wife.[28]

The customs and practices in regard to betrothals and marriages in Christ's time are fairly well known, and may be briefly summarized as follows. Women were given in marriage and the arrangements were usually made by the father or guardian; the consent of the girl, however, was sought and theoretically was necessary, but often was not heeded.[29] The father of the groom as a rule also took part in the bargaining over the dowry to be given with the bride.[30] The betrothal ceremony consisted of the groom's giving the bride a gift saying, "You are hereby betrothed to me." [31] Then a blessing was pronounced, and the young woman was considered the wife. After being put in writing, and duly witnessed,

[23] Cf. Gaechter, op. cit., 156 f.; Mishnah, Nedarim (Vows), 10, 2; Danby, p. 277; Niddah (Menstruant), 5, 6, 7; 6, 11; Danby, pp. 751 f.; Ketuboth (Marriage Deeds), IV, 4 f.; Danby, p. 250.

[24] Mishnah, Ketuboth (Marriage Deeds), 4, 5; Danby, p. 250.

[25] Mishnah, Niddah (Menstruant), 5, 4; Danby, p. 750.

[26] Cf. Billerbeck, Kommentar zum Neuen Testament aus Talmud und Midrach, II, 274 f.

[27] Mishnah, Ketuboth (Marriage Deeds), 5, 2; Danby, p. 252; Nedarim (Vows), 10, 5; Danby, p. 278.

[28] Cf. Philo, De specialibus legibus, III, xii, 72 (Loeb, VII, 519); Neufeld, Ancient Hebrew Marriage Laws, pp. 142–44; Moore, Judaism in the First Centuries, II, 121.

[29] Cf. Mishnah, Ketuboth (Marriage Deeds), 4 f.; Danby, p. 250.

[30] Cf. Willam, Mary the Mother of Jesus, p. 40.

[31] Cf. Mishnah, Kiddushin (Betrothals), 2, 1; see also Gaechter, op. cit., p. 153; Willam, op. cit., p. 42.

the engagement could not be broken off, without legal divorce proceedings.[32] It was the custom that a certain time, generally a year,[33] should elapse between the espousals and the marriage, when the bride was escorted to the home of the groom. During that interval the couple were never allowed to be alone.[34] If the bride had made any vows, they had to be made known to the groom before the engagement; for concealed vows could be made the grounds both for divorce and for dismissal without repayment of the dowry.[35] In case the bride was an heiress, the rule was that she should marry a relative outside the forbidden degree, for the purpose of keeping the property in the family, as the law of Moses commanded, according to Tobias (7:14). It was customary that all women should marry; in fact, it was considered their religious duty and highest privilege because of the fervent hope that the Messiah was to come. The age of marriage was thirteen and a half years, and most marriages took place in the autumn of the year.[36]

Presuming that Mary of Nazareth followed these customs and laws,—and most likely she did [37]—we may attempt to outline what happened in her case. Under God's grace she dedicated her virginity to Him some time after her twelfth year.[38] Then, when she was

[32] Mishnah, Kiddushin (Betrothals), 1, 1. She was henceforth considered the wife of the betrothed, in the negative sense that she was forbidden to anyone else. But she was not under his control in regard to her vows. See Gaechter, op. cit., p. 155; Mishnah, Nedarim (Vows), 10, 2.

[33] Mishnah, Ketuboth, 5. This normal interval was not obligatory; cf. Danby, p. 251.

[34] An exception was made for Judea, not for Galilee, after the revolt under Hadrian, A.D. 132–35. See Mishnah, Ketuboth (Marriage Deeds), 1, 5; Danby, p. 245; Gaechter, op. cit., p. 152.

[35] Mishnah, Nedarim (Vows), 10, 4; Danby, p. 277.

[36] The marriage at Cana (John 2:1–11) took place in April; but generally marriages occurred in October. See Gaechter, "Chronology from Mary's Betrothal," Theological Studies, II (1941), 335–39.

[37] As Gaechter (op. cit., p. 156) says, we are entitled to suppose that Mary followed the customs of the time, "until someone proves that things were different." Yet on the other hand, as Collins remarks, we must bear in mind her unique position in the history of the world; "Our Lady's Vow of Virginity," Catholic Biblical Quarterly, V (1943), 377.

[38] According to the Mishnah the vows of a girl of twelve years and one day are valid, Niddah (Menstruant), 5, 6; Danby, p. 750. It also says that the vows made by a girl could be revoked by her father and the betrothed husband together; Nedarim (Vows),

about twelve and a half years old the question of giving her in marriage would come up. As she realized that she could not oppose the views of the time and the wishes of her family she bowed to the inevitable, trusting that God would help her to keep her sacred wish.[39] She would have to inform her prospective husband concerning her desire and obtain his consent. Perhaps it was because she was an heiress that a cousin was looked for as a suitor. The choice of a kind, virtuous man would be prompted by her exceptional goodness.[40]

If St. Joseph was a relative as St. Jerome [41] seems to be right in maintaining, Joseph was of the same tribe as Mary. Indeed both were descended from the great king David; for St. Matthew's genealogy traces Joseph back to this king, and it is implied in the Scriptures, if not expressly said, that Mary was descended from this same royal stock (Luke 1:27–32; Rom. 1:3).[42] Then again, St. Luke (1:36) informs us that Zachary's wife, Elizabeth, a daughter of Aaron, was a cousin of Mary. The exact relationship of the two women is not known; but on account of the differences in their ages, that of aunt and niece readily suggests itself. Ac-

---

10, 1; Danby, p. 277. St. Thomas (*Summa theol.*, IIIa, q.28, a.4) says that the Mother of God is not believed to have taken a vow of virginity absolutely, but under the condition that it was pleasing to God. The common opinion among Catholic exegetes is that Mary's words, "I know not man" (Luke 1:34), signify that she had taken at least a resolution of perpetual virginity. Cf. the excellent treatment of the question by Collins: "Our Lady's Vow of Virginity," *Catholic Biblical Quarterly*, V (1943), 371–80. It was out of the ordinary for that time; yet there were some who lived a life of virginity, such as the Essenes, St. John the Baptist, and St. Paul.

[39] The following reasons are assigned for Mary's marriage: First, Mary being an heiress, a marriage was arranged with a near relative, so that her property would stay in the family. Secondly, her marriage with St. Joseph would protect her vow and save her from the importunities of other suitors. Thirdly, the fact that her marriage afforded protection for her reputation, and a foster father for the divine Child. See Collins, *op. cit.*, p. 378.

[40] Cf. Willam, *Mary the Mother of Jesus*, p. 467; Lagrange, *Evangile selon S. Matthieu*, p. 9 f. "A kinsman was considered the most desirable husband," writes Neufeld, *Ancient Hebrew Marriage Laws*, p. 138.

[41] *Perpetual Virginity of the Blessed Mary*, IV; NPN (2nd ser.), VI, 335.

[42] Luke 2:4 says that St. Joseph was of the house of David. Whether "house of David" in Luke 1:27 applies to the Blessed Virgin or to St. Joseph, is disputed. Lagrange holds that the application to St. Joseph is more probable; *Evangile selon S. Luc*, p. 26 f. Certainly Luke 1:32, 69 imply Mary's descent from David.

cordingly the opinion is widely held that the Mother of Our Lord was descended from the tribes of both Juda and Levi.

When the Gospel first speaks of Mary it is introducing the narrative of the Annunciation. She is living at Nazareth engaged to St. Joseph and we suppose she was about fourteen years old. Some of her sterling qualities are revealed in her conversation with the archangel. Gabriel paid an eloquent tribute to her character when he declared that her soul was enjoying the favor of God in all its fullness and was embellished with all the marks of God's friendship and love.[43] Extraordinary words of praise such as were employed by the heavenly messenger usually test stability and poise of character; yet here, far from showing any sign of susceptibility to flattery with the consequent upset to balance of judgment, Mary became perplexed rather than pleased at the laudatory words. Then the Gospel account of her subjecting the angelic words to the cold light of reason along with the two instances in which we are told she carefully stored events in her mind, these reveal her as a person who through deep thought and frequent meditation had become master and captain of her mind and heart. Also her question to the archangel after hearing him unfold the purpose for which he was sent, indicated her directness and alertness of mind as well as her faith and confidence in God. Notice her implicit trust in divine Providence in that she did not ask, for instance: Who will take care of me and my future child? How will the man to whom I am engaged be informed? or What steps will be taken to preserve my good name? Instead of demanding guaranties of protection or inquiring at all about the future, she professed herself the submissive handmaid of the Lord ready at all times to do His bidding. Here again are indicated mental faculties capable of penetrating involved problems, of dealing with considerations that were far-reaching for herself and for others, and of making prompt decisions that were sure and correct. How right she was when she esteemed the privilege of her motherhood of the divine Messiah above all other considerations and when she understood

[43] For the three attributes in the angel's salutation, see Scheeben, *Mariology*, I, 14.

that, by attuning her will to the will of God, she would be well taken care of in every way!

That Mary was possessed of the perfection of all virtues, and that as such she is described by the Evangelist, as such she was found by the angel and as such she was chosen by the Holy Spirit, this is the assertion of St. Ambrose.[44] He seems to imply that the Blessed Virgin was brought up in her own home, which he says she seldom left except to attend divine services in the company of her parents and kinsfolk. On the rare times that she did go to secular gatherings, according to this holy doctor, they were such "as mercy would not blush at nor modesty pass by." [45] On these occasions, St. Ambrose remarks, Mary "inspired respect by her bearing and address," for there was "nothing gloomy in her eyes, nothing forward in her words, nothing unseemly in her acts." [46] Mary's home life, St. Ambrose says, was characterized by "spareness of food" and "abundance of services." This is the general description he gives of the young maiden of Nazareth, that she was "humble in heart, grave in speech, prudent in mind, sparing in words, studious in reading, resting her hope not on uncertain riches but on the prayer of the poor, intent on work." [47] This early writer goes on to say that Mary gave evidence that she alone stood in charge of her own character so that her very outward appearance "might be the image of her soul, the representation of what is approved." [48] He points to the perfection of her everyday life since she attended to everything as if many were watching her and since she carried out all the requirements of high virtue "as though she were teaching rather than learning." [49] Finally he asks the faithful to pattern their lives on that of Mary because her life was a lesson and example illustrating "the clear rules of virtue." [50]

In regard to herself, Mary spoke about her humility; the words

[44] *Concerning Virgins*, 11, 9; *NPN* (2nd ser.), X, 375.
[45] *Ibid.*, p. 374.
[46] *Ibid.*
[47] *Ibid.*
[48] *Ibid.*
[49] *Ibid.*
[50] *Ibid.*

on her lips could also include her humiliations. When she called herself "the handmaid" of God, she expressed a fundamental attitude that was the basis of her humility and the support that sustained her during humiliations. God's mighty power that falls crushingly on the proud and conceited she ever bore in mind and accordingly left everything to divine Providence. "Whatsoever He shall say to you, do ye" (John 2: 5), was the advice she gave to the waiters at Cana. It is supreme wisdom for us, as Mary of Nazareth knew better than anyone else.

BIBLIOGRAPHY

Bernard, St. Super "missus est," homilia quatuor, PL, 183, 55–88.

Graham, Dom A. The Christ of Catholicism, pp. 275–93.

Landucci. Maria ss. nel Vangelo (Rome, 1945) .

Maas, A. J. "The Blessed Virgin Mary," Catholic Encyclopedia, XV, 464–72.

McGarry, William J. "A Fundamental Principle in Mariology," Theological Studies, I (1940), 396–411; II (1941), 35–52.

Roschini, G. La vita di Maria (Rome, 1945) .

Schaefer, A. The Mother of Jesus in Holy Scripture.

Scheeben, M. J. Mariology, 2 vols.

Willam, V. M. Mary the Mother of Jesus.

CHAPTER III

The Angel Gabriel

WHAT a variety of creatures almighty God has created about us to brighten our sojourn in this vale of tears! How many-colored the landscape that carpets the earth! How varied the sounds that greet the ear! How different the kinds of fish in the sea, birds in the air, and animals on land! Even stars that stud the cloudless night differ in brilliance. If there is diversity of beauty in material beings, how much the more in the realm of the spirits, those creatures without any clay in their being, whom the eternal Father has created to assist close to His throne in perpetual service and adoration! We refer to such a spirit as an angel. The word signifies "one going" or "one sent." The Bible mentions nine different groups or choirs among the celestial beings. For, besides angels and archangels, cherubim are mentioned in Genesis (3:24) and Ezechiel (10:1–19), the seraphim are referred to by Isaias (6:6), and St. Paul (Col. 1:16; Eph. 1:21) adds the names of five other orders: thrones, dominations, principalities, powers, and virtues. Within these main divisions, moreover, there is still great variety and even the lowest rank of these "thousands and thousands" who stand before the throne of the Lord of hosts, has grandeur and magnificence beyond our conception.

Angels are often mentioned in the Bible, especially in the New Testament. Indeed they are intimately associated with the person and doctrines of our divine Lord. The announcements to Zachary, Mary, Joseph, and the shepherds were brought by angels. Angels sang at the birth of Christ. The flight into Egypt and the return to the Holy Land were made at the bidding of an angel. Our divine Lord received refreshment from angels when He was exhausted by His fastings and temptations and He was strengthened by an angel after His terrible agony in the garden. It was an angel with countenance like lightning and raiment like snow who rolled back the stone of the empty sepulcher shortly after the dawn of the first Easter Sunday, while later that morning an angel announced the Resurrection to the holy women. Lastly, two angels in white garments appeared to make a last pronouncement at the scene of the Ascension; and many angels around the throne take part in the praise of the Lamb.

On His part, our divine Lord repeatedly spoke of the angels. He told Nathanael at the outset that he would see angels ascending into heaven and descending therefrom. He gave an illustration of the importance of children in God's sight by pointing to the fact that their guardian angels always behold the face of the eternal Father; He also gave an example of the angels' interest in human beings by mentioning their rejoicing on the conversion of sinners. He told that the soul of Lazarus was taken to heaven by angels and that the just in heaven are equal to angels. As for Himself, our Savior claimed He could have as a body guard more than twelve legions of angels. Although He stated that the angels do not know the date of the General Judgment, yet He foretold they would sound the trumpet for it. The great part they would take on this Day of Judgment was outlined by Him: they would accompany the Son of man in His capacity as judge; before them He would make acknowledgments to the good for their profession of faith and would repudiate those who had denied Him through false shame; and then the angels would superintend the separation of the good from the bad, like a shepherd separating the sheep from the goats, or like a harvester winnowing the wheat from the chaff, or like the fisherman selecting the good fish and rejecting the bad.

The Sacred Scriptures tell us the names of three archangels: Michael, Raphael and Gabriel. The name Gabriel—the root of the word *gibbor* has the connotation of "strength," *el* is "God"— seems to mean "the mighty man of God," "the hero of God," or "the warrior of God." Although this has a militant sound, and although might and power are attributed to him in the sacred text, yet his missions to earth were of peace and mercy. In the eighth chapter of Daniel he is described as standing before the prophet "as it were in the appearance of a man." He interprets for the prophet the vision of the horned ram. In the following chapter he instructs the prophet about the mysterious meaning of the seventy weeks that would intervene before the coming of the Redeemer. Here he also foretells that Christ will be slain, and Jerusalem with its sanctuary destroyed. He is mentioned as "flying swiftly" (Dan. 9:21), and the following description probably applied to him: "A man clothed in linen, and his loins were girded with the finest gold. And his body was like chrysolite, and his face as the appearance of lightning, and his eyes as a burning lamp; and his arms, and all downward even to the feet, like in appearance to glittering brass: and the voice of his word like the voice of a multitude" (Dan. 10:5 f.).

It was the privilege of the bright heavenly warrior, St. Gabriel, to usher in the dawn of Christianity in his exalted mission of bringing to earth the two announcements, of the birth of St. John the Baptist and of the birth of our Blessed Lord. In addressing holy Zachary he asserts his function of standing at the throne of God: "I am Gabriel who stands before God and am sent to speak to thee"; and he brooks no delay or hindrance in the fulfillment of his message. At the most solemn moment of the temple ceremonies in the holy place itself he delivers his announcement concerning the Baptist. In strong contrast to this, the greatest tidings ever vouchsafed to men, he proclaims in a lowly home in a despised hill town of Galilee. His greeting to the Virgin of Naz-

areth, "Hail, full of grace," a tribute from an angelic spirit, extols
the greatness of her personal holiness. During his appearance to
Zachary, Gabriel speaks three times as he outlines the career of
the Baptist; when he speaks to Mary he addresses her also three
times, foretelling the eternal reign of her divine Son. Although he
reassures her with the words, "Fear not," we are not told that she
was alarmed by his appearance; she was only puzzled at his extraordinary words of praise. On the other hand, holy Zachary was
struck with fear by the apparition of the bright figure of the angelic
"hero of God" standing at the right side of the altar of incense, and
had to be told that there was no cause for alarm. Fear had also struck
Daniel, who trembled and fell on his face before the archangel
until the latter touched him and raised him to his feet.

It is not expressly stated in Holy Scripture, but tradition has it
that it was Gabriel who appeared to St. Joseph to calm his doubts,[1]
and that it was this angel who brought the good news of the Savior's birth to the shepherds. Tradition also supports the view that
it was the same celestial spirit who "strengthened" our Blessed
Lord in the Garden of Olives. When St. Paul (I Thess. 4:15) foretells that Christ's descent from heaven on the Last Day will be
"with the voice of an archangel and with the trumpet of God," it
is the popular belief that this archangel will also be Gabriel who
will call forth the dead from the grave and sound the trumpet to
inaugurate the day of God's truth and God's glory.

Of Gabriel, Milton [2] wrote:

> "one of the seven
> Who in God's presence, nearest to his throne,
> Stand ready to command, and are his eyes
> That run through all the Heavens, or down to the Earth,
> Bear his swift errands over moist and dry,
> O'er sea and land."

---

[1] Cf. Durand, *Evangile selon S. Matthieu*, p. 8.
[2] *Paradise Lost*, III, 648 ff. The poet here borrowed the number seven from Apoc. 8:2;
Tob. 12:15.

Since angels are mentioned through the whole Bible from beginning to end, "like to an angel of God" is a popular biblical expression, it was most fitting [3] that an angel be selected to bring such
important messages to man as these contained in the announcements to Zachary and to Mary. First it maintained the order
established by God by which divine things are brought to men by
means of angels. Secondly, it was becoming for the restoration of
human nature, to be announced by an angel since it had been
vitiated through the cajoling of a fallen angel. Lastly, it was suitable
because of the virginity of Mary of Nazareth as virginity is associated with the angelic nature. It is highly credible that, as St.
Gregory the Great states, the bearer of the highest message was
no common angel.[4] Although he may not be the highest in rank
of all the celestial choir, he is considered the highest of the special
angels known as archangels whose function is to announce sublime
things. Because his name connotes power and might it seems fitting that he should be chosen to announce the coming of the Lord
of hosts. Thus this same sacred writer mentions the meaning of the
name and gives the following reason for his being called Gabriel,
"because he was to announce Him who deigned to appear humble
that He might destroy evil powers." [5]

The following description of Gabriel as he addressed the Virgin
Mary is attributed to St. Augustine: "glowing countenance, gleaming robe, and wondrous step." [6] St. Jerome also held that Gabriel
had appeared in the form of a man; referring to the Virgin Mary,
he writes: "whom Gabriel found alone in her chamber and who
was frightened, it seems, by seeing a man there." [7] Likewise St.
Ambrose mentions the bodily form of the archangel when he

[3] Cf. St. Thomas, *Summa theol.*, IIIa, q. 30, a. 2.
[4] Homily 34, *On the Gospels*; De testimoniis in Evang. secundum Lucam; *PL*, 79, 1058.
[5] Homily 34, *On the Gospels*, II, 9; *PL*, 79, 1058.
[6] St. Augustine, *Sermon on the Annunciation*, III; cf. St. Thomas, *Summa theol.*, IIIa,
q. 30, a. 3.
[7] Letter 107, 7, to Laeta; *Select Letters*, ed. by F. Wright, p. 355. In another place St.
Jerome says that Mary "was filled with terror and consternation," thinking the messenger
to be a man; but when she learned that he was an angel she conversed fearlessly" with him.
Letter 22, to Eustochium, 38 (*Select Letters*, ed. by Wright, p. 147).

writes that Mary was disturbed "as though at the form of a man, but on hearing his name recognized him as one not unknown to her." [8]

When speaking about Mary's reaction to Gabriel's greetings, the two Fathers just mentioned, as well as others, attribute her disturbance to the sight of the archangel and not to his words. This error arose from a faulty reading in the Gospel text. The accepted Greek text for the beginning of the verse (Luke 1:29) may be translated, "but she was troubled by this discourse"; yet the Vulgate rendition may be translated: "who when she heard was troubled at his discourse." Certain of the Greek manuscripts had an interpolation here; namely, "having seen." This no doubt came about under the influence of Luke 1:12; and "Zachary seeing was troubled." The interpolation found its way into most of the Latin versions; the Vulgate, however, changing "having seen" into "who when she heard." Thus, finding the faulty reading in the Gospel text they were using, certain Church Fathers were misled into believing that the Virgin Mary was frightened at the sight of Gabriel. Although there is no mention about Mary's seeing the archangel, it is generally accepted that we are to understand that he came to her in an external, somewhat human appearance. [9]

For his appearance in bodily form to Mary, the following reasons are outlined by St. Thomas: [10] As the message concerned the invisible God taking the form of a visible creature, it was fitting that the messenger should be an invisible creature in visible form. Then the dignity of her whose consent was sought would call for an angelic vision perceptible to the bodily senses. Lastly, it is in keeping with the certainty that was required for this greatest of all events, the Incarnation, that the Virgin of Nazareth be vouchsafed a vision of great solemnity, the bodily appearance of an archangel.

[8] *Concerning Virgins*, II, 11; NPN, 2nd ser., X, 375.
[9] Cf. Plummer, *The Gospel according to St. Luke*, p. 22; Lagrange, *Evangile selon S. Luc*, p. 29; Valensin-Huby, *Evangile selon S. Luc*, p. 13.
[10] *Summa theol.*, IIIa, q. 30, a. 30.

St. Gabriel was remarkable for his promptness in carrying out God's will. In executing all three of his commissions on earth, he took on the appearance of a man, but he must have been so glorious a sight as to leave no doubt that he was an angel. Indeed his sudden appearance and disappearance would of themselves confirm this fact. Moreover, we must not forget that the bright "hero of God" was especially the angel of the Incarnation. He interpreted for Daniel the seventy weeks that were to precede the coming of Christ. He brought to earth the message of the coming of the great Precursor. Finally, he was the mouthpiece of God in securing Mary's consent for the coming among us of the Son of God. Naturally we associate him most directly with the annunciation to Mary when we lovingly commemorate this event in the Angelus. In the Canon of the Mass, also, when we supplicate the God of omnipotence to command that the sacrificial gifts be brought "by the hands of thy holy angel to Thy sublime altar in the presence of Thy divine Majesty," we may mean if not Michael, or Raphael, this angel of the incarnate Word, glorious Gabriel.

It is of interest to note that as early as the second century there is a fresco in the cemetery of St. Priscilla in which an angel appears in the Annunciation scene. Then on the triumphant arch of St. Mary Major there is a fifth century Annunciation scene in which Gabriel is depicted as soaring through the air toward the Virgin Mary. From the sixth century we have a mosaic in the Church of St. Apollinaris, Ravenna, representing Gabriel dressed in military chlamys and carrying a military standard.

Is it not remarkable that we have so many words spoken by Gabriel? How precious should be all the utterances of a visitor from the realms of bliss! According to the Book of Daniel, while referring to his function as that of instructor, Gabriel speaks of the divine Messiah to come as "the Prince." Then in the Gospel history he tells Zachary his own name and his office of standing in God's presence, and expressly says that he was sent by God to bring him the good news of the birth of a son who will be famous.

Yet, in the account of his appearance to Mary, although it begins by saying that the angel Gabriel was sent to her by God, the text does not mention that he told her his name. Of course, he must have given his name to Mary; there was an opportunity of doing so, when he spoke of her aged kinswoman, St. Elizabeth, whose husband he had visited six months previously.

The archangel Gabriel set the example of respect and devotion to the Mother of God by giving her, without being asked, a proof of the genuineness of his message and by supplying us with the very words of praise we address to her. The angel of the Incarnation further taught that the greatest respect and homage should be paid our divine Lord, for he drew attention to His great holiness and His royal divinity as Son of God; and he foretold the everlasting character of His mission and reign. Concerning God, Gabriel points to His omnipotence when he says: "for nothing shall be impossible with God." Is not the great power of God suggested by the very meaning of the name, Gabriel, "the strength of God"? And do not the great number and variety of the angelic spirits in heaven bespeak God's almighty power? The omnipotence of God is clearly reflected in the realms of heaven as well as in the planets and the sun and the thousands of millions of worlds in our material universe.

God can do all things. This truth guides us in the proper approach to the New Testament. How utterly wrong, therefore, are those who contend that a human form cannot be assumed by God! That it is possible and easy for God to become incarnate is a question to be decided by those who have profoundly studied the possibilities of being and becoming. The great expert on this subject, St. Thomas Aquinas,[11] declares that God could have become every human being, not merely one; and that He chose to become one human being and through that one to redeem all others. One of the greatest minds of all times, the great St. Augustine, had said that, if God so willed, He could become man without even being

[11] *Ibid.*, q. 3, a. 7.

born of a woman; "for as He could be born of a woman without a man, so could He also have become man without the woman." [12]

The Virgin Mary, it seems, expressed no fear at the appearance of Gabriel, and was later unperturbed by the account of the shepherds' vision of angels. The probable reason for her composure is that she had accustomed herself to be mindful of the blessed presence of the angels; as St. Ambrose remarks: "she was a stranger as to man, but not as to the angel." [13] It was St. John Chrysostom [14] who pointed out that angels did not appear to the scribes and Pharisees because of their corruption; and that, although appearing in sleep to St. Joseph, they made an outward appearance to the uncultivated shepherds because of their innocence. The angels remind us of heavenly things, our Father's home, and the Ruler of the angelic host Himself.

Because it was an angel who brought to earth the great news of the Incarnation, the name Angelus is rightly given to the popular prayer which begins with *angelus* in Latin ("the angel" in English). Gabriel is given another honor when the Mass of his feast has the same Gospel account as is found in the Mass of the Annunciation. As we follow his lead in offering words of salutation and praise to Mary of Nazareth for the graces God bestowed on her, we have opportunities each day to call to mind the blessed archangel of the Incarnation. His superb tribute to the peerless one among the daughters of Eve should be repeated by us with love and devotion; indeed it should be sung by us with sweetest melody.

By Almighty God's decree,
    Down the fields of starry space,
Camest thou, fleet Gabriel,
    Messenger of light and grace.

Valiant, wise, beyond our ken,
    Versed in lore of prophecy

[12] *Sermons on New Testament Lessons*, 1, 3; *NPN*, 1st ser., VI, 246.
[13] *Loc. cit.*
[14] In *Catenae Graecorum patrum*, on Luke 2:13; Vol. II (Oxford, 1844).

What inspired Daniel saw
  Was interpreted by thee.

Holy Zachary at prayer,
  Where the temple glories shone,
Heard with awe thy gladsome news
  Of the coming of Saint John.

More sublime Thy wondrous part
  In Redemption's ritual,
Bringing Mary promised word
  That no other tongue might tell.

Honored thus by the Most High,
  Gabriel, we hail thy name;
In our prayers the Angelus
  Rings forever with thy fame.

Hear us, help us, Gabriel,
  Ere the evil powers smite;
Rout anew the rebel horde,
  With the lightning of thy might.

And when Judgment hour is nigh,
  And we list thy trumpet's sound,
Shepherd us, we humbly pray
  Where celestial joys abound.

                              Patrick MacDonough

BIBLIOGRAPHY

Gregory the Great, St. Homily 34, On the Gospels, II, 7–15; *PL*, 76, 1248–53.

Lagrange, J. M. Evangile selon S. Luc, p. 20.

Plummer, A. The Gospel according to St. Luke, p. 16.

Pope, H. "Angel," Catholic Encyclopedia, I, 476–81.

Stoll, R. The Gospel according to St. Luke, pp. 3–13.

Valensin and Huby. Evangile selon S. Luc, pp. 5–10.

CHAPTER IV

The Priest's Vision

AS a memorial to himself and at the same time in an effort to win favor with the Jews, King Herod the Great in the year 22 B.C. decided to rebuild the Temple.[1] Indicative of the distrust in which he was held is the fact that, before beginning to raze the old edifice, he had to collect in Jerusalem a great part of the material for the reconstruction.[2] By filling in valleys and by supporting platforms of masonry on huge piers and arches, he enlarged the Temple area to about thirty acres, double its original size. An irregular quadrangle,—it is longest on the west side and wider in the north than in the south—was enclosed by a great wall nearly forty feet high on three sides, but ten feet less on the east. In this outward wall there were in the west four gates,[3] in the south two gates dividing the wall into three equal parts,[4] one gate centrally located in the north,[5] and another one at the northeastern corner.[6] Besides, battlements were located at intervals and, as a special feature,

[1] E. F. Sutcliffe (A Two Year Public Ministry Defended, p. 152) gives the following chronology: After two years of preparation, Herod began the building in February, 20 B.C. The sanctuary was completed in July, 19 B.C., but the halls and porticoes took eight years to complete. Work on the Temple, however, continued until about A.D. 63. See also Hollis, The Archaeology of Herod's Temple, p. 1.

[2] Josephus, Antiquities, XV, xi, 2. For the sources and for a fuller treatment, see Appendix, p. 344.

[3] According to Josephus, Antiquities, XV, xi, 5.

[4] Huldah Gates, Mishnah, Middoth, I, 3; Danby, p. 590. Cf. Josephus, loc. cit.

[5] Tadi Gate, Mishnah, Middoth, loc. cit.; Cf. Josephus, Jewish War, VI, 22 (iv, 1).

[6] Shushan Gate, Mishnah, Middoth, loc. cit.

inside porticoes. Three sides had double porticoes, the eastern one being known as Solomon's Porch. On the south four rows of marble Corinthian columns, 162 in all, formed three aisles and supported cedar-lined ceilings. This magnificent basilica extended uninterrupted along the whole south wall and was known as the Royal Porch. By the use of the best Grecian styles for the construction of the outer walls and porticoes, King Herod reached the height of his architectural achievement. He had the service of a thousand priests specially trained for the purpose in the construction of the holy house, which was according to traditional lines. This part was finished in a year and a half, and the completion of the other buildings occupied eight years. Indeed construction work of some kind continued for thirty years after our Lord's death.

Approaching from the south and entering the eastern passage of the twin gates, one passed under the Royal Porch to emerge on a large open space paved with various kinds of stone. Standing in the court of the Gentiles, a person could note that on the south and on the east it was extensive and that a low stone wall marked off a large square area for Jews only.[7] The Temple buildings lay due east to west, extending almost from one outer porch to the other and occupying almost half of the Temple enclosure. The inner courts and buildings appeared to be square in shape and rose successively in height, ending in the west with the holy house that towered 100 feet above the court of Israel. Other objects worthy of special attention were the two gates (the Great Gate and the Nicanor Gate), the gate houses of the Court of Israel, and the elevated platform around it, and the gold vine and gold-plated door of the holy house.

Entering at the east through the Great Gate one came into an open square-shaped court with colonnades of pillars that supported balconies on three sides, the women's court.[8] Going further west

---

[7] Called the Soreg, *Mishnah*, Middoth, II, 3a; Danby, p. 592. This may afterward be replaced by a finely wrought stone trellis mentioned by Josephus, *Jewish War*, V, 193 (v, 2). See Hollis *op. cit.*, pp. 227, 263.

[8] This may not have been built in Our Lord's time. See Hollis, *op. cit.*, p. 158.

one came to the famous Nicanor Gate [9] with its folding door of Corinthian brass. The gate was reached by a beautiful semi-circular flight of fifteen steps, the first ten of which led to a platform that went round the 450 feet square court of Israel. In this latter court that had open spaces to accommodate great crowds there were in the outer walls strong gate houses, splendid porticoes, and numerous chambers.[10] In the center was the oblong-shaped priests' court.

In the eastern part of the priests' court was the great forty-eight foot square altar, the place of slaughter with its rings, hooks, and tables being to the north. Then west of the altar, built on the highest part of the ground and probably over the sacred rock was the holy house [11] or sanctuary proper, reached by three flights of steps. It was a snow-white limestone structure that dominated all the other buildings. A remarkable feature was the porch that was 30 feet deep and 150 feet wide, projecting beyond the main building 30 feet on each side. Behind the porch were to be found the holy place and the holy of holies. The latter was half the length of the former and was a thirty-five foot cube, both empty and windowless. The holy place contained the altar of incense along with the seven-branched candlesticks to the south and the golden table of show bread to the north. This holy house was the crowning glory of the Temple, standing as it did 150 feet high. The whole effect was like that of a snow-capped mountain, and in the early morning the sunlight reflecting from the famous gilded porch looked like the sun's own rays. Distinguished by its "immense riches" [12] and "adorned with beautiful stones and offerings" (Luke 21:15), Herod's Temple was rightly considered one of the world's wonders.

[9] Called after the donor or designer who came from Alexandria. See Hollis, *op. cit.*, p. 272.

[10] See Hollis, *op. cit.*, p. 209.

[11] Vagueness in the sources gives rise to different conceptions of the holy house. It is not certain whether it was built over the sacred rock or whether the altar was over this rock. See the reconstruction by Hollis, *op. cit.*, plate XVIII, p. 213.

[12] "Immensae opulentiae," Tacitus, *Histories*, V, 8.

Priests and Levites were in charge of the Temple and its services.[13] Some of the priests lived in Ophel, the section of the Holy City immediately south of the Temple; the others lived in different parts of the Holy Land, many of them in Jericho. The chief functions of the priests were the following: the offering up of all sacrifices, the incense service twice a day, the replenishing of the oil lamps on the golden candlestick, and the weekly renewal of the loaves of proposition on the golden table. As to the sacrifices, some were private, such as vow offerings and free will offerings, others were public. Especially important was the continual or daily burnt-offering of a yearly lamb every morning and every midafternoon,[14] this offering being doubled on Sabbaths, new moons, and festival days.[15] To discharge these various duties at the Temple, the 20,000 priests had been divided into twenty-four groups or "courses" (I Par. 24: 7 ff.). Each group was stationed at the sacred edifice for an entire week twice a year,[16] all, of course, taking part at the great feasts.[17]

It was probably in the early part of September of the year 9 B.C. or four and a half years before King Herod's death, that a priest was on duty at the Temple when an angel from heaven appeared to him with an extraordinary message. This priest belonging to the group called Abia which had been reconstructed after the Babylonian captivity (II Esd. 12:4), was Zachary and his wife was Elizabeth, like him a member of the same priestly family of Aaron. We are told that at the time of the heavenly occurrence they were both advanced in years and had not been blessed with children, a condition considered by the Jews not only an affliction but even

13 Cf. Bonsirven, *Le Judaisme Palestinien au temps de Jésus-Christ*, II, 129–34.

14 *Mishnah*, Pesahim (Passover), 5, 1; Danby, p. 142. Ordinarily for the afternoon service the slaughtering began at half past two and the offering at half past three.

15 *Mishnah*, Taanith (Days of Fasting), 4, 1–3; Danby, p. 199. The "whole offering," one of the most holy things, was burnt whole on the altar fire. *Mishnah*, Zebahim (Animal Offerings), 5, 4; Danby, p. 474.

16 Each course was divided into "fathers' houses," each to take care of the duties of the day, *Mishnah*, Yoma (Day of Atonement), 4, 1; Danby, p. 166; Josephus, *Life*, 2 (1).

17 *Mishnah*, Sukkah (Feast of Tabernacles), 5, 7; Danby, p. 181.

a malediction. This couple, however, had borne their cross with resignation,[18] and were blameless in their goodness of life and their strict observance of all the requirements of their religion. Their home was in a town now called Ain Karem, about four miles south-west of Jerusalem; but during the week of duty at the Temple the aged priest may have slept in the guard house, or hearth room, at the northwest corner of the court of Israel where there were divans of stone slabs for the older priests; the younger ones slept upon mats laid on the ground.[19]

For guarding and protecting the Temple, Levites were stationed at twenty-one specified places, and priests were placed at three important posts.[20] Each night rounds of inspection were made by the officer of the Temple, for which he made use of lighted torches. The senior priest of the group in charge of the day's services slept with the keys of the Temple in his hand in the large vaulted house of the burning hearth,[21] the westernmost of the three chambers on the northern side of the inner court. Here at cockcrow the officer of the Temple, after knocking at the door of the chamber, called out: "Let him who has immersed himself come and cast lots." [22] Thus began the morning service during which in all four lots were cast [23] to designate priests for the various assignments.[24] Thus at cockcrow those priests who were to take part in the drawing of lots for the morning ceremony bathed and put on their

[18] Their piety is seen in contrast to the Mishnic instruction, that a husband should divorce his wife if after ten years of married life she did not bear him any child. *Mishnah*, Jebamoth (Sisters-in-law), 6, 6 f.; Danby, p. 277. Great care was taken that a priest's wife should come from a priestly family. Cf. Josephus, *Against Apion*, I, 31 (9).

[19] *Mishnah*, Middoth (Measurements), 1, 8; Danby, p. 591.

[20] *Mishnah*, Tamid (Daily Whole-offering), i, i; Danby, p. 582; Middoth (Measurements), 1, 1 f.; Danby, p. 589. See Hollis, *op. cit.*, Plate XIX, p. 241.

[21] It received its name because of the fact that fire was continually maintained there, on account of its use as a dwelling house and perhaps also on account of underground baths. See Hollis, *op. cit.*, p. 256, also Plate XXI, p. 271.

[22] *Mishnah*, Tamid (Daily Whole-offering), 1, 2; Danby, p. 582.

[23] *Mishnah*, Yoma (Day of Atonement), 2, 204; Danby, pp. 163 f.

[24] The first lot assigned those who removed the ashes from the altar and brought faggots for the altar fire; the second gave thirteen assignments, including the slaughtering, and the casting of the blood on the altar base. The third chose the priest who offered the incense, and the fourth those who carried the members of the sacrificial animal from the ramp to the altar. (*Ibid.*)

sacred vestments, which consisted of short breeches and a narrow-sleeved white linen tunic, the byssus, that reached to the ankle. The tunic was gathered at the waist by an embroidered, colored girdle. Their feet were bare but their heads were covered with a white linen turban. Once vested, they crossed the court of Israel to the chamber of hewn stone [25] where they waited for the casting of the lots. The following prayers were in their hearts if not on their lips.[26]

In the morning I offer my prayers to Thee and I wait. . . . But, by the abundance of Thy mercy, I shall enter into Thy house, I shall worship with reverence at Thy holy temple, O Lord. (Ps. 5:5, 8)

> Enter His gates with praise, His courts with a hymn;
> Glorify Him, bless His name.
> For the Lord is good, His mercy is forever,
> And His faithfulness from generation to generation.
>
> Ps. 99 (100):4 f.
>
> Offer sacrifice and go into His courts,
> Adore the Lord in holy attire,
> Tremble before Him, all the earth;
> Say among the heathen: the Lord reigns.
>
> Ps. 95 (96):9 f.
>
> I wash my hands in innocence,
> And I walk around Thine altar, O Lord,
> That I may proclaim Thy praise
> And recount all Thy wondrous deeds,
> O Lord, I love the abode of Thy house,
> And the place where Thy glory dwells.
>
> Ps. 25 (26):6–8

When the morning light had illumined the eastern sky as far as Hebron,[27] a yearling lamb was brought from a subchamber

---

[25] *Mishnah*, Tamid (Daily Whole-offering), 2, 5; Danby, p. 584.

[26] Translation of the Psalms (here and p. 190) is taken from the New English Translation of the *New Latin Version from the Hebrew* (W. H. McClellan), Benziger Bros., New York, 1946. All other Biblical translations are from the Douay Version.

[27] *Op. cit.*, 3, 2; Danby, p. 384; Yoma (Day of Atonement), 3, 1; Danby, p. 164.

at the northwest corner of the Temple.[28] It was slain in the place of slaughter north of the altar; to the northwest of the second ring in the morning, to the northeast of this ring in the afternoon.[29] The blood of the victim was received in a basin and was sprinkled on both sides of the northeastern and southwestern corners of the altar.[30] Then after the meal offering the priests gathered in the chamber of hewn stone for a short religious service.[31] There followed each morning the incense offering before the burning of the victim's members, whereas this order was reversed in the midafternoon.

The Gospel text is silent about whether it was in the morning or the evening that the apparition appeared to Zachary. The crowd of people (Luke 1:21) mentioned as present in the Temple at the time might indicate that it was the Sabbath day or it might signify that it was in the afternoon, when a better attendance could be expected than in the morning. Be that as it may, after the slaying of the sacrificial lamb for the daily burnt offering, came the casting of lots for the appointment of the priest to burn the incense. It was done in the following manner. The priests stood in a circle, holding up their hands with one or more fingers outstretched. The prefect announced a certain number, as, for example, seventy, and, taking off the turban of one of the priests, he counted the raised fingers from him. When the selected number was reached that

[28] The chamber of lambs was the northwestern one of the house of the burning hearth. The northern half of this house was on unconsecrated ground. The lamb, which had been inspected the previous night, was given a final inspection and made to drink out of a golden cup. *Op. cit.*, 3, 3; Danby, p. 384.

[29] *Mishnah*, Tamid (Daily Whole-offering), 4, 1; Danby, p. 585; Middoth (Measurements), 3, 5; Danby, p. 594. For the account of the slaughtering shed with its pillars, blocks, rings, and hooks, see Hollis, *op. cit.*, pp. 312–14, and Plate XXIX, p. 340.

[30] *Mishnah*, Tamid (Daily Whole-offering), 4, 1; Danby, p. 585. Minute regulations are here given about the cutting up of the sacrificial lamb. It was placed north and south with its head to the south and its face to the west. Its heart was slit to let out the blood. Nine priests stood in line each receiving a member, and the members were carried solemnly to the west of the altar ramp, where they were salted.

[31] There took place the recitation of a benediction, the Ten Commandments and the Shema, and also the pronouncing of three benedictions with the priestly blessing.

person was the one to perform the function.[32] On this occasion it was Zachary's fingers that made up the announced number.

During all the years of his ministry, Zachary had never before enjoyed the privilege of performing this most important function of the day,[33] which brought with it both temporal and spiritual blessings. So with supreme joy in his heart yet with a most attentive mind, he set about his sacred duties. Following the established custom, he first chose two of his priestly colleagues as assistants, one to take the censer filled with live coals, the other to carry the gold incense ladle containing a gold saucer with its half pound of incense.[34] Preceded by two ministers whose duty it was to clean the altar of incense and to fill the lamps on the candlestick, Zachary and the two assistant priests solemnly ascended the steps to the holy place. While they passed from the altar to the porch a loud note of the organlike megrefah had been sounded.[35] Its purpose was to summon the priests, Levites, and "stationary men" to their respective positions and to enjoin silence on all sides at this solemn hour of incense and prayer. It also was a signal for the priests to prostrate themselves after the incensing.

Inside the sanctuary the live coals were spread on the altar of incense. This altar was made of acacia wood covered with plates of gold and stood in front of the holy of holies. Then when the golden saucer of incense was given into Zachary's hands, the four attending priests withdrew to stand on the steps of the Temple porch, leaving him alone in the sanctuary. At the command of the presiding priest, "offer the incense," he spread the precious material on the burning coals, beginning at the farther end facing the holy of holies.[36] As the fragrance filled the whole place, he prostrated himself before God, the whole multitude in the courts

[32] Cf. *Mishnah*, Yoma (Day of Atonement), 2, 1; Danby, p. 163.
[33] *Op. cit.*, 2, 4; Danby, p. 164; Tamid (Daily Whole-offering), 5, 2; Danby, p. 587. The priest selected for the incense was considered enriched with favors and blessings.
[34] *Mishnah*, Tamid (Daily Whole-offering), 5, 4; Danby, p. 587.
[35] *Ibid.*, 5, 6; Danby, p. 587.
[36] *Ibid.*, 6, 3; Danby, p. 588. Zachary was instructed to do this so that he would not be burned.

outside falling on their faces before the Lord and spreading their
hands in silent prayer.

In this most sacred spot, on this solemn occasion, Zachary poured
out his soul to his Creator, not merely for himself, but for the
salvation of his people and for the coming of God's Messianic
kingdom. The mounting incense represented this prayer, and the
burning of a mixture of so many substances—thirteen went into
its composition [37]—signified the consecration of all things to God.
Incense was also symbolic of God's acceptance of the prayer. We
can safely surmise the special prayer that with the incense ascended
from the heart of Zachary and from the hearts of the multitude
at this hour.[38] Zachary no longer hoped for a son in his old age;
but both he and the people groaning under Herod's oppression,
we may be sure, were ceaselessly petitioning the throne of God
for the speedy coming of the Messiah to establish God's kingdom
and to bring about the salvation of Israel.

God's answer to his prayer surpassed anything that could be
thought of or expected. For, lo, at the right of the altar of incense,
the brilliant, majestic figure of an angel appeared. Terror over-
powered the old priest. Calling Zachary by his name and calming
his fears, the angel gave him the following message. He will have
a son whose name will be John. This child will distinguish himself
in the cause of God. He will lead an ascetic life filled with the
Holy Spirit from his mother's womb. He will be another Elias;
for he will prepare the people for the coming of the Lord by con-
verting their hearts, so that their good lives may reflect the virtuous
deeds of their ancestors.

The aged priest, though not doubting the power of God, nevertheless, asked for a sign. Abraham and Moses had asked for a

[37] According to Josephus, *Jewish War*, V, 218 (v, 5). See Edersheim, *The Temple*,
p. 134. The House of Abtinas, the easternmost of the three chambers on the south of the
inner court, was for the incense.

[38] Some authorities have thought that Zachary's prayer was for the speedy advent of
the Messiah; others are of the opinion that the prayer was for a son; still others have said
it was for both intentions as both were answered. See Lagrange, *Evangile selon S. Luc*,
p. 15.

sign and were not held blameworthy; but greater perfection was expected of Zachary in view of the new era which was at hand when faith would above all be required. It would have been more perfect for him to have put implicit trust in God's messenger. Therefore the sign given to him was not only to convince him but also to serve as a punishment for his lack of faith in the words of the angel. Before giving the sign, however, the heavenly visitor declared he was Gabriel who stands in the presence of God. The apparition then was indeed the great archangel sent from the court of heaven to convey to Zachary the message that the time was at hand for the fulfillment of the divine plan. Then he gave Zachary the sign he had asked, namely, that Zachary would be afflicted with dumbness "until the day wherein these things shall come to pass" (Luke 1:20).

Meanwhile the people and the priests in the courts outside became perturbed that the aged priest tarried so long in the sanctuary, it being a matter of apprehension if the sacred ceremonies were not discharged expeditiously in the holy place. When they saw him coming out on the steps, making signs and unable to join with the four other ministers in pronouncing the threefold blessing (Num. 6:24–26) over Israel from the steps of the porch as was the custom, they knew that he had seen a vision. This blessing, be it noted, was the only occasion on which the ineffable name of God could be uttered, and it was pronounced as a single blessing while the priests held their hands above their heads.[39] For the conclusion of the service there was the pouring of the drink-offering, which was a signal for the Levites to chant the psalm of the day.[40] This they did in unison with the voices of boys. Their singing was introduced by the clash of a cymbal; and at the close

[39] *Mishnah*, Tamid (Daily Whole-offering), 7, 2; Danby, p. 588. In the provinces three blessings were given, a substitute word for the holy name of God had to be used, and hands were lifted shoulder high.

[40] For the seven days of the week the psalms were 23 (24), 47 (48), 81 (82), 93 (94), 80 (81), 92 (93), 91 (92). See *Mishnah*, Tamid (Daily Whole-offering), 7, 4; Danby, p. 589.

of the three sections of the psalm, trumpet blasts gave notice to the people for further prostrations.[41]

After his week's service at the Temple, the mute priest returned home. Some of the Fathers of the Church think holy Zachary did not communicate the news of his vision to his wife even by writing. Yet it would be strange for so important a matter not to be made known to one who was so vitally concerned. When St. Elizabeth discovered that she had conceived at her advanced age, she praised God, saying: "Thus hath the Lord dealt with me in the days when He deigned to take away my reproach among men." Sarah and Rachael had both rejoiced over the birth of a child; but Elizabeth's joy is expressed, not at the birth of a son, but at the time of conception which was itself miraculous. The sacred text records that Elizabeth immediately went into seclusion to pass five months alone, in a little villa or country house. The saintly woman's great faith in God and her gratitude to Him are shown in these five months of solitude. Perhaps also, she and her mute husband wished to keep the secret confided to them until God willed it to become known.

With what wisdom God arranges all things! Parents of spotless integrity and personal holiness were selected to stand at the threshold of the new era of mercy and grace. As Israel had been chosen God's own holy people to produce the Messiah, and as the priesthood had been a gift to one family to represent the holiness of the nation, how appropriate was the selection of a member of that priesthood to be the father of the Forerunner of Jesus Christ! What more suitable place for the first blush that would herald the dawn of the era of God's special friendship and favor than the inner sanctuary of the Temple? What better time than the sublime hour of incense which signified the acceptance of the daily sacrifice and prayers of the people enjoined by God Himself? What more suitable person as witness and participator than the priest burning the incense in the holy place with the priests, the Levites, and the

[41] *Op. cit.*, 7, 3; Danby, p. 589.

people in prayer? Almighty God honors the Old Law and shows its true value as a foreshadowing of the New and a preparation for it.

As the Messiah was, above all, to be the great High Priest of all time, to offer on the cross the one clean oblation, as the world religion He was to establish was to be founded on, and centered in, the Christian priesthood, it was fitting that the priesthood of the Old Testament should be honored, and that a representative be selected to be the father of the great Baptist. It was fitting, too, that Gabriel's appearance and announcement should take place at the time of the daily sacrifice of a lamb without blemish, which symbolically was the prefiguring of the unending sacrifice of the Mass.

The holy place of the Temple filled with the cloud of "odors" of the incense; the aged priest prostrate in prayer; the great archangel Gabriel standing at the right of the altar; this tableau of the holiest of the earth and the celestial spirit, most fittingly marks the prelude of Christianity. The message itself, so startling in its contents and manner of delivery, comes like a bolt of lightning from the sky. As the first manifestation of the New Testament, it falls on the focal point of the old revelation, the Temple. Thus the Christian era begins with the best of the old dispensation. "Confirm, O God, what thou hast wrought in us. From thy Temple in Jerusalem" (Ps. 67 [68]: 29, 30).

THE MISHNAH, A PRIMARY SOURCE

The Mishnah is here used as a primary source of information on the religious background of the time of Our Lord. According to Jewish tradition it was compiled by Judah, the patriarch (A.D. 135 to A.D. 220), called Rabbi, meaning the rabbi par excellence. How much of it he wrote is a matter of dispute, and it is certain that later additions have crept in.[42] He was, however, the editor of the chief collection of the rules and regulations that marked the passage of the Jews from the Old Testament to what is known as Judaism. Especially during the peaceful years between A.D. 70 and 135,

---

[42] Strack rightly states: "Certainly in its present compass the Mishnah cannot go back to Rabbi." *Introduction to Talmud and Midrash,* p. 20.

the Pharisees rose to the supreme leadership that molded and fashioned the Jewish religion. Under them the oral law was established in authority alongside the written inspired word. In reassembling and editing the oral traditions of the rabbinical schools, Rabbi took the leading part, and his compilation became recognized as the authoritative work. Some of what was not contained in the Mishnah (repetition or teaching) was soon afterwards gathered into the Tosepheta (Supplement). Later additions and commentaries on the Mishnah appeared in the Talmuds, the Palestinian one about A.D. 500, the Babylonian one two centuries later.

It must be stated that it is "a matter of extreme difficulty" [43] to assess the historical value of any of the traditions handed down in the Mishnah. In making use of it as a primary source for the social and religious conditions of Our Lord's time the warning of such men as de Grandmaison,[44] Prat,[45] and Bonsirven [46] must be heeded, namely, that naturally there would have been a tendency towards unification, perfection and idealization in handing down oral traditions; and a tendency would be evident not to lag behind Christian thought and Christian ideals. In the early Christian centuries, however, there prevailed among the Jews a strong hope for the rebuilding of the Temple and for the restoration of its services. Great care, therefore, would be taken to pass along to posterity exact accounts of the Temple building and of its ritual of worship. These traditions would be "less exposed to the possibility of revision under the influence of later fashions of interpretation." [47] Accordingly such tractates as Yoma, Middoth, Tamid and parts of Bikkurim and Shekalim may be considered accounts of eyewitnesses of the Temple services, coming down from times prior to the destruction of the Temple. They may be classed as primary sources along with the works of Josephus and the Old Testament Apocrypha.

For the origin and historical value of the Mishnah and for the dates of the rabbis mentioned there, see H. Danby, *Mishnah*, pp. v, xxxii, 799–800; H. Strack, *Introduction to the Talmud and Midrash*, translation from fifth German edition (Philadelphia, 1931), pp. 12–60; M. Mielziner, *Introduction to the Talmud*, 3rd ed. (New York, 1925), pp. 4–30; Joseph Bonsirven, *On the Ruins of the Temple*, translated from the French (London, 1931), pp. 1–7; G. F. Moore, *Judaism in the First Centuries of the Christian Era* (Harvard

[43] Danby, *Mishnah*, p. xiv.

[44] *Jésus-Christ*, I, 9 f.

[45] *Jésus-Christ*, p. 44 note.

[46] *On the Ruins of the Temple*, pp. 26–31. Modern scholars warn us that what the rabbis of the Mishnah have to say concerning the times of the second temple must all be used with great caution.

[47] Danby, *op. cit.*, p. xv note.

University Press, 1927), I, 150–155; A. Vincent, *Judaism*, translated by J. D. Scanlon (London, 1934), pp. 12–41.

BIBLIOGRAPHY

Fillion, L. The Life of Christ, I, 243–55.

Maas, A. A Day in the Temple.

McClellan, W. The Psalms, a Prayer Book, translation of new Latin version from the Hebrew.

Oesterley, W. A Fresh Approach to the Psalms.

Stoll, R. The Gospel according to St. Luke, pp. 6–13.

Strack and Billerbeck. Kommentar zum neuen Testament aus Talmud und Midrasch, II, 55–95.

Valensin and Huby. Evangile selon S. Luc, pp. 5–10.

CHAPTER V

God Becomes Man

THE ANNUNCIATION

Come, strike the harp and let the trimbrel sound
　In praise of her, the Lily of the Vale!
From Lebanon soft music breathes around;
　The flowers of Esdraelon make sweet the gale.
Sing us of her who fore-ordained by God
　To be the Mother of His only Son,
Bowed her bright head, obedient to His nod
　And answered, full of grace, "Thy will be done."
The glory of the Godhead on her beamed;
　The moon became a footstool for her feet;
The sun, her radiant slave, far brighter gleamed;
　The stars shone forth, a crown for her most meet!
The Seraphim, tall flames, about her stood:
　For she was Queen of Heaven, all beautiful and good!
　　　　　　　　　　　　　James B. Dollard

Six months after the conception of John the Baptist had been announced to Zachary by the angel Gabriel, the same heavenly messenger again was sent to earth by almighty God. On this occasion the communication he bore was to complement the previous one and to mark the fullness of time. The scene of the angel's second visitation was not famed Jerusalem with its glittering palaces, its majestic Temple and its great walls, but the obscure little town of Nazareth, eighty-five miles to the north, nestling in the Galilean hills that overlooked the plain of Esdraelon. This time it was not to a priest in the holy place, enveloped in the smoke of incense as he offered the prayers and sacrifices of the people, that the heavenly messenger appeared. It was to a modest Jewish maiden, Mary of Nazareth, whose cousin was Elizabeth, the expectant mother of John the Baptist, amid the simple surroundings of her quiet home. Yet, however lowly the surroundings and however modest and unassuming her own personal appearance, Mary of Nazareth was really "the rose among thorns" and "our tainted nature's solitary boast"; for she had been especially prepared and endowed with God's choicest favors and graces for the greatest office ever allotted to a human being, her maternity of Christ. At the time she received the angelic message, she was betrothed to Joseph, by a betrothal which marked her as his legal bride. It was therefore during the period while she was waiting to be conducted to his home, namely, while she was still living with her parents or relatives, that the angel Gabriel appeared to her. What was she doing at that breathless moment when generations waited on her word? Was she busily working on her trousseau? Was she meditating on the great prophecy of Isaias: "Behold a virgin shall conceive and bear a son and His name shall be called Emmanuel"? (Isa. 7:14.) We cannot ascertain the aspirations and reflections of Mary's soul on that great day of days when there suddenly stood before her the archangel Gabriel with glowing countenance, gleaming robe, and wondrous step.

Although among the Greeks there is a tradition that it was at the fountain that she was first accosted by the heavenly messenger, yet the sacred text is silent about this. It rather seems to imply what is stated by St. Ambrose,[1] that when the angel came she was at home in privacy without any companions whatever to disturb or distract her. Gabriel saluted her with words we have lisped at

[1] *Concerning Virgins*, II, 2; NPN, 2nd ser., X, 375. St. Ambrose goes on to say that it was Mary's custom to be alone, and then he asks: "For how could she be alone who had so many books, so many archangels, so many prophets?"

our mother's knee and love to repeat throughout our life, following the example of the angel: "Hail, full of grace. The Lord is with thee. Blessed art thou among women" (Luke 1:28).

These wonderful words of greeting could not be addressed to any human being except Our Lady. They could not apply to anyone tainted with sin. They declare that she is adorned with all perfection, especially moral and spiritual, that she possessed God, hence is the most highly favored among the daughters of Eve. They would have been out of place had not this Jewish girl reached supreme heights of holiness. These sentiments were expressed by an angelic spirit sent by almighty God, not by a mere fellow human being, and thus they were of transcendent value. Mary's reaction to this extraordinary greeting was natural to her modesty and humility. Although it is not mentioned that she was startled by the appearance of the angel, it is said that she was troubled at his greeting.

The address of great praise that gave her the title, "full of grace" instead of her own name, did not upset the poise of her mind. Rather her reason reigned supreme and carefully examined the words of the angel to discover their meaning and their application to her. Before she spoke, the heavenly messenger continued his address. Assuring her that she had no occasion for alarm and giving the reason for the favors and graces she enjoyed, he came to the heart of his great announcement. Mary was to be the Mother of the Son of God, whom she was to call Jesus. The career of this future Son, the great Messianic King whose reign was to last forever, was outlined in scriptural language. "He shall be great, and shall be called the Son of the Most High; and the Lord God will give Him the throne of David His father, and He shall be King over the house of Jacob forever; and of His kingdom there shall be no end" (Luke 1:32 f.).

What a contrast to the predictions made for John the Baptist in the angel's announcement to holy Zachary! He foretold that John was to be great in the service of God. Jesus will be great and transcendent Himself. John will go before the Lord like a second Elias; his function will be to prepare the people for the Lord. Jesus will be recognized as the Son of God and will be so called. He will be the Ruler of the everlasting Messianic kingdom, so earnestly expected as promised to a descendant of Jacob and foreshadowed by the reign of King David. What marvelous news conveyed in biblical language that opened up such horizons for the humble Mary of Nazareth! [2] Yet at this astounding information, what self-composure and directness of mind were revealed by her! Particulars about the great glory of this future Son ought to have stirred her curiosity. Rather only one short question falls from Mary's lips, concerning her own personal condition. She asks for information pointing to her state of virginity and her resolution to continue in it. Her question: "How shall this be done, because I know not man?" (Luke 1:34) indicates, according to Catholic exegetes,[3] that she had taken a vow of chastity, or at least had dedicated her virginity to God. If she had not, since she was already betrothed, she would naturally ask about hastening the arrangements for her marriage. The words, "I know not man," signify "I am vowed to remain a virgin"; just as the saying, "I do not drink wine," means "I am pledged against it."

Here Mary does not ask for a sign as Zachary had done, doubting the words of the angel. Rather she believes in the angelic message

[2] St. Gabriel did not present to Mary the theology of the Incarnation in methodical, systematic form, but sketched the horizons with references to the Messianic prophecies. Cf. Valensin-Huby, *Evangile selon S. Luc*, pp. 13 f.

[3] Joüon, "L'Anonciation, Luc. 1:26–38," *Nouvelle revue théologique*, LXVI (1939), 793–98, has pointed out that an analysis of the whole Annunciation account makes it clear that Mary there makes a proposal to remain a virgin. In the first part, verses 26–29, we have the greeting and the perturbation of the Virgin. In the second part (30–33), there are outlined the Davidic origin and Messianic character of the promised son; but there is no clear statement about His divinity. Accordingly Mary was led to suppose that the Messianic child would be born of her and St. Joseph. How natural, therefore, was her question about her virginity (34). In the third part (35–37) is found a satisfactory answer to her question when the angel promised the virgin birth while announcing the divinity of the future son. Donatus Haugg, *Das erste biblische Marienwort* (Stuttgart, 1938), contended that Mary's words in verse 34 merely mean that she was pointing to the fact that she was not yet married. This view has met many opponents. See Collins, "Our Lady's Vow of Virginity," *Cath. Bib. Quart.*, V (1943), 371–80.

and, as a prudent, intelligent person, inquires about the manner in which it is to be carried out. Her case was quite different from that of the aged priest, and presented certain special difficulties of a delicate nature. He had a wife and had before him biblical examples, such as Sarah and Anna who were sterile and yet afterward bore children. It should have been much easier for him to accept the angel's announcement than for Mary, who was a young virgin unacquainted with marriage. More than that, for her guidance there were no examples to show how a virgin could conceive and bring forth a child. It was right and natural for her to ask for enlightenment on such an important matter that concerned not only herself but also the man to whom she was betrothed. She is to be praised for her good judgment as well as for faith, while Zachary is unpraiseworthy for his incredulity and for demanding a sign. Accordingly Gabriel did not ignore the remark of the Virgin as he did that of the priest, but graciously acceded to her request. About how the Incarnation was to take place, he explained with these awesome words. "The Holy Ghost shall come upon thee and the power of the Most High shall overshadow thee: and therefore the Holy One to be born of thee shall be called the Son of God" (Luke 1: 35).

The Holy Spirit of God that brooded over the primal waters in the beginning and by His creative force made the world, with all things living and inanimate, was Himself to be responsible. Like the cloud before the ark of the covenant, His presence would overshadow her. As the mother bird covers her nestlings with her wings, the divine power was to possess her and was to produce fecundity in her. As a shadow depicts the form of the objects from which it proceeds, so the power of the Holy Ghost was to reproduce the image and splendor of the Exemplar.[4]

---

[4] Cf. St. Gregory of Nyssa, *Oratio in diem natalem Christi; PG* 46, 1142. St. Gregory the Great gives this explanation: Shadow is formed by light and by a body. The Lord through His divinity is Light who deigned to become a body through the medium of a person in whose womb He assumed human nature. *De testimoniis in Evangelium S. Lucae, IV; PL,* 79, 1058.

The Gospel wording is reminiscent of the Isaian prophecy: "Drop down dew, ye heavens, from above, and let the clouds rain the just; let the earth be opened and bud forth a Savior" (Isa. 45–48) . Some of the Fathers hold that the expression, "the power of the Most High," applies to the Son of God. According to this application, which is said to be "exegetically permissible and most probable," [5] we have the following explanation by St. John Damascene. [6] He first says it was the Holy Ghost who came upon Mary to cleanse her and give her "abundant strength to conceive and bring forth the Godhead of the Word." And then, according to Damascene, "the truly abiding wisdom and power of the Most High, the Son of God, who is consubstantial with the Father, overshadowed her in the form of divine seed, and formed for Himself from her spotless and most pure blood a body animated with a rational and intellectual soul." This was done, he says, at one and the same moment by the Holy Ghost in accordance with the will of the Creator.

According to the angel's words it is with the power and operation of the Holy Ghost that the effusion of the Son of God from the bosom of the Father into the earthly bosom of Mary will take place. The angel could add, therefore, that on this account Jesus will be "the Holy One." [7] Thus the august word of homage that rises from the ranks of the seraphim before the majestic throne of God is to be immediately attributed to the Word assuming human nature.

Because this announced supernatural conception was to be so

[5] Scheeben, *Mariology*, I, 83. The author explains that this view is in more perfect accord with the depth and harmony of the Scriptures; because in this view the Second Person of the Trinity is not given a mere passive role, and in this view the Holy Spirit is the mediator of the action.

[6] *De fide orthodoxa*, III, 2; PG 94, 985; NPN, 2nd ser., IX, 47. The encyclical *Mistici Corporis* (on the mystical body), 31, says that at the first moment of the Incarnation "the Son of the eternal Father adorned with the fullness of the Holy Spirit the human nature which was substantially united to Him, that it might be a fitting instrument of the Divinity."

[7] On the question whether "holy" is subject or predicate see Vosté, *De Conceptione Originali Jesu Christi*, p. 15.

stupendous a miracle, the angelic messenger gave Mary a sign, although she had not asked for it. He revealed to her that her cousin Elizabeth, had conceived a son and was already in the sixth month of her pregnancy, although thought to be incapable of child-bearing; because, added the angel, "nothing shall be impossible with God." As St. Leo remarks, Elizabeth receives unexpected fertility "in order that there might be no doubt that He who had given conception to the barren would give it even to a virgin." [8] When Mary was thus satisfied on the question of her virginity and when she heard the wonderful news concerning her cousin, in all faith and confidence she answered that, as the handmaid of God, she rejoiced to do His bidding. "Behold the handmaid of the Lord, be it done to me according to thy word" (Luke 1:38). The Almighty rewards us with salvation and eternal union with Him only if we cooperate with His grace. Thus we may say, so to speak, that He waited on His creature's "Fiat" for the performance of His supreme act of love toward us. [9]

At Mary's assent and submission to God's will, the greatest event in human history took place: divine nature became wedded to human nature, God became man; "the Word was made flesh and dwelt among us." This does not mean that the nature of God was changed into flesh, "but that the Word took flesh into the unity of His Person." [10] That is, the Second Person of the most adorable Trinity assumed a human soul and body, and in this hypostatic union there was one divine Person, Our Lord Jesus Christ. In accomplishing this the three divine Persons of the Trinity took part; God the Father giving the authority and the mission; God the Son assuming human nature; and God the Holy Ghost being the efficient cause. We say, therefore, that Christ

[8] Sermon 3 On the Nativity, NPN, 2nd ser., XII, 130.

[9] Burrows points out that Mary's "Let it be done unto me," was reminiscent of Old Testament formulas of resignation, such as we find in I Sam. 3:18; II Sam. 15:26; Isa. 39:8. The meaning would be richer and fuller if, according to Luke 1:35, Mary would be understood to have renounced the honor of motherhood (Gospel of the Infancy and Other Biblical Essays, pp. 29 f.).

[10] St. Leo, Sermon 7, On the Nativity; NPN, 2nd ser., XII, 140.

was conceived of the Holy Ghost because this Spirit of sanctification consubstantial with the Word was the active principle in forming the body of Christ from the most pure blood of the Blessed Virgin Mary. Although the Trinity effected the conception of Christ's body, yet it is attributed to the Holy Ghost because the latter is the love of Father and Son, because it was through grace that He brought the Son of God to assume human nature, and because He who was conceived was the Holy One.[11] Christ's conception was supernatural because of the active principle, the supernatural power of God, but it was natural from the material, Mary's purest blood. It is to be held that from the very beginning, "it was the flesh of the Word of God, it was flesh animated with a rational and intelligent soul." [12] We should also bear in mind that this conception was virginal, that it was without original sin, and especially that it was of one who was both God and man.

By becoming the mother of Him who was the Son of God, who was God, Mary became the Mother of God. The words applied to the Messiah, "God with us," had a deeper significance for her than for anyone else. It was reality. The ark of the covenant where God's presence was localized was but a shadow of the reality in her virginal womb where God was assuming flesh. There was a new spiritual creation when Mary became a second Eve, the mother of all God's spiritual children adopted into the kingdom of God.

It was most fitting that the Son of God be born of a virgin, symbolized by "a garden enclosed," "a fountain sealed up," "the bush that was on fire and not burnt," and "the place wet with dew while all the ground beside it remained dry." It was in keeping with the dignity of God the Father and God the Son that no human father would be interposed to have the privilege of the fatherhood of Jesus. "For He who was of the Father, yet without a mother, was born of a woman without a father's cooperation." [13] Or again, "as Eve was brought forth from a man alone, so Mary

---

[11] Cf. St. Thomas, *Summa theol.*, IIIa, q. 32, a. 1.
[12] Cf. *ibid.*, q. 33, a. 2.
[13] St. John Damascene, *Exposition of Orthodox Faith*, IV, 14; NPN, 2nd ser., IX, 85.

of herself alone brought forth miraculously the Son of man." [14] Indeed the first man Adam received flesh from earth without a human father, "so also it was quite possible for the Son of God to take to Himself the substance of the self-same flesh, without a human father's agency." [15] Besides, as St. Augustine points out, "it was fitting that our Head, by a notable miracle, should be born, after the flesh, of a virgin that He might thereby signify that His members would be born after the spirit, of a virgin Church." [16] Christ took flesh from a woman so that the entire human nature might be ennobled and this truth of the Incarnation made more manifest. The announcement was first made to Mary, and her consent was sought because it was most appropriate for the spiritual wedlock between the Son of God and human nature that her mind be informed and her obedience given. By being conceived by a virgin who before she knew who was to be born of her had determined to continue a virgin, Christ "chose rather to approve than to command holy virginity"; [17] for in preserving Mary's virginity, both childbearing would be honored and virginity "would receive a higher honor." [18] The great event, the Incarnation, took place during the time of Mary's betrothal so that Mary's name might be protected and the divine Infant might have a guardian and a foster father. [19]

The announcement of the conception of St. John was made to Zachary because he was to be the father. The announcement of the conception of Jesus was made to the Virgin Mother because there was to be no human father. A holy priest, offering incense in the holy place, was the recipient in the first place, to show that all expectations and foreshadowings of the Old Law were to be fulfilled. A pious Jewish girl in a simple home received the greatest of all messages to demonstrate the truth that holiness can be found

---

[14] St. Cyril of Jerusalem, *Catechetical Lectures*, XII, 29; NPN, 2nd ser., VII, 86.
[15] Tertullian, *On the Flesh of Christ*, XVI; ANF, III, 536.
[16] *On Holy Virginity*, 6; NPN, 1st ser., III, 419.
[17] St. Augustine, *op. cit.*, 4; NPN, 1st ser., III, 418.
[18] St. Gregory Nazianzen, *Theophany or Birth of Christ*, 13; NPN, 2nd ser., VII, 349.
[19] St. Jerome, *Perpetual Virginity of the Blessed Mary*, 4; NPN, 2nd ser., VI, 333.

in every walk of life. The message to Mary is closely related to the message to Zachary, each having reference to the other. Both constitute the greatest and most important revelation ever made by God to man, for they contain the tidings of man's redemption. Mary's faith stands out against Eve's conduct "in order that the disobedience which proceeded from the serpent might receive its destruction in the same manner in which it derived its origin." [20] Also since sin came to the human race through the woman, it is fitting that the woman, Mary, should crush the head of the serpent.[21] Likewise it was right that the Son of God make His human appearance through a woman that our liberation be manifest in both sexes, and that we should know certainly that He was truly man as well as truly God. Further, as St. Augustine points out, He came therefore as a man, "to make special choice of that sex, and was born of woman to console the female sex." [22]

With the greatest awe and reverence Christians have ever contemplated the sublime moment when the divine nature was wedded to the human as the Word became flesh. Human language fails us when we try to express our joy and gratitude for this supreme act of God's love, far beyond our understanding, which has filled the world with happiness. Neither are we able to realize, much less to describe, the magnitude of the ecstatic love of Mary of Nazareth, as all alone with her great knowledge at first, she was wrapt in contemplation of this greatest mystery, God tabernacled within her, assuming human nature.

This great event, when God assumed human nature to redeem it from corruption and to lift it up to Himself, is lovingly commemorated thrice each day in the beautiful devotion of the Angelus, and is yearly celebrated by a feast on March 25. This greatest

[20] St. Justin Martyr, *Dialogue*, 100; ANF, I, 248.

[21] "The poison to deceive man was presented him by woman; through woman let salvation for man's recovery be presented," writes St. Augustine. (*Sermons on N. T. Lessons*, 1, 3; NPN, 1st ser., VI, 246. Likewise Tertullian says: "What had been reduced to ruin by this sex, might by the selfsame sex be recovered to salvation." *On the Flesh of Christ*, XVII; ANF, III, 536.

[22] *Sermons on N. T. Lessons*, 1, 3.

fact in all human history is also recalled when we repeat the Hail Mary. We can never sufficiently thank almighty God for the great condescension on His part and the great privilege and benefit conferred upon us in His becoming man. He made certain our faith, raised our hope and increased our charity. While curing our presumption and pride, He destroyed the empire of Satan. Yet he did not lessen His own majesty or our reverence of Him; "but on the contrary, inasmuch as He wished to draw nigh to us by taking flesh, He greatly drew us to Him." [23] Since it was through the Incarnation that we were given the power and privilege of becoming the special adopted children of God by being incorporated in the mystical body, we should gratefully recall this fact as thrice a day we repeat the Angelus. The daily reflection on the great dignity to which we were raised in becoming a partner in the divine nature should induce us to heed the imperative warning of St. Leo: "Refuse to return to the old baseness by degenerate conduct." [24]

BIBLIOGRAPHY

Bardenhewer, O. "Mariä Verkündigung," Biblische Studien, X (Freiburg, 1905) .

Fillion, L. The Life of Christ, I, 255–65.

Haugg, D. Das erste biblische Marienwort, Lc. 1:34 (Stuttgart, 1938) .

Joüon, P. L'Evangile de N.S. Jésus-Christ, pp. 282–87.

Lagrange, J. M. Evangile selon S. Luc, pp. 25–40.

Prat, F. Jésus-Christ, I, 46–52.

Simon, H. Praelectiones biblicae, I, 138–45.

Stoll, R. The Gospel according to St. Luke, pp. 13–20.

Valensin and Huby. Evangile selon S. Luc, pp. 11–17.

Vosté, J. M. De Conceptione Virginali Jésu Christi, pp. 6–17.

[23] St. Thomas, *Summa theol.*, IIIa, q.1, a.2.
[24] *Sermon* 1, 8, *On the Nativity; NPN*, 2nd ser., XII, 129.

CHAPTER VI

Mary and Elizabeth

AFTER Mary had given her consent to become the mother of the Savior of mankind, through the operation of the Holy Spirit the miraculous conception of the Son of God took place within her. She was now, so to speak, alone with God. She, alone, knew the wonderful thing which had occurred. She was, therefore, not only the first, but for a time the only human worshiper of the God-man. Her ardent devotion satisfied the incarnate Word and made up for the absence of other adorers. She poured forth her very soul in fervent aspirations of love, thanksgiving, and praise. This closest relationship, of mother to child, and most intimate association with God endowed her with special and extraordinary knowledge suited to her exalted position. On the one hand, with the keenest understanding of the nothingness of man, she descended into the lowliness of her being which had been raised to the inestimable dignity of sublime motherhood. On the other, she realized to a great extent, the extraordinary privilege which she enjoyed and the benefit that accrued therefrom: the glory of God and the salvation of mankind.

Did she reveal her secret to anyone? Certainly she was not commanded to be silent about the apparition of the archangel and his wonderful message. Yet, as divine Providence was ever her guide, we should expect that she would withhold what had been imparted to her from heaven from all except those who, of necessity, should be told. If St. Anne, her mother, was still living, she would have been the recipient of her daughter's confidence. Mary would have told her also of the sign which she did not ask or need for herself, that her aged cousin Elizabeth was with child. This information also would suggest to both mother and daughter that it was God's will that Mary should visit her cousin.

The journey would require four days, and arrangements for an escort would have to be made, probably some elderly man, a relative or friend of the family, and a woman companion. St. Joseph, her betrothed husband, would have to be informed of the trip; although, from what we know of the contemporary custom of forbidding engaged couples to see each other alone during the betrothed period, we can say with certainty that he did not accompany the Blessed Virgin on this journey. If the angelic communication took place at the traditional time at which it is celebrated, March 25, there would be numerous pilgrims making the journey to the Holy City for the feast of the Pasch, and Mary would find plenty of company in one of the festive caravans. We are certain that she went directly to Ain Karem; for St. Luke says: "And Mary rising up in those days went into the hill country with haste to a city of Juda" (Luke 1: 39). Afterward she would have attended the Passover celebration from the home of St. Elizabeth, only four and a half miles from Jerusalem.

Picture the Blessed Mother making this journey with a festive band of pilgrims, perhaps chanting the sacred psalms which proclaimed God's mercy toward the Jewish people and their hope in the coming of the Messiah. Knowing that they were fulfilled in Him, unnoticed in their midst, she secretly applied these prayers to her divine Son. The sentiments of the sacred songs, the historical memories evoked by the holy places through which she passed while she was journeying south through Palestine, would have inspired her to ecstatic heights of sublime meditation and contemplation.

The cities of Juda exult because of Thy judgments.
Walk through Sion and go round about it,
Count its towers, scan its ramparts, look over its strongholds,
That you may tell the future generation: So great is God.

Ps. 47 (48):12–15

Toward the end of the journey, after she had passed close to the Holy City, in full view of Herod's citadel, she would turn southwest and traverse the brown hills of Judea, planted with vines and olive trees. Towering above them she could see Nebi Samwil, associated with the great prophet Samuel, whose life had witnessed a great crisis in Jewish history. Surely thoughts of the prophet would arouse in the pure heart of the Virgin intense feelings of piety and patriotism. She would recall the extraordinary circumstances of his birth and ponder the beautiful Messianic canticle of his happy mother, Anna, to extract its sweetest honey and dedicate it lovingly to the Emanuel tabernacled within her.[1]

At last the young Virgin came to the town where the holy priest Zachary and his saintly wife lived. Tradition points to modern Ain Karem as the place. It also states that at this time the aged couple were not in the town but at the villa, a few hundred yards away, where the picturesque Church of the Visitation now stands. For five months St. Elizabeth had been in retirement in the seclusion of her villa, where she could give herself wholly to recollection and pious acts of thanksgiving. In this quiet retreat the Blessed Virgin sought her. The sacred text says of Mary's arrival, "And she entered the house of Zachary and saluted Elizabeth" (Luke 1:40). The Gospel's silence about any greeting to Zachary implies that he was not present on the occasion; of course he was still struck with dumbness. Mary probably offered the customary salutation: "Peace be to you!" But what an effect this had upon her aged kinswoman! First her child was affected, for the unborn Baptist recognized his Lord and leaped for joy, already beginning His career by pointing Him out. According to some scholars, by this

[1] Cf. Burrows, *The Gospel of the Infancy and Other Biblical Essays*, pp. 7–27.

visit of the Son of God, Himself as yet unborn, John was sanctified in his mother's womb; hence, although he had been conceived in original sin, he was born free from this stain. Yet the Church has made no pronouncement on the matter and therefore it remains uncertain. It is to be doubted that the yet unborn John received the use of his reason.[2] But it is certain that the grace of the Holy Ghost overflowed on the aged mother to inspire her with knowledge that her young cousin was bearing the incarnate Son of God. She uttered a great cry and pronounced in ringing tones the remarkable salutation:

Blessed art thou among women, and blessed is the fruit of thy womb.
And whence is this to me, that the mother of my Lord should come to me?
For behold as soon as the voice of thy salutation sounded in my ears, the infant in my womb leaped for joy.
And blessed art thou that hast believed, because those things shall be accomplished that were spoken to thee by the Lord.

Luke 1:42-45

The mother of the Baptist is thus the author of part of our Hail Mary. After Gabriel, she is the first to declare the Virgin Mother blessed among women. After Mary herself, she is the first to pay respect to the God-man. Without any exception she was the first to call Mary the Mother of God. St. Elizabeth's humility stands out when we consider the differences in the ages of the two women. Her great respect for her young cousin shines forth in every word of her canticle, as apostrophe to the Virgin. In a way it may be considered the first Christian hymn. She pays special

[2] St. Thomas (*Summa theol.*, IIIa, q.27, a.6) holds that St. John did not have the use of reason before his birth. On the other hand, St. Augustine (Epistle 186, ad Dardan, 7-17; *PL*, 33, 840-48), inclines to the affirmative view; so also does St. Jerome (Letter 107, to Laeta; *Select Letters*, ed. by Wright, p. 345). Previously St. Irenaeus had written; "Whom John, while yet in his mother's womb and He in that of Mary, recognizing as the Lord saluted with leaping" (*Against Heresies*, III, xvi, 4; ANF, I, 442). Against those who scoffed at him for believing that Elizabeth could know that the Savior of the world was present on the testimony of her unborn son, Origen has the following to say: If this belief of his was foolishness to others, it was for him both wisdom and the occasion of salvation. "For unless Christ's birth was heavenly and blessed, and unless it had something divine about it and surpassed human nature in all men, His teaching would not have spread throughout the whole world." Homily VII, In Lucam, PG, XIII, 1818.

tribute to the young mother's faith in the message of the archangel. And after her example the Fathers of the Church love to point to Mary's faith and obedience in contrast to Eve's unbelief and disobedience. To mention the second century Fathers, St. Justin Martyr,[3] and St. Irenaeus,[4] the first compares Mary's faith and joy with the disobedience and death for which Eve was responsible; the second speaks of the knot brought on by the first mother's disobedience and unbelief which was undone by the Virgin Mother's obedience and faith.

Under the stimulus of the occasion, but in a more subdued tone than that of her cousin, Mary burst into a spontaneously composed psalm of praise to the all-powerful, all-holy, all-faithful God for the benefits the Incarnation brought to herself and to the whole human race. The main theme of her sacred song is the Lord God. It circles round His great white throne, never leaving it. Starting by glorifying the Lord, the Virgin Mother strikes the keynote of all true Christians. Propitiations and petitions have a place in our liturgy; but for those who, by the Incarnation, are raised to the exalted dignity of co-heirs with Christ in His celestial kingdom, the first and most appropriate duty is that of praise to the magnanimous God. Glory to God is the purpose of all religion as it is the reason for the creation of all things.

It must always be borne in mind that, because she was at the moment so intimately united with God in her sublime maternity, the Virgin's hymn of praise was of inestimable value. After the opening organ peal of praise she chants the rest of the canticle in the Greek aorist or timeless tense; either because it was the moment when the Word became flesh within her that marked the greatest event in history, that witnessed "the great things" accomplished

---

[3] *Dialogue*, 100; ANF, I, 249. About the same time (A.D. 150) the *Epistle to Diognetus*, 12 (ANF, I, 30), refers to Mary as Eve incorrupted and as a virgin. For Mary in contrast to Eve, see Scheeben, *Mariology*, I, 211–14.

[4] *Against Heresies*, III, xi, 22; ANF, I, 455. He treats the matter again, *op. cit.*, V, xix, 1. Tertullian states the matter succinctly: "The delinquency which the one occasioned by believing (the devil), the other by believing (the angel) effaced" (*On the Flesh of Christ*, XVII; ANF, III, 536).

for her and for all generations; or because these great mercies of God about which she sings are unrelated to time. In the first four lines she uses twice both the words "my" and "me," thus designating her own great personal privilege in being the Mother of the Son of God. He was to her above all a Savior to exempt her from even the stain of original sin; and with this Savior and in Him and because of Him her soul has been rapt in ecstasies of joy. She chants in acknowledgment of her utter unworthiness, which seems to imply, as the Persian sage of the fourth century, Aphraates,[5] points out, that it was because of the greatness of her humility she was chosen to be the Mother of God. Yet because of the great dignity conferred on her personally [6] she proclaims, on the other hand, the prophecy that all future generations would pronounce her "blessed"—surely fulfilled in our Church's praise of her.[7] In the same breath she returns to God to couple His name with the word "Holy," which she borrows from the angelic chorus round His throne.

The Virgin Mother then expands and expatiates on her theme. Becoming both historian and prophetess,[8] she sings that the Incarnation has marked the triumph of God's power and holiness and goodness. She proclaims that the principles of divine government will hold true to the end of time. She declares that in taking flesh from her, God has already entered the arena of the world. His almighty arm has already struck out to decide the contest

[5] De humilitate, 5; Patrologia Syriaca (ed. Graffin), I, 418. St. Jerome attributed Mary's selection to her purity, Letter 22, to Eustochium, 38 (Select Letters, ed. by Wright, p. 147).

[6] Some scholars are of the opinion that the Magnificat reflects painful experiences which Mary may have already endured. Being so different from other maidens, she may have suffered from evil-minded, haughty neighbors. Cf. Gaechter, "Chronology from Mary's Betrothal," Theological Studies, II (1941), 169; Willam, Mary the Mother of Jesus, p. 9.

[7] Cf. Fonck, "Magnificat in ore Virginis Assumptae," Verbum Domini, II (1922), 227–32.

[8] Liddon's expresses the matter thus: "She is surveying the wide field of human history; she sees God's Arm of power displayed in it conspicuously; she notes the changes which God makes in the fortunes of dynasties and nations; and His rule of action in the kingdom of grace" (The Magnificat, pp. 57 f.).

between the proud, self-satisfied mighty ones and the lowly, self-sacrificing poor. The former have been crushed and scattered like chaff before the wind, while the latter have been lifted up to enjoy the full fruits of victory. Thus Mary, like the mother of Samuel, emphasizes the contest which the evil-minded wage against God in all ages, and takes a stand with Him against His enemies, especially those in high places, the same stand that her divine Son afterward so illustriously took by word and example.

Finally, the inspired Mother seemingly strikes a somewhat nationalistic note, when she recalls that the Incarnation was a divine visitation to and reception of Israel; yet her thought is far-reaching and universal. For "Israel," God's special child, here not only designates the chosen people but also Christ's followers who by faith are likewise the seed of Abraham, as St. Paul points out in his Epistles (cf. Gal. 6: 15; Rom. 4: 12; Eph. 2: 11–14).[9] She sings that the assuming of flesh by God is the loving condescension of God's unbounded mercy to all His faithful followers for all time, as He had promised to Abraham, Isaac, Jacob, and David. Thus the Virgin Mother ends her incomparable canticle, stressing the note of God's fidelity to His promises to her ancient forefathers, which she proudly recalls. But her improvised poem is best appreciated in itself:

> My soul doth magnify the Lord:
> > And my spirit hath rejoiced in God my Savior
> Because He hath regarded the humility of His handmaid; for behold from henceforth all generations shall call me blessed.
> Because He that is mighty, hath done great things to me; and holy is His name
> And His mercy is from generation unto generations, to them that fear Him.
>
> He hath showed might in His arm: He hath scattered the proud in the conceit of their heart.

[9] Here was a remarkable fulfillment of Isa. 42:1. See Zorell, *Psalterium ex Hebraeo Latinum*, p. 290.

He hath put down the mighty from their seat, and hath exalted the humble.

He hath filled the hungry with good things; and the rich He hath sent empty away.

He hath received Israel His servant, being mindful of His mercy:
As He spoke to our fathers, to Abraham and to His seed forever.

Luke 1:46-55

This inspired devotional outburst of the Virgin Mother is Hebrew poetry as we find it in the Old Testament,[10] for here is parallelism or contrast with a certain amount of freedom. A noteworthy feature of the poem is that it is a mosaic of Old Testament texts, principally from the psalms and Anna's Canticle, in such a way as to show not verbal dependence but absorption through deep meditation. It is most remarkable that this garland plucked from the ancient Scripture also happens to be the richest flowering of the garden afterward cultivated by her divine Son, illustrating again the completion and perfection of the Old Dispensation in the New. Indeed, Mary's short poem is an epitome of the Gospel. She states in a word, that Christianity is God's coming to the aid of Israel, the Church, which is comprised of the poor in spirit and the humble of heart. Her singing of God's holiness and His mercy to the God-fearing in fulfillment of His promises is in harmony with the constant theme of the sermons of Jesus. What is distinctively Christian is the honoring of the Virgin Mother herself because of her unique privilege. Her joy in her Savior points to the supreme fruit of Christianity. She is God's lowly handmaid again as at the Annunciation, revealing humility and obedience. Her sublime faith especially shines through every line of this hymn in which she sings of the victorious results already accomplished by the Incarnation. This proclamation of victory, be it noted, was made before Her divine Son had performed any miracle, even be-

[10] We follow the Latin translation of the Biblical Institute (*Liber Psalmorum cum Canticis Breviarii Romani*, pp. 344 f.) in making three strophes or divisions. Zorell (*op. cit.*, p. 288) gives four strophes.

fore He was born. No wonder that every great composer of religious music has set to music the "Magnificat," the greatest Christian hymn, the hymn par excellence of the Incarnation. No wonder the Church chants it in the daily Vespers, of which it is the core and center. It should be recited after every Mass, after every Holy Communion, in fact after every ceremony attendant upon Christian grace.

Having joyfully received her young kinswoman, acknowledged her the Mother of the Redeemer, and heard Mary's inspired canticle, St. Elizabeth left the seclusion of her retreat at the villa and went back to her home in the town of Ain Karem, accompanied by the Blessed Virgin. Concerning the length of time of the Visitation, the Gospel narrative has this to say: "Mary abode with her about three months, and she returned to her own house" (Luke 1: 56). The text could mean that she waited for the birth of St. John, or even a week or two longer. However, there is a Greek tradition which says that Mary left for home just before the nativity of the Baptist; this supposes she felt that she had accomplished her mission of grace and charity in aiding her aged kinswoman until such time as a special attendant would be engaged. Despite this tradition most scholars are hesitant in admitting that the Virgin Mary did not wait for the birth and even of the circumcision of the Baptist. Yet there may have been a special reason impelling her return home just before the birth of St. John, or shortly after. If the time of her marriage with St. Joseph was drawing near, she would have pressing, personal responsibilities demanding her presence in her own home. So Mary left Ain Karem and made the three or four days' return journey to Nazareth.

That blessed Mary stayed with her cousin not because of seeking after faith but to show kindness, St. Ambrose points out.[11] This Father also draws attention to the harmony and charity in the visitation scene when he writes: "Elizabeth was indeed the first to hear the voice of Mary, but John was first to feel his Lord's

[11] *Concerning Virgins*, II, ii, 12; NPN, 2nd ser., X, 379.

gracious presence. Sweet is the harmony of prophecy with prophecy, of woman with woman, of babe with babe. The women speak words of grace, the babes move hiddenly, and as their mothers approach one another, so do they engage in mysterious converse of love; and in a twofold miracle, though in diverse degrees of honor, the mother's prophecy in the spirit of their little ones." [12]

How melodiously is the Christian era being ushered in to the strains of music and song! How sweet is its coming amid the rich aroma of the perfume of courtesy and charity! Devotion and grace pervade the atmosphere surrounding the two kinswomen, an atmosphere of the Old Testament suffused with the golden rays of the new dawn. Above all, the divine influence of God's presence, hidden as in a tabernacle, is there. The unborn Baptist acknowledges it. The aged wife of Zachary is inspired to feel it and to pour fervent benediction on the Word-made-flesh and His Mother. The young maiden picks up the sacred music in a lower tone, but of most sublime quality, and produces melody of captivating timbre for all succeeding generations, as the thrush in springtime pours its silvery notes over the slumbering valley. St. Elizabeth teaches us devotion to Jesus and Mary. The young Mary edifies us not only by her faith and practical charity, but also by her pious use of the Sacred Scriptures, and by the exalted sentiments of the Magnificat. The aged kinswoman had retired to seclusion in thanksgiving; for the greatest favor of all times the Virgin of Nazareth expressed her thanksgiving in charitable works. These activities, however, did not rob her of her intimate life of union with God; for while God was really living in her, her heart throbbed in love for God and her soul thrilled with ecstatic joy for her Savior.

BIBLIOGRAPHY

Becker, T. The Hidden Life of Christ, pp. 36–43.
Burrows, E. The Gospel of the Infancy and Other Biblical Essays, pp. 27–34.

[12] *On the Christian Faith*, IV, ix, 15; *NPN*, 2nd ser., X, 277.

Gaechter, P. "The Chronology from Mary's Betrothal to the Birth of Christ," Theological Studies, II (1941), 162–70.

Joüon, P. L'Evangile de N.S. Jésus-Christ, pp. 287–91.

Lagrange, J. M. Evangile selon S. Luc, pp. 40–54.

Ollivier, M. The Friendships of Christ, pp. 148–68.

Plummer, A. The Gospel according to St. Luke, pp. 27–35.

Prat, F. Jésus-Christ, I, 62–67.

Simon, H. Praelectiones biblicae, I, 145–50.

Stoll, R. The Gospel according to St. Luke, pp. 20–25.

Valensin and Huny. Evangile selon S. Luc, pp. 18–25.

Ain Karim

CHAPTER VII

The Birth of St. John the Baptist

IN confirmation of the tradition pointing out Ain Karem as the scene of the Visitation, we have the descriptive words of the Gospel narrative, "the hill country" of Judca,[1] that fits this place. There is also the statement of Pliny that "mountain region" was the name of the district of which Jerusalem was the capital.[2] Then we have the additional knowledge that further collaborates the Gospel description, namely, that to the citizens of the Holy City the country that lay immediately to the west was known as "mountain land." Ain Karem, therefore, should hold our reverent interest because it was there that the incarnate Word, assuming flesh of the Virgin Mother, passed three months, and it was there that St. John the Baptist was born. Its location at some distance to the south of Nebi Samwil with the pleasant, fertile valley of Sorec, planted with fruit trees, stretching east and west, is in strong contrast to the Holy City.

According to a tradition that is somewhat late, as we would expect, the holy father of the Baptist had a country home in a

[1] Torrey says that the word "city" in Luke 1:39 should be "provincia." The Hebrew word of the original source, *medina* is given its Gentile meaning instead of its Palestinian one. (*The Four Gospels*, a new translation, p. 305). On the other hand, St. Luke may have been following biblical style, as in II Sam. 2:1; Jer. 9:11.

[2] Orinen in qua fuere Hierosolyma, *Natural History*, V, 15 (*Loeb*, II, 273). Cf. Josephus, *Jewish War*, IV, 448 (viii, I); and *Mishnah*, Shobiith (Seventh Year), 9, 2; Danby, p. 49. The only serious tradition about the birthplace of St. John is that attached to Ain Karem, as Prat rightly remarks, *Jésus-Christ*, I, 63.

pleasant valley to the west of the town to which his wife Elizabeth had retired to spend five months of prayer and thanksgiving for the favor of a child. It was here that she made the beautiful apostrophe to the Virgin, and it was here that Mary's great song for the favor of the Incarnation was first heard. Over the grotto, which was originally Zachary's house, there rises today a church, picturesquely perched on a rocky plateau at the foot of the mountain. A church has been there on this site since the fourth century. The present structure, however, is not the original for there have been numerous changes and reconstructions. In the fifth century a Greek church was erected over the site of Zachary's home in the town of Ain Karem, a little to the east, and about ten minutes' walk from the villa. In the basement of this second church there is preserved the grotto where the Baptist was born. Hence this church is called the Church of the Nativity of St. John; that on the site of Zachary's villa is called the Church of the Visitation.[3]

After the exchange of greetings between St. Elizabeth and her young kinswoman, they returned to Zachary's house in town, where this Greek church now stands. Here St. Elizabeth awaited the birth of her promised child. With what tenderness and affection the Blessed Virgin looked after her cousin! How much did St. Elizabeth and her aged, mute husband appreciate the assistance of the Virgin Mother of God! The "Virgin's fountain" calls up a picture of the Blessed Virgin carrying water for the little household; but this was only one of the many services which the young cousin rendered to the aged couple. Above all, her presence was a means of educating and instructing them concerning the great Messianic mystery soon to be accomplished.[4] For imparting information to holy Zachary who it seems was deaf as well as dumb,

[3] Cf. Meistermann, *Guide to the Holy Land*, pp. 402–406.

[4] Origen tells us that the Blessed Mother remained three months with Elizabeth "so that by a certain ineffable virtue the Savior in His close association might sanctify John and likewise Zachary, that the latter may utter his evangelical pronouncement. During the three months Zachary gradually received helps and aids that he might make the prophecy concerning Christ when he called Him 'the redemption of his people Israel'" (Homily 9, *In Lucam*; PG, 13, 1822).

communication by signs must have been resorted to; or perhaps they used the wooden tablets coated with wax whereon messages could be written with a pointed instrument. But between the Virgin Mary and Elizabeth there could be the easy flow of conversation. Judging from their first mutual greetings and from the Benedictus spoken later by Zachary, we are sure that the holiest and most exalted topics composed their conversations as well as their prayers and meditations. The Blessed Virgin Mary had ample opportunity of giving a detailed account of the wondrous message of the archangel Gabriel and of explaining that by the assumption of human nature within her by the Son of God, the golden age of the reign of grace had already begun for mankind and that indeed the Christian victory over the forces of evil had already been won. What sublime sentiments of faith and hope must have been expressed! What a great source of inspiration and sanctity must have been the continued presence of the incarnate God tabernacled within Mary! How the unborn Baptist must have been influenced! No wonder that a greater prophet than he, never was born.

As was previously stated, we are not sure whether the Virgin Mother departed for her home in Nazareth before or after the birth of the Baptist. That event caused a sensation in the locality because of the advanced age of the parents. Its miraculous nature must have heightened the rejoicings of relatives and congratulations of neighbors, all of whom seem to have taken a special interest in the case. Even before the birth of the infant they had agreed among themselves on a name. According to the fixed law, on the eighth day after birth the child was circumcised. During this ceremony, which marked a holy alliance with God and communion with Israel, a name was given to signify further dedication to the Almighty and recognition of His holy benefits. In the case of an only child the grandfather's name, as a rule, was given. But as Zachary was so old there was little likelihood of confusion, and the friends of the family had agreed on the name Zachary. Elizabeth, however, interfered with this plan, saying, "Not so, but he shall be called John" (Luke 1:60). This shows that she was acquainted with the account of the angel's vision to her husband and believed. The friends protested that none of her relatives were called by this name and consulted the mute father by signs. The latter asked for a writing tablet and wrote, "John is his name." This decisive reply was an act of faith in and obedience to the words of the archangel. By it Zachary's dumbness was removed. Immediately he spoke, praising and blessing the beneficent Lord: [5]

Blessed be the Lord God of Israel: because He hath visited and wrought the redemption of His people

And hath raised up a horn of salvation to us, in the house of David His servant:

As He spoke by the mouth of His holy prophets, who are from the beginning:

Salvation from our enemies, and from the hand of all that hate us:

To perform mercy to our fathers and to remember His holy testament,

The oath, which He swore to Abraham our father, that He would grant to us,

That being delivered from the hand of our enemies, we may serve Him without fear,

In holiness and justice before Him, all our days.

And thou, child, shalt be called the prophet of the Highest: for thou shalt go before the face of the Lord to prepare His ways:

To give knowledge of salvation to His people, unto the remission of their sins:

Through the bowels of the mercy of our God, in which the Orient from on high hath visited us:

To enlighten them that sit in darkness, and in the shadow of death: to direct our feet unto the way of peace.

Luke 1:68-79

Zachary's inspired outburst is a prophetic song of thanksgiving for the bountiful effects of the Redemption. As Mary had begun her canticle by magnifying God, so Zachary, making the best use of his newly acquired powers of speech, also begins by blessing

---

[5] We follow the *New Latin Translation* (*Liber Psalmorum* of Pontifical Biblical Institute, pp. 345 f.) in making two divisions. Zorell makes three (*Psalterium ex Hebraeo Latinum*, pp. 290–91).

the Lord, teaching us that the primary and most important use of the tongue is to bless the Creator and owner of all things. Showing that he had learned from Mary of the Incarnation and of the work of the Redemption that had already begun, Zachary blessed God for espousing the cause of his people and for sending a mighty Savior.[6] He goes on to sing of God's faithfulness to promises made to his holy ancestors and to His part of the solemn covenant made with Abraham the father of his race. He chants how man is set free from all danger of enemies of body and soul and in God's presence, moved by holy fear, can dedicate his whole life to fruitful works of piety and charity.

Then addressing his infant son, holy Zachary declares that he will be called the prophet of God; St. John was indeed the last of the prophets. Besides, he was the herald of the Messiah, pointing Him out and making the last immediate preparation of His coming. His father refers to this function as it was foretold by the archangel Gabriel and also by Isaias (40:3) and Malachias (3:1). The aged father predicts that his son will spread the knowledge that salvation is at hand, and that by repentance sins would be forgiven. Indeed, the merciful heart of God will be manifested in this new day that has dawned, vouchsafed by the coming of the heavenly Light that dispels the darkness of sin and error and illumines the road to peace.

By specifically mentioning the forgiveness of sin, Zachary indicates that the darkness to which he refers is the spiritual gloom of sin and error; the deliverance of enemies he twice mentions is to be taken in the spiritual sense and not in a physical, worldly way. Man's enemies are principally those opposed to his eternal interests as the new Messiah would emphasize later. The Jewish people were then under the bondage of Rome. Once centuries

[6] "Horn" is used metaphorically to signify might and abundance (cf. Ps. 131:17), as "visit" is employed for God's special protection and help. "To sit in darkness and in the shadow of death," means thick gloom. "The Orient" is the same as "the rising." This word "rising" or "orient" was a Messianic name signifying that the Messiah would usher in a new period of great light. This light-giving visitor would illumine the right road that leads securely to peace. Cf. Zorell, Psalterium ex Hebraeo Latinum, p. 291.

previously they had been delivered from the hands of Pharaoh and the Egyptians. But now, through the mighty Savior of the house of David, they are to be set free from the bondage of sin and Satan into which they were led by the first parents. Zachary uses "redemption," a temple word derived from "ransom" which soon, through the usage of Our Lord and the apostles, would become the technical term for the price which Jesus Christ paid to win the deliverance of the human race from the thralldom of the devil and its restoration to filial adoption by God. Because it is found in the opening words of Zachary's psalm and because the ideas it connotes are repeated frequently throughout, the Benedictus is rightly considered the song of thanksgiving for the redemptive effects of the vicarious life and death of our Blessed Lord. The reference to the unborn God-man as "abundance of salvation" that brings about the redemption of His people is an expression of high esteem and of great regard for Christ. A tribute to Our Lord is found also in the figure of the rising sun or heavenly body ushering in a new day of golden light and sunshine. By contrast with St. John, whose function is to prophesy and prepare, the exalted nature of the Messiah stands out markedly and pre-eminently.

Thus it is clear that Zachary had learned a great deal from the Virgin Mother. In their inspired canticles, both begin by praising God in his capacity of Savior. Zachary mentions the power of salvation. Mary speaks of God as stretching forth His all-powerful arm. Both, by using a past tense, sing that the work of salvation has already begun and that it is independent of time. Both chant that the effects flow to the God-fearing, the righteous, and the humble; both hold that the source is the great mercy of God, and both affirm that it is a fulfillment of the prophecies and the solemn promises made to the ancient members of their race.

The Magnificat is more personal in tone; it is more exalted in ideas and it is better Hebrew poetry. The Benedictus borrows more from the prophets. It is more nationalistic with such expressions as "God of Israel," "His people." Again, Zachary's psalm is sacerdotal as we would expect from a son of Aaron associated with the temple service. In contrast, Mary's exalted song which hovers near the great white throne, is regal as becoming the Mother of God, and is based mostly on the psalms as appropriate to the daughter of David.[7] Another striking difference is that whereas the aged priest prophesied about his son, the young Virgin foretold the favor in which she herself would be held by future generations. It has been said that the Benedictus is the last prophecy of the Old Dispensation and the first of the New.[8] But this is not so, for Mary's prophecy came before, and holy Simeon made a prophetic utterance after.

It seems appropriate that holy Zachary's song in thanksgiving for the Redemption should be assigned to Lauds, that part of the Office which specifically chants God's praises. Most fittingly, too, it is said in the ritual of the dead, if not at the graveside then at the end of the absolution service in the church. Over the sacred remains of the dead just before they are consigned to the gloom and dust of the tomb, are chanted the words of the aged priest, blessing God for His redemptive work, for lovingly sending His Son to forgive sin, and to shed besides eternal light, blessed peace. Also the reiteration of the privilege of spending one's life in works of piety, free from fear and danger, is reassuring to the living as it is applicable to the dead. The Benedictus is therefore a panegyric over the Christian life; it is a song of victory over death and sin, and it is a shout of triumph for Christ's conquering grace.

The golden rays of the "rising Sun" gild the tableau of the birth of St. John the Baptist. In the mercy and grace that are diffused, the aged priest and his saintly wife share. Yet their deep piety, their lively faith, and their ardent hope serve to accentuate the pre-eminent virtues of the expectant Virgin Mother who has been visiting them. St. Jerome [9] well points out this contrast when

---

[7] Plummer (*Gospel according to St. Luke*, p. 3) writes "while the tone of the Magnificat is regal, that of the Benedictus is sacerdotal."

[8] Plummer, *loc. cit.*

[9] *Against the Pelagians*, I, 16; NPN, 2nd ser., VI, 457.

he writes: "Elizabeth and Zachary may teach us, according to most certain testimony, how far inferior they are in sanctity to Blessed Mary, the Lord's Mother, who, in the consciousness she has of God dwelling within her, freely proclaims: 'Behold from henceforth all nations shall call me blessed.' " The aged couple therefore help to bring out the excellence of Mary; and, in turn, her great luster comes from standing in the full rays of the glorious dawn. Her brilliance like that of the moon, was reflected, the reflected glory of the Sun of Justice.

The extraordinary events which took place at the house of Zachary produced a marked effect upon the countryside. A salutary fear of God took possession of the people. Even beyond the confines of Ain Karem, among the hill country folk of Judea, the circumstances of the birth of St. John and those attending his circumcision were reported and discussed with wonder. In astonishment people asked one another what would be the future of this marvelous child. They rightly expected that the future held extraordinary things in store for Zachary's son, upon whom the almighty hand of God was so visibly present.

BIBLIOGRAPHY

Buzy, D. St. Jean-Baptist, pp. 49–63.
Fillion, L. The Life of Christ, I, 274–79.
Joüon, P. L'Evangile de N.S. Jésus-Christ, pp. 291–97.
Lagrange, J. M. Evangile selon S. Luc, pp. 54–64.
Plummer, A. The Gospel according to St. Luke, pp. 35–44.
Simon, H. Praelectiones biblicae, I, 150–53.
Stoll, R. The Gospel according to St. Luke, pp. 25–32.
Valensin and Huby. Evangile selon S. Luc, pp. 27–30.

CHAPTER VIII

St. Joseph's Vision

RETURNING to the home of her parents in Nazareth after three months spent with St. Elizabeth, the Blessed Virgin Mary was confronted with a pressing problem, one which deeply troubled her sensitive nature. Her betrothed could no longer be ignorant of the fact that she was with child. Then on learning this fact, as he did not know the circumstances, he became greatly disturbed. In brave silence she shared his trial. Because of the endurance of this trial in silence and bravery on the part of one of "such perfect delicacy," St. John Chrysostom rightly exclaims, "wondrous indeed was that Virgin." [1] The excellence of her character appears again here. Far from giving way to distracted dismay, she contains her soul in patience and confidence, just as she displayed self-control and directness of mind when she received the announcement from St. Gabriel.

Among the Jews of that time, as previously mentioned,[2] an engagement had all the binding force of marriage. When a young man chose a young woman for his spouse, she was accorded to him by her father generally by written agreement, duly witnessed. From that time she was under his law and was considered his wife, as in the sacred text (Matt. 1:20; Luke 2:5) the Virgin Mary is called the wife of St. Joseph while they were only betrothed. The

[1] *Sermon*, IV, 9, *On the Gospel of St. Matthew; NPN*, 1st ser., X, 24.
[2] Cf. *supra*, chap. 2, p. 22.

marriage ceremony was merely the solemn procession in which the bride was led to the home of the bridegroom. This generally took place about a year after the engagement, during which time the parties did not see each other alone; indeed breaches of chastity between them were considered sinful.[3] On the other hand, betrothal conferred full marital rights; so much so that if a child was born during it, the child was considered legitimate; and if the espoused husband died, the espoused wife, like a widow, had the right to claim the full amount of the sum stated in the document of engagement.[4] Unfaithfulness was considered adultery and was punished according to the ancient law of Israel (Deut. 22:23 f.) by public denunciation and death. Although this severe penalty was not applied in all its rigor at the time of Christ, yet it is certain that for the breaking of an engagement legal proceedings were required, as for divorce itself. These proceedings could be either public or private.[5]

[3] Cf. *Mishnah*, Yebamoth (Sisters-in-law), 13, 1; Danby, p. 237.

[4] *Mishnah, Ketuboth* (Marriage Deeds), 5, 1; Danby, p. 251.

[5] The tractates of the *Mishnah* that would be of special interest to us here are: Gittin (Bills of Divorce) and Kiddushin (Betrothals); Danby, pp. 307–29. Among other matters we learn here the three ways a wife was to be acquired (Kiddushin, 1, 1); the ways parties were to be betrothed (Kiddushin, 21), and what was to happen if the woman was under a vow (Kiddushin, 2, 5). That the offspring of betrothed couples need not be illegitimate is implied (Kiddushin, 3, 12). The reason alleged for divorces are given, and for the dissolution of marriage the giving of a bill of divorce was required (Gittin, 9, 10). Holy Writ had said that a husband could absolve his wife from her vows (Num. 30:7–15).

That a girl preserved her virginity before and during her betrothal, was required especially in Galilee. If she lost it, and there was evidence of this fact when she was taken to the home of the bridegroom, then a bill of divorce would be made out. So that in an ordinary case a man in St. Joseph's position would have procured two witnesses to the evidence of the unfaithfulness of his betrothed and brought them to the Jewish magistrates to have the nuptials dissolved. The gifts of espousals would have to be returned to him by her father and as well punishment meted out to the girl. Cf. *Mishnah*, Sanhedrin, 7, 4; Danby, p. 392; and Ketuboth (Marriage Deeds), 7, 6–10; Danby, p. 255; Neufeld, *Ancient Hebrew Marriage Laws*, pp. 144, 176–88. According to the Babylonian Talmud (ed. Rodkinson, VIII, 194), death was decreed for anyone who violated a virgin betrothed to another. Cf. Josephus, *Against Apion*, II, 201 (24).

The Gospel case of course was most extraordinary. St. Matthew's statement that during the period of her engagement, that is, before she was conducted to the home of her husband, Mary was found with child of the Holy Ghost, has as its complement St. Luke's accounts of the Annunciation and Visitation. What occurred in the home of holy Zachary would be considered by the relatives of the Blessed Mother as a proof of

The Virgin Mother had not informed her betrothed that she was bearing the Son of God through the operation of the Holy Ghost. She trusted in God to make this known in His own time. So far He had revealed the miracle only to St. Elizabeth and holy Zachary. Would it be vain for us to speculate as to how St. Joseph became informed? To compute how long she was with child at this time might help us. It would have taken the Virgin Mother about two weeks to make preparation for her departure to her cousin's home. The journey to Ain Karem would take the greater part of a week. She remained there three months and the return journey would take nearly another week. Thus when she arrived home it was toward the end of the fourth month of her pregnancy. At this stage [6] it certainly would be confirmed by her mother who could also verify the extraordinary fact that she was still a virgin. This might be the meaning of St. Matthew (1:18): [7] "When as His mother Mary was espoused to Joseph, before they came together, she was found with child of the Holy Ghost."

The fact that the Blessed Mother had preserved her virginity, together with the confirmatory events that had taken place in Zachary's home and that had been "spoken abroad in all the hill country of Judea," would testify to the great truth of the announcement by the angel Gabriel that Mary was with child of the Holy

the truth of Mary's statement as to her own condition. Indeed in the Gospel text there is a slight suggestion that it was these relatives who discovered that she was with child of the Holy Ghost, her virginity remaining intact. Those close to Mary would come to the decision that the time was at hand to inform the person vitally interested, St. Joseph. It seems that the Blessed Mother waited on God's providence in regard to the imparting of the news of her great selection. If St. Joseph asked her about it, she would surely tell him the truth. Evidently it was from Mary's relatives he received the information about her condition, and his trial took place before he had the opportunity of speaking to her personally.

[6] At this stage Mary's pregnancy would not be noticed. See Gaechter, "The Chronology from Mary's Betrothal to the Birth of Christ," *Theological Studies,* II (1941), 352.

[7] Lagrange (*Evangile selon S. Matthieu,* p. 10), Gaechter (*op. cit.,* p. 354), Vosté (*De Conceptione Virginali Jesu Christi,* p. 20), and others dissent from the view of St. Jerome (*Comment. in Matth., ad loc.; PL,* 7, 25; *Perpetual Virginity of Blessed Mary, NPN,* 2nd ser., VI, 336) that it was St. Joseph who found that the Virgin Mother was with child of the Holy Ghost for the reason that those who were engaged did not see each other alone during the engagement. Although St. Matthew does not give Gabriel's annunciation to Mary, this verse 1:18, implies it.

Ghost. Then if the year of the engagement was expiring [8] (which seems a likely explanation of the return of the Virgin Mother to Nazareth just before or after the birth of John the Baptist), St. Joseph would have been informed, and the extraordinary occurrences in the hill country of Judea would have been brought to his notice, if he had not already heard of them. Thus was created the problem for the intended husband. Of one thing he was certain: the purity and holiness of his betrothed. This would make him the more anxious to find out and to do God's will. In this extraordinary situation he had resort to earnest prayer, beseeching God to show him what to do. Thus he came to the conviction to put far from his thoughts all idea of public repudiation, desiring rather to break the engagement quietly and secretly, to give Mary her liberty and at the same time to save her from any public defamation. The reason given for St. Joseph's wish to come to such a decision is that he was "a just man." The word "just" in the Sacred Scriptures generally means, virtuous or righteous. Here it includes the connotation of kindness, which would be in harmony with St. Joseph's conduct not only on this occasion but during his whole life. What he determined to do showed him to be also a man of self-restraint and free from jealousy, "the most tyrannical of passions." [9]

However, this anxiety and embarrassment was not of long duration,[10] perhaps only a day or two. While he was still pondering the

[8] Gaechter proposes the following chronology. Mary's engagement took place in October. The Annunciation came eight months later, namely, in June of the second year. After the three months' visit to St. Elizabeth, Mary returned to Nazareth in September two weeks before her marriage to St. Joseph. Our Lord was born five months later, that is, in March of the third year, namely, 7 B.C. (op. cit., p. 368).

[9] St. John Chrysostom, Sermon IV, 7, On the Gospel of St. Matthew; NPN, 1st ser., X, 23.

[10] That St. Joseph was in real doubt, not suspecting the Blessed Virgin of unfaithfulness and yet not knowing what to think, and that in his doubt his prudence guided him to make the decision not to proceed with his marriage but to dissolve the engagement, is the view generally held by Catholic scholars. Some Catholic authors offer the following explanation of St. Joseph's doubt. St. Joseph became acquainted with both the fact of Mary's pregnancy and the cause of it, according to Matt. 1:18. His holiness and humility made him most desirous of avoiding the drawing of public attention to Mary's condition;

matter, his doubts were allayed by the vision of an angel. It may have been Gabriel whom God sent to address him in his sleep in these words: "Joseph, son of David, fear not to take unto thee Mary thy wife, for that which is conceived in her is of the Holy Ghost. And she shall bring forth a Son; and thou shalt call His name Jesus. For He shall save His people from their sins" (Matt. 1:20 f.).

Thus St. Matthew supplements St. Luke's account of the Annunciation. In both cases an angel of God brings the heavenly message that God is to become man in Mary through the Holy Ghost. In one it is brought to the Virgin Mother; in the other to the foster-father. It was fitting that Mary be informed before the miraculous conception by an angel in person to whom she could express her consent. As so great faith was not required of St. Joseph, since he knew Mary to be truthful and innocent, he was told of the miracle afterward and during his sleep. St. Joseph is addressed as "son of David" to remind him that all the Messianic rights of the house of David would descend through him on his

---

and more than that, caused him to deem himself a most unworthy and unsuitable consort of a woman so august as to be with child of the Holy Ghost. Like St. Peter's desire for Our Lord to depart from him, St. Joseph wished to retire before this ineffable occurrence and out of holy fear and reverence for God to break off his engagement with such a holy person so closely associated with God. On account of this holy fear and dread, the angel directed St. Joseph not to be afraid to take to himself Mary his wife, and also for this reason the sacred text states that he did as the angel ordered him.

This explanation for St. Joseph's doubt is defended by R. Bulbeck, "The Doubt of St. Joseph," *Cath. Bib. Quart.*, X (1948), 296–309. It must be said about it that it is supported by only a few ancient authorities: Eusebius (*Quaestiones evangelicae ad Stephanum*, 1, 3; PG, 22, 835); a sermon attributed to Origen (*Homilia in Vigilia Nativitatis Domini*, PL, 95, 1164), and St. Ephraim (quoted by Bulbeck as Moes, p. 22). It is not correct to say that St. Basil (Homily, *In sanctam Christi generationem*, 3 f.; PG, 31, 1463–65) gives this explanation.

St. Jerome and most Catholic commentators present the view that St. Joseph was left in real doubt. According to this view, which seems to fit better the Gospel texts, St. Joseph, not knowing the cause of Mary's pregnancy, was subjected to a real trial in which the goodness of his character proved itself. For here, as St. Basil (*op. cit.*, PG, 31, 1465) remarks, he shows that not only he was not opposed to her who was full of the Holy Ghost, but also he was not unworthy of her.

Lagrange (*Evangile selon S. Matthieu*, p. 13) warns us to keep in mind on the one hand that St. Joseph did not suspect Mary of adultery, and on the other that he did not as yet know of the conception of the Holy Ghost.

foster-child. He is bidden to proceed with his marriage to Mary, joyful news to him.

But a greater source of happiness was the ineffable dignity he was to enjoy as the husband of the Blessed Mother who, he was told, was bearing the incarnate Son of God. The angel Gabriel had announced to Mary the name of her Child. Now the news is brought from heaven a second time, and Joseph, as the legal father, is informed. Most appropriate is the name Jesus, the Greek form of the Hebrew name, Jeshua, which means "God is Savior," for the divine foster-child was to be the Savior of the world. The Evangelist St. Matthew goes on to say that thus was fulfilled what the Lord spoke through the prophet Isaias, 7:14: " 'Behold a virgin shall be with child, And shall bring forth a son, and they shall call His name Emanuel' which is interpreted, 'God with us' " (Matt. 1:23 f.). This prophecy could be fulfilled by none other than Jesus Christ.[11] No one else was born of a virgin. And no other was really and truly "God with us." Since he was of divine nature He had no need of a human father but was conceived of the Holy Ghost. As to the human generation of Jesus, this prophecy, "Behold, a virgin shall be with child," certainly applies as He was born of a virgin who was married to St. Joseph after His conception.

When the latter was apprised of this miraculous conception, in accordance with the instructions of the angel he immediately took the Virgin Mother to his house. If the time of their engagement was expiring he could do this without exciting curiosity. Thus in the eyes of the public and before the law he took responsibility for the Child. Henceforth he was reckoned one of the "parents" of Jesus. He was called the "father" of Jesus, who became known as the "Son of the carpenter."

[11] On the prophecy of Isaias and its fulfillment, see Lagrange, *Evangile selon S. Matthieu*, pp. 14–17; Vaccari, "De Signo Immanuelis Isaias," *Verbum Domini*, XVII (1937), 45–49, 75–81; Feuillet, "Le signe proposé à Achaz et l'Emanuel," *Recherches de sciences religieuses*, XXX (1940), 129–51; Lattey, "The Emanuel Prophecy," Isa. 7:14, *Cath. Bib. Quart.*, VIII (1946), 369–76; "The term Alma in Isa. 7:14," *Cath. Bib. Quart.*, IX (1947), 147–54; Power, "The Emmanuel Prophecy of Isaias," *Irish Ecclesiastical Record*, LXX (1948), 289–304.

That the prophecies be fulfilled in his foster-child, St. Joseph was of the seed of Abraham, of the tribe of Juda, and of the house of David. Both St. Matthew and St. Luke give the genealogy of our divine Lord. But it is quite different in each Gospel, owing to the different points of view. St. Matthew begins his Gospel with a genealogy. Since Abraham was the founder of the Jewish people and since the promise made to him was fulfilled in Christ, St. Matthew presents a list along Old Testament lines from Abraham to St. Joseph, "the husband of Mary." He makes three divisions of fourteen generations each; that is, fourteen generations from Abraham to David, fourteen from David to the Babylonian captivity (here he omitted three names), and fourteen from the Babylonian captivity to Christ (in the last case "Joathan" precedes Jechonias or else the latter name is to be mentioned twice). Four women are mentioned, Ruth who had been a pagan, and Thamar, Rahab, and Bethsabee, all sinners, in strong contrast to the immaculate Mother and to her divine Son, who came to redeem sinners.[12] St. Luke gives his genealogical list at the beginning of his account of the public ministry. He adopts the simple way of simply mentioning names beginning with St. Joseph, who he says, was the supposed father of Jesus, and going back all the way to Adam and even to God as Creator. He thus would indicate the universality of the redemption.

Comparing the two lists, we find that they agree for the period from Abraham to David. From then on, St. Matthew traces the line through Solomon, whereas St. Luke traces it through Nathan, another son of David. Salathiel had Jechonias as his father, according to the First Gospel; but according to the Third Gospel, Neri was the father (possibly explained by levirate marriage). But the most striking difference is that in St. Matthew, St. Joseph's father is Jacob, whereas in St. Luke, Heli is the father. These differences were noted early in the Church, and Julius Africanus

[12] St. Jerome writes that the women sinners are mentioned "so that He who came for the sake of sinners, by being born of sinners, might blot out all sin" (*Comment. on Matt.* 1:3; *PL*, 23).

(who wrote about A.D. 220) gives an explanation for "he has nothing better or truer to offer." [13] He explains that the relatives of Our Lord drew up those genealogies from memory and from documents that were rescued from destruction by Herod, and that they "come down to St. Joseph with considerable intricacy indeed, yet quite accurately." He gives the reason for the divergence in regard to the father of St. Joseph thus: "Joseph's grandmother, Estha, married twice. By her first husband, Mathan, she had a son named Jacob. By a second husband, Melchi, she bore another son named Heli. This Heli died childless and by the leviratical law his step-brother had to marry the widow of Heli. From the second marriage, St. Joseph was born. Thus Jacob was the real father of St. Joseph, and Heli his legal father. This explanation is according to the Jewish legal institution which provided that, if a man married his brother's widow and had a son by her, that son would count his mother's first husband as his legal father. In the question of inheritance of rights which could be transmitted from brother to brother or from an adopted father as well as from father to son, what would be demanded by the Jews was St. Joseph's genealogical [14] descent whether directly or through a collateral line from King David.

Our Lord is called the Son of David in the Gospels. Indeed St. Matthew begins his account by giving Him this title. The division into three groups of fourteen members each in his genealogy is made seemingly because the Hebrew letters making up the name of David, if considered as numerals, when added together amount to fourteen. The genealogies probably both belong to St. Joseph and are authentic records showing his Davidic descent. Julius

[13] Eusebius: *Ecclesiastical History*, I, vii; NPN, 2nd ser., I, 94.

[14] We are accepting the complicated explanation of Julius Africanus because he was a soldier of broad interests and because he had the opportunity of obtaining a genuine tradition handed down by the relatives of Our Lord, namely, while he was stationed at Nicopolis in Palestine. There are objections against it. See Arendzen, *The Gospels: Fact, Myth or Legend?* pp. 110–27; Lagrange, *Evangile selon S. Matthieu*, pp. 1–8; Durand, *Evangile selon S. Matthieu*, pp. 2–6; Hetzenauer, *De Genealogia Jesu Christi*; On the levirate marriage, see Epstein, *Marriage Laws in the Bible and Talmud*, pp. 76–144.

Africanus, St. Justin Martyr, St. Irenaeus, and St. Ignatius of
Antioch affirm the constant tradition that the Virgin Mother was
of the same tribe of Juda. This is also insinuated in the Gospels
and Epistles. So well recognized was the Davidic descent of Our
Lord that grandsons of his cousin were brought before the Emperor
Domitian because they claimed to be descended from David.[15]
The foster father actually had, besides other privileges, the right
to confer legal status of descendant of David upon Our Lord.

Contrary to all Jewish custom, St. Matthew mentions in his
genealogy the mother Mary, and adds, "of whom was born Jesus
who is called the Christ." The Evangelist concludes his account
of St. Joseph's vision thus: "And Joseph rising up from sleep,
did as the angel of the Lord had commanded him, and took unto
him his wife. And he knew her not till she brought forth her
first-born son, And he called His name Jesus" (Matt. 1:24 f.).
"First-born son" is the term used because of the ceremonies attached to any first-born son. It does not imply that other children
were born. We know that there were none, for Mary and Joseph
lived in chastity, not only for the first five months of their married
life, as the text testifies, but also to the end of it. This truth is
not contradicted by the Scripture use of the word "till" in the
quotation given above. In Gen. 8:7, we have a similar use of the
word when we are told that the raven did not return to the ark
"till the waters were dried up," which does not imply that the
raven returned at all.

It is certain that a great witness to Christ's miraculous conception of the Holy Ghost was St. Joseph himself. He was vitally concerned since he was betrothed to Mary when it took place. Therefore St. Chrysostom [16] correctly reaches the following conclusion
from St. Joseph's conduct: Unless Joseph had fully persuaded himself that what was done was of the operation of the Holy Ghost,
"he would not have kept her with him and ministered to her in

---

[15] Eusebius: *Ecclesiastical History*, III, ix, 107; NPN, I, 148.
[16] *Sermon IV, 5, On St. Matthew*; NPN, 2nd ser., V, 22.

all other things." After asking how St. Joseph could be called "just" if he would conceal the crimes of his wife, St. Jerome [17] asserts that it is a "testimony to Mary's integrity that Joseph knowing her chastity, and admiring what had occurred, concealed by silence what he did not understand." St. Ambrose [18] likewise points to Mary's husband as the trustworthy witness of her purity "in that he would deplore the dishonor, and avenge the disgrace, were it not that he acknowledged the mystery." As this same writer also remarks, on account of the fact that she was engaged, Mary's words are all the more credible, for the motive of lying is removed. St. Joseph's doubt thus serves to our advantage, strengthening our faith here as does the apostle Thomas' incredulity concerning the Resurrection.

In providing a husband for the Virgin Mary before the birth of Christ, divine Providence arranged a witness to the virgin birth, furnished a shield of protection for Mary's good name, supplied her and her Child with a provider, and concealed the knowledge of the virgin birth for a certain period even from the devil, according to St. Ignatius of Antioch (beginning of the second century) .[19] The arrangements certainly saved the Virgin Mother from attack of evil gossip which would be long-lived in a town like Nazareth. Thus here our divine Lord seems to have preferred, as St. Ambrose puts it, "that some people should doubt His own origin rather than His mother's honor." [20] One of the best men of all time was selected for the exalted position of foster-father of the Son of God; a most virtuous man, especially remarkable for his kindness, his sublime chastity, his implicit obedience, and his staunch faith.

St. Joseph was born probably at Bethlehem, the ancestral city of his family. When he grew up, he adopted the trade of carpenter. In pursuit of a livelihood so it seems, he traveled north and settled

---

[17] *Comment. in S. Matth.* 1:19; PL, 7, 25.

[18] *Commentary on Luke* 1:26 f.; PL, 15, 1559. St. Basil comments that St. Joseph's espousals to Mary took place that he might become the domestic witness to her purity. Homily *In Sanctam Christi generationem*; PG, 31, 1463.

[19] *Epistle to the Ephesians*, 19; translation by Kleist, p. 67.

[20] *De virginibus*, 42; PL, 16, 3:6.

in Nazareth, where he met and espoused the Blessed Virgin. The name Joseph is interpreted "may God add," and was quite common at the time of Our Lord on account of the popularity of the famous eleventh son of Jacob. The apocryphal "Gospel of the Nativity of Mary" [21] says that St. Joseph was picked as the husband of the Blessed Virgin from eligibles of the descendants of David by a dove coming down from heaven and resting on the rod he carried. Thereupon the rod blossomed forth. According to another work of the same [22] unreliable character, "The History of St. Joseph the Carpenter," composed in Egypt in the fourth century, St. Joseph was a widower and previously had four sons and two daughters. In this spurious account St. Joseph was chosen by lot from twelve old men of the tribe of Juda and was one hundred and eleven years old when he died. Despite their strong appeal to artists, these apocryphal works have always been rejected by the Church. Hence the data they supply for St. Joseph's age must be rejected. If he died from ordinary old age, before Christ's public ministry, he would have been in his forties when he married Mary. It is more likely that he was in his twenties or even younger.

BIBLIOGRAPHY

Bulbeck, R. "The Doubt of St. Joseph," Catholic Biblical Quarterly, X (1948), 296–309.

Durand, A. Evangile selon S. Matthieu, pp. 1–10.

Epstein, L. Marriage Laws in the Bible and the Talmud, pp. 3–25, 77–144.

Filas, F. The Man Nearest to Christ, pp. 68–76.

Fillion, L. The Life of Christ, I, 279–89.

Knabenbauer, J. Commentarius in quatuor s. Evangelia, pp. 47–58.

[21] Both these works are to be found in *The Apocryphal New Testament*, being the Apocryphal Gospels, Acts, Epistles, and Apocalypses; translated by M. James (Oxford, 1945), pp. 38 ff.
[22] See note 21.

Lagrange, J. M. The Gospel of Jesus Christ, I, 28–31.
————. Evangile selon S. Matthieu, pp. 2–18.
Maas, A. The Gospel according to St. Matthew, pp. 9–15.
Neufeld, E. Ancient Hebrew Marriage Laws, pp. 142–88.
Prat, F. Jésus-Christ, I, 507–12.
Ricciotti, G. The Life of Christ, pp. 234–36.
Simon, H. Praelectiones biblicae, pp. 153–56.
Vosté, J. M. De Conceptione Virginali Jesu Christi, pp. 17–29.

CHAPTER IX

The Birth of Christy

THE birth of our divine Lord did not take place at Nazareth but ninety-five miles to the south, at Bethlehem in Judea. The reason for His being born so far away from home was that the Blessed Mother and St. Joseph had to journey to Bethlehem in compliance with a decree issued by no less a person than Caesar Augustus himself. He ordered the enrollment of the whole world, that is, his empire, in which there were fifty million people, of whom about one-tenth were Roman citizens. In his long reign from 30 B.C. to A.D. 14, Augustus gradually acquired a great deal of the power and authority which his granduncle, Julius Caesar, was accused of desiring and he finally became what Pompey wished to be.[1] Holding control of the army and of finance, he brought peace and prosperity out of chaotic conditions of civil war, and by his restoration of the previous constitutional order and the distinction between the classes, Italy was made dominant and he himself was established as the First Citizen. He received the name imperator (commander) from the army, the title Augustus (augmenter) from the senate, and Princeps or First Citizen from the people. His rule became a one-man rule, although theoretically

[1] Cf. Rostovtzeff, *A History of the Ancient World*, II, 193; G. H. Stevenson, "The Imperial Administration," *Cambridge Ancient History*, X, 182–216.

95

under the old constitutional forms of magistrates, senate, and popular assembly.

The wealthiest man in the Empire, Augustus operated both his own wealth and that of the state for the good of the state like a business manager on a gigantic scale. He was able to bring a considerable prosperity and security to the provinces by his wise control of tax farmers and his regulation of the direct tax. One of the greatest administrators of all time, and a pioneer in the bureaucratic form of government,[2] he made frequent inventories of the man power and assets of the Empire; and was able at his death to leave a Breviarium, or summary, of the resources of the state.[3] Under his direction a census not only recorded the name of each person, but also his age, profession, and wealth; and this of course was for the purpose of taxation. Poll taxes were levied on men from 14 to 65 years of age and on women from 12 to 65 years of age; all, however, were registered in a census, even newly-born infants.

From certain records, it appears that registrations of the citizens of Italy were made in 28 B.C., in 8 B.C. and A.D. 14.[4] As to non-citizens in the provinces, there is evidence from the middle of the first Christian century to indicate that a census of them according to family was held every fourteen years.[5] The Acts of the Apostles (3:37) refers to a census of Palestine during which took place the revolt of Judas the Galilean. This was in A.D. 6 when Quirinius was for the second time made legate of Syria, his first time as legate having been in 3 B.C. Thus fourteen years before

[2] Cf. Ramsay, "Luke's Narrative of the Birth of Christ," *Expository*, XV (1912), 389; Marsh, *The Founding of the Roman Empire*; Holmes, *The Architect of the Roman Empire*.

[3] Cf. Suetonius, *Divus Augustus*, CI, 4; *Loeb*, I, 287. Tacitus (*Annals*, I, 11) tells us it contained a summary of the resources of the state, the number of Romans and auxiliaries in the armies, the size of the navy, kingdoms, provinces, tributes, customs, the public expenditure and largesses. Dio Cassius mentions that Augustus made a census in which he included even his own property. *Roman History*, LIV, 35; *Loeb*, VI, 373.

[4] Cf. Holzmeister, *Chronologia vitae Christi*, p. 29. Augustus mentions that a lustrum was offered at the end of three different censuses of citizens. *Res gestae Divi Augusti, Monumentum Ancyranum*, II, 8; ed. by Shipley (*Loeb*, pp. 357 f.)

[5] See Appendix 3, p. 335.

A.D. 6 would be the year (October, 9 B.C. to October, 8 B.C.). We naturally ask the question whether the series of censuses every fourteen years for non-citizens in the provinces was first inaugurated in 8 B.C., and whether this is the reason why it is called "the first" by St. Luke in the Nativity Gospel. The word "first" would also be appropriate if the census at the time of Christ's birth was the first one ever held in Palestine by the Romans.[6] According to this calculation the year 8 B.C. witnessed a census of the non-citizens of the provinces and also a census of the citizens of Italy. Accordingly the words of the Gospel text, "the whole world," could validly be employed. Several scholars, such as Lagrange,[7] hold that the Gospel passage can be translated: This census was made prior to that held under the governorship of Syria by Quirinius. However, there is another explanation that is in accordance with a more natural meaning of the text.

At the time of Christ's birth the Holy Land was a dependent monarchy under Herod the Great. The reason for the extension of the census to Herod's kingdom may have been that Augustus was contemplating its incorporation into the Empire. At any rate, Herod, who styled himself "Friend of the Emperor," would not dare oppose but rather would facilitate a census ordered by the Emperor, especially toward the end of his reign when he was fast losing the favor of Augustus. His many family troubles were one cause of irritation. Then in 9 B.C. his invasion of Nabataea aroused the suspicions of the Emperor, who intimated to Herod that, though he had treated Herod up to then as a friend, he would henceforth deal with him as a subject.[8] Such a treatment would be the extending of the census to Palestine in 8 B.C. We do know that in this same year Herod strove to regain favor at court by establishing in his kingdom an oath of fealty to the Emperor,[9] and by giving

[6] Clement of Alexandria would imply this when he writes: "When first the census was ordered to be taken up in the reign of Augustus" (*Stromata*, I, xxi, 147); ANF, II, 333.

[7] Cf. *Evangile selon S. Luc*, p. 66.

[8] Josephus, *Antiquities*, XVI, ix, 3. Here it is said that Augustus in his anger humiliated Herod by not receiving his messengers on two occasions.

[9] Josephus, *op. cit.*, XVII, ii, 4.

presents to the legate of Syria, C. Sentius Saturninus.[10] Hence he would do all in his power, and even take more measures than usually, to make the census a success. Indeed the will of Herod,[11] which presents such a close survey of the resources of his kingdom, would suggest a recent census, namely, one made within a few years of his death.

According to the Gospel narrative Publius Sulpicius Quirinius (Cyrinus) was ruler of Syria when the census that included Palestine was made. This man, according to Josephus,[12] was a person of "great dignity," not only because he had been consul but also "on other accounts." A brief outline of the career of Quirinius is found in Tacitus,[13] who narrates that on the occasion of his death the next emperor, Tiberius, requested the Senate that this "brave soldier" be given a public funeral. He was the outstanding military leader of his day, was twice legate of Syria and was proconsul of Asia. As chief of staff and as tutor, he accompanied Gaius Caesar to the East in A.D. 4.

Quirinius was appointed military commander of Syria shortly after his consulship in 12 B.C., and may have held this position for four or five years. In this capacity, he would hold superior rank to the civil prefect, and matters of census such as household enrollments would come under his jurisdiction. In this case, then, in the year 8 B.C., which we have selected as the year of Christ's birth, there would be two governors of Syria, the civil prefect or legate, Saturninus, and the military prefect, Quirinius.[14] The latter would

---

[10] *Ibid.*, ii, 1.

[11] *Ibid.*, vi, 1; viii, i.

[12] *Ibid.*, XIII, i, 1.

[13] *Annals*, III, 48 (*Loeb*, II, 597–99). He says Quirinius was a harsh, intrepid soldier who became unpopular in his old age.

[14] We do know that, while Sabinus was finance officer of Syria, there was another procurator, Varus, whose function it was to look after Caesar's properties in the province. Cf. Josephus, *Jewish War*, II, 16 (ii, 2); and *Antiquities*, XVI, ix, 1. On the two kinds of procurators, see Oesterley, *History of Israel*, II, 382 note, 464 f. In the Augustan age conditions were unsettled and administrative practice was not governed by hard and fast rules. Ex-praetors and ex-consuls were put in charge of provinces as occasion required. Cf. Anderson, "The Position Held by Quirinius for the Homanadensian War," Note 2 (*Cambridge Ancient History*, X, 877 f.). Yet this author says that the second tenure of

conduct the census in Palestine; indeed he was such a distinguished military commander that it was natural for St. Luke to mention him as being in charge of Syria where, we know, he had brought a war to such a successful conclusion that he was honored by being allowed to wear the robes of a triumphator. In the early Christian centuries when the lists of the legates of Syria were available and the career of Quirinius was well known, St. Luke's statement as well as his reason for not mentioning the civil legate would be understood. Thus Tertullian, although he knew that Quirinius was mentioned by St. Luke, states that the census was taken up by Saturninus and he implies that the census record was in his day in the hands of the Romans.[15]

When extending the universal registration to Palestine and giving orders for the first Roman census there, the Emperor may have expected that these orders would be resisted and that there might even be open revolt. Perhaps this was why he had his best military commander at hand to cope with any situation that might arise. Yet this first census, unlike the second one, did not lead to rebellion, perhaps because it was not accompanied by the imposition of taxes. Decrees for the registration would be drawn up in different languages and would be posted in the principal cities and towns of the Holy Land. The authorization of enrollment according to family descent might have been a concession to Jewish religious and patriotic sentiment.

St. Joseph and the Virgin Mother had been married about five months when they learned of this edict of the Emperor. They gave it prompt obedience, recognizing in it the hand of God. In being born away from Nazareth, the future Child would be saved from

Syria for Quirinius would be unparalleled. But the will of the emperor was supreme; through his friendship all precedent would be broken. (Cf. Tacitus, *Annals*, VI, 39).

[15] *Adv. Marcion*, IV, 19; ANF, III, 378; *Ad Judaeos*, IX, *op. cit.*, III, 164. While Quirinius was a harsh, severe soldier, Saturninus was a man of moderation. A consul and a man of great influence, he tried to save from death the two sons of Herod. Josephus, *op. cit.*, XVI, xi, 3. See W. Rees, "Cyrinus the Governor of Syria," *Scripture*, III (1948), 76–83.

evil gossip; and in being registered in Bethlehem as a descendant of David, He would be establishing His Messianic claim.

During most of the four-day journey south, the expectant Mother may have ridden on the back of an ass; but the journey would not have held any extra difficulties for her; being exempt from original sin, she did not suffer from certain of its consequences. On the last day of this journey she would pass just west of the Holy City, close to the citadel of Herod with its three massive towers. What fervent prayers arose from her soul as she caught glimpses of the magnificent Temple! What emotions welled up in her heart as within two miles of her destination she passed the tomb of Rachel, who died giving birth to Benjamin! Then following the road that turns southeast, as she approached the ancestral city her mind must have adverted to the announcement of the angel that her Son would restore and perpetuate David's kingdom, indeed, would reign there forever. Yet a disappointment awaited her; she was to find out that not only was there no hospitality but no accommodations available at the inn. There must have been a great number who proudly laid claim to descent from King David and who naturally kept their genealogical lists carefully. Because of the great crowd at the inn and in its courtyards, it would have provided no privacy. Mary and Joseph had to make the best of the situation and take shelter in a cavern or grotto formed by an overhanging cliff or rock. The chief distinguishing mark by which it was well known was a manger to hold fodder for domestic animals. This cave may have been attached to the inn; for today in Bethlehem many houses are built on caves, which are used for domestic animals. Here, in a place almost open to the elements, the greatest event in the history of the world took place, the birth of the Son of God; probably not on the day of arrival, but within a few days, according to the words of the text, "while they were there."

Unlike the apocryphal Gospels, the inspired historian keeps a discreet and reverential silence in regard to details. But he does say that it was the Blessed Mother herself who wrapped the long, nar-

row strips of cloth around the infant Savior and put him in the
only available place, the manger. The fact that she ministered to
the new-born Babe indicates that she was her own attendant and
did not suffer childbirth pains, a consequence of the sin of our first
parents. "She was both mother and midwife," as St. Jerome says.[16]
That the Blessed Mother miraculously remained a virgin in giving
birth to the Son of God is the view of the Fathers of the Church;
because, as they point out, the "infused power of the Divine Spirit
had to preserve in spotlessness and holiness that sanctuary He had
chosen for Himself." [17] St. Jerome, quoting Isaias, 1:3, is our authority for the presence of the ox and the ass.[18] Drawings that depict
animals at the scene of the Nativity have come down to us from the
fourth century. Our Lord's Virgin Mother and His foster father
were the first worshipers of the God-man. But on the same night
others were informed of the great event and were brought to the
crib in a miraculous way.

A desert sloped east from Bethlehem for twenty-five miles, extended as many miles north and stretched many times that distance
south. Here was favorable ground for flocks; and the shepherds
who lived there necessarily led a nomadic life. Because they had
little or no opportunity to become acquainted with legal prescriptions and sacred laws, these wandering shepherds incurred scorn
in certain quarters; [19] yet they were sincere, God-fearing people
whose calling in life brought them dangers and hardships. Bethlehem was a favorite rendezvous for them because of its proximity
to Jerusalem, the market for their flocks. In the valleys east of the
town snow falls rarely; in any event the severities of winter do not

[16] The Perpetual Virginity of the Blessed Mother, 10; NPN, 2nd ser., VI, 338. Cf.
also St. Gregory of Nyssa, Oratio I, In Christi resurrectione; PG, 46, 601.

[17] St. Leo, Sermon, XIII, 2, On the Nativity; NPN, 2nd ser., XII, 130. For some evidence of the view of the early Church on this matter, see J. C. Plumpe, "Some Little-
known Early Witnesses to Mary's Virginitas in Partu," Theological Studies, IX (1948),
567-77.

[18] Letter 108, 10, to Eustochium; NPN, 2nd ser., VI, 199. Origen says the same thing;
Homily 13, in Lucam; PG, 13, 1832. Animals are found in the representations from the
fourth century on; see Lowrie, Art in the Early Church, p. 97.

[19] Cf. Mishnah, Kiddushin (Betrothals), 1, 10; Danby, p. 323; Babba Kamma (First
Gate), X, 9; Danby, p. 10.

arrive as a rule before the first of January. In the last month of the year flocks would be collected at night within improvised folds where careful watch would have to be kept because of robbers or wild beasts. To lessen the number of hours during which each watcher would have to be exposed to the chilly, damp night, shepherds would naturally band together and agree to take turns in the vigils.

Thus it was that on the night of Christ's birth certain shepherds were in the vicinity of Bethlehem engaged in their work of guarding their flocks, when without any previous indication a brilliant heavenly light dispersed the midnight darkness and lit up the surrounding sky. In the dazzling brightness there appeared an angel, apparently in bodily form, who calmed the fears of the shepherds terrified by such a startling spectacle. He told them he was bringing a most joyful message, intended not only for themselves but for all the people, that in the neighboring town of Bethlehem there had just been born a Child who was no less than the Messiah, Savior and Lord. The shepherds were informed that this wondrous Infant could be found in King David's town, for He would be wrapped in swaddling clothes like other new-born babes; yet, instead of being in an ordinary crib, He would be lying in a manger.

So far only one angel had made an appearance; then suddenly along with the bearer of the great good news there appeared a whole multitude of angels who filled the midnight air with their voices singing the first Christmas carol. The words, simple in themselves yet sublime in meaning, were remembered by the shepherds: "Glory to God in the highest and on earth peace to men of good will." The glory of God, the purpose of all things, especially of religion, was furthered immeasurably by God assuming human nature when homage most perfect and infinite could be offered to the divine Majesty. Blessed peace, consolation, and security of conscience are bestowed on us by the Holy Ghost as a result of the merits of the God-man. They are the expression of the good will or pleasure of our heavenly Father, yet to a certain extent they depend on our good dispositions. Indeed in the text "good will" is left undetermined. Certainly by cooperating with God in faith and in baptism man can now through Jesus become a special adopted son of God inheriting peace here and hereafter. This blessed peace had been debarred by the estrangement between God and men brought about by sin for which man himself was not able to supply a remedy. The newly born divine Infant by His relationship to both God and man was "to bring both to friendship and concord, and to present men to God while He revealed God to man." [20]

Angels had sometimes visited the earth as ministers of God's punishments on men. The first Christmas night, on the contrary, their errand was one of blessed joy and consolation. As they chanted their words of praise and harmonized their expressions of exultation, mere dwellers of this valley of tears were permitted to hear the celestial chorus; because now God was on earth as man, because reconciliation was being effected between God and man, and because, with the opening of the heavenly courts to man, the angel's number depleted by the fall of Lucifer would be filled up [21] and companionship between men and angels would be established.

After the disappearance of the angels and the return of darkness to the midnight sky, the shepherds decided, without there being any need of discussion on the matter, that they should act in accordance with the wonderful information they had received and make a visit to the new-born Savior. The mentioning of "the manger" indicated the place where He was to be found, and it was with haste they made their way there. On finding the divine Infant they began to spread the good news; not only to the Blessed Mother and to St. Joseph, but to all they met they repeated the account of seeing and hearing angelic visitors. The tale of the shepherds was received in amazement on all sides, as indeed it should be. Differently from the others, however, for Mary the shepherds'

[20] Irenaeus, *Against Heresies*, III, xviii, 7; ANF, I, 448.
[21] St. Gregory the Great, *Moralium*, XXVII, 7; PL, 76, 404; cf. *De testimoniis Evangelii*, X; PL, 79, 1058.

vision of angels occasioned deep thought, contemplation, and the remembrance of the archangel's great visit to herself. The Gospel text adds that the shepherds returned to their folds praising God for all they had seen and heard.

A bend of a mountain saddle that forms a depression between two peaks, is the site of Bethlehem. The eastern peak on which the Basilica of the Nativity is located, is the lower of the two, and slopes away toward the Dead Sea. Except from the northwestern approach, the high location, about 2,500 feet above sea level, is surrounded with pleasant valleys and affords long views of scenery. One of these valleys, probably the scene of the story of Ruth and Booz, was fertile enough to justify the name, "The House of Bread." Bethlehem had been an outpost of the mountain country to the south, but lost its significance because of its nearness to Jerusalem. However, it continued to be a market place, and a meeting place for the nomads of the desert that stretched to the east.

Bethlehem today has a population of about 10,000, mostly Christians; and it is well graced with Christian institutions. Its oldest and most venerable monument is, of course, its Basilica of the Nativity of Our Lord with chapels dedicated to St. Joseph, the Holy Innocents, the Magi, and St. Jerome. A mile northeast of Bethlehem, the Shepherd's Field is pointed out, which has been marked by a church since the fourth century. Farther north toward Jerusalem there has been found the remains of the Flock Tower identified by St. Jerome.[22] The center of all is the Grotto of the Nativity over which the basilica is built. Here the exact spot of Christ's birth is marked by a vermilion star with the Latin inscription, "Here Jesus Christ was born of the Virgin Mary."

Brought up in Palstine a hundred years after Christ, St. Justin Martyr could speak of the "neighboring cavern of Bethlehem." [23] A hundred years later, according to Origen,[24] the cave of Bethle-

---

[22] *Letter* 108, 10 *to Eustochium NPN*, 2nd ser., VI, 200. On the Shepherd's Field, see Prat, *Jésus-Christ*, I, 90 note; Meistermann, *Guide to the Holy Land*, pp. 323–30.

[23] *Dialogue with Trypho*, 78; ANF, I, 237.

[24] *Against Celsus*, I, 51; ANF, IV, 418.

hem with its manger where the infant Christ was laid was known and pointed out even by strangers to the faith. In the second century Emperor Hadrian had erected in Bethlehem a pagan shrine to Adonis. The first Christian emperor, Constantine, and his mother St. Helena, about A.D. 330, built over the place of the Nativity, the basilica, which with modifications stands today, one of the oldest of all Christian churches. Then about A.D. 400 we have the witness of St. Paula, who tried to express her emotions in the presence of the cave and its manger.[25] That he had the privilege of kissing the manger and of praying in the cave is testified by St. Jerome; [26] although he regretted that in his day the original soft limestone manger had been replaced by one of gold and silver.[27] At this shrine, one of the oldest and most firmly established historically, pious pilgrims down the ages have thronged to honor the birth-place of Christ.

The circumstances attending the birth of our divine Lord teach respect for civil authority. It was because of obedience to civil law that the great event took place in Bethlehem. He was Himself subject to registration, and would pay the poll tax after He was 14 years of age. The Persian sage, Aphraates, writes, "as by poll tax he was enrolled among them, He will also succor them." [28] That the divine Infant was actually registered seems to be confirmed by the fact that St. Justin Martyr could write to the Roman Emperor that the place of Christ's birth "you can ascertain also from the registers of the taxing made under Quirinius your first procurator in Judea." [29] A direct blow for all time was struck at vain

[25] Cf. St. Jerome, letter 108, 10, to Eustochium; NPN, 2nd ser., VI, 200.
[26] Ibid.
[27] Homilia de Nativitate Domini; Analecta Maredsolana (ed. by Dom. Morin), III, 393. Pointing to their poverty, St. Jerome here says that Mary and Joseph came to Nazareth without any beast of burden. For the history of the Basilica of the Nativity, see Finegan, Light from the Ancient Past, pp. 438–42; Abel, Bethlehem, le sanctuaire de la Nativité, pp. 19–207.
[28] Select Demonstrations, V, On Wars, 24; NPN, XIII, 361. Ambrose said that Christ had to be enrolled according to custom; Commentary on Luke 3:23; PL, 15, 1590. Of course the poll tax would not apply until after A.D. 6.
[29] First Apology, 34; ANF, I, 174.

worldliness and empty pomp by the fact that the owner of all things was born in a place of stark simplicity utterly devoid of any comforts. After contrasting the cave with mansions, costly halls, and roofs that intercept the light of the sun, St. Jerome exclaims: "Behold in this poor crevice of the earth, the Creator of the heavens was born." [30] Detachment from things of the earth is also taught by the fact that the high and mighty were not present at the great event. On the contrary, around the crib were God-fearing semi-nomads, with their simplicity, sincerity, and firm faith; the silent guardian, St. Joseph, with his staunch faithfulness and downright goodness; and the immaculate Virgin Mother with her intense and warmly ecstatic love. The newly born God-man was satisfied with what He received on the first Christmas night.

The annual commemoration of His birth should increase our love of God and neighbor, and should fill us with hope and optimism. Christmas, a day of family reunions, should not be allowed to pass without our seriously reflecting on all that it means for us, following the example of her who was nearest to the divine Infant. From the shepherds we may learn the lesson of making good use of our Christian inheritance and of being zealous for the spread of our religion. Following the example of both the shepherds and the angels on each Christmas we should bless and praise the greatness of the good will and the immensity of the condescending love of God in His coming among us as a little infant to win our love for Himself. This coming of the Almighty in the form of weakness set the pattern divine we are to follow in humbling ourselves in the service of our neighbor, that we may be exalted hereafter.

BIBLIOGRAPHY

Becker, T. The Hidden Life of Christ, pp. 44–67.
Confraternity Commentary on the New Testament, pp. 238–40.
Dalman, G. Sacred Sites and Ways, pp. 16–55.

[30] Letter 46, 11; NPN, 2nd ser., VI, 64.

Panorama of Bethlehem from the wall of David

Fillion, L. The Life of Christ, I, 289–310.
Lagrange, J. M. Evangile selon S. Luc, pp. 65–81.
————. The Gospel of Jesus Christ, I, 33–39.
Lebreton, J. The Life and Teaching of Jesus Christ, I, 16–25.
Leo, St. Sermons on the Feast of the Nativity, NPN, XII, 128–44.
Meistermann, B. Guide to the Holy Land, pp. 296–330.
O'Shea, D. The Holy Family, pp. 22–44.
Prat, F. Jésus-Christ, I, 82–91.
Ricciotti, G. The Life of Christ, pp. 236–45.
Valensin and Huby. Evangile selon S. Luc, pp. 31–38.
Vincent and Abel, Bethlehem, le sanctuaire de la Nativité, pp. 19–207.

CHAPTER X

Circumcision and Name

WHEN almighty God changed Abram's name to Abraham, with the promise that he was to increase and multiply so as to be the ancestor of many kings and nations, He established a convenant the sign of which was to be the circumcision of all male descendants. This rite, thus authorized and commanded by God, was preserved by Moses in his legislation. Although not a mark of sin, yet circumcision bore a relation to sin inasmuch as it suggested the necessity of self-sacrifice and pledged the one circumcised to the observance of the Law. Circumcision marked the formal induction into membership of the chosen people.

St. Luke tells us that when the divine Infant was eight days old He was circumcised. The ceremony took place either within the house or in the synagogue at Bethlehem, and the minister was probably either St. Joseph or a priest.[1] It caused the first shedding of the precious blood and it left the divine Babe in pain and discomfort for several days. Sympathy must surely have been felt in the hearts of the Blessed Mother and St. Joseph during the time that the infant Savior suffered.

As the all-holy God, without the shadow of sin, the Christ Child certainly was not bound by the Law that required circumcision.

[1] Most probably within the eight days St. Joseph procured a house or made the cave somewhat houselike. Cf. Prat, *Jésus-Christ*, I, 92.

He waived His right of exemption, however, and endured the pain inherent in this rite to atone for sin. He came "in the likeness of sinful flesh and of sin" (Rom. 8: 3), that "He might be a propitiation for the sins of the people" (Heb. 2: 17); that "He might redeem them who were under the law; that we might receive the adoption of the sons" (Gal. 4: 5). He would accomplish redemption by pain and the shedding of blood. The first loss of the precious blood was indicative of the mode of procedure of the true Christian Messiah. It intimated that by suffering and death He was to establish the golden age of God's grace on earth.

Indeed the reasons why our divine Lord submitted to the rite of circumcision are many; they have been outlined by St. Thomas.[2] In the first place it shows beyond the shadow of a doubt that Christ had a real human body like ours. The reality of his true humanity is no longer held in doubt; but of old it was denied by the Manichaeans with their doctrine that Jesus' body was an imaginary one, by Apollinaris with his view that the sacred humanity was of the same substance as the Godhead; by Valentinus, in whose opinion Christ's body was brought with Him from heaven.

Secondly, circumcision came originally as a command from God, who ordered that Abraham and all his male descendants be circumcised as a mark of faith (Gen. 17: 10–14). In submitting to the rite, therefore, our Savior gave approval to this ancient institution and at the same time indicated that He was a true descendant of Abraham. If Our Lord were not circumcised, the Jews would find here an excuse for not accepting Him; for we know how insistent they were that the early converts of St. Paul be circumcised.

Another reason for Our Lord's circumcision was that it was prescribed by the law of Moses (Lev. 12: 3). Indeed in itself it was a ceremony that publicly professed a man's purpose of keeping the law; as St. Paul says, "I testify again to every man circumcising himself that he is a debtor to the whole law" (Gal. 5: 3). We know that our Savior exactly carried out all the requirements of the law

---

[2] *Summa theol.*, IIIa, q. 37, a. 1.

of the Lord (Luke 2: 39), giving us here an example of obedience, as He gave a like example when obeying His parents or the civil authorities.

Then, lastly, as circumcision, being sign of penance for sin, continued as a healing remedy until it became void and unnecessary in the great substitution of the sacrifice of the cross; and as Christ came in the likeness of sinful flesh, He did not wish to seem to reject the remedy whereby sinful flesh was wont to be healed. Lastly, He was "made of a woman, made under the law" (Gal. 4: 4), not only to approve it, but also to perfect it and to bring it to an end in Himself. As He underwent death to destroy the spiritual death of sin and to supply spiritual resurrection, and as He subjected Himself to the law to annul it and to furnish the freedom of the children of God; so also He submitted to circumcision to free us from its burden and to accomplish a spiritual circumcision in the cleansing of sin. So that our circumcision is "not made by hand, in the despoiling of the body of the flesh, but in the circumcision of Christ" (Col. 2: 11).

Blood, that was taken to represent life (Lev. 17: 11), was poured out in plenty on the altar of sacrifice in the Temple of Our Lord's day. There were numerous private offerings and there were the daily morning and evening sacrifices, not to mention the slaughtering of tens of thousands of lambs each year at the Passover. The purpose of all this was to strive to fulfill toward the Creator obligations of homage, thanksgiving, repentance, petition. Yet God was not satisfied with these gestures. Lavish and spectacular as these sacrifices were, they were not an adequate fulfillment of man's obligations. Indeed in the case of the offense to God's majesty by sin, man of himself is not able to make an adequate atonement. Man's great need was supplied when the Son of God came and made an oblation of Himself, shedding the last drop of His most precious blood on the cross. Thus His blood atoned for sin, redeemed us from the slavery of the devil and justified (Rom. 5: 9) us in the sight of God. The blood of Christ "as of a lamb unspotted and undefiled" (I Pet. 1: 19) was the purchase price of our salvation. The Epistle to the Hebrews (chap. 9) points out this effect of the shedding of Christ's blood on the cross. Heretofore, as it says, everything had to be sprinkled with blood by the high priest since "without the shedding of blood there is no remission"; but once the sacrifice of Calvary was effected, the slaughter of goats, sheep, and cattle was no longer necessary. The Great High Priest, the God-man, had offered an oblation that was perfect in every way and that was infinite in value. This one sacrifice secured for us redemption for all time and also an abundance of grace and merit. The shedding of the Christ Child's most precious blood at the circumcision was a token offering in obedience to the heavenly Father, and the commencement of the redemptive work; for, as St. Bernard says, "He began from here to bring about our salvation by shedding His innocent blood for us." [3]

The rite of circumcision lasted from the time of Abraham until the fulfillment of the promises made by almighty God to this patriarch, that is, to the death of Christ. Then, not only the children of the circumcision, but also "strangers to the testament" of the promise were brought "nigh" to God "by the blood of Christ" (Eph. 2: 12 f.). In doing away with the rite itself, our Lord did not abolish what it signified, penance for sin and dedication to God. The Council of Jerusalem decided against the necessity of the rite of circumcision for Christians (Acts 15:9 f.); and from that time this yoke was not to be placed on the neck of the followers of Jesus, as St. Paul stated: "For in Christ Jesus neither circumcision availeth anything nor uncircumcision; but faith that worketh by charity" (Gal. 5:6). It is faith that is necessary for salvation, as it was also faith that was necessary for those who lived before the time of Abraham, and for this patriarch himself before the rite of circumcision was inaugurated. Through Christ's circum-

[3] *Sermon II, on the Circumcision; PL, 183, 136.*

cision all Christians are spiritually circumcised. St. Thomas expresses this truth by saying that Jesus "took upon Himself the shadow that He might accomplish the reality." [4]

Our hearts are deeply moved at the thought that the Infant of Bethlehem suffered for us in the circumcision. He teaches us thereby the need of self-sacrifice and mortification which should serve as a scalpel to circumcise our hearts and our desires that we may follow securely in the footsteps of our suffering Savior and attain salvation.[5] The exhortation of the prophet Jeremias (4:4) to spiritual circumcision of the heart is repeated with new emphasis in the new dispensation to those who through faith have access to grace "and glory in the hope of the glory of the sons of God" (Rom. 5:2). Each year as we celebrate the feast of the Circumcision on the opening day of a new year,[6] the pattern is set for us by the child Jesus atoning for sins through pain and the shedding of blood. We ought to be inspired to dedicate anew our efforts to the avoidance of sin in accordance with the obligation assumed in our baptismal vows.

A final consideration is presented to us by St. Ambrose.[7] The ceremonies of the Old Law were in themselves types of the realities of the new order; so, as we have seen, the cleansing of the heart from the stain of sin was signified by the circumcision of the body. Nevertheless, we know from experience that the proneness to sin remains in man until his death; thus the circumcision on the eighth day is a type of that complete liberation from sin which shall be enjoyed at the resurrection.

[4] Ibid.

[5] Cf. Becker, The Hidden Life of Christ, p. 83.

[6] St. Augustine makes reference to the difference between the Christian and the pagan celebration of New Year's Day in his time, for the Christians kept the day with prayer and penance. Sermons, 197 and 198; PL, 38, 1024 ff. Cf. Sermon on the Circumcision of Christ; PL, 47, 1138.

[7] Expositio Evangelii sec. Lucam, 2:21; PL, 15, 1572; The Venerable Bede compares Christ's circumcision with His baptism. He states that Our Lord procured remedies for sin when He consecrated the water by His baptism. So, also by the circumcision He accepted, He purged us from our sins and taught that in this purging our human nature should be renovated and in fact on the last day restored, when the pest of various forms of death would be destroyed (In Lucae Evangelium Expositio, I; PL, 92, 337).

Seemingly no extraordinary occurrences attended upon Our Lord's circumcision such as were present at the circumcision of the Baptist. St. John's mother, it is recorded, received the felicitations of the neighbors who freely speculated on the future of the wonder-child. In contrast, the Virgin Mary was practically unknown to her neighbors in Bethlehem, who did not crowd in to offer congratulations on the formal induction of her divine Son into membership of the Jewish race. Yet something took place at the ceremony of circumcision which was of world-wide importance, the conferring of the name of the divine Infant.

The name of the God-man was appointed in heaven and was twice sent to earth. The archangel Gabriel brought it to Mary when he instructed her to call her future child "Jesus." Then, since Joseph as the legal father was officially the person to confer the name, an angel informed him in a dream concerning the name that should be given. The angel also explained the reason for the name, when he said, "for He shall save His people from their sins."

The name, which was given the eight-day-old Babe on the occasion of the circumcision was Jeshua, which means "God is Savior" or "God saves." [8] The Hellenized form of the name, Jesus, became popular even in the East, especially because the Gospels were in Greek. Thus we have the name for Our Lord. When we add the word "Christ" we are giving Him the title of His profession. The latter word is from the Greek and means "The Anointed." Our word "Messiah" really comes from the Aramaic and has the same meaning as the word Christ, namely, "The Anointed." We use the word "crown" or "crowned head" to designate a king, as in modern times kings are initiated into their high office by being crowned. In ancient times Jewish kings and high priests were initiated by being anointed with oil; and "the Anointed One" or

[8] Ya, or Yahweh, is the name of God; so Jeshua is made of two Hebrew words. Our word "Messiah" comes from the Aramaic word "Meshiah," the Hebrew is "Mashiah," meaning "the Anointed." Our word "Christ" is from the Greek word which also means "the Anointed." The name "Jesus" has come to us from the Greek form of the Hebrew name "Jeshua." Cf. Dalman, *Jesus-Jeshua*, 3, 6, 13.

"Messiah" or "Christ" came to be used for the great Redeemer that was expected. Our use of this title, however, designates "the august and incomprehensible mystery" [9] in the person of Jesus.

Of old the prophet Isaias had foretold that the Messiah's name would be Emmanuel (7:14), which in Hebrew means "God with us." Again Isaias (9:6) had prophesied that "His name shall be called Wonderful, Counsellor, God the Mighty, the Father of the world to come, the Prince of Peace." All these titles are included in the name "God is Savior." Jesus received and accepted other titles from His followers. The chief one, that which contained the essence of His teaching, was "Son of God." The name He frequently used for Himself was the "Son of man," since it was suitable for His method of gradually unfolding His divinity. This name was also a most appropriate one, for it recalled the prophecy of Daniel (7:13), where the Son of man is said to be associated with God and to enjoy divine qualities. Then several times Jesus was called "the Son of David," a popular Messianic title. At first Christ's disciples called Him "Rabbi." This literally signifies "my great one," but it was used for "teacher" or "master." When Jesus displayed His divine powers through His miracles, He was called "Lord." [10] The Savior accepted this title, and "Our Lord" became the general name employed for Him, especially when the emperors after Tiberius demanded the title. As Christians could not give it to a mere man connoting as it did reverence and veneration due to a divine person, they accorded it all the more readily and frequently to Christ.

The name Jesus, in a general way, contains all the other names of Our Lord. In particular it specifies the main reason and chief purposes of the Incarnation. Man needed a Savior because of the fall of Adam, the first parent. As Adam could not remedy the situation into which sin had brought him, the Son of God came in the form of sinful flesh to make atonement and besides to establish

[9] Scheeben, *The Mysteries of Christianity*, p. 333.
[10] Cf. Dalman, *The Words of Jesus*, pp. 324–31.

a rich fund of grace. The God-man is our Savior; this great truth is the fundamental meaning of the name Jesus. The Gospel story is the account of the way in which the God-man saved mankind. On the night of the Nativity the shepherds were told that there was born a Savior who is a divine Messiah. Zachary referred to Him as a "horn of salvation," and holy Simeon as "God's salvation." Mary called God "My Savior" because she received the great deliverance: through the merits of her Son she was exempt even from original sin. Isaias had predicted that "all flesh shall see the salvation of God," as it did in Christ.

It was most appropriate that the name Jesus was given the infant Savior at His circumcision. As He then officially became a member of the Jewish people, it was fitting that He should begin the shedding of His precious blood, which eventually was the ransom price for sin. Thus it seems, as Suarez [11] remarks, He was unwilling to accept the title "God-saves" until He had first shed His blood. By this first precious token of suffering He was beginning the atoning for sin and starting to build for us a great reservoir and treasure house of graces. As well as the rite of circumcision, the conferring of the name "God is Savior" also served as a dedication to the work of redemption. More than that, the name was a pledge of the complete victory of the cross.

Finally it is right for us to say as we do in our customary prayers to the divine Infant,[12] that at one and the same time both the circumcision of Our Lord and His holy name designate Him as the Savior of the world. Although it is true that Jesus really died on the cross so that by tasting death for all He might destroy "the empire of death" (Heb. 2:9, 14), yet the sufferings that accompanied His death and indeed all the sufferings of His sacred life were propitiatory and efficacious in the work of atonement. Meanwhile the evident truth has to be borne in mind that, since He was divine, any work, prayer, or suffering of His was sufficient to

[11] *Divi Thomas*, q. 37, a. 2 (Disp. XV, 2); *Opera omnia*, 256.
[12] *Raccolta*, or Prayers and Devotions, p. 62.

atone for the sins of all mankind. In the light of this truth, the labors and privations of the hidden life, the weariness and troubles of the missionary days, as well as the sufferings and agonies of Holy Week must be considered as sharing in the redemptive work and in the winning of the superabundance of grace. Hard though it is to understand why God permits His beloved children to suffer, it is a far greater mystery that He allowed His only-begotten Son to suffer. Certainly we must see here a manifestation of God's boundless mercy and love toward us, that for us He spared not even His own beloved Son; and we must hold dear as tokens of God's infinite love for us, all the trials and inconveniences of Our Lord's human life as well as the extreme sufferings of His cruel death.

What name could be adequate for God? Being far greater than anything we shall ever know about Him, God is the great Nameless One. The name we use to stand for Him in our poor knowledge of Him must be ever "great," "Holy," and "terrible" (Ps. 98 [99]: 3). In assuming human nature, however, He took for Himself the name Jesus that combines "Savior" with "God." This most appropriate of names designates our divine Lord's chief function as Redeemer and points to the great purpose of the Incarnation; for He came to seek and save that which was lost. "God-Savior" is expressive of God's mercy and forgiveness as well as of His majesty and power.

No more comforting and consoling name could be found for the God-man than "Jesus," "God-Savior," or "God saves." When we call Him by His name we are reminded of the fact that He is Redeemer and has saved us from our sins; it means the best Person saving us from our worst evil. It is a name of sweet refreshment on the lips of a sinner, connoting as it does, not dread and fear but mercy and love. It is a name of strength and power bringing us God's protection and help. As St. Peter said, "there is no other name under heaven given to men, whereby we must be saved" (Acts

4:12); and according to St. Paul (Phil. 2:10) even the demons in hell must bow at the mention of His name.

That all nations and peoples may hold in reverence and love the name that stands for our great Creator and Redeemer, should be the aim of our prayers and works.[13] Furthermore, that His holy name may be blessed and sanctified through our lives and also through the lives of others, should be our chief duty, being the purpose of our existence. Rightly must we repeat in the first petition of the Lord's Prayer, "Hallowed be Thy name." May the ineffable name of Jesus be our support and strength in life's journey, and on our dying lips our comfort and security.

> Ye flaming Powers, and winged Warriours bright,
> That erst with Music, and triumphant song
> First heard by happy watchful Shepherds ear,
> So sweetly sung your Joy the Clouds along
> Through the soft silence of the List'ning neight;
> Now mourn, and if sad share with us to bear
> Your fiery essence can distill no tear,
> Burn in your sighs, and borrow
> Seas swept from our deep sorrow,
> He who with all Heav'ns heraldry wile are
> Enter'd the world, now bleeds to give us ease;
> Alas, how soon our sin
>   Sore doth begin
>   His Infancy to cease!
>
>   John Milton

BIBLIOGRAPHY

Becker, T. The Hidden Life of Christ, pp. 77–84.
Kohler, K. "The Tetragrammaton," Studies, Addresses and Personal Papers, pp. 102–11.
Lagrange, J. M. Evangile selon S. Luc, p. 80.

[13] It must be the influence of the evil spirit that is responsible for the misuse of God's name. Sad it is that God had to legislate against the improper use of His name. As an effort at reparation the Holy Name Societies have been organized in modern times.

Lessius, L. The Names of God.

Moore, G. Judaism in the First Christian Centuries, II, 16–21.

Prat, F. Jésus-Christ, I, 92 f.

Vaccari, A. "In Festo Circumcisionis Domini N. Jesu Christi,"
    Verbum Domini, II (1922), 10–18.

Valensin and Huby. Evangile selon S. Luc, pp. 40 f.

Willam, F. The Life of Jesus Christ, p. 31.

CHAPTER XI

The Presentation

IN submitting to the pain and shedding of blood in the circumcision the infant Savior, when only a week old, indicated the pattern according to which He was to carry out His redemptive work. A month later, when forty days old, He set another example of fulfilling the requirements of the Jewish ceremonial law; for it was then that He underwent the rite of presentation in the Temple. The ceremonies and the journey of about six miles each way to and from the Holy City must have taken up the greater part of an entire day.

Moses had dedicated all first fruits to God and accordingly ordered that every first-born male be presented to the Lord (Exod. 13:2, 12; Num. 18:15–23). The purpose was both to acknowledge the ownership and dominion of God and to commemorate the liberating of the Jewish people from the hands of Pharaoh, when the destroying angel killed the first-born of man and beast in Egypt, except of those whose door posts were sprinkled with the blood of the paschal lamb. The presentation of the first-born sons signified that they were to be given for the service of the Temple; or, if not, they were to be compensated for by a specified gift. Then, as the office of priesthood and ministry of the Temple was reserved for the tribe of Levi, the custom grew up of presenting the first-born male in the Temple and of obtaining ownership of him again, or buying him back, with the stipulated price of five shekels, that is, about three dollars.

Most edifying is the example of the holy family availing themselves of this beautiful custom in praise and glory of God. Both St. Matthew (1:25) and St. Luke (2:7) call our divine Lord the "first-born son," a title that was given to a first-born whether there were other children or not. In Our Lord's case He was above the law and, since He was holiness itself, there was no need of presenting Him as holy; yet here, as usual, He did not miss the opportunity of giving honor and service to His Father. In the arms of His Blessed Mother the tender Infant is carried from Bethlehem to Jerusalem.

It is probable that the journey was made in the early hours of the morning so that the holy family might be present for the morning service of the perpetual sacrifice; namely, the offering of a yearling lamb and the incensing. They would enter the Holy City from the west through the Jaffa Gate and pass north of the citadel of Herod and the palace of the Hasmonaeans. This shortest way to the Temple would lead over the bridge that crossed the Tyropaean Valley to the western gates of the sacred enclosure. Crossing the Court of Gentiles, they used the "Great Gate" to reach the Court of Women. Here alongside the pillars that supported the gallery where women worshiped apart from the men,[1] there were twelve trumpet-shaped boxes to receive money and other offerings. The Virgin Mother approached the third one and deposited in it the price of her sacrifice. When the organ-peal of the Magrepha was heard announcing that the incense was about to be kindled on the golden altar, then she with those who were to be purified was conducted up the fifteen steps of the beautiful circular stairway that led from the Court of Women to that of Israel.[2]

[1] Cf. *Mishnah*, Middoth (Measurements), 2, 5; Danby, p. 592. From the gallery women could look through the Nicanor Gate to the altar.

[2] See Hollis, *The Archaeology of Herod's Temple*, p. 195, Plate XVII. The central gate on the south side of the inner court of the Temple appears to have been the place assigned for the offerings for the redemption of the "first-born," for this gate is called the Gate of the First-born; *Mishnah, ibid.*, I, 4; Danby, p. 590. See Hollis, *op. cit.*, p. 222.

Here these women were arranged on either side of the immense open gateway and were as near as they were ever to be to the great stone altar of sacrifice, or to the holy place and the holy of holies.[3] They could apply to themselves in a special way the prayers that arose with the cloud from the golden altar and the benedictions that came from the lips of the ministering priests with the pronouncing of the ineffable name. Indeed they could claim and appropriate the expression of joy symbolized by the drink-offering and by the hymn of praise that arose from the Levites praising God with words of God, or God praising Himself with the lips of men.

As St. Joseph paid the modest sum,—which went into the priest's treasury and could be paid to any priest in any place—the Virgin Mother must have reflected on the utter insufficiency of the amount in comparison with the ineffable dignity of her Son. She had now given Him to God for God's great work, and in redeeming Him she realized that it was merely that He might be the more consecrated to the service of the Most High. She could say again, "Be it done to me according to thy word," feeling that she was making the greatest of sacrifices in presenting a "first-born" who was the essence of salvation and happiness.[4]

The infant Savior joined in the consecration. The original Passover lamb had saved all the first-born Israelites in the land of Egypt. So this rededication and consecration was a renewal of offering and immolation of the eternal paschal lamb received by the priesthood of the Old Law to be delivered, when the hour came, to the death of the cross, in a sacrifice which was to bring to an end all other sacrifices.

A paradox may be seen in the rite of presentation; namely, the ransoming was itself a dedication of the great first-born of the sons of God among men. It is indeed well said that here there is "an

[3] Cf. Dalman, *Sacred Sites and Ways*, p. 306.
[4] See Schaefer, *The Mother of Jesus in Holy Scripture*, pp. 185 f.; also J. B. Frey, "La Signification du terme Prototokos d'après une inscription Juive," *Biblica*, XI (1930), 373–90.

antithesis of law against truth, or theologically, a divine irony." [5]

The Virgin Mother, as we have noted, was closely associated with her Son in this offering, in His presentation. She also followed closely His example in voluntarily submitting to the rites of purification. There was another law laid down in the twelfth chapter of Leviticus whereby a mother was to remain ritually "unclean" after childbirth for forty days if the child was a boy and sixty if it was a girl. At the end of the prescribed time, "the days of purification," the mother was required to present at the sanctuary of the Temple a one-year-old lamb for a burnt offering, and a young pigeon or turtle dove for a sin offering. However, if she could not afford the offering of a lamb, then instead, another turtle dove or young pigeon would be presented as a holocaust.

Surely the Blessed Mother was exempt from this law of purification, since she preserved her virginity in the supernatural conception and also in the birth of her divine Son. Not only that, but the close association and presence of God brought her pre-eminent holiness. Mary could proclaim herself the great exception to the law. On the contrary, under the inspiration of the Holy Ghost who guided her every action, she would not miss such an occasion of

[5] *The Gospel of the Infancy and Other Biblical Essays*, p. 43. In this stimulating study (pp. 17 ff.), Burrows points out the following interesting facts. The quotation from the Law as given in Luke 2:23 is not found exactly anywhere in the Old Testament. The closest to it is Num. 8:16 ff. The principle mentioned here is explained as accounting for the presentation of the Levites. There is described the real presentation, or ordination ceremony of the Levites. When the Temple was reached by the child Jesus, there is no allusion to the presentation ceremony, for indeed there was no rite of the presentation of infants in the Old Law. Samuel was presented in the house of God. St. Luke did not refer directly to the law of the redemption rite but to the general principle of the consecration of the first-born in Numbers, chapter 8. According to the ritual the infant Christ was redeemed, but "in idea and in spirit He was offered to the Lord like the Levites." The redemption of the Son of God would be meaningless, but His dedication in the Temple to His Father's service was "profoundly significant."

Likewise for the Blessed Mother the legal aspects of the rite of purification had no significance. Ancient authorities had thought the sacrifice was offered for the child, not for the mother. The doves were offerings of purification in the eyes of the law; but they had a further meaning as a sacrifice accompanying the presentation of the first-born. For here the custom of the law gives way to the Holy Ghost and the mystery of Christ. A priest of the Holy Ghost, Simeon, is present to bless the parents, and the presentation of the Child "is a prelude to the future sacrifices in which the mother will be a fellow victim."

personal humility and sanctification. Rather she gladly seized it, especially as the divine Child was giving her so great an example. Like Him, by humility and obedience in submitting to the prescription of the law, to which she was not subject, she was removing from the Jews all excuse of calumny and scandal.

It must have been a matter of poignant regret to her on this occasion that she could present only the offering of the poor, when the sacrifice of a firstling lamb would have been so symbolically appropriate, and when the best of all the earth was so little where the God-man was concerned. However, as the Fathers of the Church point out, the birds have a figurative meaning. With St. Athanasius, the turtle dove is a symbol of temperance and quietude, and the young pigeon typifies innocence and meekness.[6] St. Thomas among other things sees the confession of faith, chastity, and contemplation symbolized by the turtle dove, and gentleness and simplicity by the pigeon.[7]

What a glorious day it was in the history of the Temple of Jerusalem as the God-man first visited the great central shrine of Jewish worship! The prophecy of Malachias (3:1) was fulfilled: "when the Lord whom you seek and the angel of the testament whom you desire shall come to His Temple." There was also fulfilled the prophetic utterance of Aggeus (2:8–10) in which the Lord of hosts declared: "the desired of all nations shall come; and I will fill this house with glory." God has given the further assurance that He would grant peace in this place and that "great shall be the glory of this last house more than that of the first." Almighty God provided that the event did not pass unnoticed. Although there was nothing extraordinary about the outward appearance of the holy family, yet to the surprise of the Blessed Mother and St. Joseph two persons of great piety and holiness, both advanced in years, were vouchsafed the revelation that the little Babe in Mary's arms was the long-expected Redeemer. Thus

[6] *Comment. in Lucam, ad. loc.; PG, 27, 1396.*
[7] *Summa theol.,* IIIa, q.37, a.3. Cf. Origen, Homily 15, *In Lucam; PG,* 13, 1839.

there began here the turning of good, pious Jews away from the Temple to follow Jesus Christ, for these two saintly characters represented the best of the Israelites who were sincerely seeking to follow God's will.

The first was an old man named Simeon. He was inconspicuous in his time as far as we know; hence, most likely, he was not the person of the same name who was the son of Hillel and the father of Gamaliel. He was singled out by almighty God to stand in a position that overlooked two worlds. He represented the best of the Old Testament in his assiduous piety and ardent hope; and he had the knowledge of holding in his arms the Author of the New Covenant, the Messiah Himself. Indeed, he had been assured by the Holy Ghost that he would not die before seeing the great "Anointed One." This old man was inspired to come to the Temple and to recognize the fulfillment of the promise in the person of the little Child. He immediately took Him into his arms. What a wonderful dispensation had come! Simeon could hold the Son of God. He called upon the Lord to dismiss him, now that his fondest hopes had been realized. This is his canticle, the poetical outburst from his joyful heart.

> Now thou dost dismiss Thy servant, O Lord,
>   according to Thy word, in peace;
> Because my eyes have seen Thy salvation,
>   which Thou hast prepared before the face
>   of all peoples:
> A light to the revelation of the Gentiles,
>   and the glory of Thy people Israel.
>   Luke 2:29–32

As Mary had declared that she exulted in God her "Savior," and as Zachary had been preoccupied with "redemption" and "salvation," so here too Simeon appreciates and accentuates the "salvation" that was to liberate him and to let him die in peace. Indeed all can now pass from this world in peace, for opportunity will be given to peoples of all lands to recognize that God in

Christ reconciles the world to Himself. This reconciliation or restoration of grace means enlightenment of pagans and glory for Jews. That is, the effulgence of the golden sunshine from Him whom Simeon holds will penetrate the darkness of paganism and at the same time with its reflecting rays will gild with luster the people from whom the Infant springs. These ideas with their universal application are all found in Isaias; indeed it may be said that here we have the pith and core both of Isaias' prophecies and of Zachary's canticle. "Salvation," "Light," "Peace" are caught up as the keywords of Christianity and enshrined in a lyric gem as a tribute to Jesus (cf. John, 12:35–50). In such few words we have the headlines that briefly summarize the effects of Christ's mission and work. This beautiful though short canticle expressive of appreciation for seeing and possessing Christ is an appropriate hymn of thanksgiving for the reception of Christian grace. It is a suitable night prayer or evening song and rightly finds a place in Compline. We may well repeat it at the hour of death.

With prophetic vision holy Simeon saw the shadows of the future as well as the brightness. He informed the mother that her Child will be a stumbling block over which some will trip and fall; but for others He will be a stepping stone to sublime heights. Simeon intimates what history bears out, that the Son's enemies will be the Mother's also, and in the conflict her soul will be crushed with sorrow;[8] for Christ will be the searcher and revealer of hearts inasmuch as He will reveal everybody's true character in the test of real sincerity, "more piercing than any two-edged sword and reaching unto the division of the soul and the spirit" (Heb. 4:12). Thus, far from being promised a career of worldly glory for her

[8] Taken strictly, Luke 2:35 means that the Blessed Mother would suffer from hostile tongues, a fellow victim along with her Child. In line with this thought, "the sword of sorrow" could be a figure for an evil tongue. Yet as in the prophecy there is undoubtedly a reference to Our Lord's passion, the word seems to refer to that which pierced the Savior's side in the presence of the Blessed Mother. It is pointed out by Burrows (*Gospel of the Infancy*, pp. 43 f.) that holy Simeon's prophecy seems to be reminiscent of Zach. 12:9 ff. and Ps. 22. Accordingly the word "sword" would be capable of a generic sense with the rendering "the steel," or "the iron." Cf. Gallus, I, "De sensu verborum Luc. 2:35, eorumque momento Mariologico," *Biblica*, XXIX (1948), 220–39.

Son, Mary is told to expect opposition and sorrow. She must have been aware of this before, for the rejection of the high and mighty which she herself had already prophesied, could not be done without the price of a struggle. Indeed, her own statement that the hungry would be filled with good things was verified in the case of both these pious individuals who were here encountered in the Temple.

For another was also favored with the knowledge that the Savior of the world was visiting the sacred edifice. This was an old woman of eighty-four years, belonging to the tribe of Asher which was celebrated for its beautiful women. Her name was Anna and her father was Phanuel. After seven years of married life she had been widowed, and ever since she led a most exemplary life; for she "departed not from the temple, with fastings and prayers, worshiping night and day." "She earned 'spiritual grace,' received the title 'daughter of the face of God,' and obtained a share in the 'blessedness and wealth' that belonged to her ancestry." [9] A prophetess she was, certainly in the sense that under divine influence she instructed the well disposed. Now being specially inspired to recognize the divine Savior as she met the holy family, she gave open thanks and spoke of Him "to all that looked for the redemption of Israel." Thus those who desired and expected the Messiah heard the good news that He was already born. This pious old woman spreading the wonderful information is an outstanding example of holy widowhood. St. Augustine holds her up for admiration when he says that she is to be commended for the fact that with so great service of piety she continued her office of widowed chastity even to so great age.[10] Pointing to Anna's fastings and prayers, this same doctor of the Church warns: "How incumbent on widows to go beyond others in devoting time to prayer!" [11] In urging widows to

[9] St. Jerome, *Letter* 54, *to Furia*, 16; *Select Letters*, ed. by Wright, p. 259. This doctor is here employing the literal meanings of the names Anna, Phanuel, and Asher. In another letter (79, 10) he holds that Anna "received in her arms the Savior of the World and had revealed to her the holy mysteries which were to come."

[10] *On the Good of Widowhood*, 16; NPN, 1st ser., III, 447.

[11] *Letter* 130, *to Proba*, 29; NPN, 1st ser., I, 468.

persevere in chaste widowhood, St. Jerome also points to the example of Anna.[12] In like manner St. Ambrose states that Anna shows us "what widows ought to be," for she received praise for "being intent not less on the duties of religion than on the pursuit of chastity." [13]

Holy Simeon who "endured to carry in his weak arms that Majesty which the creatures could not endure" was, according to St. Ephraim, representative of priesthood and prophecy, "priesthood from his hands and prophecy from his lips." [14] Yet it is not said in the sacred text that holy Simeon was a priest. Rather it seems that he represented the good and pious from the ranks of the laity; as also did holy Anna. Thus it was the most devout and most sincere who were given the honor of recognizing the infant Jesus as He was presented in the Temple, just as it was the simple God-fearing shepherds who had been led to His crib. His associating Himself with the good and pious was a prelude of what to expect in the public ministry. Indeed, by attracting to Himself the very best He was already making manifest the secrets of men's hearts. As St. Irenaeus writes, "He was already despoiling men, by removing their ignorance, conferring upon them His own knowledge, and scattering abroad those who recognized Him." [15]

In submitting without obligation on their part to the ceremonies of the Old Law, our Redeemer and His Blessed Mother preached a practical sermon inculcating prompt fulfillment of religious rites and duties. In His holy childhood He "fulfilled all things as prescribed in the law of the Lord" (Luke 2:39). He was "born under the law that He might redeem those who were under the law" (Gal. 4:4) and that He might liberate us from the shackles of the law. The presentation of Jesus in the Temple teaches us to consecrate ourselves and everything we have to His Sacred Heart; for,

[12] *Letter 54, to Furia,* 16, 18; *Select Letters,* pp. 259, 263.
[13] *Concerning Widows,* 4, 21; NPN, 2nd ser., X, 394.
[14] *Three Homilies on Our Lord,* 49, 51; NPN, 2nd ser., XIII, 328. He also writes that Christ "gave Himself to be offered that by His cross the hands of them that offered Him might be sanctified" (NPN, 2nd ser., XIII, 327).
[15] *Against Heresies,* III, xvi, 4; ANF, I, 442.

as St. Athanasius [16] tells us, the great First-born presented Himself in the Temple that "we may purge ourselves and present ourselves to God." Jesus' consecration and His Mother's purification were followed by the profession of faith on the part of two witnesses; as His circumcision was followed by His being given His glorious name, and His birth in the stable by the visitation of the angelic host. "He that humbles himself shall be exalted."

> In the huge temple deck'd by Herod's pride,
> Who fain would bribe a God he ne'er believed,
> Kneels a meek woman, that hath once conceived,
> Tho' she was never like an earthly bride,
> And yet the stainless would be purified,
> And wash away the stain that yet was none,
> And for the birth of her immaculate Son
> With the stern rigour of the law complied:
> The duty paid received its due reward
> When Simeon bless'd the Baby on her arm;
> And though he plainly told her that a sword
> Must pierce her soul, she felt no weak alarm
> For that for which a Prophet thanks the Lord
> Once to have seen, could never end in harm.
>
> Hartley Coleridge

BIBLIOGRAPHY

Fillion, L. The Life of Christ, I, 326–38.

Joüon, P. L'Evangile de N.S. Jésus-Christ, pp. 301–305.

Lagrange, J. M. Evangile selon S. Luc, pp. 81–91.

O'Shea, D. The Holy Family, pp. 45–72.

Prat, F. Jésus-Christ, I, 93–97.

Simon, H. Praelectiones biblicae, I, 166–69.

Stoll, R. Gospel according to St. Luke, pp. 40–47.

Strack and Billerbeck. Kommentar zum Neuen Testament aus Talmud und Midrasch, II, 119–41.

Valensin and Huby. Evangile selon S. Luc, pp. 41–44.

[16] *In Luc. Comment.; PG,* 27, 1396.

CHAPTER XII

The Homage of the Magi

The Wise Men see the star
And follow as it leads before;
By its pure ray they seek the Light
And with their gifts that Light adore.

To Thee, O Jesus, Who Thyself
Hast to the Gentile world displayed,
Praise, with the Father evermore,
And with the Holy Ghost, be paid.
                    Sedulius (Fifth Century)

THE Gospel narrative of the visit of the Magi uses the word "house" (Matt. 2:11) to describe the place in which the child Jesus was found. Hence some scholars have been led to affirm that, shortly after the nativity, St. Joseph procured a house to which he conducted the Blessed Mother and her new-born Son. Others, relying on the ancient tradition that goes back to St. Justin Martyr,[1] have asserted that the holy family did not forsake the original cave in which the Savior was born, but continued to live there. St. Joseph, being a carpenter, could quickly make the necessary alterations to render it habitable and homelike. Thus it may have been that the Magi were led to the same Nativity grotto with its manger as were the shepherds and in almost as miraculous a manner.

[1] *Dialogue*, 78; ANF, I, 237.

On another important detail, the time of the visit of the Magi, there is no general agreement. The statement of St. Matthew that it was "when Jesus was born in Bethlehem of Juda" seems to insinuate that the arrival of the Magi was shortly after the birth of the Savior. Yet a different implication is given by the Gospel account of the slaughter, by King Herod's order, of all the male children two years of age and under in Bethlehem and vicinity. Accordingly different dates are given for the reception of the Magi. Probably the divine Child was between two months and one year old when it took place. The original purpose of the feast of the Epiphany was not to mark the exact date of the arrival of the wise men but to serve as a joint commemoration of the divine manifestations that took place at the baptism and at Cana, as well as of those occasioning the adoration of the wise men.

Throughout the Roman Empire at the time of Christ the word "Magi" had two meanings. It classified impostors who used magic and sorcery to evil purposes, and in this sense it is employed in the Acts of the Apostles (8:9). It was also the name of a priestly caste given to the study of philosophy and the natural sciences. The institution of Magi flourished in Persia where it held political influence despite dynastic changes, and where in the seventh century B.C. it accommodated itself to Zoroastrianism, a religion that abominated idolatry and professed belief in one God as well as in the immortality of the soul. In Babylon the Magi were diviners and soothsayers in the time of Daniel the prophet, who was made their prince after interpreting the dreams of Nabuchodonosor. Despite the fact that their religion forbade sorcery, some of the Magi in the course of time became devoted to the black arts. Thus in the West a bad reputation was given to their caste, and the derivation of our word "magic" is explained.

The Magi of the Gospel story belonged to the better class, famous as priests, philosophers, counselors of kings, adepts in the natural sciences. The tradition that they were kings seems to have been based on the liturgical use of Psalm 71:10: "The kings of

Tharsis and the islands shall offer presents; the kings of the Arabians and of Saba shall bring gifts." This in itself is no proof.[2] There is nothing definitely known about their number which is generally considered three on account of the three gifts. Likewise their names are unknown. Besides Gaspar, Melchior, and Balthasar, other names have been given to them. Finally, in regard to their native land, they must have come from some part of the Parthian Empire, from Media, Persia, Assyria, or Babylonia, as these countries had a Magian priesthood in the time of Christ. For Palestine of that time, any country from the Jordan to the Euphrates and beyond would be considered the East, the word used in the Gospel, and the territory adjoining the Holy Land stretching as far north as Damascus was known as Arabia.[3]

[2] See Lagrange, *Evangile selon S. Matthieu*, pp. 19–23; Prat, *Jésus-Christ*, I, 200; Drum, "Magi," *Catholic Encyclopedia*, IX, 528. Cf. Josephus, *Antiquities*, XIV, i, 4.

[3] This fact would explain why early writers regarded Arabia as the country of the Magi. That the native country of the Magi of the Gospel account was Persia was stated by such early writers as Clement of Alexandria, Diodorus of Tarsus, St. John Chrysostom, St. Cyril of Alexandria, Juvencus and Prudentius. It is strange that some of the early writers and Fathers such as St. Justin Martyr (*Dialogue*, 78; ANF, I, 238), and Origen (*Against Celsus*, I, 60; ANF, IV, 422) thought that these Magi were magicians and were converted from their evil ways by Our Lord. In this they were wrong.

About the Magi as an institution and as a definite group we have some definite information that has been handed down by early non-Christian writers. Pliny maintains that magic was born in medicine and that it combined medicine, religion and astronomy (*Natural History*; XXX, i, Latin ed. Lipsiae, 1830, IV, 249 f.). According to Herodotus the Magi were originally one of the tribes of the Medes (*History*, I, 101; *Loeb*, I, 132). This historian also tells us that the Magi interpreted dreams and signs in the heavens (*History*, I, 107, 120, 128; VII, 19, 37; *Loeb*, I, 138, 156, 166; III, 332, 350). Under Cyrus or perhaps later the Magi were invested with the priestly office. They superintended the sacrifices and a sacrifice could not be offered "without a magian." Likewise they kept the sacred fire ever burning and chanted incantations for about an hour each day (Herodotus, *History*, I, 132; VII, 113; *Loeb*, I, 172; III, 416; Strabo, *Geography*, XV, iii, 14–15; *Loeb*, VII, 175 f.). In the political field the Magi deposed Cambyses, were set as a guard at the tomb of Cyrus, and as counsellors attended Parthian and Persian kings (Strabo, *op. cit.*, XI, ix, 3; XV, i, 68; XV, iii, 7, 24; *Loeb*, V, 277; VII, 119, 167, 189).

High tributes are paid the Magi by two important early writers. Strabo attributes to them superior knowledge and states that they led an "august" form of life (*Id.* I, ii, 4; XV, iii, 1; *Loeb*, I, 87; VII, 157). They are classed among the associations of men "of the highest excellence" by Philo, who goes on to give them the following words of praise and acclaim, while outlining their function: "Among the Persians there is the order of the Magi, who silently make research into the facts of nature to gain knowledge of the truth, and through visions clearer than speech, give and receive the revelations of divine excellence (*Every Good Man is Free: Quod Omnis Probus Liber sit*, 74 [XI, 456]; *Loeb*, XI, 53).

Apparently this is how the Magi associated the new star which they saw with the birth of the "King of the Jews," the title which Our Lord received on His cross. At that time Jews were scattered over many lands, and their Messianic ideas found acceptance even in Rome, as some of the classical writers bear witness. Now the Jews associated a star with their future Messiah, for an apocryphal work [4] of the time says: "His star shall rise in heaven as a King." This association was based on the prophecy of Balaam: [5] "I shall see him but not now; I shall behold him but not near. A star shall rise out of Jacob and a scepter shall spring up from Israel" (Num. 24:17). This prophecy of the Messiah of the Jews that speaks of his splendor under the figure of a star and his power under the figure of a scepter was uttered toward the end of the forty years wandering. It is remarkable that Balaam, like the Magi, lived in the east, and came to Moab to utter his prophecy. Like them, too, he was a Gentile who had the knowledge of the true God. Also he was a soothsayer, and in this capacity God used him to pronounce a Messianic prophecy. The Magi, keenly interested as they were in astrology, would be acquainted with all ancient writings that refer to the stars. Hence, when they saw a strange star that was associated with Balaam's prophecy, they would know that it presaged the birth of the Jewish Messianic king. Whether it was in this manner, as was held by Origen [6] and by St. Jerome,[7] or whether it was entirely the result of a divine revelation, of which in any event there was a certain amount, the fact is that one day the Magi arrived in Jerusalem and asked: "Where is he that is born king of the Jews? For we have seen his star in the east and are come to adore him" (Matt. 2:2).

Men with such grave, studious countenances, wearing dress that marked them off as belonging to an eastern priestly caste, would attract wide attention in the Holy City. News of their strange

[4] Testament of XII Patriarchs, XIII, 3.
[5] See Guyot, "The Prophecy of Balaam," Cath. Bib. Quart., II (1940), 330–40.
[6] Against Celsus, I, 60; ANF, IV, 422.
[7] Comment. in S. Matthaeum, ad loc.; PL, 7, 27.

quest and their statement that they had seen a star that announced the birth of a king for the Jews would have spread quickly, causing astonishment and commotion. As nearly everyone at that time believed in the signs of the stars, the account of the Magi would have been accepted without question. That it caused annoyance, we are told in the Gospel text. Why were not the Jews glad over the news of the birth of their King? Perhaps they feared further political troubles, which they had plenty of already. We know certainly that the anxiety of Herod came from the mad, cruel jealousy that had eaten his heart to its core. Experience had taught him that the Jews believed in a Messiah and that they would revolt in favor of one who might liberate them politically. Therefore he determined from the start to put this newly-born child to death and planned a dark, cunning way to do it, the while he shrewdly procured all necessary information.

First, he called a special meeting of the chief priests and scribes (probably not a convocation of the whole Sanhedrin, but representatives of the two mentioned classes) and asked them where they expected their Messiah to be born. There could be only one answer. They quoted the prophecy of Micheas (5:2) that designated the place. As given by St. Matthew [8] it reads: "And thou, Bethlehem, the land of Juda, art not the least among the princes of Juda, for out of thee shall come forth the captain that shall rule My people Israel" (Matt. 2:6).

Having obtained the desired information, Herod acted promptly. He decided not to send spies to Bethlehem along with the Magi lest he show his hand and give evidence to the Jews that he believed in the Messiah or the Scriptures. On the other hand he must give the impression to the Magi that he was completely in accord with their simple faith and open sincerity. Therefore he called them to him secretly to obtain another necessary piece of information, the age of the Child. This he did by ascertaining the exact time of

[8] This quotation given by the chief priests and scribes differs in three minor points from the original. The prophecy refers to the Messiah and interprets the prophecy of Isaias that treats of the Virgin Mother. Cf. Maas, *Christ in Type and Prophecy*, I, 275.

the first appearance of the star. He also wished to make use of the Magi to find this newly-born King, pretending that his purpose was to worship Him.

After their secret audience with King Herod, the Magi immediately set out for Bethlehem, about six miles to the south. To their great joy the star which they had seen in the east reappeared and "went before them, until it came and stood over the place where the Child was" (Matt. 2:9), making it easy for them to find the object of their quest. When they entered "the house" indicated by the star, they saw the divine Child with Mary His Mother. Thus on this occasion the Blessed Virgin had the place of honor and the privilege of presenting her Son to the first Gentiles who prostrated themselves in worship of the God-man. As a mark of their fealty they offered Him from their treasures, gold, frankincense, and myrrh,—the latter a fragrant, transparent gum from India or Arabia. The Fathers of the Church bring out the symbolism of these gifts. Thus St. Irenaeus [9] states that the Magi showed by their gifts who it was that was worshiped: "Myrrh because it was He who should die and be buried for the mortal human race; gold, because He was a king, 'of whose wisdom is no end'; and frankincense, because He was God."

The Gospel account of the Magi's visit concludes with the warning which they received in sleep not to return to Herod. They went back to their own country by another way. A different way to return east would be in a southeastern direction toward the Herodium and Engedi and thence around the southern end of the Dead Sea. There was, however, a second desert route generally used at that time.[10] According to Greek tradition the Magi took this route, namely, due east past Marsaba to the ford of the Jordan just north of the Dead Sea.

Was the star that led the wise men one of the heavenly bodies

---

[9] *Against Heresies*, III, ix, 2; ANF, I, 423.

[10] Cf. Dalman, *Sacred Sites and Ways*, p. 23. Origen held that it was an angel who warned the Magi, and that this warning was a reward for their piety. *Against Celsus*, I, 60; ANF, IV, 423.

in its ordinary course which God used for this purpose? Was it a conjunction of the planets such as that of Jupiter and Saturn, in the region of the sign of Pisces, which occurred in the year 7 B.C.? This date would harmonize well with the chronology of Christ's birth according to our calculation, 8 B.C.[11] Against this view of stars in conjunction it has been objected that an observer could easily see that there were two stars, not one. In reply it may be said that these planets would be astrologically considered one.

Was the Magi's star one of those periodic visitors to our sky that we call a comet? For instance, the great comet of 1858 might have a period of revolution of nearly two thousand years, and thus might have come within human vision at the time of Christ's birth. Father Lagrange,[12] is inclined to the view that a comet could fulfill all the requirements of the biblical narrative; indeed Origen was [13] somewhat of the same opinion.

Was the heavenly apparition of the Nativity a meteor or shooting star that left a long, bright trail as it streaked its way through the sky in the direction of the grotto of Bethlehem? Or was it a nova or new star, such as Nova Hercules, that bursts forth as a first magnitude star and then wanes off? Was it the planet Venus that shines with rare brilliance in the southwestern sky? Or was it one of our fixed stars, such as Spica, the brightest in the constellation of Virgo, that rises about midnight December 24, or Sirius, the

[11] Cf. Maas, *The Gospel according to St. Matthew*, p. 20. In the beginning of the seventeenth century, Kepler reckoned that a conjunction of Jupiter and Saturn had occurred in December 7 B.C. This led him to an explanation of the star of the Magi somewhat based on this conjunction. A conjunction of stars rising in the east and then a conjunction again setting in the west would lead the wise men in a westerly direction, and would satisfy the text: "We have seen His star in the east." On the other hand a conjunction of stars that might have happened later again—while the wise men were in Jerusalem, for this third occurrence of a conjunction to lead the wise men to Bethlehem, it would be difficult to understand. The stars in conjunction would continue to proceed west and not south; whereas Bethlehem is south of Jerusalem. Thus the comet theory is more probable than Kepler's theory. See Corbishley, "What is known of the Star of Bethlehem," *Scripture*, III (1948), 52.

[12] *L'Evangile selon S. Matthieu*, pp. 28 f.; also "*The Gospel of Jesus Christ*, I, 45, where he notes that Halley's comet passed through the solar system on October 9, 12 B.C. Durand prefers "a meteor miraculous and transitory"; *Evangile selon S. Matthieu*, p. 13.

[13] A new star partaking of the nature of a comet or meteor. *Against Celsus*, I, 58; ANF, IV, 422.

Dog Star, the brightest of all stars in the Christmas sky? The question is a difficult one. Since a fixed star moves at the most only one degree a day, and since no comet or meteor disappears, reappears, and stands still, like the star of the Gospel, the general view has been that the Magi were led by a miraculous phenomenon of starlike appearance, as the pillar of fire which served the Israelites in the desert, or the brightness of God that lit up the Christmas midnight sky for the shepherds. However, modern Catholic scholars look for the star of the Magi among the stars already made or the natural phenomena which God used on that occasion. This would also be the opinion of St. Leo, who says that it was "a star of new splendor in the regions of the east, which, being brighter and fairer than the other stars, might easily attract the eyes and minds of these who looked at it, so that, at once that might be observed not to be meaningless which had so unusual an appearance." [14]

A Magian conception was that each good person had a heavenly counterpart or double that develops until united with him in death. It is significant that almighty God made use of this astrological view of the Magi in bringing them to the feet of His infant Son. Says St. John Chrysostom,[15] "He called them by the things that are familiar." St. Thomas [16] points out that Christ was made known by angels to shepherds who were Jews; and among the Jews appearances of angels were not rare. But to the Magi, who were accustomed to consider the heavenly bodies, the birth of Christ was manifested by the sign of a star.

It is likewise worthy of note that the wise men were rewarded for their earnest seeking after knowledge and their faith in what had been made known to them. Their earnestness and their faith are shown by their long journey, their great joy in seeing the star again, their adoration of the divine Child and the symbolic gifts which they presented to Him. In strong contrast is the conduct of

[14] *Sermon* 31, *Feast of Epiphany*, I (*Hom.* 6, 4, on Matthew); NPN, 2nd ser., XII, 145.
[15] *Hom.* 6, 4, On Matthew; NPN, 1st ser., X, 38.
[16] *Summa theol.*, IIIa, q. 36, a. 5.

the Jews and their religious leaders. The latter were the custodians and interpreters of the Sacred Scriptures; and God made use of the revelation contained therein in the guidance of the wise men. Yet, although the Jews pointed the way, they made no effort to follow the Magi. As St. Jerome [17] says, "this listless neglect of theirs holds them inexcusable." St. Leo [18] succinctly expresses the matter in the statement, "truth enlightens the wise men, unbelief blinds the experts." And St. John Chrysostom [19] tells the Jews to be ashamed, "seeing themselves anticipated by barbarians and Magi." This Father further adds, "indeed what happened then was a type of the things to come."

It was prophetic that in their tragic neglect the Jews were ranking themselves with Herod of murderous intent. Thus from the outset religious and civil leaders were arrayed against the Savior. It was prophetic, too, that the sincerest Gentiles were on their knees pouring out their offerings before the King of kings, representative, as they were, of the best of the Gentile world that in succeeding generations were to be led to Christ by the light of reason and revelation to give Him the gold of their hearts' love, the incense of their devotion, and the myrrh of their learning, art, good deeds, even life itself. Zealously searching after truth, energetically using all available means to find it, and then giving of their best to Eternal Truth when they found Him, the wise men are here our examples as well as our representatives.

Lastly, it may be said that the Magi's star was itself a prophetic symbol, leading them, as it did, to the true Light that dispelled the darkness of paganism. In this world there is contrast between light and darkness, a greater one between the mental brightness of knowledge and the palling gloom of ignorance, and the greatest

[17] Comment. in Matth., I, 2; PL, 7, 27. The Gospel text does not say that the star led the Magi from the east to Jerusalem, but it apparently says that it led them from Jerusalem to Bethlehem. This fact militates against the view that the appearance was a natural star. Moreover, as Lagrange points out (op. cit., p. 23), the words of the Magi, "in the east," should designate the eastern part of the sky; the star at its rising, rather than the country from which they came.

[18] Sermon 32, Feast of Epiphany, II; NPN, 2nd ser., XII, 145.

[19] Homily 7, 5, On Matthew; NPN, 1st ser., X, 47.

between the dazzling brilliance of grace in the soul and the dismal murkiness of sin. Hence our divine Savior appropriated to Himself the name, "light of the world," in the Gospel (John 8:12), and "the bright and morning star," in the Apocalypse (22:16). The prophecy that He was to be a "light for the enlightenment of the Gentiles" quickly began its fulfillment in the Magi. These latter were themselves significant inasmuch as they gave evidence of the widespread yearning for the golden age of truth and grace at the beginning of the Christian era. Their star [20] symbolized the beacon light of Christian faith that was to guide untold multitudes to the goal of their quest for happiness and peace.

BIBLIOGRAPHY

Arendzen, J. P. The Gospels: Fact, Myth or Legend? pp. 141–54.

Corbishley, T. "What is known of the Star of Bethlehem?" Scripture, III (1948) 51 f.

Drum, W. "Magi," Catholic Encyclopedia, IX, 527–30.

Durand, A. Evangile selon S. Matthieu, pp. 12–16.

Fillion, L. The Life of Christ, I, 339–53.

Houdous, E. "The Gospel of the Epiphany," Catholic Biblical Quarterly, VI (1944), 69–84.

Lagrange, J. M. Evangile, selon S. Matthieu, pp. 19–31.

———. The Gospel of Jesus Christ, I, 41–46.

Leo, St. Sermons 31–36, on Epiphany; NPN, 2nd series, XII, 144–52.

Maas, A. The Gospel according to St. Matthew, pp. 16–24.

Prat, F. Jésus-Christ, I, pp. 97–107; 521–25.

Ricciotti, G. The Life of Christ, pp. 249–55.

[20] Here St. Ignatius Martyr has an appropriate reference: "A star blazed forth in the sky, outshining all the other stars, and its light was indescribable, and its novelty provoked wonderment. . . . This was the reason why every form of magic began to be destroyed, every malignant spell to be broken, ignorance to be dethroned, an ancient empire to be overthrown—God was making His appearance in human form to mold the newness of eternal life" (To the Ephesians, 19; translation by J. A. Kleist; Ancient Christian Writers [Westminster, Md., 1946], I, 67). The adoration of the Magi was a favorite subject in the early Church art. See Lowrie, Art in the Early Church, pp. 81 f.; Finegan, Light from the Ancient Past, pp. 371, 386 f., 440, 450.

Bethlehem, with the church of the Nativity

CHAPTER XIII

The Child Jesus Exiled in Egypt

THE exile of the child Jesus in Egypt was occasioned by the murderous designs of the cruel King Herod aroused to frenzies of jealousy by the quest of the Magi. His blindly striking out at the life of the infant Savior in the slaughter of the Holy Innocents is in keeping with what is recorded in profane history. His thirty-seven-years' reign was marked by almost unparalleled cruelty and bloodshed. Josephus rightly called him "a man of great barbarity toward all men equally, and a slave to his anger." [1] Even the members of his own family fell victims to this raving, murderous fiend; his father-in-law, his mother-in-law, his son-in-law, and two sons, then his favorite wife, Mariamne, and finally five days before his death his one-time favorite son, Antipater. All of them except Mariamne became his victims because, in his suspicious jealousy, he regarded them as a menace to his life or his throne.

The Jewish historian just mentioned informs us that, as Herod advanced to old age and reached about seventy, "he grew fierce and indulged the bitterest anger on all occasions." [2] This description certainly fits the perpetrator of the massacre of the Holy Innocents, which took place a few years before his death. However, it is a fact that Josephus does not mention the massacre itself. The

[1] *Antiquities,* XVII, viii, 1.
[2] *Ibid.,* XVII, vi, 1.

reason for his not doing so was probably that he would consider it of not sufficient importance when he had already such a litany of tragedies to lay to Herod's account; such as the slaying of a number of Pharisees for pretending to foretell that his government would soon cease,[3] and such as the giving of the order for the death of a number of Jewish nobles so that the whole nation would be put in mourning when his own death would come.[4] There is also a special reason why it should not be a surprise to us that Josephus did not mention the Gospel incident, although giving the proper setting for it. Such "an intense self-seeker"[5] to magnify himself in the eyes of the Romans, would avoid all reference to such an inconvenient, if not dangerous, subject as Christ. Thus, although the Gospel event is not mentioned, its historicity finds additional support in the picture painted by Josephus of this most cruel king, reeking with the blood of the victims of his mad jealousy, victims, as we said, including even members of his own family.

As the sacred narrative tells, Herod cunningly hid his murderous design under a pretended zeal. After carefully obtaining all the information which the wise men would give him, he sent them to Bethlehem with the request that they inform him as soon as they found the new-born King. The Magi were warned of Herod's wicked plan and returned to their country by a different route. As their presence in Bethlehem must have been a matter of great public note, their departure would have been promptly reported to Herod, for he had spies throughout his kingdom.[6] Outwitted, his jealousy

[3] *Ibid.*, ii, 4. Herod slew those of his household who believed the predictions.

[4] *Ibid.*, vi, 5; *Jewish War*, I, 659 (xxxiii, 6). Other atrocities similar to the massacre of the Holy Innocents can be found in Josephus. Herod had the two rabbis, Judas and Matthias, and several young men burned to death for cutting down the Roman eagle (*Jewish War*, I, 655 [xxxiii, 4]). Not being able to find certain "robbers" in Trachonitis, he slew their relatives (*Antiquities*, XVI, ix, 1). Desiring that he alone should be honored, and dreading that his present or future reputation might become less glorious, he punished those of his own people who were not sufficiently obsequious to him and he treated as enemies some of his own friends and relatives (*Antiquities*, XVI, v, 4).

[5] Edersheim: *The Life and Times of Jesus*, I, 215.

[6] Cf. Josephus, *Antiquities*, XV, x, 4: "There were spies set everywhere both in the city and in the roads"; also *Jewish War*, I, 492 (xxiv, 8).

developed into a rage in which he determined to do all that lay in his power to accomplish the death of the infant aspirant to the Jewish throne. His soldiers [7] were ordered to surround Bethlehem and its environs and to slay all the male infants who were two years old or under that age. The infant Savior could not have been much more than one year old; and perhaps even younger, but, as St. John Chrysostom [8] says, "Herod was marking out the object of his chase so as to include far more in it," and this was done "for the sake of fuller security." It was a cunning effort at security that brought within the scope of the murderous decree the neighborhood of Bethlehem in which there would be about twenty small hamlets. The number of infant boys thus put to death is reckoned at about twenty.[9]

Cruel beyond measure and savage to the extreme was this mad act of slaughtering these helpless infants. The inconsolable weeping of the mothers was a fulfillment, in the typical sense of a prophecy of Jeremias (30:15), where Rachel is represented as lamenting the temporal ruin of the nation: "A voice in Rama was heard, lamentations and great mourning; Rachel bewailing her children and would not be comforted because they are not." Because Rachel's tomb was close to Bethlehem and because she had a great love for children, she could aptly typify the sorrowing mothers whose poignant grief is so touchingly and poetically described: "Rachel bewailing her children and would not be comforted because they are not."

The child Jesus escaped before the cordon of soldiers had been thrown about Bethlehem and its neighboring hamlets; for soon after the departure of the Magi, most likely that same night, an

[7] Some of these soldiers were perhaps from the same races from which many of us spring. Josephus (*Antiquities*, XVII, viii, 3; *Jewish War*, I, 672 (xxxii, 9) mentions Thracians, Germans, and Galatians (Gauls) among Herod's soldiers.

[8] *Homily*, VII, 3; *On St. Matthew*; NPN, 1st ser., X, 46.

[9] Lagrange (*The Gospel of Jesus Christ*, I, 47) estimates the number as twenty. Fillion calculates there were thirty victims (*Life of Christ*, I, 356). Prat says perhaps thirty or forty (*Jésus-Christ*, I, 110). Durand figures between twenty and thirty (*Evangile selon S. Matthieu*, p. 18).

angel appeared to St. Joseph in his sleep and gave him the following command: "Arise and take the Child and His mother, and flee into Egypt, and remain there until I tell thee. For Herod will seek the Child to destroy Him" (Matt. 2:13). We should note that St. Joseph as head of the holy family received the vision. Yet the words, "the Child and His mother," would indicate the doctrine of the virgin birth. Implicit obedience is taught us by St. Joseph, for he promptly arose and, while it was yet night, set out with the infant Savior and the Virgin Mary for the neighboring country of Egypt. No details are supplied us concerning that journey, which may have led south through Hebron or, as tradition says, west to Gaza and then south along the shore route. It would have taken the holy family about five days to reach the border; but more than three weeks would have been required in going to Cairo if they went directly there.

In old Cairo there is a crypt earlier than the seventh century which, according to tradition, was built on the site of a house occupied by the holy family. Six miles to the north of Cairo is Matara, where the Jesuit Fathers have built a church to "The Child Jesus in Exile"; close by are "the tree of the Virgin," and "the garden of balms"; yet not until the thirteenth century do we first hear that these places were associated with the holy family's visit.[10] According to *The Arabic Gospel of the Infancy* (X–XV), written about A.D. 600, the infant Jesus traveled through several cities of Egypt, performing many fantastic miracles on the way. *The Gospel of Pseudo-Matthew* (XVII–XXV), which was written about A.D. 500, attributes eight miracles to Our Lord while in Egypt; and the Latin form of the *Gospel of St. Thomas* (I–III), written about A.D. 300, describes two miracles there. Thus, the later the date the more miracles are added in these apocryphal works which have always been rejected by the Church and must be classed as mere fiction. Most beautiful fables have been invented to satisfy a pious curiosity provoked by the silence of Holy Writ, in regard to the flight

[10] Cf. Lagrange, *Evangile selon S. Matthieu*, p. 32.

into Egypt and the sojourn there. But we must bear in mind that they are without historical foundation.

The gold that had been given by the Magi was undoubtedly of service while the holy family was getting settled in a little house in Egypt and while St. Joseph was securing work for their support. Probably this was not too easy to obtain and was of a laborious nature, for as a rule special difficulties beset one's path in a foreign country. There ought to be special veneration for this land of our divine Lord's exile which previously had afforded a refuge for the chosen people. The sacred presence of the divine Infant undoubtedly brought it special graces. Hence the following observation of St. John Chrysostom [11] is appropriate: that by receiving the hunted Lord, Egypt obtains a sort of first impulse toward her union unto Him; so that afterward, when she should hear Him preached, "she might have this at least to glory of, as having received Him first." Within a few decades of the Founder's death, the Gospel message was brought to Egypt. This land has the further distinction that in it first budded the brightest Christian flowering, monasticism.

At the time of the child Jesus' exile there, Egypt had a population of about seven million people whose chief industries were glass-blowing, the making of paper, and the weaving of linen. The principal gods worshiped there were Isis and Serapis. Although the cult of animals was a remarkable phenomenon of the religion of the Egyptians, what led them to mummify their dead was the doctrine of the immortality of the soul and its return to the body. The pyramids, already twenty-five hundred years old, bore testimony to the hoary antiquity of the ancient culture. Indeed thirty successive houses of rulers could be counted, unique in all history. Then, besides the megalithic monuments, the storied monoliths and the forest of pillars in their temples, Egyptians could boast of their great Book of the Dead, of their ancient wise proverbs, and of the remarkable movement toward monotheism in the fourteenth

[11] *Homily*, VIII, 5, *On Matthew*; NPN, 1st ser., X, 53.

pre-Christian century. The explanation for the long persistence of their form of civilization is to be found not only in the protected position and fertility of soil of the narrow Nile Valley, but also in the tenacious character of the people themselves.[12] Only a few decades before the Christian era (in 30 B.C.) had the country been annexed to Rome by Augustus himself, who evidently now personally obtained the enormous revenues, and who governed through a prefect, Turianus. Lower Egypt especially came under Hellenic influence, for Alexandria with its famous library was a center of Greek culture and in fact the intellectual center of the world. In the country where Egyptian, Greek, and Roman civilizations existed side by side there were about a million Jews, two out of the five quarters of Alexandria being occupied by them. One of these Jews, a rich young man about twelve years old at that time, was Philo.[13]

It must be said that we do not know definitely in what part of Egypt the holy family sojourned, nor do we know certainly how long was their stay there. In the early centuries Jewish opponents of our Christian faith, attempting in some way to explain Our Lord's great wisdom and power, held that He remained long enough in that country to learn magic. Thus Celsus (about A.D. 178) has a Jew insinuate that Jesus "hired Himself out as a servant in Egypt," that there He acquired "some miraculous powers, on which the Egyptians greatly prided themselves," and that He returned to His own country "highly elated on account of these powers of magic to use them to proclaim Himself a god." [14] This attempt to explain Our Lord's supernatural power and wisdom is opposed to the direct testimony of Holy Scripture, which states: "But when Herod was dead, behold an angel of the Lord appeared

[12] Cf. Rostovtzeff, A History of the Ancient World, II, 188.

[13] In the garden of balm at Matara, near ancient Heliopolis, there is an old sycamore tree under which, according to pious tradition, the holy family passed a night. Yet this tree is comparatively modern. There were balm trees in Jericho at the time of Christ. Cf. Josephus, Antiquities, XIV, iv, 1.

[14] Against Celsus, I, 27; ANF, IV, 413. Similar insinuations were made by Jews later. See Grandmaison, Jésus-Christ, II, 148.

in sleep to Joseph in Egypt, saying: 'Arise, and take the Child and His mother, and go into the land of Israel, for they are dead that sought the Child's life.' Who arose, and took the Child and His mother and came into the land of Israel" (Matt. 2:19–21). Thus on the death of Herod the holy family returned to Palestine. We know rather definitely that this king died just before the Easter festival of 4 B.C., at which time Our Lord would have been only three years and a few months old, for we take the date of His birth as December, 8 B.C. On the other hand, in the assumption that He was about one year old when He went to Egypt, His stay there would have lasted about two years.[15] Some hold that the sojourn in Egypt lasted only a few months. Certainly His return to Palestine on the death of King Herod precludes the fantasy of His acquiring magic in the land of the pyramids.

The Evangelist applies to our Savior exiled in Egypt the prophecy of Osee 11:1: "Out of Egypt have I called my son." This is done in the typical sense; for the original refers to the Jewish people who typified the great central figure for whom their whole history was a preparation. To both the Savior and Israel, Egypt afforded a refuge; for both of them there was a Joseph as a protector; both had a royal persecutor; and both were rescued in a miraculous manner. While returning to the Holy Land, probably at Gaza, St. Joseph heard of Archelaus' bloodthirsty deeds and received the warning not to return to Bethlehem. In this event, he would continue his journey along the coastal road as far as Caesarea. There he would turn inland to pass through Ara and Megiddo, and then would cross the plain of Esdraelon to reach Nazareth.[16]

St. Joseph must have been glad that the exile was over and that he was again back in the Holy Land where his foster Son would grow up and manifest Himself as the divine Messiah. As he was taking the holy family back to their native land he had intended to

---

[15] Ruffini asserts that the stay in Egypt was not longer than four and not less than two years. *Chronologia vet. et. novi. Testamenti*, p. 125. Holzmeister holds it was at least one year. *Chronologia vitae Christi*, p. 49.

[16] Cf. Dalman, *Sacred Sites and Ways*, p. 233.

return to Bethlehem, or at least to Judea: such is the impression given us by the sacred text. But because of the unfavorable information and the warning he received, he did not carry out his intention of returning to that part of Palestine which in his judgment afforded the best opportunities for his foster Son to be recognized as the Messianic King, descended from King David.

The Son of God enduring the discomforts of exile is the divine Patron of all exiles for the sake of righteousness. The infant boys of Bethlehem who were massacred on the occasion of the exile were the first harvest of Christian martyrs. As buds cut off in their fresh immaturity, they blossomed forth into fragrant flowers of paradise. An all-wise Providence had given these innocent babes an opportunity for reward, incomparably greater than the temporal pain or loss endured, a privilege afterward vouchsafed to thousands who voluntarily shed their heart's blood for Christ. They preceded Him to His kingdom; as St. Irenaeus [17] well says: He suddenly removed them "that He might send them on before into His kingdom; since He was Himself an infant, He so arranged it that human infants should be martyrs." These "first fruits" to God and to the Lamb (Apoc. 14:4), who are honored in the Church, teach the hard lesson that it is what we endure for God that counts eternally.

As for the cruel murderer turned maniac, despite his evil planning and all the forces at his command, he was frustrated in his attempts on the life of the divine Child; for vain and futile is malice against the all-powerful God whose will is accomplished despite the evil intents of men or devils. In his writing, Celsus has a Jew ridicule Our Lord as God because he fled from a human being, the wicked king; adding the taunt that His blood was not Godlike, was not "ichor such as flows from the veins of the blessed gods." In dignified language Origen [18] answered this sneering attack by pointing out that it would not have been of any service

[17] *Against Heresies*, III, xvi, 4; ANF, I, 442. Cf. Tertullian, *Treatise on the Soul*, XIX; ANF, III, 200.
[18] *Against Celsus*, I, 66; ANF, IV, 426.

to the God-man, to whom God the Father bore witness, to have made use of miraculous powers in escaping from Herod. Rather, he said, it was far better that the child Jesus should go and reside in Egypt than that the divine Providence should hinder the free will of Herod, or that the fabled poetic helmet of Hades be employed, or that the soldiers sent to Bethlehem be smitten with blindness like the people of Sodom. We may add that the procedure of the whole hidden life of Our Lord was to respect God's institutions and to rely on the ordinary rulings of divine Providence, thus honoring and sanctioning His own ordinances.

In His own way the Almighty did punish King Herod. When Herod was about seventy years of age, which could not be long after the massacre of the Holy Innocents,[19] he was afflicted with diseases of the body that were regarded by his contemporaries as the judgment of God. Josephus mentions some of these bodily ailments, and the bare recital is enough to produce horror. His distemper or fever was "a fire glowing within him" to augment his pain inwardly. Outwardly he suffered a dreadful "itching," and he was tortured by a vehement appetite that could not be satisfied. His intestines were ulcerated, and dropsical tumors developed in his feet and abdomen. The lower part of his body became putrid and wormy. With a loathsome breath, the loss of his sight and convulsions of the body, his "afflictions" seemed greater than he could bear. Added to all this were civil and family troubles, so that he tried to kill himself. He died just five days after he put to death his son Antipater, in whom he had placed all his hopes.[20]

The child Jesus suffering the hardship of exile at the hands of cruel Herod teaches the lesson to both subjects and rulers that they must not ignore the truth that authority comes from God.

---

[19] Eusebius writes that it is worth while noting how divine vengeance overtook Herod "immediately, without the least delay," after his daring crime against Christ. (*Ecclesiastical History*, I, viii, 3; translation by K. Lake, Loeb, I, 66). Josephus says that Jewish diviners attributed Herod's diseases to punishment for his treatment of the rabbis, Judas and Mathias, and to punishment from God for his impiety. Cf. *Jewish War*, I, 656 (xxxiii, 5); *Antiquities*, XVII, vi, 5.

[20] *Antiquities*, XVII, viii, XI; *Jewish War*, I, 665 (xxxiii, 8).

On the one hand, authority is to be respected regardless of the character of the ruler; on the other, those exercising authority do so only for the common good. The rights of subjects which must not be infringed are upheld by the same God who gives authority. Tyrants and evil rulers in their injustices strike at God; as the unscrupulous Herod in his mad effort to safeguard his rule was striking out at the divine Infant who gave Him that rule. Subjects may appear helpless, but they are powerful to the extent that they have the Almighty for their avenger.

BIBLIOGRAPHY

Becker, T. The Hidden Life of Christ, pp. 94–102.

Fillion, L. The Life of Christ, I, 353–63.

Lagrange, J. M. The Gospel of Jesus Christ, I, 46–50.

Maas, A. The Gospel according to St. Matthew, pp. 25–29.

O'Shea, D. The Holy Family, pp. 126–49.

Prat, F. Jésus-Christ, I, 107–13.

Vitti, A. M. "S. Familia in Aegypto ubinam juxta Apocrypha constiterit?" Verbum Domini, IX (1929), 3–13.

Willam, F. The Life of Jesus Christ, pp. 37–45.

CHAPTER XIV

The Divine Child

AFTER describing the incidents that attended Our Lord's presentation in the Temple, St. Luke goes on to say: "And the Child grew, and waxed strong, full of wisdom; and the grace of God was in Him" (Luke 2:40). As the Savior was forty days old when the ceremonies prescribed for the first-born were performed and as the next incident recorded took place in His twelfth year, this succinct verse of the Third Gospel covers twelve years of the divine life. How important is every word of the sacred text for all attempts at understanding the divine Child!

First and chiefly, it is to be remembered that in this Infant whose physical development is mentioned, there was the Word-made-flesh, there was the Second Person of the Blessed Trinity begotten from all eternity, taking the place of a created personality; and under the ineffable divine personality there was a union of divine and human natures. As Jesus had been conceived of the Holy Ghost, He was therefore the all-holy God, the Son of God, divine. Even His human body had never existed except as united with the life-giving Word. His human nature had all the perfections of that nature.

Let us direct our attention next to the words of the Evangelist concerning the child Jesus, "the grace of God was in Him"—

literally, "one divine grace was on Him." We can get some idea
of this grace when we reflect that the human soul of the God-man
was embellished with all the grace necessary to fit it for its well-
assorted union with the Divinity and prepare it to be the harmonious instrument in the hands of that Divinity. From the union with
the Word "in the first moment of His conception, Christ had the
fullness of grace sanctifying His body and His soul." [1] As man
so intimately united with God, He was excellently equipped with
all those spiritual vitalities we call grace, so that St. Luke could say
absolutely, "the grace of God was in Him," and St. John (1:14)
could proclaim Him to be "full of grace." St. Thomas teaches that
no greater grace can be thought of than that with which Christ
was full.[2] What an abundance of grace He possessed!

We are further told by the Evangelist that the infant Savior was
"full of wisdom." The scriptural expression can mean either "filling Himself with wisdom" or "keeping Himself full of wisdom." [3]
The verb that is used has a completed sense signifying that fullness
was reached so that nothing was lacking. The meaning is somewhat
similar to St. Paul's, when he says of Christ, "in whom are hid
all the treasures of wisdom and knowledge" (Col. 2:3) . Our Lord,
as man, had knowledge in various ways. He enjoyed the beatific
vision that is granted to spirits perfect in charity; He had the spirit
knowledge with which the angels are endowed; and He had the
knowledge acquired through the senses, that is, by experience and
reasoning. He had a most complete and far-reaching intellectual
knowledge, which neither had its origin in the experience of sense
nor was due to the beatific vision. Christ's human mind must
have been fully developed, must have possessed every kind of perfection a created intellect can possess, simply because of His double
privilege of being a God-man in Himself, and the King of the

[1] St. Thomas, *Summa theol.*, IIIa, q. 34, a. 1.

[2] *Ibid.*, q. 7, a. 12.

[3] The middle participle with the meaning of "filling oneself." Cf. Prat, *Jésus-Christ*,
I, 121 note; Joüon, *L'Évangile de N. S. Jésus-Christ*, pp. 305 f.

human race forever and by a kind of extension, the King of the whole spirit race.[4]

Therefore in the Christ Child there was lacking only the experimental knowledge, but by His beatific knowledge He knew everything thoroughly. Thus St. Augustine could say that in the infant Jesus there was neither ignorance nor any of that mental weakness which we associate with children.[5] Indeed the Fathers of the Church point out that the God-man was perfect from the first moment of His existence. Clement of Alexandria insists that "the perfect Word born of the perfect Father was begotten in perfection according to economic foreordination." [6] St. Gregory of Nazianzen, too, speaks of Christ as being "perfect from the beginning." [7] That "He was a perfect man already in the womb," is asserted by St. Jerome.[8] Moreover, St. Augustine says that "as soon as the Word entered the womb, while retaining the reality of His nature, He was made flesh and a perfect man.[9] Likewise St. John Damascene pointed out that from the hypostatic union of the two natures, divine and human, the soul of Christ was assumed by the Word of God and therefore not only was free from all ignorance, but knew all future things.[10] The orthodox view was summarily expressed by St. Leo the Great when he said that the man received into the unity of Christ's person was in such wise "from His very commencement in the body that without the Godhead He was not brought forth, without the Godhead He was not nursed." [11]

The perfection of Christ, not only as a child but also from the first moment of His conception, is stressed by St. Thomas, who teaches that Christ in the first instant of His conception had the

[4] Cf. Vonier, *Personality of Christ*, pp. 101 f.
[5] *De peccatorum meritis*, II, 48; *Corp. Script. Lat.*, LX, 119.
[6] *Pedagogus*, 1, 6; PG, 8, 279.
[7] *Oratio 43, In laud. S. Basil*; PG, 548; NPN, 2nd ser., VII, 408.
[8] *In Jeremiam*, 31:22; *Corp. Script. Lat.*, LIX, 398.
[9] *De Trinit.*, quoted by St. Thomas, *Summa theol.*, IIIa, q. 34, a. 2.
[10] *De fide orthodoxa*, III, 12; PG, 94, 1084.
[11] *Sermon 28, On the Nativity*, VIII, 6; NPN, 2nd ser., XII, 143.

fullness of sanctifying grace; the fullness of known truth, free will, and the beatific vision.[12] This is the view of Catholic theology, for which we need quote only one authority, Denis the Carthusian, who taught that Christ from the first moment of His conception was perfect "not by reason of His age, but on account of the fullness of grace, the eminent degree of virtues, and the perfection of wisdom."[13] The scriptural texts for the doctrine of the perfection of the divine Infant are Luke 2:40 (the basis of this chapter) and Hebrews 10:5–7: "Wherefore when He cometh into the world, He saith: Sacrifice and oblation Thou wouldest not; but a body Thou hast fitted to Me: holocausts for sin did not please Thee. Then said I: Behold I come: in the head of the book it is written of Me: that I should do Thy will, O God." Here St. Paul attributes the words of the thirty-ninth Psalm to Our Lord coming into the world, that is, at the very beginning or the first moment of His conception.[14] St. Paul points out the great significance of these words, for he goes on to say that by them Christ annulled the old covenant and established the new. St. Paul also states that the will of God which Christ proposed to carry out was the oblation of His body.

We are therefore to regard the Christ Child not as an unthinking, unknowing, helpless Infant devoid of grace and merit. Rather we are to see in Him an all-holy, all-wise, and powerful Person,

[12] *Summa theol.*, IIIa, q. 34, a. 1–4.
[13] *Commentary on the Psalms*, 1; *Opera*, V, 409. From the beginning the God-man enjoyed even in His human nature the closest and highest union with God the Father, a union that would not be strengthened or perfected except only by degrees. The participation of Jesus' soul in the divine nature meant, besides holiness and grace, fully achieved glory and beatitude from the first moment of His conception that His sacred humanity was present in God's bosom ever gazing upon God's countenance, proving itself most worthy of belonging to the Son of God and giving Him an incalculable advantage over the first Adam. On the great fact of the hypostatic union which deified Christ's humanity were founded first the transfiguration of this humanity and its assimilation to God by grace and glory, and secondly the relation of the humanity to the Logos in virtue of which it became the latter's instrument. Cf. Scheeben, *The Mysteries of Christianity*, pp. 326–31.
[14] "As soon as 'the Word was made flesh' He showed Himself to the world clothed in His priestly office, subjecting Himself to the eternal Father." Encyclical *On the Sacred Liturgy*, 22.

"the brightness of God's glory," the "glory of the only begotten
. . . full of grace and truth." He was the wonder Child par excellence, and of Him, and only of Him, could it be said that "He
was full of wisdom and the grace of God was in Him." No natural
explanation is given or could be given for this extraordinary statement about an infant. Accordingly Origen says that before the
completion of the forty days of purification and before He came
to Nazareth He beheld the whole range of wisdom.[15] Moreover,
far from seeing this verse (Luke 2:40) as an expression of ordinary
growth, Origen goes on to say that it delineates the miraculous
and the divine. Against those who deny the divinity of the Savior,
he uses the text to show that, according to the Sacred Scriptures,
the divine came on earth in a human body and in a human soul.
This early writer argues that St. Luke's words, that Jesus before
being twelve years old was completely filled with the wisdom of
God, indicate that His childhood was something "wonderful"
that nature does not allow in man; for it is one thing to have a part
of wisdom, another thing to be completely full of wisdom.[16]

We know the reason for the brilliance of wisdom and the richness of grace in the soul of the Christ Child, namely, its intimate
union with the sun and source, Wisdom itself and Holiness itself.
Was it not strange that the rays of the sun of wisdom that illumined
His soul and the torrent of that fountain of grace that inundated
Him could be confined within the body of an infant? Marvelous
it was that there was not a bursting forth and an overflowing to
dazzle and astound all who saw the Babe of Bethlehem, the Child
in Mary's arms in exile, the boy among His companions at Nazareth. He who was "the power of God and the wisdom of God" (I
Cor. 1:24) used wisdom and power in displaying great reserve.
He in whom dwelt "all the fullness of the Godhead corporeally"
(Col. 2:9) veiled the glories of this Godhead under the appearance
of human childhood. Thus the great oneness of our Savior by which

[15] Homily 18, In Lucam; PG, 13, 1847; "jam totam sapientiam respiciebat . . ."
[16] Op. cit.; PG, 13, 1849.

He concealed His divine personality behind the glories of His sacred humanity was displayed all the more in His early years. For the wonder of wonders is not only that God assumed our human nature, but also that He lived a human life, subjecting Himself in His youth to the laws of growth and at the end to the death of the cross.

We may ask: What is the difference between childhood and manhood when both are considered in the immeasurable distance that divides them from Divinity? Very little, indeed. Consequently there is no reason to fear in regard to the small size of the body of the divine Infant lest, as St. Augustine says, "in it the Godhead should seem to have been straitened"; [17] or, as St. Jerome says, its littleness "should be prejudicial to divine Wisdom." [18] It is quite as easy for God to use childhood for an instrument as to use manhood. In fact, did not the Savior in the period of the public ministry show a preference for the simplicity and purity of childhood when He insisted: "Unless you become as little children you cannot enter the kingdom of heaven"? Modern scholars have strayed far from the truth when they declare that the Christ Child was an unthinking child, unconscious of His mission and nature. They are setting limits to the power and wisdom of God and they are contradicting the Sacred Scriptures, that tell us how God became man. Marcion in the second century made the same mistake when he promulgated the false teaching that God came only as a fully grown man. The truth is that the Christ Child was a divine Child, God as well as man, "full of wisdom" and the "grace of God."

The words of the Evangelist, "the Child grew and waxed strong," tell us that in bodily appearance Jesus resembled an ordinary child and that His youthful body developed year by year, gradually passing from infancy to childhood, from childhood to boyhood, and from boyhood to young manhood. For these various stages of growth there were among the Jews appropriate names that may

[17] *Epistle* 137, *to Volusianus*, iii, 8; PL, 33, 519.
[18] *In Isaiam*, III, 7; PL, 24, 110.

have been applied to Our Lord. At first a babe was called a "newly born." Next he received the name of "suckling," and when he could eat bread he was called an "olel." After two years of age he became "the weaned one." In the final steps he was given the names of "strong one," and "youth."

What of Christ's appearance? Was He different from other children? Did He display divine characteristics in His infancy? It may be said that to all outward appearances He was like other children. Rightly do statues and pictures represent Him as an ordinary child in His mother's arms. Perhaps the neighbors could say that He was strikingly handsome and bore a resemblance to His Mother. His face and His bodily form did not at all indicate His divinity. His actions, which were always wise and gracious, did not reveal what was known only to the inner circle of the holy family, that, concealed within the form of the child, were the power, the wisdom, and the grace of God. This which was proclaimed to the world and supported by the miracles of the public ministry and the miracles of the Church is known to us and must be the main theme of all our thoughts of the divine Child. St. Leo says that the Magi found the Christ Child in bodily appearance in no way different from other children: "small in size, powerless to help others, incapable of speech." [19] But in the form of a helpless child subject to heat and cold and hunger and thirst was the great reality of almighty God; for the wise men adored "the Word in flesh, the Wisdom in infancy, the Power in weakness, the Lord of majesty in the reality of man." [20] How Our Lord kept a reserve suitable to His condition as child, subjecting Himself to the economy of our nature, is explained by St. Cyril of Alexandria. Although granting that the divine Babe might easily have displayed wonderful wisdom, he holds that it would not be appropriate, for it "would have approached the miraculous," [21] and besides would be incongruous. This Father goes on to say that the mystery of the In-

[19] *Sermon 4, On Epiphany; NPN*, 2nd ser., XII, 147.
[20] *Ibid.*
[21] *Quod Unus est Christus; NPN*, 2nd ser., XIV, 212.

carnation was accomplished without noise or clash and that the God-man allowed the measures of humanity to have power over Himself.

It was a wonderful condescension that the Word incarnate accommodated Himself in what we call the divine economy of the laws that were set for the children of men. According to the ordinary laws of growth to which He subjected Himself, He grew gradually taller and stronger, and like others gradually passed through the various stages, infancy, childhood, boyhood, and adolescence. Already in the century after Christ, St. Irenaeus [22] pointed out the reason for this passing through the different stages of life on the part of the God-man. Besides showing He was truly human, He sanctified the various conditions through which we all must pass "becoming an infant for infants, thus sanctifying infants; and a child for children, thus sanctifying those who are of this age." Also at the same time for children and youths, our divine Lord was setting "an example of piety, righteousness, and submission." Thus as this early Father states, from earliest consciousness man has before him a standard that is no less than the high ideal, that of the Savior, and he must try to walk the way the Perfect One trod. Aiming at perfection is therefore not to be deferred until mature age; but rather in every stage of our earthly life we are to strive to be perfect in accordance with our dignity as children of a perfect Father in heaven.

Seven hundred years before the birth of the Savior, Isaias had uttered prophetic words that are applicable to the divine Child. This prophet had just foretold that the Messiah would bring abundance of joy into the world because through Him the rod of the oppressor would be broken and violence and bloodshed would cease. Then he went on to predict that the Messianic King would be given to the human race as a "child" and as a "son," and that from His childhood He would be acclaimed justly as the giver of wisdom, mighty God, eternal Father, and the Bringer of everlasting peace: "For a Child is born to us, and a Son is given to us, and

[22] *Against Heresies*, II, xxii, 4; ANF, I, 391.

the government is upon His shoulder; and His name shall be called Wonderful, Counsellor, God the Mighty, the Father of the world to come, the Prince of Peace" (Isa. 9:6).

"A little child will lead them," are also prophetic words of Isaias (11:6). The chapter had opened with the famous prophecy that the Messiah will be a "bud" that will shoot forth from the root of Jesse. Then with words that are reminscent of the hidden life of Our Lord, the prophecy goes on to say that the Messiah would not judge by mere external appearances (11:3), but rather His estimates would be made with fairness in favor of the poor and the needy (11:3). When the prophet declares that the Messiah would have for His weapons merely goodness and faithfulness (11:4) and that He would be equipped with the gifts of "wisdom and understanding" (11:2), the words are plainly applicable to the child Jesus. For the child Jesus' wisdom and grace are pointed to by the Evangelist as outstanding characteristics. Finally, how well verified are the often quoted words: "a little child will lead them!" The child Jesus leads all to respect the rights of even the most helpless; He leads all because He sanctified childhood through which all must pass; and each Christmas He uplifts all men, leading their thoughts to blessed peace and their heavenly Father. The apostles, disputing among themselves about their own personal qualifications for greatness, were told to acquire childlike virtues which were necessary for entrance into the kingdom of God (Matt. 18:1-5). The adornment of those desiring to have part with Christ in the hereafter, must be simplicity and purity, trust and confidence, and generosity and optimism. How true it is that "a little child will lead them." A child is set up as the model of all Christians, and the model of all children is the divine Child.[23] He alone leads both children and adults to the home of the eternal Father.

[23] Having the power of doing all things, God has the incomprehensible power of making himself weak. The exercise of this power in the holy Childhood, in the sufferings of the cross, and in the consecration during Mass was not a difficulty of faith to Cardinal Newman; but rather was an incentive to his faith. He recognized in it a truth: God's "most awful antagonism" to sin which essentially consists of pride and disobedience. Sermon on "Omnipotence in Bonds"; *Favorite Newman Sermons* (ed. by D. O'Donnell, New York, 1946), pp. 40 f.

When Our Lord was a little new baby
And lay on our Lady's knees,
He heard the bees in the clover,
He heard the wind in the trees,
He remembered making the clover
And setting the wind to blow,
He remembered putting the hum in the bee
And teaching the trees to grow.

These are the flowery fields, where first
The wisdom of Christ was nursed;
Here first the wonder and surprise
Of Nature lit the sacred eyes:
Waters and Winds and woodlands, here,
With earliest music charmed His ear,
For all His conscious youth drew breath,
Among these hills of Nazareth.

The quiet hills, the skies above,
The faces round were bright with love;
He lost not, in the tranquil place,
One hint of wisdom or of grace;
Not unobserved, nor vague, nor dim,
The secret of the world to Him,
The prayer He heard which Nature saith
In the still glades of Nazareth.

G. A. Chadwick

BIBLIOGRAPHY

Fillion, L. The Life of Christ, I, 424–79; 625–41.
Graham, A. The Christ of Catholicism, pp. 150–214.
Lagrange, J. M. Evangile selon S. Luc., pp. 92 f.
Lebreton, J. The Life and Teaching of Jesus Christ, I, 25–37.
O'Shea, D. The Holy Family, pp. 150–81.
Scheeben, M. The Mysteries of Christianity, pp. 312–37.
Vonier, A. The Personality of Christ, pp. 52–175.

CHAPTER XV

Nazareth

MAKING the eighty-five mile journey from Jerusalem to Nazareth by car along the most direct road, you can make a stop at El Bireh about ten miles from the Holy City. This village formerly had a church in honor of the holy family because of the tradition that here the boy Christ was missed by Blessed Mary and St. Joseph as they were returning home after the Passover pilgrimage of His twelfth year. As the car speeds north, the rough, sharp, rocky scenery gradually changes when the fertile plains and valleys of Samaria make their appearance. A visit may be made to Nablus (Sichem), the birthplace of St. Justin Martyr; and, five miles west of the main road to Sebaste (Samaria) where there are ruins of a church built over the sacred remains of St. John the Baptist.[1] Then at Jenin the road descends from the Samaritan hills to the magnificent plain of Esdraelon (Jezreel).

An irregular triangle [2] in shape with its longest side stretching twenty-four miles on the southern edge and its two other sides fifteen miles each, this largest plain in all Syria looks at first to be

[1] Cf. Meisterman, *Guide to the Holy Land*, p. 468.

[2] There are several plains joined together. The first extends nine miles from the sea to Carmel. Then there is the central plain having a base twenty miles in extent. Then between Jezreel and Shunem there is a sudden fall of level eastward. The general altitude of the central plain is 200 feet above sea level. In the valley that leads to Bethshan there is a gradual drop to 400 feet below sea level. See Smith, *The Historical Geography of the Holy Land*, pp. 379–410; Abel, *Geographie de la Palestine*, I, 411–13.

completely surrounded by hills. Where it tapers to the northwest under the shadow of majestic Carmel, it runs into the plain of Acre. To the east Esdraelon leads into two valleys, one on the north of Little Hermon, a mere bay of the plain; the other on its south between Moreh and Gilboa extends all the way to the depression of the upper Jordan. In the formation of this plain nature made a basin-like depression in the mountains of western Palestine, leaving like scattered islands the mountains of Thabor, Little Hermon, and Gilboa. This depression had the further reducing effect on the northern and southern range of mountains, for in both there is an increase of height as they recede from the plain. This broad expanse at the juncture of opposing nations was in successive ages of the past the battleground for Egyptians, Hittites, Israelites, Philistines, Assyrians, Syrians, Greeks, Romans, Crusaders, Saracens, Turks, and English. The great plain (I Mach. 12:49) has a brighter and happier function. It presents a pleasant, varied landscape. Where the Cison and its numerous tributaries of streams and torrents have left marshes, a rich carpet of sedge, reeds, and long grass appears. Between the many picturesque hamlets one sees in springtime wide stretches of the dark green root crops variegated with swaying golden patches of wheat, oats, and barley, to which here and there a bright touch is added by the red anemone. This is Esdraelon, an immense lawn at Nazareth's front door.

Already from the mountains of Ephraim, even at a distance of twenty-four miles can be seen high in the distant blue haze, a white speck, the home town of Christ. While the traveler is crossing the plain, the thrilling sights that feast the eye whether from the scenery nearby or from Gilboa, Little Hermon, and Thabor on the right or Carmel on the left, do not prevent him from casting longing glances on Nazareth, set like a majestic queen amid the towering hills of Zabulon which lie across the northern horizon. Finally with sharp bends the road climbs precipitously to a plateau that is 800 feet above the plain and 1,200 feet above sea level. There you can see at a glance that this plateau is hollow, that it slopes gently to the east and that it is surrounded on three sides by gracefully rising hills. The highest of these hills, Nebi Sain, looks down on the plateau from its further height of 400 feet. Nestling in this hollow plateau and climbing the broad flanks of these last foothills of Lebanon lies the home of Jesus, elevated and sheltered, picturesque and imposing.

There are many holy sites and places to be visited at Nazareth.[3] First, there is the one that calls for reverence equal to that given to the cave at Bethlehem—the grotto of the Annunciation. This has been enclosed in a church since the fourth century. In the present structure, erected as a parish church in 1730, a large stair-case of fifteen white marble steps leads down into the crypt which is the traditional site of the house of the Blessed Virgin Mary. In the vestibule of this crypt on the right is an altar dedicated to St. Ann and St. Joachim, and on the left another consecrated to St. Gabriel. Then one passes through an arcade and descends two steps into the grotto of the Annunciation, a chapel hewn out of the rock. There is an altar with a beautiful picture above it depicting Gabriel addressing the Virgin at Nazareth. Under the altar are inscribed the words in Latin: "Here the Word was made flesh," recalling the great event that took place at this sacred spot.

A few minutes' walk to the northeast brings the pilgrim to the Church of St. Joseph, built on the traditional site of St. Joseph's home. This is called the Church of the Nutrition, or Upbringing, for here Our Lord lived from the time of His return from Egypt until the beginning of His public ministry. A church has been here from at least the sixth century; it was destroyed in the eighth century but rebuilt by the Crusaders. In the early years of this century the present building was erected on the original foundations. It contains a large underground grotto with two cisterns which in ancient times were used for storing grain or water. About 200 yards to the northwest is the parish church for Greek Catholics, built on the traditional site of the synagogue which Jesus attended during

[3] Cf. Meistermann, *Guide to the Holy Land*, pp. 485–98.

His hidden life. To the southeast, where the chain of hills ends abruptly, an ominous looking knoll that shoots up to nearly a thousand feet above the great plain has the name of the Mount of the Leap, or Precipitation. From here, it is said, the enraged mob tried to cast Jesus down. In connection with this mount there is, on the road from it, a chapel erected to "Our Lady of the Fright."

The "Table of Christ," a large slab of limestone, is housed in a little chapel in the northwest section of the town. This receives its name from a tradition that upon it our Savior, after His resurrection, partook of a repast with His disciples. About five minutes' walk from St. Joseph's house brings the pilgrim to a public fountain which from ancient times has been called "the Fountain of Mary," or "the Virgin's Fountain," recalling the fact that from it the Blessed Mother and her divine Son drew water. Nearby a Greek church has been erected to Gabriel because of a false supposition that the archangel first appeared to the Virgin at this spot. Under the chapel is the original fountain, from which water is piped to the present "Virgin's Fountain."

Nazareth today has the appearance of a pleasant amphitheater. In tier after tier neat white houses cover the plateau and extend for some distance on the northern hills. The houses are set in gardens of olive, fig, and pomegranate trees with cactus hedges. On all sides are Christian institutions, such as churches, hostels, hospitals, convents, orphanages, and schools. Besides the Catholic institutions, nearly all the main non-Catholic Christian sects are represented. There are also a few buildings for the few thousand Mohammedans of the town. The population, now about 20,000, is twelve times what it was seventy years ago. This increase is due to the coming of the Christian institutions and also to the prosperity the town is enjoying because of its situation on the main road from Haifa to Tiberias.

In regard to weather, the place is favored, not having the extremes found in the tropical and subtropical Jordan valley and in the much colder mountains of upper Galilee. Sharing in the climate characteristic of all Syria in the division of the year into a dry and a wet season, the first from about April 15 to October 15, the second in the other half of the year, Nazareth rarely has rain in the summer, and seldom has snow in the winter; and when snow does fall, it lasts only a day or two. The high position is a helpful contribution to its salubrious climate; throughout the year the variation of temperature is only forty degrees. The prevailing wind is from the southwest in the wet season; in the summer a welcome pleasant breeze blows from the northwest all day until sundown. It is the occasional southeast wind, dreaded especially in October, that scorches the crops and is most oppressive.[4]

In the days of Our Lord's early life, Nazareth did not have the importance it has today, for Haifa was then only an insignificant village without a harbor. It is true that the Gospels refer to Nazareth as a "city." According to Josephus' boast there were "204 cities and villages" in Galilee, the least of which had a population of more than 15,000. The exaggeration is evident from the fact that the total population of the province was somewhat less than half a million. Although we have no evidence on which to base an accurate estimate of the number of residents of the Nazareth of New Testament times, we may say that it was probably much less than a thousand. The first-century Nazareth also did not have the attractive amphitheater appearance of the present town stretching itself around the flanks of its northern hills. It was more to the south, where the shrines, grottoes, and cisterns are to be found.[5] It was perched on a slight eminence of triangular shape whose southern point was the fountain of St. Mary's Well. This watered a valley lying immediately below it, which must have been owned and tilled by the people of Nazareth.

A little help in trying to visualize the Nazareth of Christ's day may be obtained from the general picture. The town lying half-

---

[4] The highest mean temperature is 41.2° centigrade and the lowest 0.2°. As a rule the warmest month of the year is August, and the coldest January. Fall is warmer than spring. The mean temperature for the whole year is 18.5°. See Abel, *op. cit.*, pp. 108–13; also Dalman, *Sacred Sites and Ways*, 66–68; *Arbeit und Sitte in Palästina*, I, Parts 1 and 2.

[5] Cf. Lagrange, *The Gospel of Jesus Christ*, I, 16 f.

way between the Mediterranean and the lower end of Lake Tiberias was near the center of the most important part of Galilee. Natural reasons as well as administrative purposes brought about the division of this province into upper and lower Galilee.[6] A person going northward encounters four plains and four chains of mountains, each plain and each mountain rising higher than its southern neighbor. Thus the first two sets fell into one part of the province and the second two into the other, the dividing line running across from Capharnaum towards Acre. Upper Galilee could boast of the highest peak in Palestine and the southern district could point with pride to Lake Tiberias, Esdraelon, and half a dozen other extensive plains. In the west, lower Galilee reached to within seven miles of the coast, from which it was cut off by Carmel and the coastal upland of Acre. In the south the boundary line with Samaria must have crossed the middle of the great plain; the Jordan and the district of Decapolis were in the east. Above Esdraelon, Galilee consisted of long series of hills, interspersed with upland valleys and rolling plateaus. Lake Tiberias gave a generous supply of fish; the olive and the vine grew luxuriantly on the mountain sides; and the plains and valleys were intensively cultivated or grazed. So universally rich in production was the area enclosed by sixteen miles around the capital, Sephoris, that it was declared to be the land "flowing with milk and honey." [7] This meant a comparative prosperity for almost all classes of the entire district.

Nazareth must have shared in the general prosperity around it. Although it was perched in the climbing hills, it had a central

[6] Josephus (*Jewish War*, III, 35 [iii, 1]) makes the division into Upper and Lower Galilee; the *Mishnah* (Shebath 2, 2; Danby, p. 49) mentions Upper, Lower, and the Jordan Valley. According to Dalman (*Sacred Sites and Ways*, p. 210) Galilee's southern frontier ran through the middle of the plain of Esdraelon; according to McCown (*Remapping of the Bible World*, New York, 1949, p. 36) the province extended to the southern edge of the Great Plain.

[7] Josephus, *Jewish Wars*, III, 42 (iii, 2), Antoninus, *Itinera Hierosolymitana* (ed. Geyer; *Corp. Script. Lat.*, XXXVIII, 172, 197). Smith (*op. cit.*, p. 419), says "Over the most of lower Galilee there is a profusion of bush, with scattered forest trees, holly, oak, maple, sycamore, baytree, myrtle, arbutus, sumac, and others—and in the valleys olive orchards and stretches of fat cornland." Masterman writes that "the whole of Lower Galilee is of great natural fertility" (*Studies in Galilee*, p. 9).

position and may be said to be surrounded by plains. It looked down on extensive Esdraelon and the beginning of the two valleys that led to the Jordan. Its own spur of mountain rose in the north out of the plain of Turan, which ran into the spacious plain of Asochis (Battof). Other plains and also upland valleys supported towns and cities in the vicinity. Down on the great plain only a mile and a half to the east was Iksul (Kesaloth), which seems to have been about the size of Nazareth. At the same distance to the southwest up in the hills like Nazareth itself lay a town of several thousand population, Japhia; its importance can be judged from the fact that it was protected by two walls and was called by Josephus "the largest village in Galilee."

From the top of their own hill, Nebi Sain, the townspeople of Nazareth could look down on a city only three miles to the north, Sephoris, the greatest in all Galilee [8] and the capital of the province from about 5 B.C. until A.D. 18. The year when the divine Child returned from Egypt, this city suffered in a revolt and as a result was burned to the ground by Varus.[10] Soon afterward Herod Antipas rebuilt it with new walls and a great citadel, making it "the ornament of all Galilee." [11] It became subordinate to Tiberias when the latter was made the capital, but it continued to be the largest and wealthiest city of the province.

Sephoris was surrounded by many cities and towns, all of which would be within easy reach of Nazareth. Within five miles to the north were Asochis, Cana, and Jodephat, this last a city of several thousand. Nearer to Nazareth were Ruma, Gubbatha, and Garis.[12] About ten Jewish communities were on or near the fifteen-mile road that led from Nazareth to Magdala on Lake Tiberias.[13] Four

[8] *Life*, 230 (45). He says it had a "dense population."
[9] *Ibid.*, 232 (45).
[10] Josephus, *Antiquities*, XVII, x, 9.
[11] *Ibid.*, XVII, ii, 1.
[12] We know the names of a few more villages in the vicinity of Nazareth. These villages must have been numerous. See Dalman, *Sacred Sites and Ways*, p. 104, and the maps on pp. 56, 100, and 108.
[13] Cf. *ibid.*, p. 119.

miles due east of Nazareth was Daberath; about five miles south-east were Endor and Naim; twice that distance to the south were Shunem and Jezreel. The latter was on the edge of the great plain. In the plain also were Simonias four miles due west of Nazareth, Gabatha and Besara farther west, and Tarbeneth in the southwest. In all the larger cities and towns there were many Greeks and Syrians who would be in control of most of the business and administration. This was especially true of Sephoris, with its strong Roman leanings. Within an easy day's journey from Nazareth were Phoenician and Greek cities that were Greek in constitution and culture, yet having large Jewish populations. Accordingly it may be said that Jews and Gentiles exerted a reciprocal influence on each other in "Galilee of the Gentiles."

In addition, influences that could enlarge the mental horizon of the residents of Nazareth, would come over the great highways [14] that passed through it or near it. The town was directly on the road between the two capitals, Jerusalem and Sephoris. The famous caravan road from Damascus, the great exchange market of east and west, passed through Capharnaum on Lake Tiberias, and then divided at Loubieh on the way to the coast and Egypt; one branch went directly west, while the other went south to the plain of Esdraelon, passing between Thabor and Nazareth, only a few miles from the latter. Christ's home town was conveniently situated in regard to other great highways, and because of its central position it may be said to lead to everywhere in the Holy Land. There were three routes by which the people of Nazareth could travel to Jerusalem. The shortest and customary way was directly south across the great plain to Jenin and then over the highlands of Samaria. A second way was through Wady Ara, Kefr Othnay, and the coastal road to Antipatris, thence to Jerusalem by way of Beth-horon. Then there was an eastern way through Endor, Scythopolis, and down the Jordan valley to Jericho, thence to Jerusalem by way of Bethany.

[14] See *ibid.*, p. 62; Booth, *The World of Jesus*, pp. 160–65; Charlsworth, *Trade Routes and Commerce of the Roman Empire*, pp. 47 ff.; Abel, *Geographie de la Palestine*, II, 217 ff.

This latter road would be used only in spring and winter because the excessive heat of the other seasons would make it most uncomfortable.

From the hills that support and shelter Nazareth can be seen a magnificent panorama of scenic spots. The mountains of upper Galilee and, over Safed, snow-clad Hermon greet the eye to the north. In the distant east the mountains of Gilead and Moab tower over Lake Tiberias itself hidden from view. The eye travels south over sharply rising, flat-topped Thabor and the peaked summit of Little Hermon to rest on the blue haze of the hills of Samaria. In the bright sunshine patches of the blue Mediterranean shimmer in the west around the silhouette of Carmel and above the glistening sands of the Acre plain.

Thus the town that was the scene of Jesus' hidden life was in a position to be touched by many outside influences, and it was itself secluded. It had acquired a poor reputation in regard to its ability to produce anything good or great. A native of a nearby town, Nathanael, asked, "Can anything of good come from Nazareth?" (John 1:46.) This saying of the apostle was prompted by various reasons. The town's name never appeared in the pages of the Old Testament, neither is it afterward mentioned by Josephus, who speaks about so many places in the vicinity. It was so overshadowed by nearby towns and cities that it seemed to have no religious or political importance whatever. Hence it would be easily overlooked in searching expectantly for anything significant and great. For the Messiah to come from the town of Nazareth, would be a surprise.

This, then, was the town to which the holy family retired after the flight into Egypt to live there continuously. Here our Savior as a child of a few years at the most, began the thirty years of His hidden life, all of which were passed at Nazareth. The Gospel text rightly refers to the town as the place where "He was brought up" (Luke 4:16); and in connection with the holy family, calls it "their city" (Luke 2:39). Our Lord Himself intimates it was

His own country (Luke 4:23). Here, accordingly, Jesus received more natural influences than anywhere else; rather, of course, He experienced them in His human nature. The long continuous residence of the God-man conferred on this town untold blessings. For the pilgrim who visits it the mount of the Precipitation and the crosses that surmount the Christian buildings are continual reminders of His rejection by His own and of the sadness of Calvary; but the sacred soil the Master trod so continually and the sacred sights that were so long familiar to Him, call up the bright, beautiful picture of His childhood, boyhood, and manhood, and radiate holy joy. A feeling of great happiness comes on one who tours "the nursery of the Lord," [15] where the many golden years were spent in the happy home as a member of the holy family. Above all the spots on earth Nazareth was honored by being selected as the home town of the God-man and by receiving the great glory of being coupled with the very name of the Savior, Jesus of Nazareth.

St. Matthew (2:23) writes that the prophecies of the Old Law were fulfilled by Our Lord's return from Egypt to Nazareth to grow up there and thereby receive the name "the Nazarene." This word Nazareth (*nazara*) could mean "it guards" or "consecration" or a "bud" or "flower," and these would suggest various ancient prophecies. The derivation of the word from "*netser*" ("bud") would fit Isaias 2:1: "a flower shall rise up out of his root." This derivation at first met the approval of St. Jerome when commenting on St. Matthew,[16] and also when he called Nazareth, "the flower of Galilee"; [17] yet ten years later when writing on Isaias [18] he pointed to the objection that the Hebrew word for "bud" has the letter sade (ts), whereas the Hebrew word in use for Nazareth had the letter zain (z). The fact is that we are not

[15] St. Jerome, *Letter* 108, 13; *to Eustochium; PL*, 22, 878.
[16] *Comment. in Matt. ad. loc.; PL*, 7, 29.
[17] *Letter*, 46; *to Paula, Eustochium, and Marcella; PL*, 22, 491.
[18] *Comment. in Is.* 11:1; *PL*, 24, 144.

certain of the derivation of the word "Nazareth," nor are we sure of its etymological meaning.[19]

The ancient prophecies had foretold that the Messiah would not judge by external appearances (Isa. 11:3), and that He Himself would be conspicuous by the absence of worldly appeal and the lack of worldly prestige (Isa. 53: 1–4; Jer. 11:19; Ps. 21 [22]: 6 f.; 68 [69]: 9–13). In line with these prophecies would be the home town that was secluded in geographical position, unimportant in size and commerce, unsung in history, and a byword on the lips of contemporaries. Certainly this home town did not help Jesus' cause in the eyes of worldlings. His enemies pointed to the disadvantage of His coming from the province of Galilee (John 7:41 f., 52). They called Him "Jesus of Nazareth" (Matt. 26:71) and later they called early Christians "Nazarenes" (Acts 24:5). Pilate wrote the name of the home town into the title on the cross: "Jesus of Nazareth, the King of the Jews" (John 19:19). As the royal son of King David, our Savior was born in David's city, Bethlehem. On the other hand, the place in which He lived nearly all His life and from which He made His appearance was an obscure, despised town of Galilee. These two elements of the sacred humanity, the exalted and the humble, were announced by the prophets; and St. Matthew, according to his custom refers to the fulfillment. For "Jesus of Nazareth, the King of the Jews," the chief scenes of the hidden life are Bethlehem and Nazareth, as those of the public ministry are Capharnaum and Calvary.

From the point of view of prestige, Nazareth was merely a fortress town that had lost all its importance and besides had become dwarfed by its proximity to towns and cities of distinction. Yet in regard to location, it was excellent, and seemed to be selected and prepared by the angels; for it had a nest-like posi-

---

[19] On the philological aspects of the word "Nazareth" and the derivation of Nazarene from Nazareth, see Dalman, *Sacred Sites and Ways*, pp. 56–60; Albright, "The Names 'Nazareth' and 'Nazarene,'" *Journal of Bib. Lit.*, LXV (1946), 397–401; Lyonnet, "Quoniam Nazaraeus vocabitur," *Biblica*, XXV (1944), 196–206; Lagrange, *Évangile selon S. Matthieu*, pp. 37–39.

tion held high in the Galilean hills to enjoy all their tender beauty and all the long vistas of exquisite scenery. Who can say that any place is not important when in answer to Nathanael's disparaging question we can reply: come and see what good did come out of Nazareth: the Author of all good?

BIBLIOGRAPHY

Abel, F. Geographie de la Palestine, I, 59 f.
Dalman, G. Sacred Sites and Ways, pp. 37 f.
Legendre, M. The Cradle of the Bible, pp. 52 f.
Meistermann, B. Guide to the Holy Land, pp. 435 f.
Smith, G. A. The Historical Geography of the Holy Land, pp.
    377–436.
Smith, W. The Students' Historical Geography of the Holy Land,
    pp. 51–81.
Van Dyke, H. Out-of-doors in the Holy Land, pp. 219 f.

Mount Thabor and the plain of Esdraelon

CHAPTER XVI

The Boy Jesus at Nazareth

OUR Savior was a mere child, perhaps only six months old, and certainly not more than a few years old, when He was brought to Nazareth. Here He passed His childhood, boyhood, and young manhood. The home in which He lived with His Virgin Mother and His foster father was like most of the other homes in the town. As there is plenty of limestone in the locality, some of the houses were built of rough stone set two or three feet thick. Mostly they were square with one large room, the floor of which had two levels, one about eight feet above the other, the lower one being used to accommodate the domestic animals. Also houses were of mud-brick; some were built around stone or wooden pillars with mud mixed with straw that was packed around wattle work and baked in the sun. The houses that rested on the side of a hill had an additional room excavated grotto-like out of the hill. Each house was supplied with an outside stone stairway that led to a roof of hard dry clay where in the summertime people sat in the cool of the evening and slept during the warm nights. These flat-roofed, one-story houses built close to one another in narrow streets were occasionally supplied with an open fireplace for heating and cooking purposes and sometimes with a chimney. The furniture was of the simplest kind, generally consisting only of tables for meals, stools, chests for cupboards, and low wooden bedsteads. The bed covering was probably a woolen blanket or, in the case of the very poor, a sheepskin.[1]

Among the townfolk, there were plenty of children, for the Jews of that time, unlike the Greeks and Romans, considered offspring a great blessing. The divine Child was probably weaned when He was two years old, and, like other children, for the first few years was under the direct care and supervision of His Mother. Jewish women of that day enjoyed more liberty than their Arab counterparts of today. They could go abroad freely and were not compelled to be completely veiled. In matters of religion they were not obligated to the full observance of the ceremonial laws, such as attendance at the feasts. The principal occupation of women was preparing meals and making or mending clothing. At that time bread was the main article of diet. It was eaten with various other kinds of food, such as oil, cheese, honey, olives, dates, figs, and grapes. Bread with oil was the usual breakfast. Sometimes at the principal meal, which was at sundown, along with vegetables, salted fish was served. Only rarely was meat eaten by the ordinary folk of Palestine. The chief beverages were water, milk, and rarely wine. In making their bread the women first ground the grain between two stones that fitted one into the other. The grain was placed in the hollow bottom stone and the top one was revolved by means of a handle until the grain was all flour. The meal was put in a bowl and mixed with water until dough was formed. Then yeast or leaven was added, and, after the dough rose, it was baked in an outdoor oven. It was customary to have many festival meals at which guests were invited to join with the members of the household. On such occasions it was a matter of pride for the housewife to be prepared to entertain at short notice. Thus her spare time was occupied in getting ready articles of food which had to be kept in a special cabinet.

As to articles of wearing apparel, the sandals of leather or wood

[1] Cf. Dalman, *Sacred Sites and Ways*, pp. 8, 68–73; also Booth, *The World of Jesus*, pp. 78–82.

were as a rule purchased; but the other garments were frequently woven and made by the women. The inner garment was a tunic or coat made of wool or linen. It was sleeveless, reaching to the knees and held at the waist by a girdle or belt. Over this was worn a seamless outer woolen garment wrapped around as a kind of shawl. Any income from the weaving of linen or other handiwork by the women was kept by them personally and not given to their husbands.[2] While the Blessed Mother was doing the ordinary work of the house—grinding corn, refining oil, washing clothes, spinning, weaving, cooking, and making beds—we can picture the child Jesus near her.

The games of children of that time,[3] we may suppose, often consisted of pranks at the expense of their elders. There would also be dancing and leaping in the streets and playing with nuts, clappers, bells, and "jack stones" made out of bones. Probably two kinds of ball game were in vogue in Palestine. We know there were games with tame birds and with little locusts, the whipping of tops, and the riding of donkeys and hobby horses. Gifts were customarily distributed to children on Passover eve, and at the end of the feast of Tabernacles fruits were given them to enjoy. While yet young, children of both sexes played together; but as they grew older they separated in play. Since their games consisted of imitation of their elders, girls played at cooking, and boys collected materials for Sabbath preparations. Likewise in imitation there were word and riddle games mimicking business transactions with pebbles, shells, and acorns, and there was the playing at funerals with little animals and locusts. Thus in one of His discourses Our Lord refers to children playing at marriage and funerals when some of them, irked by the peevishness of others, cried out: "We have piped to you, and you have not danced; we have mourned, and you have not wept" (Luke 7:32). Curiosity prompts us to peep through the silence of the Gospel, striving to see the boy Jesus at play. There

[2] Cf. *Mishnah*, Babba Kamma (First Gate), 10, 9; Danby, p. 347. Cf. Ketuboth, 5, 58; Danby, p. 252.

[3] Cf. Krauss, S., *Talmudische Archaeologie*, III, 107–10.

are a number of questions we should like to have answered. Did He take part in the usual games and pastimes of His day? Did He go scaling the hills around Nazareth? Did He climb the trees in the near-by forests? Did He roam through the terraced vineyards to behold the fruit and watch the vinedressers at work? Did He visit the farm lands to the south to see the sower scattering the seed in the early rainy season and the harvesting of the grain in the spring time? Did He visit the public threshing floors in the valley south of Nazareth to watch the oxen going round in a circle while doing the threshing and the men casting the corn in the air with the seven-pronged fork in the process of winnowing and separating the grain, the straw, and the chaff?

Did the boy Jesus attend the local school? That there was a school in Nazareth as well as a synagogue we can affirm without hesitation; for even small Jewish communities of that time appointed official teachers for those who had not private tutors.[4] In a town of its size, probably the public building was the synagogue which did service for a school managed by the congregation. There would also be one or more schools organized on a private basis by a teacher. It was required that all teachers be Jewish and be married men living with their families. Schools as a rule were plain; for the children as well as the teacher sat on the floor sometimes on mats or on the cloaks of boys. The younger children wore tunics, the older ones had coverings for their head. Elementary education began in the sixth year and ended with the thirteenth. The subject of study was the Bible, from which the Jewish boy learned not only religion and the history of his people, but also reading, writing, and even figuring. As the study was done aloud, information was imparted not so much by reading as by recitation.[5]

[4] Everywhere in Syria there were schools for learning reading, writing, and simple arithmetic. Cf. Heichelheim, "Roman Suria," in *Economic Survey of Ancient Rome,* IV, 171. Houses of Study are mentioned a dozen times in the Mishnah.

[5] In a Jewish town of Palestine in the first century there would be two or more schools, public or private. Synagogues served as schools and sextons frequently were teachers. Although attendance at school in any particular synagogue was not obligatory, every

About the year 570, a certain Antoninus of Piacenza made a journey to the east which was afterwards described by an unknown companion in a work called "The Itinerary of Antoninus of Piacenza." [6] The part describing the visit to Nazareth says that the pilgrims saw there in the synagogue the volume from which Our Lord learned His alphabet. It also says that in the synagogue was the bench on which He sat with other children. This bench, it is stated, the Christians were desirous of removing but were not permitted to do so by the Jews. The volume was more likely the one which Christ used when reading from the ancient Scriptures in the beginning of His public ministry. The bench in question may have been the one on which He generally sat as a grown man at regular synagogue services.

According to St. John's Gospel (7:15), Our Lord's opponents declared that He was unschooled or unlettered. Marveling at His teaching in the Temple during a feast of Tabernacles, these critics expressed themselves thus: "How doth this man know letters,

---

child had to attend one of the schools in his locality. The equipment required of each pupil was a wax tablet, a stylus, and a small parchment roll of the Law. As the Scripture rolls had to be correct, they were made by the teacher. Parents paid the teacher for the instruction of their children, but poor children were instructed gratis, and sometimes were even fed and housed besides. Children brought gifts from their parents to their teacher, who also received subscriptions from the congregation. As a matter of duty, the highest respect was paid the teacher, who on his part had to exercise patience to the highest degree. Each teacher had a class of about twenty-five pupils. Instructions began about six o'clock in the morning and lasted about four hours in the summer, somewhat longer in the winter. Pupils went home for lunch and returned to school in the late afternoon to remain until dusk. Feasts and fast days were observed to the extent that no new work was taken up and the hours of school were shorter. Then for three weeks in the summer, schools had only morning sessions. The memory was especially cultivated, and for this purpose recitations were loud and repetitious. Morning and evening prayers were recited in a sort of chorus. For truancy, disobedience, and other faults, the punishment was not to be too severe. The leather thongs, however, were used as a discipline. As some women of the time were learned, these must have received their education from special tutors at home, for girls did not attend the regular schools. Neither women nor unmarried men could be teachers. Cf. *Mishnah, Kiddushin* (Betrothals), 4, 13; Danby, p. 329; W. M. Feldman, *The Jewish Child, Its History, Folklore, Biology and Sociology*; also A. Kennedy, "Education," *Hastings Dictionary of the Bible* (one volume ed.) p. 204; R. Kretzmann, *Education among the Jews*. Josephus says that the Jews of his time did not encourage any learning except that of their sacred laws. *Antiquities*, XX, xi, 2; cf. *ibid.*, IV, 211, VIII, 12.

[6] *Itinerarium*, 5; *Itinera Hierosolymitana*, ed. by P. Geyer; *Corp. Script. Lat.*, XXXVIII, 161, 197.

having never learned?" Yet these men of Jerusalem were not acquainted with Our Savior in His childhood years. Despising the learning of Galilee, as they did, their words would mean that Jesus had not gone through the regular course of study required for the scribes. A more general expression was used by the residents of Nazareth, who could have known whether Jesus had attended school. Also astonished at His teaching, they asked: "How came this man by all these things?" (Mark 6:2.) This saying and the statements in Mark 1:22 and John 7:15 imply that Jesus had not passed through the regular schools for scribes; but they do not preclude His attendance at the local elementary schools. On the basis of Luke 2:40 St. Thomas Aquinas could state that Christ did not learn anything from men, it being more fitting for Him to acquire His human knowledge by discovery.[7] To be sure, the Blessed Mother and St. Joseph could tell their neighbors that the boy Jesus was able to read the Bible at home and thus forestall insistence on His attending the local school; yet, since almost all children of the time went to school and since the Savior became like His fellow men He conformed here also; namely, that, as He allowed St. Joseph to guide His hands in the carpenter shop, so He sat among the boys of Nazareth in the local school reciting the daily tasks and allowing the teacher to guide His hands in the formation of letters.

In the days of Christ at least a portion of the Scripture was to be found in many Jewish homes. Jewish parents took seriously their obligation of seeing that their children could read and write and be educated in the Jewish religion. This is evidenced by the Jewish writer of the first Christian century, Josephus,[8] who states that the Jews of his time considered the instruction of their children the most important affair of their lives and took great pains

---

[7] *Summa theol.*, IIIa, q.19, a.3. Origen said it was not by "education and teaching" that Christ came to the height of wisdom and power; *Commentary on Gospel according to St. Matthew*, II, 17; ANF, IX, 425.

[8] *Against Apion*, II, 178 (18); I, 60 (12). Cf. Origen, *Against Celsus*, V, 42; ANF, IV, 562.

with it. He also says that the command to do so came from Moses himself. As a result, "from earliest consciousness" Jewish children learned the sacred laws so well as to have them "graven" on the soul. Another Jewish writer, Philo,[9] almost a contemporary of Our Lord, uses similar language, when he boasts that the Jews, instructed in their laws, "from earliest youth bear the image of the laws in their souls," and when he further asserts that the Jews are taught "from their swaddling clothes by their parents, teachers, and others who bring them up." Timothy (II Tim. 3:15) knew the Holy Scriptures from his childhood.

Every opportunity was used to make the children acquainted with Holy Scripture. Choice portions of it were hung up on doorways and worn on the arm or forehead so as to be seen and learned. The Bible stories themselves would make a deep impression on children as they were related by their parents during the noonday heat or the long winter evenings. In the very practice of their faith there was a great amount of education, for theirs was a ritualistic religion, teaching through the eye in a way well adapted to the capacities of children. This practice of their religion began at an early age, for the Jewish institution known as "son of commandment"[10] that enjoined a boy of thirteen to assume religious obligations grew up centuries later. In New Testament times no definite age was yet fixed. As soon as it was convenient, parents took their children to religious functions. Later, when young manhood was reached, observance of the law was strictly required.

Once the child began regularly to attend religious services at the local synagogue, he heard portions of the Sacred Scriptures read on Mondays, Thursdays, Saturdays, holydays, new moons,

---

[9] Cf. *Legatio ad Caium*, 16. Philo states that parents are in the position of "instructors" to teach their children the various branches of knowledge and the ways of virtue. Besides reading and writing, he mentions arithmetic, geometry, music, and philosophy. He says that parents employed nurses, tutors, and instructors for their children from their earliest years. *De specialibus legibus*, II, XL, 228–33; *Loeb* (ed. Colson), VII, 449.

[10] According to the *Mishnah*, the vows of a girl twelve years and one day old were valid and those of a boy thirteen years and one day old; Niddah (Menstruant), 5, 6; Danby, p. 751.

and festival days. Here was a considerable measure of education imparted in the explanation of the Jewish feast days, in reading the Bible in the ancient Hebrew language, in the vernacular interpretations that followed, and in the homiletic lessons drawn therefrom. Thus for that era Jewish education was exceptional inasmuch as it applied to adults and was mostly religious. Jewish education was indeed unusual because the Jews centered their attention in a collection of sacred works which contained their history, laws, maxims of wisdom, prophecies, and psalms. Indeed, these works enjoyed the special privilege of containing the revealed will of God.

Shortly after his fifth year, the Jewish child began committing to memory the sacred laws contained in the fifth and sixth chapters of Deuteronomy and also the group of psalms known as the Hallel (112–117). The first day that he went to school when about six or seven years of age, he began to read the Bible. It was the custom to begin with the book of Leviticus, then proceed to the other books of the Pentateuch, and after that to the Prophets and other sacred writings. As an explanation was given with the reading, the pupils learned not only Hebrew words but also the Scriptural meaning. The Jews strove to get all their knowledge and wisdom out of the Bible, holding that anyone who did not know the sacred character of God as revealed in the inspired text could not please God. Hence their "innumerable schools of practical wisdom," as Philo [11] styles their synagogues; because the specific purpose of the synagogue, which already for a few generations had been established in all Jewish communities, was to spread a popular knowledge of the sacred writings.

The Jews of Our Lord's day had an additional reason to concentrate their energies on the Holy Book. In it they sought both solace from the cruelty of Roman oppression and refuge from the dangers of Graeco-Roman civilization. The prevalent Hellenistic ideas did not promote morality but rather countenanced gross ex-

[11] He says they were in every city and there were thousands of these schools of "good sense, temperance, courage, justice, and the other virtues" (De specialibus legibus, II, XV, 62) (ed. by Colson) VII, p. 347.

cesses against the moral law. Accordingly among the many Gentiles who inhabited Galilee there were prevalent crimes and sins condemned by the revealed word of God. Thus Jewish children were beset by many moral dangers from pagan games and sports, from the amphitheater and from pagan ideas and ideals. As an antidote to all this the effective means of strict religious education was employed. Time that might have been given to sports and games was occupied in religious training and services. The contact and conflict with the paganism of their Gentile neighbors occasioned for Galileans everyday problems. Yet the result was a strengthening of their religious spirit and patriotic zeal. They became less exclusive than their brethren in Judea, but much more earnest and daring in the causes of principle and truth.

While playing with the other boys on the hills of Nazareth, the all-holy Son of God, as a mere lad, could look down on the distant blue Mediterranean, the great sea which carried ships to Greece, Italy, and other distant countries. He could look down on the caravan routes that passed through or near His home town and see sometimes contingents of Roman soldiers, sometimes long trains of camels that linked Egypt with Damascus and the cities of Mesopotamia. He could look down on Sephoris, only three miles to the north, where under the immoral tetrarch, Herod Antipas, there clashed eastern and western cultures, and the Jewish faith and pagan religions.

Turning away from the secular and worldly sights, the boy Christ could look out from the hills of Nazareth upon sacred scenes that recalled historical events in God's tender dealing with the chosen people. There a few miles to the north was a hill that guarded the grave of the prophet Jonas.[12] Wheeling toward the west, He could see standing out Mount Carmel associated with the prophets Elias and Eliseus. On a bright day could be seen almost due west, fifteen miles away, the white speck that marked the altar of sacrifice where

[12] According to an old tradition mentioned by St. Jerome, who says it was his native place (*Prologue to Comment. in Jonas; PL*, 25, 1119). According to another tradition Jonas was buried in Edom, southern Palestine.

Elias prevailed over the priests of Baal. Turning south close under the hills of Samaria, the place "Thanach by the water of Mageddo" marked the victory of Debbora and Barac over the Canaanites. Over the blue haze of the Samaritan hills a finger could point in the direction of places beyond the reach of the eye, the plain of Dothain where Joseph was sold by his brothers and Ebal and Gerizim, the mountains of blessings and curses. Toward the east lay Gilboa, recalling the victories of Gideon over the hosts of Median. The town of Jezreel on the nearest foothill of Gilboa was the scene of Naboth's vineyard and the death of the covetous Achab and his wicked wife Jezebel. This town was also associated with the prophet Elias. Opposite Jezreel but hidden from view around the corner of Moreh, the town Shunem recalled the memory of Eliseus who there brought back to life the son of the Sunamitess. Further around the east, but only four miles away, stood up the sharp altarlike Thabor, which was made the rallying spot by Barac and which was made a fortress by the wicked King Antiochus. Finally, just before completing the circle,[13] in the northwest direction were the caves of Arbeel that witnessed the last stand of the adherents of the Hasmonean dynasty.

Thus the top of the highest hill of Nazareth, Nebi Sain, must have been a favorite spot of the boy Jesus; for there amid thorny heather and the purple anemone, "the lily of the field," He and the other boys of Nazareth could look out on such a historical panorama as to be thrilled by the recital of the heroic deeds of Gideon and Barac and the edifying accounts of the prophets Jonas, Elias, and Eliseus. Like other Jewish boys of His time, He heeded the warnings of the elders not to participate in pagan games and sports. From an early age, like other Jewish boys He wore attached to the bottom of His outer garment, the sacred fringe consisting of threads with a cord of blue entwined, or of white threads and blue threads. This was an external mark and distinguished the

---

[13] Smith (*Historical Geography of the Holy Land*, p. 433) writes that from the hill of Nazareth you can see thirty miles in three directions: "It is a map of Old Testament history."

Nazareth hills, with the Latin convent

Jews from the Gentiles with whom they could not avoid all contact.[14] To other boys He gave example and edification in the assiduous reading of Holy Scripture and in devotion to prayer, public and private.

BIBLIOGRAPHY

Albright, W. F. The Archaeology of Palestine.
Bailey, A. E. On Nazareth Hill.
Booth, H. K. The World of Jesus.
Carpenter, J. Life in Palestine when Jesus Lived.
Charlesworth, M. P. Trade Routes of the Roman Empire.
Dalman, G. Arbeit und Sitte in Palästina, I–IV.
Edersheim, A. In the Days of Christ.
Feldman, W. M. The Jewish Child.
Glover, T. R. The World of the New Testament.
Kretzmann, P. E. Education among the Jews.
Neil, J. Palestine Life, Its Light on the Letter of the Holy Scriptures.

[14] Prohibitions against business relations with Gentiles are found in the Mishnic Tractate, Abodah Zarah (Idolatry); Danby, pp. 437–45. They concern especially wine, milk, cheese, and things that would be used for idols or idolatrous worship. Even about several things mentioned, it is added: "But it is not forbidden to have any benefit from them." Cf. Dalman, Jesus-Jeshua, p. 4.

CHAPTER XVII

The Boy Jesus at Prayer

Honor and glory are given to the Creator, and graces and favors flow to man when use is made of the great privilege of addressing God in prayer. Who can estimate the glory of God and the blessings on mankind which resulted from the prayers of the God-man, whose acts were infinite in value? His petitions obtained for us numberless graces and favors which otherwise we would not have received. The sublime dignity and ineffable worth of the private prayers of Our Lord cannot be measured by us. Of course, Jesus' life was one long prayer; for His soul, perpetually united with the Father in the enjoyment of the beatific vision, was continuously wrapped in prayer sublime, above our powers of conception. We do know that the Savior in His public ministry was most conspicuous for devotion to prayers, public as well as private. For instance, it is recorded: "He went out into a mountain to pray, and He passed the whole night in the prayer of God" (Luke 6: 12).

As a boy winning favor with God and man, Jesus was most assiduous in the recital of the ordinary prayers, common to His time. How effective these prayers were on His divine lips! What significance they had when uttered by Him! What an inspiration for us all is the Christ child at prayer! By His sacred example He blessed and sanctified the simple prayers of little children and all prayers said within the sanctuary of the home. His use of prayer hallowed the ordinary prayers said by the Jewish children of the time. What were some of the prayers that came from the lips of the divine Child, that we may be inspired and edified by them?

The first sentence which a Jewish father would teach his child was the chief profession of Jewish faith in the unity of God: "Hear, O Israel, the Lord our God is one Lord." How pleased and consoled Mary and Joseph were when they heard the Christ child lisping these words, the keynote of Jewish doctrine! This verse together with a few extracts from the Pentateuch were called the Sh'ma,[1] from the opening word in Hebrew. Jesus repeated them twice a day, morning and night. The following prayer was said first: "Hear, O Israel, the Lord our God is one Lord. Thou shalt love the Lord thy God with thy whole heart and with thy whole soul and with thy whole strength. And these words which I command thee this day, shall be in thy heart. And thou shalt tell them to thy children, and thou shalt meditate upon them sitting in thy house, and walking on thy journey, sleeping and rising. And thou shalt bind them as a sign on thy hand, and they shall be and shall move between thy eyes. And thou shalt write them in the entry, and on the doors of thy house" (Deut. 6: 4–9).

This profession of faith was followed by another portion of the Sacred Scripture (Deut. 11: 13–29). This passage told how people's welfare depended on their attitude toward almighty God, and commanded that this Scripture be taught to the children and be placed on their arms, their foreheads, and the doorposts. The third selection (Num. 15: 37–41) enjoined the Israelites to add fringes to their garments as a way of recalling the obligation of keeping the commandments and the exodus from Egypt. These verses of Scripture were memorized by the child Jesus. Also, as He left or entered His home, He touched reverently the parchment on which they were written, which was in a small box attached to the doorpost.

[1] On the Sh'ma, see Kohler, *Studies, Addresses and Personal Papers*, pp. 113–21; Elbogen, *Der jüdische Gottesdienst in seiner geschichtlichen Entwicklung*, pp. 16–26; Danby, *The Mishnah*, pp. 2 f., 386.

Besides, to this morning and evening commemoration which, according to Josephus,[2] was ordered by Moses in remembrance of God's favor in delivering the Jewish people out of the land of Egypt, there were added the "eighteen benedictions" consisting of three praises, twelve petitions (now thirteen), and three thanksgivings. These have been handed down in Jewish tradition without much change, from the end of the first century, when Gamaliel II is reported as saying there was a strict obligation to recite them daily.[3] Perhaps twelve of these "benedictions" were in use in Our Lord's day.

If these prayers were lisped by the divine Child, how effective they were! And what a meaning Psalms 2 and 109 had on His lips! The holy family in their humble home of Nazareth reciting psalms together and offering up prayers in unison is a model for all family devotions. We can imagine them saying together the following psalm:

> It is good to give praise to the Lord:
>> and to sing to Thy name, O Most High.
> To show forth Thy mercy in the morning,
>> and Thy truth in the night;
> Upon an instrument of ten strings, upon the psaltery:
>> with a canticle upon the harp.
> For Thou hast given me, O Lord, a delight in Thy doings:
>> and in the works of Thy hands I shall rejoice.
> O Lord, how great are Thy works!
>> Thy thoughts are exceeding deep.

Ps. 91:2–6

Exclamations of praises to God, or blessings, as they were called, were offered frequently during the day by pious Jews at the time of Christ. There was a blessing for each dish and for each new pleasure at the table,—at least in some instances. At sight of bread, the following was spoken: "Blessed be the Lord who created the

---

[2] *Antiquities*, IV, 212 (viii, 13).

[3] *Mishnah*, Berakoth (Benedictions), 4, 3; Danby, p. 5. Cf. Lagrange, *Le Judaisme avant J.C.*, pp. 469 f. See Appendix 5, p. 354.

bread." [4] Personal benefits, phenomena of nature,[5] and consolations from reading or hearing the Sacred Scripture provoked blessings; for example, "Blessed be He who gave the Law." Before the recitation of the morning Sh'ma two blessings were offered: "Blessed be He who created the lights," and "blessed be He who loveth His people Israel"; then at the end the following was said: "Blessed be He who redeemed Israel." Frequently during His public life Our Lord pronounced blessings on food,[6] thus sanctioning and hallowing this beautiful practice. Prevailing in Christ's family circle during His hidden life was the custom of pausing often during the daily routine for this most laudable purpose of invoking blessings on various occasions.

In St. Luke's Gospel (4:16) we find mentioned that Our Lord attended the synagogue service in Nazareth when He returned to His own home town during the public life. "He came to Nazareth, where He had been brought up; and He entered the synagogue, according to His custom, on the Sabbath day and He rose up to read." The Sabbath,[7] which was announced from the roof of the

---

[4] At table the blessing for bread was: "Blessed art Thou, Lord God, who bringeth forth bread from the earth"; and that for wine was: "Blessed art Thou, Lord God, who created the fruit of the vine." *Mishnah*, Berakoth (Benedictions), 6, 1; Danby, p. 6.

[5] "Blessed is He whose power and might fill the world" (*op. cit.*, 9, 2; Danby, p. 9). On seeing the Mediterranean: "Blessed is He that made the great sea" (*ibid.*). For bad news: "Blessed is the true Judge" (*ibid.*). For the favor of rain: "Blessed is the good and the doer of good" (*ibid.*).

[6] Matt. 14:19; Mark 8:6; Luke 22:19; John 6:11. Cf. I Cor. 11:24; I Tim. 4:4; Ps. 133 (134):3.

[7] The Sabbath had been given by God to man as a day of rest and a day of religious devotion. The prophet Ezechiel (20:20) had insisted on the holy character of the day and had preached that its proper observance was an external sign that the Jews were the chosen people of God. At the time of Our Lord the Jews, whether in the homeland or dispersed in foreign countries, were known for this distinctive religious rite. The observance of the seventh day as a day of rest had already spread to many countries. Cf. Josephus, *Against Apion*, II, 282 (39); Philo, *De specialibus legibus*, II, xv, 60. At that time, however, there were no Friday night services, although the Sabbath was reckoned to begin with sundown on Friday. We cannot say for certain which of the numerous ordinances that are found in the Mishnic tractate, Shabbath (Danby, pp. 100–21) were in force in Christ's day. Cf. Bonsirven, *Le Judaisme Palestinien au temps de Jésus-Christ*, II, 172–79. The Gospels tell us that our Savior deliberately broke the minute regulations of the Pharisees, and proclaimed that the Sabbath was for man, and that the observance of it must fit into man's life. Under divine authorization, the apostles took over Sabbatical observance and transferred it to Sunday, and the Church has

local synagogue by a thrice repeated blast of a trumpet on Friday
afternoon, and by the lighting of a lamp at home at nightfall,
was especially a day of rest enjoined by the Scriptures. Although
attendance at synagogue services was not required by Holy Writ,
it became by custom the proper way of celebrating the day. Few,
indeed, absented themselves.

We can join in spirit with the boy Jesus, as with His Blessed
Mother and St. Joseph He takes part in the regular services [8] at
the local synagogue, and follow with Him some of the ceremonies
that had grown up around the reading of the Sacred Scriptures
there.

We notice in the court a laver in which the members of the
congregation wash their hands as they approach the synagogue.
Within we see a platform on the side facing the Temple of Jerusalem.[9] On it there are a chest, or ark, to contain the scrolls of
Scripture, and a reading stand on which they are to rest. There are
lamps and candelabra throughout the hall; also one can see trom-
bones and trumpets on the walls and stone benches along the walls.

The boy Jesus and St. Joseph are sitting with the men in the
middle while the Virgin Mother is standing with the women on a
balcony or on the sides behind a grille partition. The main body
of the congregation sit on benches facing the holy ark; however,
the elders or teachers and the "ruler" of the synagogue are sitting
on the first bench, facing the people. As the prayer begins, the
people stand; but these at the first bench have to turn about so
that they, too, may be facing templeward. At first the Sh'ma,
given above, is recited by all in unison. Then the precentor, whose

ordered that the chief observance be the attendance at Mass. For the Jews of the first
century the synagogue service on Saturdays was mostly for the reading and expounding
of the Sacred Scriptures. Cf. Josephus, Against Apion, II, 175 (17), 204 (25). It is
needless to add that the influence of the Christian celebration of Sunday is inestimable.

[8] Cf. Dalman, Jesus-Jeshua, pp. 38–55; Bonsirven, On the Ruins of the Temple, pp.
153–70; Le Judaisme Palestinien au temps de Jésus-Christ, II, 136–47; Moore, Judaism
in the first Christian Centuries, I, pp. 281–307; II, 21–39; Prat, Jésus-Christ, I, 370 f.

[9] Lagrange says that synagogues did not have any special necessary orientation, Le
Judaisme avant J.C., p. 291. The Synagogue at Capharnaum opened southward, facing
the Temple. Cf. Dalman, Sacred Sites and Ways, p. 142.

head is veiled, goes before the ark to offer in the name of all, not the eighteen benedictions of weekdays, but only the first three and the last three with a special one for the Sabbath as the middle prayer. After each benediction the congregation responds, "Amen"; but before the last prayer, if there is a priest present, he goes to the platform and, facing the people with uplifted hands raised shoulder high,[10] pronounces the following Aaronitic blessing in the Hebrew language: "The Lord bless thee and keep thee. The Lord show His face to thee and have mercy on thee. The Lord turn His countenance to thee and give thee peace." (Num. 6:24–26).

Then comes the chief part of the service, the reading of the Sacred Scriptures from a lectern in the forefront of the platform. This is done by a reader who stands facing the people. Beside him stands a translator, who without any book gives a rendering in the case of the Law after every verse, but in regard to the Prophets at the end of every third verse. One person reads the portion of the Prophets and recites the prayer; while the reading of the Law is divided into seven parts for seven persons, each of whom offers a benediction before and after the lesson. Moreover, the one who reads from the Prophets selects any passage he wishes to read; whereas with the readers of the Law there is a continuous reading with no choice, each taking up where the preceding paused. The readers are of different ages, some of them rather young. The boy Jesus, now about ten years of age, being one of those called on to read, does so to the great satisfaction of all, especially of His Blessed Mother. Finally, a suitable person is selected who goes to the platform and sits while he delivers a fervent sermon in the vernacular. Then the congregation is dismissed, and the boy Jesus, with St. Joseph, rejoins the Blessed Mother to return to their happy home.

There were synagogue services not only on each Sabbath but also on Mondays, Thursdays, holydays, and new moons.[11] Doubt-

---

[10] *Mishnah*, Tamid (Daily Whole-offerings), II; Danby, p. 388.
[11] Cf. Moore, *Judaism in the First Christian Centuries*, I, 296.

less the boy Christ attended all these public services. Then there were the great festivals of the year during which special prayers were offered in the synagogue at Nazareth by those who did not make the pilgrimage to Jerusalem. As Jesus' home town was a four days' journey from the Holy City, the average citizen attended the Temple celebrations only once or twice a year, but on the other occasions he was present there in spirit while he devoted himself to pious exercises and the reading of the Law in the local synagogue.

The oldest and greatest of the Jewish festivals,[12] the Pasch or Passover, fell in the spring and lasted seven days. This feast of national redemption and freedom commemorated the deliverance of the Jewish people from Egypt. Only in the Temple could the paschal lamb be slain, but the laws forbidding the eating of leavened bread and the presence of leaven in the house applied to every Jewish family. The special psalm was 134 (135).

The festival of Weeks or Pentecost followed Passover in fifty days. This was a grain harvest commemoration that was celebrated only in the Temple, where the first fruits of the grain were offered to God. To this solemn assembly of this feast of harvest were brought first fruits from wheat, barley, grapes, figs, pomegranates, olive oil, and (dates) honey. While still unplucked they were set aside as the property of the priests. There were required, besides, a peace offering, singing, and spending the night in Jerusalem.[13] In bringing up the first fruits to the Temple mount the men from smaller towns met at evening in one town to spend the night there in an open place. Early the next day they were summoned by an officer in charge to begin the solemn procession. The ox as peace offering that was driven in the front had its horns overlaid with gold and a wreath of olive leaves on its head. As they drew near Jerusalem the fruits were adorned and messengers were sent to the

---

[12] Cf. *ibid.*, II, 40–54; Bonsirven, *On the Ruins of the Temple*, pp. 170–79; *Le Judaisme Palestinien au temps de Jésus-Christ*, II, 120–29; Schauss, *The Jewish Festivals*.

[13] *Mishnah*, Bikkurim (First Fruits), 2, 4; Danby, p. 95. Those from a distance brought dried figs and raisins.

Holy City to announce their arrival. They were welcomed by officials of the Temple and by craftsmen. At the Temple mount, flute playing which had accompanied the procession ceased, and each pilgrim put his basket of first fruits on his shoulder and proceeded to the Temple court. There the Levite sang psalm 29 (30), while pigeons were sacrificed as whole-offerings. Then, while each pilgrim recited the profession enjoined (Deut. 26: 3 ff.), a priest in acceptance waved his hand under the offering, and the basket was left by the side of the altar.[14]

In the early autumn, the Day of Atonement impressed young and old with the obligation of repentance, for on that day the scapegoat was sent into the desert to symbolize God's forgiveness of sin. With this day the penitential psalms were associated especially 102 (103) and 129 (130), and the special psalm was 28 (29).

Shortly thereafter, with the beginning of the Jewish New Year (Ps. 47), when the harvest had been gathered in and the rainy season was at hand to bring future fruitfulness, the most joyous of the feasts, that of Tabernacles, was celebrated. People lived in temporary booths for eight days to commemorate the way their ancestors had been obliged to live on their flight from Egypt. The central rite of this feast was a libation of water, and a distinctive feature was the waving of festive branches with the recital of the psalms. A priest went from the Temple to the pool Siloam (Shiloh), where he filled a golden ewer with water. On his returning through the water gate, a loud trumpet blast was sounded, whereupon the people sang: "Therefore with joy shall ye draw water of the wells of salvation." The water was poured into another basin. Then at the words: "Raise up thy hand," the water libation was offered upon the altar and together with it a wine offering. During this ceremony trumpets were sounded, followed by the singing of the psalms 112–117 to the accompaniment of flutes. When the Levites sang verses 1, 25, 26, and 29 of the last mentioned psalm, the

[14] *Op. cit.*, 3, 206; Danby, pp. 96 f.

congregation shook their palm branches in the direction of the altar. This same psalm was sung on each of the seven days of the feast as the priests marched round the altar after the sacrifices had been offered. On the night of the first day was the thrilling illumination service. This was a torch dance, in which even the most prominent Israelites took part. It was held in the Court of Women, which was brilliantly illuminated. During this the Levites from the steps of the inner court sang psalms 119–133, "Songs of Ascent," with the accompaniment of various musical instruments. This celebration continued until cockcrow, when two priests at the Nicanor gate sounded the signal for departure. On leaving, however, the crowd faced about at the eastern gate when the priests recited the words: "Our forefathers in this place turned their backs on the altar of God, and their faces to the east worshiping the sun, but we turn to God."

There were also three feasts of deliverance: the feast of Dedication, or feast of lights, lasting eight days, to commemorate the victory of Judas Machabeus, for which psalm 29 was the special psalm; the feast of Nicanor, which celebrated the defeat of Nicanor; and that of Purim, recalling Esther's victory, during which psalm 7 was sung. These feasts and other religious observances, such as fasts,[15] intercalated throughout the year, were great incentives to piety and prayer for the Jews. The boy Jesus must have entered into their spirit with edification for all around Him. He took part in the services at the local synagogue whenever He did not go to Jerusalem to attend the Temple celebrations. He chanted the sacred hymns of praise and thanksgiving to the eternal Father at one time amid festive pilgrims of many lands, at another amid farming folk of secluded Nazareth.

> Rejoice to God our helper:
>   Sing aloud to the God of Jacob.
> Take a psalm, and bring hither the timbrel:
>   the pleasant psaltery with the harp.

[15] The special psalms for new moons were 97 (98) and 103 (104). See Oesterley, *The Psalms*, I, 101.

Blow up the trumpet on the new moon,
   on the noted day of your solemnity (Ps. 80 [81]:2-4).
Blessed be he that cometh in the name of the Lord.
   We have blessed you out of the house of the Lord.
The Lord is God, and He hath shone upon us.
   Appoint a solemn day, with the shady boughs, even to the horn of
      the altar.
Thou art my God, and I will praise Thee:
   Thou are my God, and I will exalt Thee (Ps. 117 [118]:26-28).
I will sacrifice to Thee the sacrifice of praise,
   And I will call upon the name of the Lord.
I will pay my vows to the Lord
   in the sight of all His people:
In the courts of the house of the Lord,
   in the midst of thee, O Jerusalem (Ps. 115 [116]:17-19).

The law that required the presence of male Israelites at the
Temple for the feasts of the Pasch, Pentecost, and Tabernacles
would not apply to those as far from Jerusalem as the residents of
Nazareth. They made the pilgrimage to the Holy City once a year;
perhaps those engaged in agriculture repaired there for the feast
of Booths, and artisans, such as St. Joseph, went there at the feast
of Passover; or perhaps the most devout attended the most solemn,
Passover. In this connection the Gospel narrative merely states
that "His parents went each year to Jerusalem at the solemn day
of the Pasch." Thus St. Joseph may have attended at the Temple
on the other two occasions enjoined by law, but the Virgin Mary
accompanied him at the Passover feast.

From about His seventh year, the child Jesus was probably taken
on the yearly Passover pilgrimage, for it was customary for children
to take part as soon as they were able to eat of the paschal lamb a
portion that was as large as an olive. The visit of His twelfth year is
specially mentioned on account of the episode which occurred.
Indeed, it is implied that He had made previous visits, since otherwise the parents would make sure that He was with them when
they were starting out on their return trip to Nazareth. In this
yearly pilgrimage, that lasted in all thirteen days, to celebrate the

feast that had most significance religiously and nationally, a feast that was so replete with symbols and types of Himself, the boy Christ gave all, both young and old, an example of public service to almighty God. For there each year He commemorated with solemn ritual His Father's feast in His Father's house, not only as an individual or as part of a family group, but also in company of fellow townspeople and in conjunction with the representatives of the whole Jewish nation at home and abroad.

BIBLIOGRAPHY

Bonsirven, J. On the Ruins of the Temple.
———. Le Judaisme Palestinien au temps de Jésus-Christ.
Boylan, P. The Psalms, 2 vols.
Dalman, G. Jesus-Jeshua, Studies in the Gospels.
Edersheim, A. The Temple: its ministers and services as they were at the time of Jesus Christ.
Elbogen, I. Die jüdische Gottesdienst in seiner geschichtlichen Entwicklung.
Lagrange, M. J. Le Judaisme avant Jésus-Christ.
Moore, G. F. Judaism in the First Centuries of the Christian Era, 2 vols.
Oesterly, W. A Fresh Approach to the Psalms.
———. The Psalms, 2 vols.
Schauss, H. The Jewish Festivals from Their Beginnings to Our Day.
Schechter, A. Lectures on Jewish Liturgy.
Vincent, A. Judaism.

CHAPTER XVIII

The Boy Jesus at the Passover

IT is approaching the middle of the lunar month of the vernal equinox, the time of the year for the great feast of the Pasch, or Passover. In the quiet, secluded town of Nazareth, on all sides preparations are being made for the pilgrimage to the divinely chosen place, Jerusalem, to celebrate this, the greatest of the Jewish feasts. Men are busy repairing roads, mending bridges and whitewashing sepulchers. Women are getting clothes ready and preparing foods, while houses are being carefully searched for all leaven, which is to be destroyed. In the local synagogue special lessons and prayers mark the advent of this feast commemorative of historic deliverance and freedom. Most eager and expectant are the young as they joyfully look forward in anticipation of the treats in store for them: the great crowds and strange sights of the Holy City, the thrill of God's great house, the ceremonies conducted there by priests and Levites, and the famous rabbis discussing erudite topics. The hearts of young and old beat faster as the deepest sentiments of religious fervor and patriotic emotion are aroused whenever the conversation turns to the ardent hope that the Messiah may make His appearance at the coming feast to liberate the Jewish people from the galling shackles of Rome, or that, at least, Elias may return to act in the capacity of herald to proclaim the advent of the Messiah and the approach of redemption.

At last the day of departure arrives. Pilgrims intent on proceeding in a group for better protection begin to gather outside the town on the road that leads down to Japhia. We notice that the majority are on foot. A few have camels and donkeys, and one or two are wealthy enough to afford a chariot. Those on foot wear sandals, have staffs in their hands, leather wallets hanging from their waists, and waterskins and food containers on their shoulders. Some bring along a lamb, others a goat, many carry money on their person. A family made up of the "parents," now about thirty years of age, and the boy Jesus, now twelve, approach and take a place with the artisans in the group. When all are assembled, a leader is selected who stands before the caravan and calls out: "Arise ye and let us go up to Zion, unto the Lord our God." [1] He then leads the way while the festive group follows in joyful mood singing psalms, among which is the following:

> How lovely are Thy tabernacles, O Lord of hosts!
> My soul longeth and fainteth for the courts of the Lord.
> My heart and my flesh have rejoiced in the living God.
> For the sparrow hath found herself a house,
> and the turtle a nest for herself where she may lay her young ones.
> Thy altars, O Lord of hosts, my King and my God.
> Blessed are they that dwell in Thy house, O Lord:
> They shall praise Thee forever and ever.
> Blessed is the man whose help is from Thee:
> In his heart he hath disposed to ascend Thy steps.
>
> Ps. 83 [84]:2–6

The members of this festive group are going to follow the shortest route which goes directly south and which will afford opportunities of obtaining food and lodging. They intend to make a little better than twenty miles a day and expect to reach their destination in four days. Stops will be made at towns to buy bread from

---

[1] *Mishnah*, Bikkurim (First Fruits), 3, 2; Danby, p. 96. Some texts have "the house of" as in Isa. 3:3, the prophecy concerning the influence of the Lord's house.

the bakers' shops; wells and springs will be visited for water; and the pilgrims will frequently be the recipients of hospitality at the camps and inns where they pass the night.

The whole period of daylight from sunrise to sunset will have to be utilized in shortening the way; yet each day there will be a long midday rest during which the noon meal will be eaten. As they proceed along their festive way the pilgrims do not heed their fatigue after the long hours of walking or the hardships and difficulties of the journey; for they are buoyed up with the thought that they are on the way to the city of David, as "the foundations thereof are in the holy mountains: the Lord loveth the gates of Sion above all the tabernacles of Jacob. Glorious things are said of thee, O City of God" (Ps. 86:1–3). They are thrilled, too, with the anticipation of praying in the great Temple; for truly "better is one day in Thy courts above thousands. I have chosen to be an abject in the house of my God, rather than to dwell in the tabernacles of sinners" (Ps. 83:11).

With the progress of the four days' journey over the difficult road, soft from recent rains, the number of the pilgrims grows more and more as other festive caravans join in from the villages or towns or even from distant countries. At certain places groups are so close together as to form one long procession extending for miles, and their joyous hymns re-echo through the neighboring hills and valleys. At other points the road is choked with herds of cattle for the Temple sacrifices or with long trains of camels carrying spices and herbs from Mesopotamia. In the final stages of the journey pipers lead the way, and with mounting enthusiasm the pilgrims march to music.

The Holy City is sighted with its four hills, 2,500 feet above sea level, yet basinlike because of higher ground, with its strong walls and its towers rising forty feet above them, with the citadel of Herod and its three massive towers, with the tower of Antonia partly jutting out from the northwestern corner of the Temple area, and with the glorious Temple buildings themselves surmounted by the holy house whose white stones and gold plates sparkle in the sun. No wonder a reverent hush falls on the multitude as they feast their eyes on this entrancing spectacle. Finally, at the city gates they are greeted by representatives of Jerusalem,[2] and with the accompaniment of musical instruments they join in the singing of Psalm 121 (122):

> I rejoiced at the things that were said to me:
> "We shall go into the house of the Lord"
> Our feet were standing in thy courts, O Jerusalem
> Jerusalem which is built as a city, all compact in itself.
> For thither the tribes go up the tribes of the Lord,
> The testimony of Israel, to praise the name of the Lord
> Because their seats have sat in judgment seats upon the house of David.
> Pray ye for the things that are for the peace of Jerusalem!
> And abundance for them that love thee!

Coming from the north, the pilgrims turn east under the shadows of the imposing towers of Herod's palace and enter the city by the Garden Gate. Here began the second north wall that protected the vulnerable northwest portion of the city. On the way toward the Temple they go directly east, passing on their right the palace of the Hasmoneans, the gymnasium, and the council chamber of the Sanhedrin. This road leads to a western gate to the outer Temple wall, crossing the valley by a bridge. Even in the front of the eastern gate reverence and respect had to be shown; but the most ardent of the pilgrims, making haste to "appear before the Lord," leave with others their traveling equipment and shoes, to enter the Temple ground on which they are most careful not to spit.[3] Keeping to the right and making a circuit, they cross the busy, spacious Court of Gentiles to the Beautiful Gate, where they distribute alms to lame and blind beggars who loiter there. Then

---

[2] *Mishnah, loc. cit.*, 3, 3; Danby, p. 97. This passage mentions rulers and prefects and treasurers of the Temple. It also mentions "craftsmen" who expressed themselves as follows: "Brethren, men of such and such a place, you are welcome." Josephus mentions "harpers and choristers with their instruments" (*Jewish War*, II, 321 [xv, 4]).

[3] It was forbidden to enter the Temple mound with staff, sandal or wallet, or with dust on one's feet. *Mishnah*, Berakoth (Benedictions), 9, 5; Danby, p. 10.

they enter the Temple building itself and pass through the Court of Women to the Court of Israel. There, standing before the great altar of sacrifices with eyes fixed on the veil of four colors, they worship in the presence of God.

The contingent from Nazareth with the members of the holy family are now in Jerusalem. Some of them are pitching tents in squares and open places, others are seeking lodging in the city or suburbs. The first thing evident about the city is the great crowd everywhere; [4] for to the usual population of a hundred thousand is now added several thousand pilgrims. What variety, too, is seen among these Jews and Jewish converts from almost every part of the known world, from Asia Minor, Babylonia, Media, Cyprus, Greece, Egypt, and even Rome! How different the languages spoken and how distinctive the dress! The brilliant colored dress of the Babylonian women is in striking contrast to the bleached linen of their Palestinian sisters. Rich merchants and bankers, gorgeously arrayed, who have come by boat from distant lands, now brush shoulders with poor native peasants of Palestine, while local cattle and sheep dealers mix freely with traders who have brought camel trains from afar. All consider themselves equal during the feast. Occasionally detachments of newly arrived Roman soldiers pass by, come in from Caesarea with the Roman procurator who has taken up his quarters at the fortress Antonia, a reminder that the scepter has passed from Juda and that, therefore, one should expect Him who is to be sent.

The following morning as the boy Jesus and St. Joseph go through the city they encounter a scene somewhat like the follow-

---

[4] Josephus refers to a vast crowd from the country at a Passover service (*Jewish War*, II, 10, [i, 3]). In *Antiquities*, XVII, 9, 3, he adds that there were more sacrifices offered at the Passover than at any other feast. The figures he supplies are greatly exaggerated and are considered fantastic. A similar judgment is passed on the figures in the Talmud, 600,000. Cf. Pesahim, V, *Babylonian Talmud*, ed. Rodkinson, V, 121. Tacitus (*Histories*, V, 13) says that the number of those within beseiged Jerusalem was 600,000. The number of pilgrims estimated by modern scholars varies from 15,000, given by Herford (*Judaism in New Testament Period*, p. 148), to 100,000, mentioned by Schauss (*The Jewish Festivals*, p. 48). As to the permanent residents of Jerusalem at that time, estimates range from 50,000 to 100,000. The higher figure is accepted by McCown "The Density of Population in Ancient Palestine," *Journal of Bib. Lit.*, LXVI (1947), 436.

ing: The Temple area projects on the northeast side of the city so that some of its western flank is a suburb. The city itself (differing from the walled city of today) lies to the south of the Temple and rests on two ridges of hills [5] running north and south; the Tyropoeon valley dividing them. Since the western hill is higher and broader than the eastern, the western section is known as the Upper City. Most of the markets and business streets are here. It is easy to know whence come the names of the streets; from the trades or merchandise to which they are set apart. Thus the butchers and bakers and tailors,[6] and sandalmakers, have their streets. There are little side streets for goldsmiths, blacksmiths, and coppersmiths. Streets are set aside for dealers in timber, wool combers, weavers, and cheesemakers. Even donkey drivers have their own street. The great market is lined with booths that sell goods from Rome and Alexandria, as well as from the homeland and the Middle East. One dealer sells fish from Lake Tiberias, another cakes from wheat grown in Mount Ephraim, and another a syrup made from wine. A goldsmith offers a special ornament for the head, calling out: "Buy gold Jerusalems as a souvenir of the Holy City." [7] But the greatest noise arises from the bargaining in the cattle market near the Temple mount. The narrow streets are so steep that they have to be supplied with numerous steps. As to the houses, they are all much alike; flat-roofed square buildings two floors in height. Yet there are several palaces and numerous synagogues. Despite the buying and selling, there is an appearance of great seriousness and festive devotion in the faces of the crowds. Most of the people walk in the middle of the street, they are the ritually pure; those classed

[5] There were four hills in Jerusalem; but as Josephus (*Jewish War*, V, 137–41 [iv, 1]); *Antiquities*, XIII, 215–17 (vi, 7) says, the southeastern one Akra, was reduced in height so as not to dominate the Temple courts, and thus was combined with the Temple hill to form one hill. The northern hill, Bezetha, was outside the wall at this time. The Temple hill was not as high as either the northern or the western hill, but it dominated the Tyropoeon Valley on the west and the Kedron Valley on the east. Cf. F. J. Hollis, *Archaeology of Herod's Temple*, pp. 10 f.

[6] Tailors, barbers, washermen and shoemakers were allowed to work until midday on the eve of Passover, *Mishnah*, Pesahim (Passover), 4, 6; Danby, p. 141.

[7] A tiara shaped like Jerusalem, called "golden city" in the *Mishnah*; Shebbath, 6, 1; Danby, p. 104.

ritually impure walk on either side.[8] Then all who are looking forward to entering the sanctuary and to partaking of the sacrificial
meal take all precautions of avoiding contact with the heathen as
well as of touching the dead. For this reason the streets are carefully cleaned every day.[9]

In this setting of din and bustle the boy Jesus and St. Joseph go
forth to select and purchase a paschal lamb [10] at the cattle market
and to obtain other necessaries for the paschal meal. Follow them
that afternoon as they proceed to the Temple with St. Joseph leading the lamb. They reach the court of the Temple and join thousands of others who have also brought lambs. The thousands of
sacrifices are performed in three divisions and last from about three
o'clock to five in the afternoon.[11] When the Temple court is filled
with the first section of the people, the Levites close the gates. To
keep order and prevent accidents, twelve Levites holding silver rods
are inside the court.[12] The blowing of trumpets is a signal for each
pilgrim to slay his own animal. Does the boy Jesus put His hand on
the Passover lamb and slaughter it Himself, while turning west
toward the holy house? More likely it was St. Joseph who did this.[13]
The fat of the lamb is cast on a pyre kept perpetually burning with
fuel from fig, nut, and pine trees. As to the blood, it is caught in
basins and passed along rows of priests until cast on the base of the
altar of sacrifice.[14] These priests are dressed in red so that no blood

[8] *Mishnah*, Shekalim (Shekel Dues), 8, 1; Danby, p. 161.
[9] See Franz Dolitssch, *Jewish Artisan Life in the Time of Jesus*, pp. 58–62; and Hayym
Schauss, *The Jewish Festivals*, pp. 50 f.
[10] The Passover lamb must be a male from sheep or goats. Other festal offerings could
be males or females and could be from oxen.
[11] On the eve of Passover, the daily whole-offering was slaughtered at half past one in
the afternoon and offered at half past two. After that took place the Passover offerings.
Mishnah, Pesahim (Passover), 5, 1; Danby, p. 141.
[12] This detail and two others, the clothes worn by the priests and their thirty days of
rehearsal, are given in a letter of Versovius, the translation of which is given in an appendix in the *Babylonian Talmud*, ed. Rodkinson, V, 143–47.
[13] Each slaughtered its own offering; but a priest caught the blood; *Mishnah*, Pesahim
(Passover), 5, 6; Danby, p. 142. The lamb's head was to the south, its face to the west.
Tamid, (Daily Whole-offering), 4, 1; Danby, p. 585.
[14] *Mishnah*, Tamid (Daily Whole-offering), 4, 1; Danby, p. 585. Cf. Dalman, *Jesus-
Jeshua*, p. 123.

stains are evident. They wear short sleeved coats reaching to their knees. Their feet are bare, but their heads are covered with a small cap tied round with a turban several feet long. They have been rehearsing their parts in the service for thirty days and now can perform them with precision and great speed.

The rows of priests extend from the place where the paschal lamb is slaughtered to the altar. The first and last rows carry silver basins, and the intermediary rows golden ones. The blood of the sacrifice is caught in one of these basins and passed along the row of priests until it reaches the priest standing next to the altar. Empty basins are returned along the rows of priests, the whole being so arranged that a priest receives a full basin in return for an empty one. While this spectacular ceremony is going on, Levites, standing on a platform, sing the Hallel psalms 112–117 to the accompaniment of musical instruments. The assembled throng repeats the first clause of the six psalms, and after each line they shout "Alleluiah." However, when they come to the last psalm, 117, they also repeat with the Levites verses 25 and 26: "O Lord, save me: O Lord give good success. Blessed be he that cometh in the name of the Lord." Thus resound through the Temple edifice praises and thanksgiving to God for His greatness and goodness and His power as displayed in the Exodus. After the sacrifice the slain lambs are hung on the walls north of the altar or if these are not available, on sticks supported on the shoulders of the pilgrims. The carcasses are skinned and the fat of the entrails and other sacrificial portions placed on a tray to be burned by a priest at the altar (Lev. 3: 3–5) ; and then with mirth and gladness each pilgrim leaves the Temple precincts, each carrying on his shoulder the slain sacrifice wrapped in its own skin.[15]

As evening falls, in all the courtyards of Jerusalem can be seen clay baking ovens shaped in the form of a cylinder. Inside each, spitted on fragrant pomegranate wood [16] in the form of a cross, a Passover lamb is being roasted. At the same time busy preparations

---

[15] *Op. cit.*, 5, 10; Danby, p. 143.
[16] A metal spit was not permitted. *Op. cit.*, 7, 1; Danby, p. 145.

are also going on with the sweet sauce, bitter herbs, and other requirements for the meal. In the streets people are repairing to their rendezvous in their best attire, wealthy women wearing jewels and rich embroidery. Nobody is left out, the poor being invited by the rich. Parties of festive fellowships have been arranged prior to the feast, and in the name of each the paschal lamb is slain in the Temple, and now as a group they are about to partake of the sacrificial meal. It is against tradition for last-minute guests to join a group in the evening; [17] and the festive bands must consist of ten or more pilgrims so that the Passover lamb will be wholly consumed. [18] The sacrificial meal must take place within the confines of the Holy City: hence every large room in Jerusalem is now being fitted out in preparation for the thousands of paschal celebrations. It is easy to find accommodations, for the city is considered the common property of all the people; and tonight the owners are glad to give rooms for festive parties without charge. Even for divans and bolsters no payment is asked. However, as a recompense, guests will gladly leave skins of animals and vessels used during the meal.

It is about nine o'clock in the evening. The full moon of spring is shedding a soft, silvery light on the city roofs and on courtyards where the embers of a fire that had just roasted the paschal lamb still smolder. The lamb itself is now in the festive hall where everything is in readiness for beginning the meal. Since the lamb was slaughtered in the Temple, it belongs to the "holies of a lower degree" that must be partaken of in purity; so there is the ceremonial washing of hands. The group now recline on sofas, each one's left hand resting on soft cushions while the right is used to take food and drink from a table or tables. The meal begins with a cup of wine mixed with water. Then, after the right hand is washed, lettuce dipped in a tart liquid is eaten. This is followed by the principal part of the meal, which, of course, is the partaking of the

---

[17] Op. cit., 1, 3; Danby, p. 147.

[18] On the following day the bones and sinews were burned. Op. cit., 7, 10; Danby, p. 146.

paschal lamb.[19] With the sacrificial lamb unleavened bread and
bitter herbs are eaten as a reminder of the ancient hardship endured
in Egypt. No plates or spoons are used, but bread does service for
both. When a knife is employed, care is taken that no bones of the
animal are dented or broken. Before the different dishes appropriate
blessings are invoked. The following is pronounced over the lamb:
"Blessed is He who sanctifies us with His commandments and ordered us to eat the Passover." With the serving of the second of the
four cups of wine, a son of the household, usually the youngest boy
present, asks the question: "Why is this night different from other
nights?" Then beginning with the disgrace and ending with the
glory, the story of the Exodus is unfolded and the ritual of the
evening explained.[20] It was usual to serve four cups of wine, other
cups, however, could be taken, but not between the third and
fourth cup.[21] Psalms 112 and 115: 1–8 were sung before the paschal
supper; but now are sung Psalms 113 (9–26), 114, 115, and 116
after the meal, the last part being chanted antiphonally with the
children present. Then, without revelry [22] the various groups break
up while the majority of the feasters return to their lodgings, some
visit from one group to another, and others go to the Temple to
pray; for this is one of the nights of the year when the gates of the
Temple are kept open by the Levites, as well as the gates of the
city.

Who are the other members of the group with whom the holy
family shared the Passover lamb? Perhaps the youthful Lazarus
and his sisters. Is it the boy Christ who, on this occasion of His
twelfth year, asks the question, "Why is this night different from
other nights?" Does He go to the Temple after the Paschal meal

[19] A portion at least as large as an olive must be eaten. *Op. cit.*, 8, 3; Danby, p. 147.
A festive company may not be made of women slaves and minors. *Op. cit.*, 8, 7; Danby,
p. 148.
[20] *Op. cit.*, 10, 4; Danby, p. 150. The Passover, the unleavened bread, and the bitter
herbs had to be explained.
[21] *Op. cit.*, 10, 7; Danby, p. 151.
[22] *Op. cit.*, 10, 8; Danby, p. 151. The traditional interpretation is that the meal ends
without "dessert." Also the meal must be finished by midnight. *Mishnah*, Zebahim
(Animal-offerings), 5, 8; Danby, p. 475.

to spend the night there in prayer? These are questions we cannot answer. But this much we can know: He certainly enters most enthusiastically into all the details of the symbolic ritual of the Passover.

On the following day, the 15th of Nisan, the boy Jesus wholeheartedly begins the celebration of the feast of unleavened bread, which will last seven days in all, to commemorate the bitter hardship endured by the Jews in the land of Egypt and the deliverance therefrom. On the first day there is a special slain thank-offering, the second Chaggigah, besides the usual "sacrifices of joyousness" for gifts received. Then on the next day, the 16th of Nisan, the young Savior joins in the spirit of the beautiful ceremony expressive of God's ownership and dominion when crowds march into the Temple with the newly-cut sheaf of the first barley, which is taken by the priest and waved over the altar to signify its being given to God. The four succeeding days, the so-called minor festivals, see many of the pilgrims who live at a distance depart for home. Not so the members of the holy family; as implied in the Gospel text, they stay on to the end of the feast to celebrate the 21st of Nisan, a major feast of holy convocation.

Frequently during these seven days' stay at Jerusalem, the holy family are to be found in the great house of God, mingling their voices with the great chorus of hymns and prayers that arise from the Court of Israel. They are to be seen frequently at the regular morning and evening sacrifices and at the special services conducted in the Temple. As in this one pilgrimage to God's appointed shrine they commemorate three feasts, those of the Passover, of unleavened bread, and of first fruits, the thoughts of the members of the holy family turn with all Israel to what is suggested and implied by the symbolic ritual enacted: deliverance and redemption. They alone, however, realize that the earnest prayer of pious Israelites that God should soon send His Messiah to inaugurate His golden reign of peace and power was in process of being granted in the person of Our Savior.

By His presence and example the boy Jesus consecrates anew these ceremonies of the paschal pilgrimage and gives them a new meaning. Through type and prophecy He sees and looks forward to the fulfillment when the Passover meal will be the occasion of His giving His body and blood as the spiritual food of men, and when as the Lamb of God He will shed His blood for the remission of sin and for eternal redemption. Indeed, He is looking forward to the great fulfillment, when in His Father's heavenly home His well-beloved from all lands will be gathered around the marriage feast of the King's Son to enjoy it securely and eternally.

BIBLIOGRAPHY

Callan-McHugh. The Psalms Explained for Priests and Students.
Dalman, G. Jesus-Jeshua, pp. 86–184.
———. Sacred Sites and Ways, pp. 285–307.
Danby (ed.). The Mishnah, Pesahim (Feast of Passover), pp. 136–51.
Eaton, R. Sing Ye to the Lord.
Knox, R. The Psalms.
Liber Psalmorum cum canticis Brevarii Romani (nova editio) of the Pontifical Biblical Institute.
McClellan, W. H. Psalms, Latin-English Edition.
Oesterley, W. A Fresh Approach to the Psalms.
Schauss, H. The Jewish Festivals, pp. 38–55.
Smith, G. A. The Historical Geography of the Holy Land, II, 521–55.

Shepherding near Nazareth

CHAPTER XIX

The Boy Jesus among the Doctors

SEVERAL times before IIis twelfth year Christ had probably accompanied the Virgin Mother and St. Joseph on their yearly Passover pilgrimage and had returned with them to live the ordinary life at Nazareth. These parents had become accustomed to His traveling with the pilgrim contingent from Nazareth. Naturally, like other boys, He occasionally passed from one group to another of relatives and friends during the journey to and from Jerusalem and during the stay in the Holy City. Just as there was a fixed hour and place for the starting of the pilgrimage, so also for departure from Jerusalem the appointed time and meeting spot were well known to all the members. Most likely as the sacred city was disgorging its thousands of festive visitors there would be a certain amount of confusion. Then the unit of about a hundred from Nazareth must have had another unit immediately before and immediately after it as it moved out. When the Nazareth contingent was finally clear of the city on its way home, it probably extended for several hundred yards on the road; thus it was difficult to make a canvass of all the members to ascertain whether anybody was missing until the first camp place was reached at the end of the first day's journey. On the occasion of the departure for home in the pilgrimage of Jesus' twelfth year, His parents did not pay attention to the fact that they did not see Him, knowing that He was aware of the place and hour of departure and feeling He would notify them if for any reason He was not joining His returning townspeople. The Blessed Mother and St. Joseph held their place in the line of march, persuaded that He was somewhere in the Nazareth contingent. Only at nightfall, when all the groups of relatives and acquaintances could be contacted as they were preparing to camp, did His "parents" make inquiries among all the people of the company with whom He was at all likely to be, and discovered to their great dismay that He was missing.[1] Worry and solicitude tore at the hearts of the Blessed Mother and the foster father during the first night while they waited for dawn to continue the search for the missing Boy. All the next day they sorrowfully retraced their steps making inquiries along the way. Then in the Holy City, which they reached that evening, He was not to be found at the usual lodging places. On the third day, after searching for Him through the streets of the city, they unexpectedly came across a scene in the Temple where He was the central figure among the doctors. Who were these "doctors" introduced into the picture?

After the time of Esdras there grew up a body of biblical scholars who devoted themselves to the study of the Sacred Scriptures, especially the five books of Moses, known as the Law. They became an independent class, and by the time of Our Lord were a profession in themselves, learned in the sacred text and the real teachers of the people. They were known as doctors or teachers of the Law, scribes, jurists, or lawyers. Extraordinary respect and reverence were paid them, as is shown by the titles of honor accorded them in address, such as the usual one, "My Master." This

---

[1] The traditional place of the missing is el-Bireh. As this camp site is only nine miles from Jerusalem, the presumption is that the Nazareth contingent got a late start from the Holy City. If a full day's journey (Luke 2:44) had been completed, the place would be el-Lubban, which is in Judea close to the border of Samaria. Cf. Dalman, *Sacred Sites and Ways,* p. 216.

is the literal meaning of the word "rabbi," which after Our Lord's time became the name of the class as well as a title of address. The chief function of the scribes was the teaching of the Law. The method they used was mostly repetition or memory work. But they also taught by asking questions, which they often answered themselves, and by having their pupils propose questions. The pupils sat on the ground, while the teachers sat on an elevated platform.

In their zeal for the strict acceptance of the Law the scribes elaborated what they called a "hedge" around it by preserving oral traditions and interpretations which they claimed went back to Esdras and even to Moses. With their contention that oral tradition was of equal standing with the sacred text, the Savior took sharp issue in His public ministry. He asserted that the oral tradition of the scribes was opposed to the spirit of the inspired word. He condemned these fabricators of laws for their hypocrisy in making heavy burdens for the people which they themselves eluded by subterfuge. He counseled the people to follow the advice of the scribes but not their example. Indeed the wisdom of some of the earlier ones is enshrined in the pages of the Old Testament, since it was inspired by the Holy Ghost.

As to the two famous scribes, Shammai and Hillel, the first was already dead when Christ was twelve years of age; but the second would be about seventy-five years old if he was still living. In contrast to the stern Shammia, Hillel was noted for his mildness as can be seen from one of his maxims handed down, "Be a disciple of Aaron, a lover and maker of peace, love men and attract them to the Law." According to some scholars, Hillel's son was Simon, and his grandson was Gamaliel I. This latter was the teacher of St. Paul (Acts 22:3); and we can have a great respect for his prudence and judgment from the advice he rendered on the occasion of the trial of the apostles (Acts 5:34–39). This Gamaliel could have been among the teachers and Nicodemus among the pupils when the boy Jesus was found in the Temple.

Within the great Temple enclosure, in one of the porticoes of the sacred edifice, especially when great crowds were in the Holy City for important feasts, the learned doctors of the Law discoursed on erudite subjects to an entranced audience.[2] We know from the Gospels that Our Lord took advantage of this practice to preach to the people within the sacred precincts before, during, and after the various feasts. "He was teaching daily in the Temple," says St. Luke (18:14), speaking of the last week of Christ's earthly life when He made use of the house of God as the place to expound His doctrines to the Jews from at home and abroad who were preparing to attend the last, tragic Passover. Now in His twelfth year, He deliberately separated Himself from those who had the privilege of being His earthly relatives to associate Himself with the official teachers of the Jewish religion. This He did, be it noted, not merely for one hour or one day but for three days. During this period of time He may have obtained food from one of these scribes or their friends and He may have lodged with one of them at night. In any case it was at great inconvenience to Himself as well as at the expense of great sorrow to those nearest and dearest to Him that He took part in this group discussion of religious topics conducted by the scribes within the sacred precincts of the Temple. To form an opinion on the nature of this discussion or on the part that the boy Christ played in it, one has to examine carefully the concise wording of the Gospel narrative which notes the effect produced on the doctors and the blessed parents.

First, from the words, "They found Him in the Temple, sitting in the midst of the doctors" (Luke 2:46), it is clearly indicated that the scene which the Virgin Mother and her spouse encountered in the sacred edifice was not that of a class of pupils around a teacher. Let us note that the sacred text does not say that the boy Jesus was among the pupils; rather it expressly states that He was among the teachers and in a central position among them,

---

[2] It was told of Rabbi Johanen ben Zakai that he sat in the shade of the Temple and lectured all day. He used the open court because he could not find a room large enough to accommodate his audience. *Babylonian Talmud*, Pesahim (Passover), ed. by M. Rodkinson, V, 38.

which is the meaning of "in the midst of." The text also says that
He was hearing them; and further that He was propounding questions to them, and in turn He was giving answers to their questions.
The effect, not only on the doctors but on all others who were
listening is thus summarily described: "And all that heard Him
were astonished at His wisdom and His answers." Here is a case
where the Greek word used in the text is not adequately expressed
by a single English word, but requires several words. The word
which is translated "astonished" signifies "to be beside oneself
with wonder," to be bewildered or stupefied with astonishment
because of a preternatural occurrence. Hence the learned rabbis
and all who were witnesses of the scene were looking at the boy
Jesus as at a great prodigy displaying inexplicable, preternatural
intelligence. Be it remembered that it is not peasants or citizens of
a country town who are astounded by a mere boy of twelve, but
the most learned people of that time, the well-trained, erudite
rabbis of Jerusalem.

The Virgin Mother and St. Joseph who joined the outskirts of
the crowd around the boy Christ also joined in the bewilderment.
There is, however, a different word used to express their wonderment. It denotes a combination of feelings—shock, fear, amazement—and can be translated as "awestruck." This extreme reaction
of His "parents" to the scene which greeted their eyes can be explained by the fact that it was entirely unexpected, for they had
grown accustomed to His acting as an ordinary boy. This was the
reason, too, why it was with extreme anxiety and solicitude that they
sought for Him through the crowds on the way back to Jerusalem,
through the suburbs and through the streets of the Holy City. Then
on the third day of their sorrowful search, their hearts torn by care
and sorrow, they suddenly come upon this scene of their boy Jesus,
modest in mien and behavior, sitting among the doctors, discours-
ing with these learned men, the noticeable feature of the whole
scene being the fact that these famous teachers of Israel were
wearing a look of stupefaction and amazement because of the

preternatural intelligence He was displaying. No wonder His parents were momentarily filled with awe; in fact, their shocked reaction speaks eloquently for the extraordinary character of the affair as they knew Him better than anyone else. Hence a mere display of precocity could scarcely account for the great amazement which the scene brought to them.

What really happened was therefore probably the following. The twelve-year-old Jesus had deliberately stayed behind when the group from Nazareth left for home. It must have been on the day of departure that He began His discussion with the doctors. It was an ordinary occurrence for a boy to question the Jewish experts of the Law, as these men loved to be consulted by anyone. But this proved to be no ordinary affair. Nor was it a few clever questions with a few witty answers. It continued for several hours each day for three days; to be sure not at night, when the Temple was closed. It was a free discussion, and of course not a lecture. He proposed questions which led through intricate and important problems. At first the scribes did not suspect the depth and directive force of these questions; finally, however, they began to question one another regarding the answers to the boy Jesus' questions. Then, when no answer could be given by the leading rabbis of Israel, to the profound astonishment of all, the beardless Youth who had proposed the subtle questions began to answer them with lucidity and aptness. The best and sincerest of the scribes became intensely interested as did also many of the audience. As Jesus continued to meet questions with additional questions and thus to lead the discussion, His masterly control over learned subjects and the brilliant flashes of His profound insight into dark problems were gradually made evident to all. From His position in the audience He was invited to take a seat in the center of the learned teachers themselves, which He did with modesty and grace. There sitting in their midst He continued His searching questions; He continued to listen to the attempts at answers; and He continued to give

crystal clear explanations revealing a most extraordinary understanding.

The keenness of His mind and His insight into the most baffling
problems convinced these masters that in this mere Boy they had
found an expert. A great part of their amazement arose from the
fact that there was no haughtiness about this Boy-prodigy, rather a
winning modesty of bearing and a kind forebearance toward the
opinions of others. This with the golden words of wisdom and grace
which fell so naturally from His lips made a happy combination.
Who is this Boy who in the gutteral Galilean accent proposes such
pointed questions and gives such brilliant answers? Where did He
come from? How did He acquire this profound knowledge? How
explain this powerful intellect, and this mastery over erudite subjects? How appealing His modesty and how captivating His words
which warm the human heart and lead it to God! In His display
of heavenly wisdom, in His elucidation of the approach of God's
kingdom, how marvelous! How miraculous! Never before did
anyone speak like this Boy. Questions and exclamations of stupefaction were heard on all sides among the doctors and the audience.

In all sober history there is nothing like the account of the boy
Jesus among the doctors. Lately there has been a tendency to min-
imize the episode, to dwarf it to the mere showing of precocity and
flashes of budding genius. Yet the Evangelist, here as everywhere
our infallible guide, used the strongest word to express the utter
astonishment of the learned jurists, a word which indicates that the
occurrence which they witnessed was inexplicable by natural causes.
Popular pictures do not do justice to the Gospel wording in depicting the astonishment of the doctors. Indeed, cold canvas [3] must
fail in portraying the strongest human emotions.

The Fathers of the Church as a rule use the word "disputing"
when referring to what Christ was doing among the doctors. Origen

[3] The scene has been painted by many artists, such as Da Vinci, Dobson, Doré, Dürer,
Giotto, Hofmann, Hunt, Luini, Mazzolino, Veronese, Adrian Van de Werff, Thumann,
Tissot. In many of the paintings, the boy Jesus is not sitting but standing.

especially supplies us with several worth-while comments. He points out that the subjects brought up by Jesus' questions were answered by Himself and that these answers of His were a matter of wonder even more than the questions, however marvelous these may have been.[4] For Origen it was because Our Lord was yet young that He is found sanctifying and instructing teachers and also because of His youth He is found not teaching but questioning; for it is the part of youth to listen rather than to make a display of teaching. Yet Origen insists that the questioning of the doctors by the Christ was not that He might learn anything, "but that He might instruct while questioning."[5] This writer further observes that from the same fountain of knowledge and science come both the art of wisely interrogating and the art of making wise answers, and that Jesus had first to be a master of the erudite subject before He could expound it by question and answer. The result according to Origen was profitable instruction for the doctors because they were prompted to make inquiries and thus to obtain information on certain matters which they did not previously know.[6]

St. Jerome is ingenious and succinct when he states that the boy Jesus in the Temple "interrogating the elders on questions of the Law rather taught while He prudently asked questions." Likewise the Syrian scholar, St. Ephraim,[7] expresses the same thought in his characteristic way: Our Lord "lowered Himself and asked that He might hear and learn what He knew; that He might by His questions reveal the treasures of His helpful graces."

We would greatly like to know the topics that were discussed between the boy Christ and the doctors. It has been suggested that they were scriptural subjects, intricate points of law, knotty paschal questions, or pressing problems concerning the Messiah. Perhaps specimens of the discussion may be found in the accounts of the public ministry, such as the provocative questions about the

[4] *Hom. XVIII, In Lucam; PG*, 13, 1848.
[5] *Hom. XIX, In Lucam; PG*, 13, 1851.
[6] *Hom. XX, In Lucam; PG, loc. cit.*
[7] *Hymn on the Nativity*, II; *NPN*, 2nd ser., XIII, 228.

son of David being called Lord (Matt. 22:41–46). Would Jesus' reply to His Mother's anxious question be a specimen? It was a deep, mysterious saying that was to be understood only in the light of His entire life.

We may be sure that the subjects of discussion were not frivolous, nor were they taken at random. Rather they had order and purpose and were constructive as well as informative. Before the preaching of St. John the Baptist the scribes sat in the chair of Moses, and under God's providence were the official guides of the chosen people. To a group of these official teachers the young Messiah devoted a few days of instruction in His own way by question and answer—the customary method of that time. It was an evangelical prelude to the great message which the Jewish nation was to hear proclaimed on the hillsides of Palestine twenty years later. Thus, in taking a hand in the training of some of the official advisers of the Jews He was participating in the great work of preparation for the coming of the kingdom of God, the work for which the prophets had done their share, and the Baptist was to give such signal service. Jesus was Himself preparing soil for the sowing. Who can tell where the Gospel seedlings which He planted in the minds of the group of jurists and their audience may have fructified? In a young Lazarus? In Nicodemus? In Gamaliel? In a parent of a future apostle? The Holy Spirit had inspired holy Simeon and the prophetess Anna to recognize the Messiah in the infant of forty days. Through their knowledge of astrology or astronomy the Magi had been led by God from the east to adore the divine Child. Now the Son of God, Wisdom Himself, when twelve years of age, breaks the long silence of the hidden life to take a hand in the cause of truth and grace with the experts on the Sacred Scriptures in the house of God.

The modest, docile example of Jesus asking questions to learn the opinion of the doctors is pointed to by St. Gregory the Great in his warning to the weak and inexperienced lest they attempt to teach: "He is found not teaching, but asking questions. By which example it is plainly shown that none who are weak should venture to teach, if that Child was willing to be taught by asking questions, who by the power of His divinity supplied the word of knowledge to His teachers themselves." [8] The young especially may well hold before them the model of the boy Jesus in their application to school work and in the improving of their minds. For the patience and perseverance required during the wearisome hours of the class-room, teachers can find inspiration and encouragement in the Gospel account of the boy Christ in the role of teacher for three days. For an incentive to zeal in spreading the Gospel and bringing salvation to souls, there is the personal example of Jesus delivering His evangelical prelude in spite of inconvenience to Himself and sorrow to His nearest and dearest.

BIBLIOGRAPHY

Fillion, L. The Life of Christ, I, 374–87.
Lagrange, J. M. Evangile selon S. Luc, pp. 93–97.
Prat, F. Jésus-Christ, I, 124–29.
Strack and Billerbeck. Kommentar zum neuen Testament aus Talmud und Midrasch, II, 141–47.
Temple, P. The Boyhood Consciousness of Christ, pp. 121–34.
Valensin and Huby. Evangile selon S. Luc, pp. 45–49.

[8] *Pastoral Rule*, III, 25; PL, 67, 98. In another place (*In Ezech.*, 1, hom., II, PL, 76, 796) he writes: "So that men in infirm age would not dare to preach, He deigned in His twelfth year to ask men who by His divinity always teaches the angels in heaven."

CHAPTER XX

The Boy Jesus' Words

THERE has been preserved for us one saying of Our Lord uttered apart from the public ministry; only once did He break for us the long silence of His hidden life. That instance was when He replied to His Mother's anxious question, why He had tarried in Jerusalem at the cost of three days of sorrow and solicitude on the part of herself and St. Joseph. His reply was a short one; but it mentions His unique relationship with God the Father and His obligation to be engaged in the Father's interests. Because of the reference to both His nature and His mission, this succinct saying can serve as an excellent heading for a treatise on Christ's life and work. This early self-interpretation, affording us a welcome glimpse into the first thirty years of His sacred life, gives us the key to that whole life. These few precious words of Jesus are testimonials of His zeal, His spirit of sacrifice, His irrevocable dedication to His Father's will, the guiding principle of His life, springing from His relationship as the eternal divine Son of God.

The earliest recorded saying of Our Lord was prompted by a question from the Virgin Mother as she was recovering from the effects of sudden awe and amazement brought on by finding her twelve-year-old Son sitting among the astonished doctors of the Law. The sorrow that had weighed heavily upon her and her spouse, St. Joseph, for the three days they had wearily and anxiously sought for Him, came back to her mind. She referred to Jesus as "Son," and she called St. Joseph "Thy father" because he was the legal father. She was not insisting on her rights, but only intimating them. Nor was she looking for an apology; she was asking for an explanation: "Son, why hast Thou done so to us?" She was expecting an adequate explanation and she received one.

By replying, "How is it that you sought Me? Did you not know?" The Christ boy drew attention to the fact of His virgin birth and to the unique relationship in which He stood to God, whom He alone could call "My Father" in the strictest and fullest sense. In saying further, "I must be about My Father's business," He pointed out that, because of His unique dignity as the only-begotten Son of God, there was necessarily an identification between His Father's interests and His and there was a special necessity for Him to be ever inseparable from His Father's will. He was recalling the reason why He came into the world, which is so well put in His mouth in the words of the Psalmist (39:8 f.): "Then said I, behold I come; in the head of the book it is written of Me that I should do Thy will, O My God." As a dutiful child in the happy home at Nazareth, leading an ordinary life, He was doing the Father's will. That same Father's will now called for an evangelical prelude here in the Temple, even though it proved to be the occasion of heart-rending sorrow to those so dear to Him. Thus it was a hint of what was to come, of what must be expected and hence prepared for. From this lesson Mary learns to be ready for her dreadful ordeal, to stand heroically and unflinchingly at the foot of the cross, considering it a privilege to suffer with God. Mary has no choice but to cooperate with His work of redemption.

Thus, to explain the necessity for being the occasion of three days of worry and sorrow to His Blessed Mother, the boy Jesus gave so complete a justification that she could understand it fully only when the shadow of the cross had finally passed over His life. Mary realized then the meaning of that boyhood saying. She realized that it had been only human and natural for her to draw attention to the exalted privilege which she enjoyed in being His Mother, the Mother of the incarnate Word; but that, on the other hand, it was right for the God-man to draw attention to the fact that not human standards and measures must be His, but rather the most extraordinary rules and methods. She was delighted, then, that human rights and feelings were sacrificed in the interests of that great Messianic mission which her Son, by a divine decree, had of necessity to carry out. She realized that anything she suffered was compensated for by the solace and consolation of the Boy's wonderful words with which He upheld His sublime nature and mission. This saying she dearly cherished. It not only comforted her; it became the guiding principle of her life, helping her to consider it her high privilege to suffer not only in the outburst of zeal of the twelfth year, but also when the hour came for her Son to drink the chalice of suffering to its bitter dregs.

The name of God on the lips of the boy Jesus was "My Father." The Savior of the public ministry preached a threefold grade of God's fatherhood: By creation God was Father of all; He was especially Father of the disciples on account of adoption and participation in the divine nature; the special and unique grade was reserved for Himself as the eternal Son of God become man. He never included Himself in the title for God, "Our Father," which he taught His disciples to use. He Himself always said, "My Father," and He called Himself "the Son." This corresponded with the words, "My beloved Son in whom I am well pleased," which the Father addressed from the cloud. It also corresponded with the titles "His own Son," "the Son of God," "the only-begotten Son of God," which His disciples used of Him in His lifetime and which have been repeated ever since. In giving us His most important revelation that in the nature of God there are three divine persons, Father, Son, and Holy Ghost, the chief burden of His preaching and His central doctrine was that He Himself was the true, eternal Son of God. In accordance with His teaching He addressed God as "My Father." Indeed, this name "Father" was His most frequent name for God and the one that dominated His whole thought of God. So that His usage of "My Father" for God expressed what was most characteristic in His teaching, namely, His own divine sonship. Yet this is the name for God which we hear from the lips of the twelve-year-old Savior. It is uttered by Him in a completely matter-of-fact way. It is accentuated because it is coupled with the sacred word "must" and because it is contrasted with the closest of human ties. Thus, for the first time, we hear from Christ, the profession of the most sublime truth, His ineffable, unique relationship with God the Father.

Christ's first words contain a reference to His divine mission as well as to His divine nature. Because He is the Son of God, He must do God's will. This will required that, instead of accompanying His parents, and departing for home, He remain in the Temple to take a hand in the work of preparation for the kingdom of God. He must be about His work at any cost, even though it means pain to those bound to Him by the closest of human ties. Thus by His actions He was giving a foretaste and, as it were, a demonstration of His future career and was laying down a policy of His whole life.

The Savior of the public ministry loved to repeat that He was always doing the will of His eternal Father. Thus He declared: "I came down from heaven, not to do My will, but the will of Him who sent Me" (John 6:38). "I do always the things that please Him" (John 8:29). Indeed He considered it His very meat to do God's will: "My meat is to do the will of Him who sent Me" (John 4:34), "I seek not My own will, but the will of Him who sent Me" (John 5:30). He repeatedly said He did only what the Father wanted: 'The Son cannot do anything of Himself, but what He seeth the Father doing (John 5:19), "The works which the Father has given Me to perfect" (John 5:36). More than that, He stated that all that He did was commanded by God: "This commandment have I received of My Father (John 10:18), "As the Father hath given Me commandment, so do I" (John 14:31;

15:10), "I do know Him and do keep His word" (John 8:55). Jesus even declared that He must do God's will and God's works: "I must work the works of Him who sent Me" (John 9:4). He frequently uses this word "must" to express the fact that because of a divine decree there was an obligation on Him to carry out the mission received from His Father, especially to suffer and to die on the cross. Thus He used this strong word "must" when He wished to express this obligation of spreading the gospel in other towns of Galilee (Luke 4:43), and when He insisted that of necessity He was to suffer and to be rejected (Luke 9:22; 17:25). A divine decree that no civil government could prevent foreordained that He meet His death at Jerusalem (Luke 13:33; 22:22; John 10:18). This decree was, of course, found in the Sacred Scriptures which must needs be fulfilled before He would enter into His glory (Luke 22:37; 24:26, 44).

Christ's will was in such a thorough accord with the will of His Father that He could not separate Himself from that will and was obedient to it, even to the death of the cross. This was as a necessary consequence of the union in Him of the divine and human natures. The human nature in Him was carried along in the current of the divine so that everything about Him was for the Father and, to express this disposition of His soul, He could say: "I live by the Father" (John 6:58; 14:10). This fundamental disposition is voiced in the saying of the boy Jesus, where it is supported by the strongest of words, "must," and where it is put forward in opposition to the closest and dearest of human ties, that of parent to child.

According to some interpreters, Christ's words are to be understood in the sense that there was no need for the parents to search for Him since He was easily to be found in His Father's house. In this view the Savior implies that God's house is His own house and that as Son He is over the Father's household and at home in the Father's house. During the public life He cleansed this same Temple and in indignant words hurled against the pro-

faners, He used this expression for the Temple, "My Father's
house." Already in His twelfth year He briefly interrupts the hidden life to take charge, so to speak, of the teaching in the Temple
and to assert that, as the Son, He is to be found in His Father's
house. Thus, in His calling the Temple His Father's house, He
lays claim to the dignity of the Son of God in the highest sense
of the word, as Messiah and as God's only-begotten Son.

Yet it seems that in the ellipsis found in the saying of the boy
Christ, there is to be understood something more than the Temple.
For an ellipsis is employed to indicate a place only when it is evident
that it is not necessary to mention such a place. Now, the Temple
was not popularly known as the Father's house. Then, as the Gospel text states, when Jesus was found in the Temple He was hearing the scribes and questioning them. Would we not expect,
therefore, that, in giving the Blessed Mother and St. Joseph the
reason for not accompanying them as they returned home, Jesus
would indicate not only the place where He was to be found,
but also what He was doing there, what detained Him there? Moreover, the Gospel account itself insinuates that the saying of Christ
was more complex and more comprehensive than a mere indication of the place where He was to be found; for it adds the
significant remark that "His parents" did not understand it. So
that this first recorded saying like many others of Our Lord was
understood only in the light of His whole life. Let us recall that
the apostles did not understand the many references to Christ's
death and resurrection when He first uttered them. Neither did the
Virgin Mother and St. Joseph understand the boy Jesus when He
announced a policy that was to dominate His whole life and that
was insisted upon in so many sayings during the public ministry;
namely, that at all costs He must be always engaged in the Father's
interests. Those were "the word and will of the Father from which
the Son cannot separate Himself." [1]

[1] Dalman, *Sacred Sites and Ways*, p. 301. Our Lord's will was unalterably holy and
perfectly attuned to the will of His Father. Cf. Scheeben, *The Mysteries of Christianity*,
p. 330; St. Thomas, *Summa theol.*, IIIa, q.13–15.

Christ's answer to His mother, according to St. Cyril of Alexandria,[2] shows that He was more than human and teaches her that she was the chosen handmaid to become His mother in giving birth to Him, but that, by nature and in truth, He was God and the Son of the heavenly Father. St. Ambrose [3] also holds that the Blessed Mother learned from her divine Son; as a pupil she was here corrected by Him, for she had demanded what was human. Likewise, St. Augustus [4] takes the Savior's words addressed to His parents to mean that He does not wish to be their Son in such a way that He would not be understood to be the Son of God; nor, by indicating God as His Father, does He wish to deny they are His parents.

Indeed, already in the early part of the fifth century, St. Cyril of Alexandria pointed to the words "My Father" in the saying of the boy Jesus and argued that, because He made use of them instead of "Our Father" or "the Father of all," He showed He was divinely born of God from all eternity and that in becoming man He retained His divine nature and divine sonship.[5] Following this Father of the Church, Catholic scholars see in the first recorded saying of Our Lord an expression of His divine sonship. They also agree that here Christ mentioned His Messianic mission. Indeed, the staying behind and the three days' discussion with the doctors entailed hardship for Jesus and sorrow and anxiety for His dear parents. Then, in answer to the question that asked for the reason, He justified His action on the basis of His virgin birth and His divine sonship. Here, then, was some part of His mission, a part of His life of endurance or vicarious life offered for the redemption of mankind.

Jesus' tarrying in the Temple without the permission or authority

---

[2] *Commentary on Luke, ad. loc.; PG, 72, 509.*

[3] *Ibid., Corp. Script. Lat., 32, 75.*

[4] *Concordance of the Gospels, II, 10; PL, 35, 342 f.*

[5] *De recta fide ad reginas; PG, 76, 1320.* Theodoret of Cyprus wrote that Our Lord in His first words, while defending Himself, "quietly reveals His divinity." *On the Incarnation; PG, 84, 73.* For the comments of the Fathers on Luke 2:49, see Temple, *The Boyhood Consciousness of Christ,* pp. 3–12.

of Mary and Joseph could not be justified if He were an ordinary boy. His display of preternatural wisdom before the learned rabbis marks Him off as superior to all other boys and to all other men. Then His saying was not that of an ordinary boy or that of any ordinary man. Indeed, a saying that claimed in an emphatic way an obligation to God that superseded the closest of human ties, a saying that was deep and mysterious beyond the comprehension of His parents, this saying assertive of divine independence, is the saying of a divine person.

The words that Jesus employed to explain why He stayed behind to cast gospel seedlings among the rabbis of Jerusalem could be used by Him in every moment of His divine life. The emphatic assertion of the twelve-year-old could well apply to His birth at Bethlehem, His flight into Egypt, His subjection to the requirements of the Law, His humble life at Nazareth, and the missionary activities of His public life. Especially, the first recorded saying could have been said on the cross most appropriately, for it is a dedication of Christ's sufferings and death, and a consecration of His whole life. Certainly the assertive saying of the boyhood years reveals the dedication and consecration of the hidden life to the Father and stands out as the high point of the hidden life. It is the voice of the long silent years preaching to men of all generations the obligation of prompt, ungrudging, unflinching dedication to the continual acknowledgment of the sovereignty of God.

In this short saying of Jesus there is, therefore, a wealth of meaning. In these few words we find the purpose of His life proclaimed in an assertive manner. We find enunciated a policy of the public life: that the greatest human sacrifices must be made to carry out the will of God. We find the boy Christ already reaching the climax of His most sublime teaching in His expression of eternal divine sonship. If anything approaching this earliest recorded saying was uttered by the Christ before the doctors, it is no wonder that they were beside themselves with amazement. Indeed, the depth of this saying is in harmony with St. Luke's previous statement about the child Jesus, that He was "full of wisdom."

Although the subjects discussed in the scene before the doctors have not been handed down, there have been preserved, fortunately for us, the words which Jesus spoke in answer to His Blessed Mother's question. They are words worthy of the Son of God united to His eternal Father in love, in thought, and in action. They are words worthy of the Messiah, the divine Messiah come to establish God's reign of grace, concerned only with His mission and work. Our Savior's short saying is a great self-revelation to which one could devote deep study and profound contemplation. His display of intelligence before the doctors and His self-revelation in His first recorded words are the counterpart of His manifestation in the adoration of the Magi. This saying of His, which casts illuminating rays on His person and office, is the crowning feature of His entire hidden life. What a tribute to its profound and far-reaching significance is the fact that even for His Virgin Mother who, being closest to Him, knew more of God's secrets than any other human being, the Son's saying is clarified only by His life and death! Also what a tribute to its mysterious richness that this explanation of His reason for tarrying in the Temple was cherished so lovingly in her heart!

Jesus' words teach us that our first and chief concern should be God's will in all things. Our eternal Father, who made us and conserves us and therefore owns us in every way, we must obey and serve above all. We are to bear in mind that we are closer to Him than to anyone else, and accordingly our greatest obligation is to Him. We are to remember on the other hand that other people, no matter who they are, are closer to God than to us and are much more bound to God than to us (Matt. 10:35 f.). In the heroic person of the Son of God we have a most sublime example which should daily stimulate us toward the accomplishment of God's will; for, intent on being about His Father's business, He shed the last drop of His blood, thus saving men and bringing them to the knowledge of God's truth.

BIBLIOGRAPHY

Becker, T. The Hidden Life of Christ, pp. 108–11.
Fillion, L. The Life of Christ, I, 385–87.
Lagrange, J. M. The Gospel of Jesus Christ, I, 50–53.
O'Shea, D. The Holy Family, p. 210–12.
Simon, H. Praelectiones biblicae; Novum Testamentum I, 179.
Stoll, R. The Gospel according to St. Luke, pp. 50 f.
Temple, P. The Boyhood Consciousness of Christ.

CHAPTER XXI

The Boy Jesus and His Parents

AT the close of the episode of the boy Jesus in the Temple, the Evangelist writes: "And He went down with them and came to Nazareth and was subject to them" (Luke 2: 51). The form of the verb "was subject to" in the original signifies voluntary and continual obedience on the part of Jesus during the succeeding years at Nazareth where He resumed the role of living "the life of the many." As one who had declared His own divine sonship, He did not owe obedience to those who were privileged to be His earthly "parents"; for as Creator He superseded all laws that He Himself made. On the other hand, He respected His own institutions and economies and sanctioned responsibilities arising therefrom. It was only when the obligation of His mission required it for a few days during His visit to the Temple in His twelfth year that He acted above human parental authority and above natural law. Yet this was followed by His free resumption of His place as a member of the holy family, the lowest place to all outward appearances. He began again and continued to give obedience and to pay respect to St. Joseph His legal father, in the eyes of the townspeople of Nazareth His real father. He also gladly began again His life of devotion and loyalty to His Virgin Mother, cheerfully carrying out her wishes and always catering to her needs. As

St. Jerome writes: "He venerated the mother of whom He himself was the parent, and He cherished the foster-father whom He himself had nourished; for He remembered that He had been carried in the womb of the one and in the arms of the other." [1]

But the sacred text adds: "His mother kept all these things in her heart" (Luke 2:51). The force of the words implies the continuous, loving storing away in Mary's memory of the events of Christ's twelfth year. We were previously told that the incidents of Christ's birth had been lovingly laid away in the mother's memory for correlation and reflection, "but Mary kept in mind all these words, pondering them in her heart" (Luke 2:19). These two texts are indications that she herself is the final authority for the accounts of the holy Infancy found in the Third Gospel.

The angelic manifestations to the shepherds at the Nativity were revolved in the Mother's mind and were found to be in harmony with the great truth announced by Gabriel that her Son was the Son of God. Again the sacred historian thought it worth while to inform us that Mary preserved in her memory the incidents of Christ's twelfth year; although from a merely human point of view we would expect she would wish to forget; such as His deliberate staying behind at the expense of prolonged worry to herself and St. Joseph and His mysterious answer to her anxious questions, seemingly offering no apology. Then, on the one hand, He had manifested preternatural knowledge before the learned rabbis and had expressed His divine sonship that required His inseparable dedication to the Father's interests; yet, on the other hand, the fact was that He returned to His ordinary home at Nazareth and continued to subject Himself to her and the foster father. "All these things," were mysteries she stored away carefully in her motherly heart where she adored the divine will. The pain and loss of the three days of anxious searching were not remembered with resentment but with joy for the privilege of enduring a trial in the cause of her divine Son and His eternal Father.

[1] *Letter*, 119; *Corp. Script. Lat.*, LV, 425; *Select Letters* ed. by E. Wright, p. 375.

The inspired text,[2] therefore, recording how the Blessed Mother treasured the words and actions of Christ's twelfth year, which in the case of any merely human boy would be counted disobedience, is a Scriptural indication that Mary considered her Son to be really and truly the Son of God. Christ's conduct and His words justifying it were accepted by His mother not as coming from a twelve-year-old boy but as belonging to the all-perfect Son of God who had been conceived by the Holy Ghost.[3] Thus the statement that the Virgin Mother stored away in her heart the details of the episode of her Son in the Temple furnishes the key to her whole life. It shows that the incident had a profound influence on her, insinuates that the mysterious words of the boy Christ more than compensated for the ordeal of the three days' loss, and indicates that her life was one of devotion and service to Jesus.

From among the daughters of Eve, Mary had been chosen for the greatest of privileges, as His Mother, to be nearest and dearest to the God-man. How direct she was in question about her perpetual virginity when the archangel Gabriel delivered his remarkable message! What exceptional knowledge befitting her exalted position did she reveal in her Magnificat! How firm her faith in the word of the archangel, praised by Elizabeth! How

---

[2] Some ancient commentators, such as Scholia Vetera (In Lucam; PG, 106, 1187) and Theophylactus (Ennaratio in Evangl. Lucae; PG, 125, 725), commenting on Luke 2:19, point out that Mary revolved the incidents of the holy childhood in her mind and found that they were in harmony with the great fact that her Son was the Son of God. See St. Jerome's remarks on this verse; Homilia de Nativitate Domini; Anecdota Maredsolana, III, 1, 394. Also many Commentators deduce from Luke 2:51 that Mary accepted the conduct and words of the boy Jesus not as coming from one of twelve years but rather that she understood they came from a most perfect Person. Commenting on this verse, 2:19, the Venerable Bede states that when Mary saw the Son of God in the crib she compared what she saw and heard with what she had learned from St. Gabriel, and had read in the Scriptures (In Lucae Evangelium Expositio, I; ad. loc.; PL, 92, 335–6).

[3] Such are the comments on Luke 2:51, as given by Origen, Homilia, 20, In Lucam (PG, 13, 1852); Euthymius Zigabenus, Comment in Lucam, ad loc.; (PG, 129, 889); Symeon Metaphrastes, Oratio de Sancta Maria, 25 (PG, 115, 550); Theophylactus, Ennaratio in Evang. Lucae, 2:51 (PG, 123, 733). In later life, of course, the Blessed Mother's faith and knowledge, as well as her charity were revealed when she asked her divine Son for the miracle of Cana. Likewise, her faith and knowledge, as well as marvelous self-control, were manifested by her brave stand at the foot of the cross.

implicit her trust and confidence in God while she waited for Him to reveal the secret of the Incarnation to her spouse, St. Joseph! When he proceeded with his intended marriage, he took responsibility for Mary's Child; and in the eyes of the law of his time and among the neighbors he was considered the real father. He took up his duties as foster father and protector with holy joy and carried them out with alacrity. But always he kept humbly in the background. In the finding in the Temple he preserved a reverential silence, allowing the Virgin Mother to speak for him as well as for herself because of her close relationship to the divine Savior.

Good pious Jews these parents were. They carefully carried out the requirements of the sacred laws and promptly obeyed all directions of God concerning their wonder Child. They were naturally surprised when they found that others, as Simeon and Anna, were vouchsafed a knowledge of what He was. The prophecy of opposition for the Son and sorrow for the Mother did not open up the future in detail but must have left a lingering shadow. There were joy and consolation when the Magi, heaven-sent, presented their pledges of loyalty and acknowledged His kingship. Yet these were quickly followed by the sorrow occasioned by the deaths of the Holy Innocents and the hardship of exile in Egypt. During the golden years as Jesus grew from childhood to boyhood in the happy home of Nazareth, presumably nothing was spoken among the members of the holy family about His nature and mission. The parents were to merit by faith in Him and dependence on God's providence. To all appearances the Christ boy lived like an ordinary boy. There was so little of the extraordinary about Him that the manifestation before the doctors in His twelfth year constituted a shock to Mary and Joseph. They had become accustomed to His natural way of living and did not expect anything out of the ordinary to happen.

For their Son's tarrying behind on this occasion no one can charge His parents with neglect. The boy Jesus deliberately stayed behind when they thought He was as usual with the caravan from

Nazareth returning home. The Gospel text explicitly states this: "When they returned, the child Jesus remained behind in Jerusalem; and His parents knew it not" (Luke 2:43). It was natural that they became alarmed when they missed Him, for they could not imagine what happened to Him. It was natural that their hearts were torn with sorrow and solicitude as they searched for Him all the way back to Jerusalem and through the streets of the Holy City. Separation from Him was agony and the word the Blessed Mother used when she said, "Thy father and I sought Thee sorrowing," expressed great torturing worry. She called Him "Son," but she implied, while asking for the reason of His doing so, that she was aware He had deliberately stayed behind.

The Blessed Mother's sorrow and amazement were changed into holy joy by the succinct words of Jesus. These conveyed more than an adequate explanation. They afforded comfort and consolation, at the same time bringing confirmation of her faith in Him. His mention of God as His Father recalled the virgin birth and conception of the Holy Ghost. His reference to His mission to be carried out at all costs was prophetic of His public ministry. It was only after her poor heart had been transpierced with the sword of sorrow, when she saw Him carry out His Father's mission to the bitter end, that she fully understood the boyhood saying. She cherished it as part of her education. When she was giving it to St. Luke she recalled that at its first utterance she had not understood it since it did not make known to her fully the divine mystery that later unfolded itself.

Our Lord was, of course, the Blessed Mother's great teacher, educating her for the exalted roles of Queen of Martyrs and Co-operatrix in redemption. The privilege of being the Mother of God was not to exempt her from the sad experiences which she accepted in the proper spirit and which led to Calvary. There was the embarrassment before St. Joseph was told that she was with child of the Holy Ghost. There was the birth of her Son in a cave without ordinary comforts. There was the tarrying in the Temple which cost three days of intense suffering. These and other trials were gradually preparing her for the long, cruel hours at the foot of the cross where she would stand so valiantly, the perfect heroine.

The personal example of her divine Son was the sustaining support for the Virgin Mother. The God of all power and majesty had emptied Himself of His glory in assuming human nature. He hid Himself within her virginal womb; He became a helpless Infant; He subjected Himself to the ordinary laws of growth and human economy; He endured pain in the circumcision and hardship in exile; He lived a simple, humble life as an ordinary youth at Nazareth. Only once, for a brief time, did He exercise His divine independence when the gospel necessity called for it. This was at the cost of sorrow for those nearest and dearest to Him for whom in His heart He must have felt the greatest sympathy; but He took the brave stand, and declared that all must be sacrificed for His eternal Father's interests. All this was not only comfort and solace for her, but also encouragement and inspiration.

Above all, as Mary watched her divine Son subjecting Himself to her and His foster father, doing the daily errands of the home at Nazareth as one having the lowest rank in the household, she was edified beyond measure.[4] His very living of the life of an ordinary individual in an obscure town deepened her humility. His obedience made obedience a joy for her. His manner of doing ordinary, everyday work made her realize that holiness consists of doing ordinary things well. His patient dependence on God's providence strengthened her trust and confidence in that providence. Thus, profiting from His exalted example, she became the first and best pupil in the school of Christ.

Was she not the first to request the Messiah to perform a miracle? When she saw Him surrounded by His first disciples, her great faith in Him and her charity toward others prompted her to make an appeal that occasioned the first public manifestation of the

---

[4] As St. Ambrose states, far from being puffed up, the more Mary recognized her merit, the more fully did she pay her vows, the more abundantly did she perform her service . . . and fill up the mystic time." Concerning Widows, IV, 25; NPN, 2nd seer., X, 395.

Savior's power. When our divine Lord proclaimed that spiritual kinship with Him depended on doing God's will and pointed to His disciples as His mother, sister, and brother, he did not insinuate that the Virgin Mother was remiss in striving after the accomplishment of God's will. Rather, in always seeking to do the will of God she followed most closely in the footsteps of her divine Son and enjoyed the closest spiritual relationship as well as that of motherhood. Thus when He preached the high ideal that the kingdom of God must be put above family ties, as He did, for instance, in the words: "I have come to set man at variance against his father. . . . He who loves father and mother more than Me, is not worthy of Me" (Matt. 10:35–37; cf. Deut. 33:9), in this He was reflecting praise on His Blessed Mother for she lived most closely to this ideal. One proof is that she lovingly preserved the boyhood saying although it occasioned three days of extreme anxiety, and a further proof is that when the supreme test came, she met it as the great high priestess offering herself in sacrifice at the foot of the cross and her Son in sacrifice on the arms of the cross. No wonder, then, that she was to be found so deservedly among the chosen disciples when the Holy Spirit descended upon the infant Church on Pentecost.

In the episode of Christ's twelfth year, as we have seen, St. Joseph remained silent. But he was not passed over in silence. Giving him all the honor and dignity that went with his position as the legal father of Jesus and as her own spouse, the Blessed Mother used the words, "Thy father and I." In answering her question the boy Jesus addressed both His foster father and His Blessed Mother. He drew attention to what they should be aware of, that being above human measures and standards as the Son of God He had the obligation of acting above human obligations whenever the interests of His eternal Father required it. His words, mild and respectful in tone, contained a delicate contrast. When He said "My Father," He was opposing "Thy father and I," opposing the claims that arise from His close relationship with God as Son against the claims arising from the closest human relationships; not that He was disowning these human relationships, but that He was insisting on His superior rank over them. He was pointing out that in certain instances He must act without reference to them because of His unique relationship with the eternal Father.

When the sacred text states that "they did not understand" these earliest recorded words, it refers to St. Joseph as well as his spouse. As these words had outlined the policy to be followed throughout His whole earthly life, as made clear only in the light of the cross, they were not understood by St. Joseph when he heard them from the lips of Jesus. Perhaps they were never fully understood by him; although, like the Virgin Mother, he must have pondered over them during the return journey to Nazareth and during the remaining years of his life.

St. Joseph had shared the agony of his spouse when the boy Jesus was missed from the returning caravan after the Passover. Both are examples for those who suffer because of something they do not understand. The foster father too was stunned when unexpectedly he encountered Jesus in the midst of the learned doctors of the law, provoking discussion by His questions and answers. The sacred text states that Joseph and his virgin spouse made the thirteen-day pilgrimage to Jerusalem for the Passover, each year, and they give edification thereby. At the Temple services with the pilgrims he chanted the psalms beside the boy Jesus and must have received many a favorable comment because of Jesus.

It gave great honor and glory to St. Joseph to be considered one of the parents of Jesus and to be mentioned as such and to be called His father in the Sacred Scriptures. In truth, he was the legal father and the adoptive father, and as such was the fatherly protector and provider of Jesus and His Blessed Mother. This office of his began before the Nativity, and from the crib at Bethlehem it was his great privilege to take the infant Savior into his arms. He provided for the care and support of both the Madonna and her Child and arranged for their homes at Bethlehem, in Egypt, and at Nazareth. It was St. Joseph who was warned by the angel to take the Child and His mother into Egypt; and it was he who was notified by the angel that the time for return had come. Then back in the Holy Land, being dissuaded by another warning from settling in Bethlehem to which he seemed desirous of going, St. Joseph made the decision that brought the holy family back to Nazareth. Our Lord honored St. Joseph with His companionship, working and praying with him, always obeying him, and giving him filial affection. St. Joseph received from Him the great lessons of humility, obedience, and submission to God's providence. Although he did not have the privilege of living to witness the miracles of the public ministry, the foster father was present at many of the miraculous occurrences of the holy childhood and heard the boy Jesus make a profession of His divine sonship. He had the inestimable privilege of dying the happiest of deaths with Jesus and Mary at his bedside. Intimately associated with our divine Lord's hidden life, especially the holy childhood and boyhood, St. Joseph was remarkable for his chastity, kindness, and goodness. Through his working for Jesus and Mary and through his close association with them he was led to the sublime heights of union with God. Silent and unobstrusive, the hard-working provider and head of the holy family is the patron of Christian family life and also the patron of the universal Church.

One of the best of men as he was, and the best of women as his spouse was, yet for the Son of God to subject Himself to these two, who were mere creatures, is one of the great mysteries of the world. His submission, voluntary and complete in all things, means that as a boy and youth Christ placed Himself at the disposal of His parents; and did their will promptly and gladly. He carried out their behests and desires all day long as the routine of things required. One time He is helping His Blessed Mother by bringing water from the fountain or by turning the grinding stone; at another He is giving a hand to His foster father in the carpenter shop. On the one hand we have here the loving condescension of God, and on the other the exceedingly great dignity of the parents. "Both amaze us, both are marvelous" exclaims St. Bernard.[5] St. Ambrose also expresses this sentiment: "No wonder that the great Teacher should practice! And shall we marvel how He who was subject to His mother was about His Father's business? His subjection to His mother proceeded not from weakness, but from dutiful affection." [6] Here dutifulness does not mean the abrogation of sovereignty but a perfection of it, just as mercy is an adornment to the crowned head. Here Jesus was doing His Father's will when He was obeying His parents at Nazareth just as well as when He was instructing the doctors in the Temple. Yet the fact that the God-man subjected Himself to these earthly parents is an astounding one. The Scripture text recording it is one of those that should be written in letters of gold.

Our Lord's voluntary and complete submission to His parents follows the pattern of His whole life. Outwardly it was in obedience to an edict of Augustus that He happened to be born in Bethlehem. Then He fulfilled all the requirements of the Jewish ceremonial laws in the circumcision and the presentation. The laws of economy and growth governed Him. He paid the tax to the Temple and ordered the paying of tribute to Caesar. He was obedient to the Scriptures and to His Father even unto the death of the cross. Thus from cradle to grave He teaches us the hard lesson of obedience.[7]

[5] Homily I, on Missus est Angelus; PL, 183, 60.
[6] In Lucam 2:50; Corp. Script. Lat., XXXII, 75.
[7] When referring to Mary and Joseph, St. Luke is careful to keep in mind the doctrine of the virgin birth of Christ which was announced by the archangel Gabriel. The Blessed Virgin Mary is in the fore front, and St. Joseph in the background throughout the early chapters of the Third Gospel. Although the Evangelist speaks of Zachary and his wife— and in the account of the child Samuel, Anna is always called the wife of Eleana—yet he nowhere calls Mary the wife of St. Joseph. She is called the betrothed before Christ's birth (1:26; 2:5); and after the Nativity the usage is "Mary and Joseph," "His parents," "His father and mother" (2:16, 27, 41, 43, 33). St. Luke does not follow the model of the account of Samuel (I Sam. 2:21) in stating that Mary had other children, for the reason that she remained a virgin after the birth of Christ.

Nazareth, well of the Virgin Mary

BIBLIOGRAPHY

Bartmann, B. Christus ein Gegner des Marienkultus? pp. 42–61.
Bernard, St. Homilia de laudibus Virginis Matris; PL, 183, 55–88.
Bossuet, J. B. Devotion to the Blessed Virgin.
Caldos, R. "S. Josephi dignitas et sanctitas ex locis evangelicis probata," Verbum Domini, VII (1937), 133–37.
Encyclicals and Apostolic Letters on "St. Joseph" and "the Holy Family."
Filas, F. The Man Nearest to Christ.
Ollivier, M. The Friendships of Jesus, pp. 85–115.
O'Shea, Denis. The Holy Family, pp. 182–221.
Temple, P. The Boyhood Consciousness of Christ, pp. 135–50.

CHAPTER XXII

The Holy Youth

A PECULIARITY of St. Luke's style is that occasionally he leaves his meaning to be found out from what he has already written or even from what afterward is set down. We should bear this fact in mind when we come to the brief sentence that is used to span and summarize twenty years of our divine Lord's life: "And Jesus advanced in wisdom and age, and grace with God and men" (2:52). A mere dozen words that record so long a period and such comprehensive subjects as grace and wisdom constitute a text which is naturally cryptic and profound. For its meaning and its emphasis it should be explained in the light of the whole Gospel, especially of what had just previously been written, verses 40 to 51, to which it is joined by the conjunction "and."

Verse 40 speaks of the Child of forty days after He had been presented in the Temple: "And the Child grew and waxed strong, full of wisdom, and the grace of God was in Him" (2:40). This is similar to verse 52 inasmuch as it refers to Our Lord's bodily growth, wisdom, and grace, yet it is somewhat more definite. In regard to wisdom the original Greek uses a present participle which can mean either that the child Jesus was kept full of wisdom or that He was keeping Himself full of wisdom. Even with the rendering "filling Himself with wisdom," since the verb employed means to fill completely so that nothing is lacking, it has to be interpreted to mean that the child Jesus did become full of wisdom. As to grace it is said absolutely and definitely that the grace of God was in Him.

Then the episode of the Passover pilgrimage of the twelfth year illustrates the wisdom and the grace of the boy Jesus. There were prayers and canticles and pious exercises and ritual ceremonies during these thirteen days of festive celebration. There were highest ideals and holiest purposes exemplified and expressed in His deliverance of the prelude of His future gospel before the doctors at the expense of sorrow and worry to those nearest and dearest, and in His profession of the divine sonship, an expression of irrevocable dedication to the Father's will. Here in the Temple scene the majestic figure of the twelve-year-old Savior stands out against the background of bewilderment of the most learned doctors of the law; yet, more than that, against the background of non-understanding by those who should know Him best, His parents, indicating the possession of wisdom and grace beyond human measurements.

It was the young Savior full of wisdom and grace who returned with His parents to Nazareth and it was of such a one that the Evangelist wrote: "And Jesus advanced in wisdom and age, and grace before God and men" (Luke 2: 52). The literal meaning of the Greek word for "advanced" is "to cut forward" and the imperfect tense of the verb is used to express continuous action. In the light of what has already been written by St. Luke, his statement that the youthful Savior was continuing to cut His way forward in wisdom and age and grace must mean that, as He continued along the course of age, His actions were all redolent of wisdom and grace, that is, He continued to grow up a most wise and gracious youth.

We look in vain in St. Luke's text for the word "increased." A different word, "proceeded," is to be found there because the Evangelist had previously said that the Christ child was full of wisdom and grace, and had just described the Temple incident illustrating this plenteous overflow of wisdom and grace. Nor can the implication of a more and more outward manifestation of wisdom and grace be read into our difficult passage. The simple, plain fact is that less display of wisdom and grace followed. Indeed, the Gospel episode of the Passover visit is the only recorded outburst of self-revelation by Christ during all the long years of the hidden life at Nazareth. Extraordinary manifestations of His plenitude of wisdom and grace were not vouchsafed after His return from the paschal celebration of His twelfth year. This fact excludes any interpretation of "more and more" from the word "advanced," because "more and more" would imply that each year Jesus was appearing more and more extraordinary.

Besides, Catholic theology teaches that our divine Lord's soul, as befitting a soul united to Divinity, had the full perfection of its own life from the first moment of its existence and did not depend on bodily development for the exercise of its faculties, intelligence, and will. Indeed, as St. Thomas says, His human soul possessed from the very beginning the fullness of known truth. According to Catholic doctrine, our divine Lord enjoyed from the very beginning both the beatific vision and infused knowledge. It also holds that then, through the exercise of His human mind which naturally formed ideas from images brought to it by the senses, Christ learned in a new way. This latter kind of knowledge, known as acquired or experimental knowledge, increased accordingly as the Savior made use of His senses and intellectual faculties.[1] But much more than this mere experiencing, which continued throughout the Savior's whole life, is expressed in the broad, comprehensive terms of Luke 2:52. The statement that Jesus continued to cut His way along in wisdom and age and grace signifies that as He proceeded along in years His actions were characterized by, and ornamented with, wisdom and grace; or, in other words, He grew up a holy youth according to the highest standards of perfection.

The Evangelist covers, be it noted, the first twelve years of our Savior's life with one verse (2:40) in which he mentions the fullness of wisdom and grace in the divine Child. Then he bridges over another twenty years also with one verse, which points out, as I have

[1] See St. Thomas, *Summa theol.*, IIIa, q.9–12.

said, the perfection of the hidden life. There is a complete absence of reference to teachers or schools. Yet the Acts of the Apostles (7: 22) mentions that Moses was instructed in all the wisdom of the Egyptians, and that St. Paul was brought up in Jerusalem "at the feet of Gamaliel" (22: 3) . St. Luke knew that he was deliberately omitting mention of schools and teachers in Christ's young life. Thus he certainly implies that they had no great part in that life. Origen wrote that "Christ has not studied literature, not merely that of the Greeks, but not even that of the Hebrews, as the truth-loving Scriptures testify regarding Him." [2] When the Evangelist fails to make any mention of education, we can safely deduce that Our Lord did not attend a course of studies in scribal schools. This deduction is all the safer when we realize further that from what he did write St. Luke precluded this higher education from the divine life. For he says that the Christ child was filled with wisdom, so much so that when He was twelve years old He astounded the learned rabbis, those of Jerusalem itself. This is certain, that in St. Luke (2: 52) emphasis is laid on the good use of wisdom and grace during the adolescent years of Our Lord, since an earlier verse of the same Gospel attributes to the child Jesus the fullness of wisdom and grace.

In writing his early chapters St. Luke seems to be influenced in a literary way by the biblical account of the birth and youth of Samuel. There he found a text that spanned the adolescent years of the prophet: "But the child Samuel advanced and grew on, and pleased both the Lord and men" (I Sam. 2: 26) . In making use of the already inspired words, the only addition the Evangelist made was, "in wisdom." This was not to stress any growth in wisdom but to emphasize the possession of it, for he had already said that the Christ child was full of wisdom.[3] Indeed both the possession of wisdom and growth in it on the part of Christ can be deduced from the comprehensive passage of St. Luke; just as Our Lord's possession of all grace, accompanied by a certain growth in grace through the accumulation of

[2] *Against Celsus*, VI, 16; ANF, IV, 580.
[3] Cf. Burrows, *The Gospel of the Childhood*, p. 34.

meritorious acts, can be found in the expression, "He advanced in grace."

In regard to the precise meaning of the words, "Jesus advanced in wisdom," Catholic scholars are divided into two groups. One holds that they signify merely external manifestation; and the other that they refer to progress in acquired or experimental knowledge. Could both meanings be included in the passage? Perhaps our Savior accommodated His beatific knowledge and His infused knowledge to the stages of His experimental knowledge. In the latter there was progress, and this progress would be manifested externally and known through His words and actions. As St. Thomas teaches, it is only in regard to the effects that our divine Lord may be said to increase in wisdom and grace: "In the course of time He did more perfect works to prove Himself true man, both in the things of God and in the things of man." [4] Better and wiser acts were done by Him as He advanced in years, as was in accord with the economy of the human nature to which He submitted. Thus, for instance, His actions in His fifteenth year displayed more prudence and intelligence than those of His seventh year. Indeed, as St. Gregory the Great pointed out, Christ waited for His twelfth year to question the doctors, for "wisdom is supplied in the age of perfection." [5] He supplied Himself with all the requirements suitable to each stage and development as St. Justin had early stated: "For even at His birth He was in possession of His power and as He grew up like other men, by using the fitting means, He assigned its own (requirements) to each development." [6] That our Savior accommodated His display of wisdom to the different stages of His growth is expressed so well by St. Cyril of Alexandria, when he writes that it was in perfect accord with the economy of the Incarnation and its humble state that "He should seem to be filled with wisdom, in so far as the manifestation of the wisdom dwelling within Him proceeded as by addition, most congruously to the stature of the body." [7]

[4] *Summa theol.*, IIIa, q.7, a.12.
[5] *Super Ezech. hom.* 2; PL, 76, 796.
[6] *Dialogue with Trypho*, 88; ANF, I, 243.
[7] *Ad reginas de recta fide*, II, 16; NPN, 2nd ser., XIV, 212.

What is meant in Luke 2: 52, therefore, is that during the years following His twelfth year all the acts of the God-man were meritorious for us and that each one of them was perfect in its own way according to the highest standards of holiness. One of the virtues of the hidden life at Nazareth to which the Savior returned receives a special mention in the Gospel, His ready and continual obedience to His earthly parents (Luke 2: 51). This may have been singled out for particular notice because humility and voluntary subjection constituted a dominant characteristic of the God-man according to St. Paul (Phil. 2: 7) and according to Our Lord's own words: "Even as the Son of man is not come to be ministered unto, but to minister" (Matt. 20: 28). From the first moment when He said "Behold I come" (Heb. 10: 5–7), until He could say "It is consummated," He rendered supreme obedience to the Father. The young Nazarene not only as a child but even as a young man at all times joyfully carrying out the behests of Mary and Joseph, is an exalted example of supreme wisdom that highly merited before God and men. Indeed the virtues preached by the Savior of the public ministry, were, as we would expect, practiced by Him during the hidden years. For, "the Son who is perfected forevermore" (Heb. 7: 28), set a personal example of what was most perfect. Especially the fundamental Christian virtues that were later enunciated in the Sermon on the Mount were followed in the ordinary, everyday life at Nazareth. Poverty of spirit, purity of heart, meekness of disposition, peace spread on all sides, willingness to endure for justice' sake and readiness to forgive injuries, all these were in the blessed home of Nazareth, all radiating from the adolescent Jesus. He subordinated earthly considerations, ordinary pleasures, business, even His relationship with those dearest to Him to the interests of His eternal Father. Prayer, public and private, pilgrimages and attendance at synagogues were a prominent part of the life of the young carpenter of Nazareth. In a word He, who later exhorted His followers to aim at the perfection of their heavenly Father (Matt. 5: 48), led a perfect life at Nazareth.

This virtuous manner of life was certainly wisdom, for "wisdom" has a broad meaning, especially a spiritual meaning (cf. Jas.

3:17; Luke 11:49; I Cor. 1:24). It is not merely the perception of religious truths, it is likewise chaste, peaceful, prudent living; it is walking in God's presence in holiness and righteousness; it is leading a perfect spiritual life according to God's standards; it is the peaceful sowing for the production of a rich harvest of holiness (Jas. 3:18). No wonder that St. James, the blood-relative of Our Lord and the witness of His secluded years of obedience and example, in the beginning of his pastoral letter to Jewish Christians in all lands, after exhorting to the steadfast endurance of trials for the attaining of full perfection, admonishes all who lack wisdom to pray for it with unflinching faith: "But if any of you want wisdom, let him ask of God. . . . And it shall be given him" (Jas. 1:5).[8]

As to grace, it is the good will of God; it is His presence in the soul; it is God Himself there. Because the soul of Christ always enjoyed the beatific vision and possessed the indwelling of the Holy Ghost, and because it possessed unchangeable closeness with the Deity in the hypostatic union, it had the fullness of grace in its highest possible excellence and in its greatest possible extension, so that the Lamb that was slain was worthy to receive "honor and glory and benediction" (Apoc. 5:12). The fact that Jesus was God as well as man elevated to the highest degree the value of everything He did, even the least and most obscure of His actions during His hidden life. We note that the hour when He was about to begin His public ministry was the time chosen by the heavenly Father to proclaim His pleasure in His beloved Son in the words: "Thou art My beloved Son; in Thee I am well pleased" (Luke 3:22). Jesus had been advancing in the

[8] In the Prayer of the Office of the Finding of the Child Jesus in the Temple, the petition is for wisdom: "O God, Who wast pleased that the lowly childhood of Thy Son should be glorified by wisdom from Heaven, grant unto us to be so filled with the spirit of wisdom that we may walk before Thee in lowliness unfeigned. Through the Same our Lord Jesus Christ, Thy Son, Who liveth and reigneth with Thee in the Unity of the Holy Ghost, One God, without end. Amen." (*The Roman Breviary*, translated by John, Marquess of Bute, I, 922.) In the Collect of the Mass of the Holy Family, the petition is to follow the example of the holy family: "Lord Jesus Christ, who being made subject to Mary and Joseph didst hallow domestic life by Thine ineffable virtues; grant that we, with the assistance of both, may be taught by the example of the Holy Family and may attain to its everlasting fellowship, Who livest and reignest world without end. Amen." (The Raccolta, no. 258, p. 185.)

favor of God during all the years at Nazareth, and what may have seemed drab and insignificant as the Nazarene plied the tools at the carpenter's bench, was highly meritorious in the eyes of His Father.

In addition, Jesus' hidden life procured for Him the favor of men. This last expression means that, while He was growing up and during all the years that He lived in His own community at Nazareth, He held the respect and love of all. He was animated by the principle that recognized the Person of God in the person of His neighbor as well as the will of God in the will of His parents. Thus, in His courteous and gracious manner, with all, He was kindness itself, and in His everyday life He exemplified the most perfect charity. Yet there was no vulgar display; for His kind deeds, like His prayers and fastings, were performed not for popularity or public applause, but in secret. This modesty of demeanor together with His graciousness of manner won for Jesus many friends. It is recorded (Luke 4:22) that later His townspeople bore testimony to His goodness and integrity of life. All this showed that He stood in high repute in His community, enjoying the approval of all honest men. In a word, the God-man, during His growing years, in the obscure town of Nazareth, walked the most perfect way of righteousness. Although seemingly "one of the many," He was unique in His life of highest perfection and supreme merit. A perfect youth and a perfect young man, He lived day in and day out according to the most sublime principles of perfection.

We must always bear in mind that there must of necessity be aspects of the God-man that are above and beyond our limited powers of understanding. Hence we should all the more gladly welcome the guiding posts that have been set up by an infallible hand, in the pronouncements of the Church. We may confidently assert the following propositions.

1. The soul of Christ, during His life here below, possessed the knowledge which the blessed possess, by reason of the beatific vision.

2. The soul of Christ was ignorant of nothing, but from the be-

ginning knew in the Word all things past, present, and future, that is, all that God knows by knowledge of vision.

3. The doctrine of the ancients on the universal knowledge with which the soul of Christ was endowed from the beginning is to be favored in Catholic schools, and not any recent view that would set limits to the knowledge in Christ's soul.[9]

The sun is said to progress during the day as it seems to move continually across the sky; yet its bright rays come to us with varying degrees of temperature. Our divine Lord, during His progress through His years on earth, continually shed golden rays of sunshine; for the acts of the divine life, hidden and public, were continually winning merits for us while at the same time setting an exalted example. Yet the true majestic brilliance of His wisdom and grace was hidden (Col. 2:3); and the rays that did shine forth were regulated according to a planned economy and voluntary limitation.[10] All advance which the God-man made and externally manifested was in perfection, as "a Son who is forever perfect" (Heb. 7:28). This is why the Evangelist emphasized the wisdom and grace of the growing years.[11]

The hidden years of Our Lord's life, being the exemplification of the high ideals of the Sermon on the Mount, teach us, what all revelation teaches us (Jas. 4:5), that the Holy Ghost who abides in our souls jealously requires from us our undivided loyalty and devo-

[9] Holy Office, June 5, 1918. Cf. condemned propositions in Decree, *Lamentabile*, July 3, 1907. Cf. Danzinger, *Enchiridion*, propositions 32, 34, 35.

[10] St. Gregory Nazianzen explains the Gospel expression of increase in wisdom and grace, by gradual display. "How could that which is perfect from the first become more perfect, but that they (wisdom and grace) were gradually disclosed and displayed?" *Panegyric on St. Basil*, 38; NPN, 2nd ser.) VII, 408. The same explanation is given by St. Cyril of Alexandria. He declares that "advance" in Luke 2:52 does not mean an increase of wisdom, because there is no lacking in qualities of any dignity in God; the word implies that "God, the Word, accommodated the manifestations of wisdom step by step with the age of His body." *Comment. in Lucam*, 2:52; PG, 72, 507, St. Athanasius explains that it was Christ's human nature that advanced and goes on to insist that "Wisdom Himself did not advance; rather He advanced in Himself." *Oratio III, Contra Arianos*, PG, 26, 433.

[11] Isaias (11:2) foretold that the Messiah would have the spirit of wisdom and of knowledge. Wisdom and knowledge are also gifts of the Holy Ghost with which Christians are endowed.

tion. That no creature may come between the human soul and Himself, our eternal Father has set Himself up as our model, demanding that we aim at the highest perfection, "Be ye, therefore, perfect as also your heavenly Father is perfect" (Matt. 5: 48) . Always striving to draw near to God, we must detach ourselves from the world and must purify our hearts with acts of humility and contrition. Our faith in God and love of Him should find expression in deeds of practical charity. Thus with Jesus and like Him we should go forward in wisdom, age, and grace before God and man.

BIBLIOGRAPHY

Fillion, L. The Life of Christ, I, 382–409.
Graham, A. The Christ of Catholicism, pp. 29 f., 174–214.
Joüon, P. L. Evangile de N.S. Jésus-Christ, pp. 308 f.
Lagrange, J. M. Evangile selon S. Luc., pp. 97 f.
Prat, F. Jésus-Christ, I, 129–37.
Temple, P. The Boyhood Consciousness of Christ, pp. 151–65.
Vonier, A., The Personality of Christ, pp. 90–131.

CHAPTER XXIII

The Carpenter of Nazareth

WHILE most of the Jews in the Holy Land in Our Lord's time were occupied in agriculture, a certain number were engaged in the handicrafts. Usually the two occupations were combined since artisans cultivated small farms besides attending to their regular trade, and since owners of large estates produced on their grounds merchandise for the home market. Indeed Galilee's fertile soil was an incentive for craftsmen to give part time to the gainful pursuits of raising crops, fruits, and domestic animals. Then opportunities to make a living through various occupations were opened up by the commercial enterprises of the Gentiles and by the extensive building programs of the Herods. In regard to construction operations near Nazareth we have only to recall that, during the hidden life of Christ, Antipas first rebuilt neighboring Sephoris, making it "the ornament of Galilee," and later built the new city of Tiberias on the shore of Lake Genesareth.[1]

The fertility of Galilee was, according to Josephus, such as not to encourage idleness. There was a call to industrious activity in the warning of the Book of Ecclesiasticus (7:16): "Hate not laborious work nor husbandry ordained by the Most High." When St. Paul set an example and gave the recommendation, "that you do your own business and work with your own hands" (I Thess. 4:11; 2:9; II

[1] It seems that 18,000 men were continuously employed in construction work on the Temple; see Josephus, *Antiquities*, XX, ix, 7.

246

Thess. 3:8; I Cor. 9:1–15), he was but following the custom and teaching of the time. With few exceptions the rabbis used to work at a trade. Thus we hear that Hillel was a woodcutter, that Shammai was a carpenter, and that others were shoemakers, sandalmakers, smiths, potters, or builders.[2] It is certain that in Our Lord's time craftsmanship was held in high regard, and that a secure and profitable living was obtained by the handicrafts. Craftsmen were so numerous that whole villages and towns were occupied by members of the same craft; and in some of the cities, streets were given the names of the craftsmen who did business there. There were even trade guilds of some sort as well as business companies and associated workers. Certain groups of weavers, dyers, and tailors were so organized that they were able to have their own trademark on clothes.[3] However, it must be noted that, while advocating the learning of a trade for the young and esteeming highly the profession of a tradesman, contemporaries of Our Savior did not associate wisdom with those who were entirely engaged in such activities; for Ecclesiasticus (38:25, 39) advises us not to look for judges or propounders of parables in the ranks of artisans and craftsmen.

On the occasion during His public ministry when Our Lord visited Nazareth and preached there in the synagogue, the astonished townspeople asked one another: "Is not this the carpenter, the son of Mary?" (Mark 6:3); the parallel passage in St. Matthew (13:55) gives the question this way: "Is not this the carpenter's son? Is not His mother called Mary?" Thus incidentally in the first case, and in the second only indirectly, the Sacred Scriptures refer to the trade to which Jesus applied Himself during the hidden years of His life; and

[2] A rabbi who lived at the end of the last prechristian century, Shemaiah said: "Love labor." (*Mishnah*, Aboth, 1, 10; Danby, p. 447). It can be said that at the time of Christ, labor was held to be not incompatible with the study of the Law. Furthermore it may be rightfully said that in Our Lord's day manual labor and brainwork were considered an inseparable pair. As evidence we quote Rabban Gamaliel son of R. Judah: "Excellent is the study of the Law together with worldly occupation, for toil in them both puts sin out of the mind." (*Mishnah*, Aboth, 2, 2; Danby, p. 447).

In regard to rabbis taking up trades, Delitzsch tells us that the Talmud mentions over a hundred rabbis who were artisans and bore artisans' names (*Jewish Artizan Life in the Time of Jesus*, p. 78).

[3] See Heichelheim, *An Economic Survey of Ancient Rome*, IV, 189 ff.

the impression is given that it was not of importance what calling He took up in order to make a living. Since in the household which He selected for His upbringing, the head of it was a carpenter, He willingly and gladly followed the same occupation. It was part of His subjecting Himself to His earthly parents that He gave a helping hand in the carpenter's shop until soon He spent the whole day working there. It was a tradition that a son follow his father's trade; indeed there has been handed down the expression, "a carpenter and a carpenter's son." Frequently in Palestine for those going to learn a trade, contracts of apprenticeship were drawn up which stated what the apprentice was to learn and the time he had to give to service, generally ten years.[4] Such a contract would not be required in the case of Our Savior unless St. Joseph died shortly after the twelfth year pilgrimage to the Temple. Although we have no reason to suppose that the death of the foster father occurred so early, it could be inferred that it did take place several years before the opening of the public ministry from the fact that the people of Nazareth called Jesus "the Son of Mary," which they would not have done if St. Joseph were alive, or even if he had died shortly before. If this inference is correct, then for several years our Savior through His work as a carpenter was the main support of Himself and His Blessed Mother.

What kind of work was done by Our Lord? For the answer we must first examine the meaning of the Greek word [5] in the Gospel text that we translate "carpenter." It signifies a worker in any hard material such as wood, metal, or stone. Thus it would designate an

---

[4] *Ibid.*, 198.

[5] See the treatment of the word, $\tau\acute{\epsilon}\kappa\tau\omega\nu$ by Sutcliffe, "St. Joseph's Trade," *Irish Theol. Quart.*, X (1915), 196–99. Originally this Greek word meant "a producer." The root meaning is kept in $\tau\acute{\epsilon}\chi\nu\eta$, art or craft, and in the Latin word, textor, a weaver. In regard to the usage of $\tau\acute{\epsilon}\kappa\tau\omega\nu$, it was employed to mean artisan, craftsman or mechanic; and as a rule the material of the work was added in the genetive case. There are in the classics many cases where the word was used by itself for artisan or carpenter. In these cases where there is no noun of qualification the meaning either of artisan or carpenter may be gathered from the context (Cf. Wis. 13: 11). There is no question therefore about the word itself being used for carpenter. Now in the Gospel text we find the word unqualified. Since the meaning "artisan" would not be appropriate, namely, would not have sense, the word there definitely has the meaning of "carpenter." See also Hoepfl "Nonne hic est Fabri filius" *Biblica*, IV (1923), 42.

artisan or mechanic and would include not only a carpenter but also a smith, a mason, or a builder. The tradition that St. Joseph was a worker in wood, that is, a carpenter is "a well established one." [6] That Our Lord worked at the trade of a carpenter is the common tradition of the Church, universally accepted today.[7]

From a carpenter's shop would come forth household furniture, such as doors, tables, window frames, cedar chests for cupboards, and bedsteads. Of course farm implements would be produced there,

[6] Prat, *Jésus-Christ*, I, 131 note.

[7] Sutcliffe has assembled the evidence for the trade of St. Joseph and has sifted it with a critical hand. "St. Joseph's Trade, an Enquiry into the Evidence," *Irish Theol. Quart.*, X (1915), 179–201. He has also treated separately the question whether Our Lord worked as a carpenter, "The Divine Carpenter," *Irish Theol. Quart.*, XI (1916), 147–63. A brief summary of the evidence of the trade of both Our Lord and St. Joseph is as follows:

St. Hilary, St. Peter Chrysologus, The Venerable Bede, and Anselm of Laon use words and expressions that imply that St. Joseph's trade was that of a worker in metal, a smith or blacksmith. It might be said, however, that these writers are mostly interested in the spiritual lesson to be drawn from the scriptural texts involved. It may also be claimed that they were misled by the Latin translation of the Gospels in use, which has *faber*. The common meaning of this word is smith or blacksmith.

On the other side of the question, that St. Joseph's trade and that of Our Lord was a carpenter is supported by the early Syriac and Coptic versions which use the word "carpenter" in their translations. This view receives great strength from the testimony of St. Justin Martyr who is a witness from Palestine in the middle of the second century. On this side may be quoted St. Ambrose of the fourth century who suggests this view. Clearly on this side are the fifth century writers, Theodoret and Sozomen and the Arian author of the *Opus imperfectum* of the fifth or sixth century. Also from the fifth century onward there are representations in art of St. Joseph with a hatchet. Cf. E. Lowrie, *Art in the Early Church*, 154 f.)

The Greek word in the Gospel texts is definitely in favor of the view of carpenter. Especially we may claim moral certainty when we have in addition to the previously quoted evidence, the common tradition of our Church, the voice of the Christian Church today (see Sutcliffe, "St. Joseph's Trade," *Irish Theol. Quart.*, X (1915), 193–97. Indeed our English translations in use all have the word carpenter in the text.

It is possible that the tradition of the beginning of the third century may be quoted by the Apocryphal Gospel of St. Thomas (Greek form) 13, when it says that St. Joseph made "plows and yokes." In the middle of the second century, the apocryphal Prote-vengelium of James, 9, 13, alludes to St. Joseph's "hatchet" and his work of "building." In this connection we may quote Dalman (*Sacred Sites and Ways*, p. 70), who says that although there was a special word for "mason" in the Aramaic language, the word for the trade of Our Lord and St. Joseph employed in rabbinic and in Christian-Palestinian writings was *naggar*, a mason and worker in wood. Dalman here points out that in a town like Nazareth, besides the builders or masons, there must have been one or more workers in wood who put up the roof-beams of a house, did the ordinary carpentry work and worked on plows and yokes for farmers. Such would be the work of St. Joseph; and Our divine Lord according to the custom of the time would follow in St. Joseph's footsteps.

such as handles for hoes, flails, pitchforks and sledges, the wooden plow and the wooden yoke for oxen. Carpenters would take part in the construction of house frames, that is, the erection of the large beams, generally of sycamore or poplar, upon which shorter ones sometimes of oak or terebinth rested to support a layer of thorns and clay that served as a roof. The walls of houses would be put up by masons and builders; but there would be workers in wood for the selecting, preparing, and setting of the roof beams.

In searching for any genuine tradition about the kind of work Jesus turned out as a specialty,[8] we are fortunate to have the testimony of a competent writer who lived in the Holy Land just a hundred years after Our Lord's time. The importance of this witness, St. Justin Martyr, is to be gauged by his closeness in time of Our Lord's and by his home in central Palestine. These circumstances taken together make it highly probable that he would fall heir to a genuine tradition. He says the following in regard to the work of Christ: "He

[8] Because of tradition and the mention of Our Lord as a carpenter by the townspeople of Nazareth, all Catholic scholars today hold that the Savior worked as a carpenter during His hidden life. In times past, however, "a considerable body of opinion" (Sutcliffe, "The Divine Carpenter," *Irish Theol. Quart.*, XI [1916], 154) was against this view, principally because of the objection to Our Lord's being engaged in a worldly trade.

In one of his scoffs at Christianity, Celsus brought together in a confused way, the tree of life in the garden of Paradise, Our Lord's being nailed to the cross, and His trade as a carpenter (Origen, *Against Celsus*, VI, 34; ANF, IV, 588). In answering this attack, Origen states that Celsus was blind to the fact that in none of the Gospels in use in the churches of his day was Jesus Himself "ever described (ἀναγέγραπται) as being a carpenter" (*op. cit.*, VI, 36; PG, 11, 1352.). For this statement of Origen two explanations are given; either he forgot the reference in St. Mark (6:3); or the St. Mark's Gospel with which he was acquainted did not have this reference. The latter is the generally accepted opinion today. Could it be that Origen's words only mean that the canonical Gospels have no detailed account of Our Lord as a carpenter, and that they do not bring out any symbolism of His trade in connection with His dying on the tree of the cross?

In commenting on Proverbs 30:19 that Solomon could not figure out the ways of a man in his youth, St. Ambrose says about Our Lord: "This is the Man whose ways in youth cannot be known. For who can estimate what works He did while living on this earth as a man?" (Sermon XLVI, *De Salomone*, IV, 14; PL, 17, 721.) This general statement cannot be used as an argument against the view that Our Lord worked as a carpenter. Neither can St. Augustine's remarks that the townspeople of Nazareth believing Our Lord to be the son of a carpenter "naturally also took Him to be a carpenter" (*Harmony of the Gospels*, II, 42; NPN, 1st ser., VI, 144). This is vague and the implication is not valid, for the townspeople could know definitely whether or not Jesus was a carpenter.

was deemed a carpenter, for He was in the habit of working as a carpenter among men, making plows and yokes, by which He taught the symbols of righteousness and active life." [9]

As Nazareth was a country town surrounded by small farms and as it overlooked the large and well cultivated plain of Esdraelon, the carpenters of the town, we may suppose, would be occupied chiefly in supplying or repairing farm implements. This is an additional reason for giving credence to St. Justin when he says that Jesus specialized, as we say, in the making of plows and yokes. Even in our day one can witness in this plain of Esdraelon the same kind of plowing with a wooden plow drawn by two oxen as in the time of Christ. Such a plow did little more than scratch the surface, yet it suited the terrain. This ancient type of plow [10] would of course be crude; it would be made out of a large piece of light but tough wood, and to its tip would be attached a small iron share to protect it from being broken by stones or roots. It was supplied with one handle, which had to be carefully and firmly attached to the share, enabling the dexterous plowman to guide the plow with one hand, while using the other to manage the oxen with a goad or pointed stick. Even more labor would have to be expended on the yokes for oxen. The narrow strips of wood on the side and the flexible but durable bars that hung over the necks of the animals had to be properly balanced and carefully shaped and planed so that they would not chafe the patient beasts of burden.

The plowing season started after the early rains in the middle of October and continued during the winter months until the end of the rainy season in the middle of March. The usual method was to plow about half an acre, then scatter the seed broadcast, and afterward plow the seed under. The little plow of that time did not make much of a furrow, so that frequently the plowing was repeated, or

---

[9] *Dialogue with Trypho*, 88; ANF, I, 244.

[10] A new type of plow and new methods of plowing were introduced by the Greeks. See Dalman, *Arbeit und Sitte in Palästina*, I, 261 ff., 400 ff.; II, 130 ff., 644, and Plates 18–39; also Gow, "The Ancient Plough," *Journal of Hellenic Studies*, XXXIV (1914), 249 ff.

several plows followed one another, each rooting out a little more soil. Especially in the common land held by all, there was group plowing. During the winter season, when nearly all the plowing was done, the Carpenter of Nazareth would be kept busy, mending plows and plowshares. The summer months would be reserved for the turning out of new farm implements in readiness for the next season.

Except on Sabbath days and feast days, Jesus worked daily at the carpenter's trade for about twenty years. This physical labor developed the hard hands and strong arms of a working man and built up the robust body of the Savior that could stand the journeys, the long hours of preaching, and the long hours of attending the sick during His missionary years. These twenty years of His life given to hard work might have received a veiled reference in His words: "Come to Me all you who labor and are burdened and I will give you rest" (Matt. 11:28). Often indeed during His labors as a carpenter, He had felt the "burden of the day and the scorching heat" (Matt. 20:12), and had experienced fatigue from the hardship of physical toil. Here again He was "one tried as we are tried in all things" (Heb. 4:15).

Jesus' trade would bring Him to neighboring streets of Nazareth or to near-by towns where He could take part in setting up the frame of a house. Sometimes too, for the repairing or making of farm implements He must have received calls to visit farms on the sloping hills, or to make trips to the furrowed fields of the great plain. Most of His work, however, would be done in His carpenter shop which had a location separate from the home, thus sparing the family the noise made by the tools or by the customers in the course of bargaining.[11] The stock of tools was of a primitive sort, namely, one or two of the following: saw, axe, hammer, mallet, chisel, and plane.[12]

[11] The custom in the Graeco-Roman world was to have the shop apart from the home. See Prat, *Jésus-Christ*, I, 130.

[12] The *Mishnah* mentions the following instruments and articles in connection with the carpenter: The plane and the shavings (Babba Kamma, 10, 10; Danby, p. 347), axes and saws (Arakhin, 6, 3; Danby, p. 549), the vice (Kelim, 16, 7; Danby, p. 627), saw-handle, cord, press, bow-handle of a drill frame of a large saw, bow-string, mole-

To the carpenter shop of Our Lord, woodcutters for stipulated sums would bring large logs and slender rods from select trees that grew in the forest districts to the east of the town or in the forest that crowned the northwestern hill of Nazareth.[13] Accordingly, as they were required for the various articles of house or farm usage, the pieces of wood would be placed on the carpenter's bench. After the hatchet and saw had worked the material to the proper size, the plane would have to be used extensively. Thus with skill and labor that brought beads of perspiration to the sacred brow, rough timber would be fashioned into handles, doors, chests, plowshares, and yokes. At noon Jesus would leave the shop and return for the frugal meal prepared by the Blessed Mother. Occasionally during the day, Jesus' work must have been interrupted by peasants who came into the carpenter shop to look over the farm implements He had Himself made or had purchased at a market.[14] Did some of them drive hard bargains to get articles for less than they were worth? Did others take away goods with the promise of payment, a promise they had no intention of keeping? We may presume that average human frailty was sometimes present in the customers at Nazareth. Yet, we may be sure that often articles were given to the needy both by our Blessed Lord and by His Blessed Mother. Moreover, we may be certain also that all were pleased with the durability and excellent workmanship of the goods turned out by the gentle Carpenter.

In a town like Nazareth one or two carpenters [15] or workers in wood would be kept busy at their trade throughout the year. When trying to make even a rough estimate of living expenses and income,

---

trap (*id.* 263; Danby, p. 636), the plummet and its cord (*id.* 29, 3; Danby, p. 648), a box, a chest, a cupboard (Babba Kamma, 9, 3; Danby, p. 344), and a door with a hole at top or bottom (Oholoth, 13, 3; Danby, p. 668).

Some of the parts of a plow mentioned in the Mishnah are: tail-piece, knee or handle, metal rings, plow-guides or plow flanks, the cross bar and the collar-piece or thick ropes (Kelim, 21, 3; Danby, p. 636).

[13] Cf. Dalman, *Sacred Sites and Ways*, p. 69; Booth, *The World of Jesus*, pp. 83–86.

[14] According to the *Mishnah*, Shebitth (Seventh Year), 5, 61; Danby, p. 45, a plow or a yoke could not be sold in the seventh year.

[15] The words in St. Mark (6:3), "the carpenter, the son of Mary," might mean that Our Lord was the only carpenter in Nazareth. Cf. Sutcliffe, "The Divine Carpenter," *Irish Theol. Quart.*, XI (1916), 148.

we must bear in mind that, although the denarius, considered of the same value as the provincial drachma, was equivalent to about seventeen cents, the purchasing power of money then was perhaps fifty times what it is now. The average daily minimum expense for an adult in Palestine in Our Lord's day was about half a denarius, and the ordinary wage for a laborer was one denarius. If one denarius could support a working man and his family, a log of wood should have cost about one denarius, and so should the little iron plowtip. Allowing two days of work to turn out a new plowshare, we may suppose it would sell for at least five denarii. A yoke should also sell for about the same price. In regard to the costs at the time, the price of one peck of wheat was about one denarius; that for a loaf of bread was about one-twentieth of that sum. Then for clothes: a head-cloth cost four denarii; the yearly sum required to buy clothes for a woman of the laboring class was fifty denarii. Thus the lease of a house for four months was four denarii, and yet meat was comparatively expensive, for it took fifty denarii to purchase a carcass of cattle.[16]

The question may well be asked whether the Savior of the public ministry ever referred to His work as a tradesman. Our Lord was speaking from personal experience when He contrasted the splinter with the beam (Matt. 7:3), and when He made reference to the difference between green and dry wood (Luke 23:31). The yoke that He turned out in His carpenter's shop got a mention when He advised, "Take up My yoke upon you. . . . For My yoke is sweet and My burden light" (Matt. 11:29 f.); and also when He said in a parable, "I have bought five yoke of oxen" (Luke 14:19). He once referred to a plow: "No man putting his hand to the plow and looking back, is fit for the kingdom of God" (Luke 9:62); and at another time He referred to plowing (Luke 17:7). Also He spoke of building a tower (Luke 14:28), a house (Matt. 7:24, 27; Luke 6:48, 49), and a watchtower and hedge of a vineyard (Mark 12:1). Once He mentions a candlestick (Matt. 5:15). A curious doubtful saying is found in a papyrus, but not in the Gospels: "Raise the stone

---

[16] See Heichelheim, *op. cit.*, IV, 178 ff.

and thou shalt find Me; cleave the wood and there am I." [17] Whereas
there are illustrations from business and banking in the parables, we
do not find there any references to carpentry itself. This fact is not
strange; for it was only incidentally that Our Lord took up his trade;
and His gospel of redemption and salvation for all men was far above
and beyond the scope of any one trade and the horizon of any mere
tradesman.[18]

When Our Lord at Nazareth proclaimed Himself the Messiah,
people took offense [19] because He had been simply a carpenter and
because He belonged to a family they considered ordinary. In the
second century, Celsus poured ridicule on Christianity because it
was founded by a mere artisan.[20] Again, two centuries later, on the
occasion of the eastern expedition, A.D. 363, an admirer of Julian
the Apostate, the sophist Libanius, it is said, asked a Christian in
derision, "What is the carpenter's son doing now?" The answer
came back foretelling Julian's death, which was soon to take place,
"Sophist, the Creator of all things whom you in derision call carpenter's son is making a coffin." [21]

[17] Cf. M. James, *The Apocryphal New Testament*, p. 27.

[18] As Delitzsch points out it is impossible to picture Our Lord with the carpenter's rule
in his hand; for His public ministry "utterly precluded the continuation of the trade."
Jewish Artisan Life in the Time of Jesus, p. 85.

[19] When the townspeople of Nazareth referred to Our Lord as "the carpenter" (Mark
6:3) and "the carpenter's son" (Matt. 13:55), it was not with the purpose of holding
the profession of carpentry up to ridicule. Carpenters are not listed among the despised
classes in the *Mishnah* (Kiddushin, 4, 14: Danby, p. 329). On the contrary artisans were
held in honor, so much so, that famous rabbis learned trades. Our Lord's trade as a
carpenter and the standing of His family were well known to His fellow townspeople.
They were acquainted with Jesus almost all the years of His life; and they could think
of no natural explanation to account for His words of wisdom and grace. They considered
both His trade as a carpenter and the rank of His family incompatible with the exalted
position of the Messiah. Thus they rejected His claim in their synagogue.

Our Lord's enemies at Capharnaum made no mention of His trade when they rejected His exalted doctrines because of knowing His family (John 6:42). Neither did His
enemies at Jerusalem bring up the matter of His trade when they spoke disparagingly
about where He was from, and His lack of rabbinical training (John 7:15, 27). The
trade of a carpenter was an honorable one and was not scoffed at by Our Savior's countrymen.

[20] Origen, *Against Celsus*, I, 28–30. Celsus ridiculed Our Lord also with being born
in a village. *Ibid.*, I, 29; ANF, IV, 409.

[21] Cf. Theodoret, *Ecclesiastical History*, III, 18; NPN, 2nd ser., III, 105; also Sozomon,
Ecclesiastical History, VI, 2; NPN, 2nd ser., II, 347.

Due reflection brings out the reason why our Blessed Lord chose to live as a carpenter during the long hidden life. Since He became man to sanctify and redeem us, He took up a life of toil and labor to be all the more like us who live by labor and toil. In this respect He conferred a dignity on what has to be done by all of us. He has also shown that the greatest perfection is not incompatible with ordinary, everyday work.

The world's toilers have this consolation, that the Son of God chose to be considered the son of a carpenter. In the light of the truth that the sufferings of this life are not to be compared with the joys of heaven and that the excellence of man lies in the practice of virtues which are within the reach of all, we can see that God seems to favor with His graces those who suffer hardship. Did not our Lord Himself call the poor blessed? [22] Was it not those bent under the heavy burden of labor that He especially invited to come to Him for consolation? Did He not extend His tenderest charity to the lowly and oppressed? (Cf. Jas. 2:5.) Accordingly, Pope Leo XIII,

---

[22] The economic condition of a carpenter in a town like Nazareth would be somewhat of the same level as that of the average resident there; or perhaps his condition would be a little better than the average. We would expect that unlike the majority of the townspeople a carpenter would not have to hire himself out as a laborer at certain times of the year, as there would be sufficient employment for him at this trade throughout the year. Besides, the information the Holy Scripture gives us about the Blessed Mother's relationship to a priestly family, that of St. Elizabeth, would be an indication that Mary's family was a respectable one.

In a psalm which may apply to the Messiah, we read "I am poor and in labors from my youth" (Ps. 87 [88]:16). This text is not to be used as an argument for the economic condition of Our Lord's hidden life; for the reason that the original Hebrew has a different meaning. The new translation (McClellan's Latin English edition) from the Hebrew gives the rendering: "I am afflicted and near death from my boyhood."

There have been some who have thought that Our Lord spent the first thirty years of His life in prayer without engaging in any kind of work; and there have been others who have been of the opinion that the Savior's hidden life was passed in abject poverty with its constant struggle and strain. That both of these extreme views are wrong the available information we possess would incline us to hold. Jesus' life was one of great simplicity and frugality, especially when contrasted with our modern standards. It may be said that as in almost every age in the past so in Our Lord's day a carpenter who was busy at his trade was able to make a fair living out of it.

It must be admitted that by His engaging in the carpentry trade the God-man honored artisans of all time. For to quote Delitzsch, to them "belongs the honor that the Savior of the world sprang from an artisan's house. The first king of Israel was taken from behind the plow; the second king of Israel was called from the sheepfold; and the second David, the Messiah of Israel, was called from the carpenter's shop" (*op. cit.*, p. 86).

when writing on the dignity of labor, held up for the consolation of the working class the divine example: "As for those who do not possess the gifts of fortune, they are taught by the Church that, in God's sight, poverty is no disgrace, and that there is nothing to be ashamed of in seeking one's bread by labor. This is strengthened by what we see in Christ Himself, who whereas He was rich, for our sakes became poor; and who being the Son of God and God Himself chose to seem and to be considered the son of a carpenter— nay, did not disdain to spend a great part of His life as a carpenter Himself. Is not this the carpenter, the son of Mary?" [23]

Following the example of our heavenly Father, who designed and built the universe,[24] and the example of the Son of God, who

[23] Encyclical, *Rerum Novarum* (*On the Conditions of Labor*). *Five Great Encyclicals*, p. 12.

[24] St. Ambrose (*Expositiones in Lucam*, lib. VII, 2; ad Luc. 3:25; PL, 15, 1671–2) explains the reason why Jesus' foster father was an artisan. He says that this trade was a type that showed forth the eternal Father who made the whole world. St. Ambrose goes on to observe that as the human cannot be compared to the divine, the perfect fulfillment of this type is found in the heavenly Father as the artisan of good souls working on them "with fire and the Holy Ghost." He removes our vices; He destroys unfruitful trees with the axe; He cuts off the mean and the sordid; He preserves the sublime, lasting fruits; He melts frozen hearts with the fire of the Spirit; and He forms for various uses the different kinds of ministries in the human race. These ideas of St. Ambrose that suggest that St. Joseph was a carpenter are repeated in works of later ages.

In a sermon on the Nativity falsely ascribed to St. Ambrose, but probably belonging to St. Maximus (fifth century), attention is drawn to the work done by St. Joseph, and comparisons are made with the work of the foster father of Our Lord and that done by the heavenly Father: Clearly an artisan is God the Father who produced the works of the whole world; also clearly He showed Himself an artisan in giving the plans for the construction of Noah's ark. An artisan is He who ordered the tabernacles of Moses, instituted the ark of the covenant and built Solomon's temple. I should say He is an artisan who melts frozen hearts, dissipates proud thoughts and brings forth the fruits of humility. The one artisan used the hatchet on trees; as in the Gospel we read that John said "For now the axe is laid to the root of the trees. Every tree therefore that doth not yield good fruit shall be cut down, and cast into the fire" (Matt. 3:10). The other Artisan does the final work so that He might build up into structures useful trees of heavenly construction, and that the unfruitful rejected trees He might completely burn with firery flames (*Sermon VI, De Natali Domini*, 7; PL, 17, 637).

Somewhat similar ideas, but expressed with more art and eloquence, are found in a sermon falsely attributed to St. Augustine (*Sermon 135, in Epiphania Domini* V, 5; PL, 39, 2012). The allegorical or spiritual significance of St. Joseph's trade is pointed out by the *Opus imperfectum super Matthaeum*, Homily, I. "Thus Mary was espoused to a carpenter since also Christ the spouse of the Church was to bring about the salvation of all men and to accomplish all His work through the wood of the cross. (Found with the works of St. John Chrysostom, PG, 56, 630 f.)

worked at the constructive trade of carpenter, man should devote himself to useful and profitable pursuits. Gainful occupations, besides serving as preventives that ward off occasions for temptations, furnish the means of enjoying the Godlike privilege of being able "to have something to give to him that suffereth need" (Ephes. 4:28).

BIBLIOGRAPHY

Booth, H. The World of Jesus, pp. 83–86.

Dalman, C. Sacred Sites and Ways, pp. 68–71.

Encyclicals, Rerum Novarum and Quadragesimo Anno; Five Great Encyclicals (Paulist Press, New York, 1939), pp. 1–30; 125–68.

Filas, F. The Man Nearest to Christ, pp. 54–59.

Hoepfl, H. "Nonne hic est fabri Filius," Biblica, IV (1923), 41–55.

Sutcliffe, E. F. "St. Joseph's Trade. An Enquiry into the Evidence," Irish Theol. Quart., X (1915), 179–201.

———. "The Divine Carpenter," Irish Theol. Quart., XI (1916), 147–63.

Plowing scene near Nazareth

CHAPTER XXIV

The Carpenter and His Neighbors

DURING His long thirty years at Nazareth, Our Savior must have met and spoken with almost all the members of the hundred families of His home town. They were like most of the residents of the many other towns that surrounded Sephoris: small farmers, fruit growers, and laborers, skilled and unskilled.[1] He became well acquainted with them, and they with Him. His work brought Him into many of their homes and also brought many of them to His shop. He installed or repaired a chest or cupboard here and there. He made a new lamp stand for one customer or helped another with a roof. He supplied the peasants with a wooden plow and gave them new parts for their oxen yoke. Also he must have frequently visited the little farms in the valleys, on the great plain of Esdraelon, and on the great marshy plain of Asochis. Especially He must have

[1] In Our Lord's day there were some towns and villages of the Holy Land given over to one business and occupied almost exclusively by men of the same trade, such as potters or workers in bronze. Because of the forests on the neighboring hills, so convenient to Nazareth, this town could easily have been the exclusive home of wood-cutters, carpenters, and joiners. On the other hand, the question on the lips of the residents of this town, when Jesus returned there during the public ministry, was: "Is not this Jesus the carpenter?" and not: "Is He not one of us?" This seems to indicate that the majority were not of the same profession. At any rate it was the custom of the time for tradesmen of the same handicraft to group their homes and shops on the same street of towns and cities.

frequently gone into the Jewish villages near Nazareth, such as Kesaloth (Iksul), [2] a mile and a half southeast, or Japhia, at the same distance to the west.

He must have paid visits to such villages as Lubieh and Garis in the vicinity, or to Gabatha and Simonias on the Esdraelon plain, or Daberath on the northern flank of Thabor. The three greatest cities of Lower Galilee (Sephoris, Tiberias and Gabara) [3] predominantly non-Jewish in population contained each several thousand Jews, yet we do not read in the Gospels that the Savior of the public ministry ever preached in these cities. He did bring the glad tidings to many of the two hundred villages and towns especially in the section lying between Nazareth and Capharnaum. The communities in this district we may suppose He knew during His hidden life; for He must have called upon them as the Carpenter of Nazareth. This part of Lower Galilee appears "as a plain broken by wave upon wave of rounded hills." [4] Nazareth lay between two great plains, that of Esdraelon and that of Asochis, but numerous other plains lay in the valleys that ran east and west between the ranges of hills. Plowed lands for the various crops and fields of sesame, saffron, and flax could be seen in the valleys, and on the hillsides groves for the cultivation of olives, grapes, dates, figs, and pomegranates.

To the neighboring towns, many of them much larger than His own and within a few hours' journey, must Jesus have gone with plows and yokes for oxen and other articles made in His carpenter shop. The market days, Mondays and Thursdays, would be occasions, and probably a donkey or mule would be used as the beast of burden. Then in the market place of these towns the Carpenter would sell His goods either for money or in barter for other goods. Here would be displayed grain crops (wheat, barley and spelt), a

[2] Cf. Josephus, *Jewish War*, III, 39 (iii, 1).

[3] Cf. Josephus, *Life*, 123 (25), i, 203 (40). He says that Sephoris was the heart of Galilee and was surrounded by numerous villages; *Life*, 346 (65).

[4] Masterman, *Studies in Galilee*, p. 6. Cf. also Merrill, *Galilee in the Time of Christ*, pp. 23–33.

variety of vegetables (carrots, cucumbers, onions, radishes, lettuce, horse-radish, lentils, beans, and chick-peas) ; [5] and an abundance of fruit (grapes, olives, figs, pomegranates, citrons, cherries, nuts, plums, dates, apples, and pears). Jobbers could be heard arguing over wine and oil; and fowl, such as doves, pigeons, chickens, geese, and ducks, would add to the din. There would be peddlers selling clothes, and idle laborers loitering in expectancy of employment. In these Jewish towns the stores would sell home products; especially in those shops operated by Syrians and Greeks there would be for sale inexpensive imported goods, such as cloth, dried fish, Syrian wine, new glassware and cheap pottery. They might also display expensive articles: Corinthian metal lamps, Indian cloths, Chinese silks, precious wood, carpets, jewels, spices, manuscripts of the Holy Scriptures.[6] Butchers and bakers would also be found in these towns. Everywhere Roman officials would be stationed to exact taxes on what was bought and sold [7] and what was carried in or out of town. Likewise in these towns one would meet town clerks, court secretaries, interpreters, and professional scribes. After transacting His business, the Carpenter of Nazareth would return home around the gentle slopes of the Galilean hills, by many a shaded lane and picturesque path, calling out greetings and blessings on friendly workers in the bright farms and smiling orchards.

The people with whom Our Lord dealt, the peasants of small holdings, were at that time classed among the poor, for a person who did not possess at least 10,000 denarii (equal to $2,000) could not be considered rich.[8] When a person accumulated at least twice that amount he was definitely in the latter class. The word "rich" in Our Lord's day was applied to those who could operate their

---

[5] The Talmud and other ancient sources mention these and other vegetables. There were several varieties of aracus, lentils, bean, kidney-bean, chick-pea, vetch, and lupin. See Heichelheim, "Roman Syria," in *Economic Survey of Ancient Rome*, IV, 130.

[6] See Heichelheim, *op. cit.*, pp. 183 ff.

[7] At least in Jerusalem; Cf. Josephus, *Antiquities*, XVII, viii, 4.

[8] Cf. Heichelheim, "Roman Syria," in *Economic Survey of Ancient Rome*, IV, 180; Furfey, "Plusios and Cognates in the New Testament," *Catholic Bib. Quart.*, V (1943), 243–63.

business on their own money; the word "poor" was applied to those who were not freed from daily toil, but had to make their living with their own hands. Thus, even in the latter class there were generally scribes, teachers, physicians, and skilled laborers. The poor, however, were not in all cases the needy. Most of Our Lord's neighbors, the people in Nazareth and the towns near-by, were peasants possessing or renting perhaps five or ten acres of ground which they worked themselves with the help of their families. Even artisans, besides their own work, would cultivate fruit and vegetable crops. A large group of small tenants also hired themselves out daily as agricultural laborers. There were others who merely labored either at a specific work or for a certain time. In seasons of hard times these suffered most in the community. Some of them drifted to brigandage, and many of them were forced to become slaves to relieve their debts. The large estates had a number of slaves. Yet these slaves, although sometimes employed in agriculture or the skilled handicrafts, were generally used in domestic service (cf. Luke 17:7). Sometimes freed slaves became immensely wealthy.

Among those considered rich were peasants who lived by lending money or seed, landowners who supplied the home market, and proprietors of large estates who sublet to tenants for half or a third or a fourth of the produce. One who owned a hundred grain fields, a hundred vineyards, and a hundred slaves was certainly reckoned a rich man. Large estates were often under a single manager. Although sometimes worked by slaves and hired laborers, they were often leased to tenants or serfs. Frequently they were operated for the purpose of lending seed or money, and sometimes they had attached to them workshops that sent goods such as pottery to merchant shops.[9]

Our Lord's home province was intensely cultivated in His day. Josephus tells us that the country for about ten miles around Nazareth was considered a paradise flowing with milk and honey.[10] A

[9] Cf. Heichelheim, *op. cit.*, p. 147.
[10] See above, chap. 15.

certain amount of rotation of crops was practiced as a help to the soil. Moreover, progressive methods of fertilization and the production of seed grain that had been introduced by the Greeks were gradually being adopted.[11] Galilee produced an excellent wheat crop, which was ranked next to that of Judea; but it came first in regard to olive oil and was considered the home of the olive. Its yield of wine merited words of praise and commendation. Despite all this, it was said that the most profitable kind of cultivation in Galilee was that of fruits and dates.[12] Frequently prohibitions had to be issued against the exportation of wine, olive oil, and flour, as these were required for home consumption.[13] To help supply the ordinary diet, figs likewise were extensively cultivated. In addition, the Galilean peasant kept bees, doves, and poultry, and raised sheep and cattle. As in most farming of a small nature, the raising of cattle was considered the staple element [14] and brought cash for household expenses. These small holders would receive for two pigeons about $.20, for a lamb about $.50, for a sheep about $5.00, for a donkey about $20., and for a cow about $30. The cost of a slave was about $34, and $5.00 would buy a suit for a slave; yet the cost of a roll of Sacred Scripture with a mat was as high as $85. These figures [15] give us some idea, even if meager, of prices at that time; provided it be kept in mind that the purchasing price of such money was many times greater than it is today.

The owners of many of the farms and orchards in the vicinity of Nazareth were rich Gentiles, who lived in palaces which for protection were often within city walls. The largest city and the capital of Galilee, Sephoris,[16] had a big share of the important managers of estates and rich business men. This city in the heart of the province was only three miles northwest of Nazareth and must have been often visited by our divine Lord. He could look down on it

11 Cf. Heichelheim, *op. cit.*, p. 126.
12 *Ibid.*, pp. 136 ff.
13 Cf. *ibid.*, IV, 140.
14 *Ibid.*, p. 153.
15 For a more complete list, see *ibid.*, pp. 183–88.
16 Josephus, *Life*, 103 (21); *Jewish War*, III, 34 (iii, 1).

when He climbed the hill that sheltered His own town from the northern winds of winter. Herod Antipas rebuilt it and its royal citadel, after it had been burned to the ground in the revolt at the beginning of his reign. He and his court lived there until he constructed the new city of Tiberias when Jesus was about fifteen years old. Here one could meet courtiers and soldiers, Roman colonists and retired veterans, descendants of old Greek, Syrian, and Arab settlers, and newly arrived students and visitors, as well as Jewish priests and rabbis. This city had a large Jewish population and soon grew to a great Jewish center. It had several synagogues and many public buildings, including barracks, temples, theaters, and amphitheaters. In one section there were large boarding houses several stories high that served as hotels; in another there was a market with an upper and lower street where merchants and craftsmen, such as weavers, had their own booths. One could purchase various kinds of imported goods (frankincense, perfumes, dyeing materials, precious stones, silks, cottons, new types of blown-glass vessels, and glazed pottery of green and brown hues).[17] Here the businessmen had their clubs, and there were trade unions and a guild for theatrical artists who presented the regular Greek plays. Here all the festivals of the Roman state as well as local feasts were celebrated with horse racing, musical shows, dancing displays, theatrical productions, and gladiators' contests with wild beasts and prisoners of war.[18]

Sephoris, had not only a royal bank but also an archives office [19] for recorded deeds and debt contracts, because new methods of banking had been introduced to the Near East by the Greeks.[20] Although goods were sometimes exchanged on the barter system, yet money was as extensively used as it was down to a few centuries ago. In Palestine, Roman, Greek, Syrian, and Jewish currencies were in circulation, the Jews having to limit their coinage to issues

[17] Cf. Josephus, *Life*, 107 (22); Heichelheim, *op. cit.*, pp. 190, 207; Rostovtzeff, *Social and Economic History of the Hellenistic World*, II, 1024.
[18] Cf. Heichelheim, *op. cit.*, pp. 208 ff.
[19] Josephus, *Life*, 38 (9).
[20] Cf. Heichelheim, *op. cit.*, pp. 224–27; Rostovtzeff, *op. cit.*, II, 844–70.

in bronze.[21] For exchange purposes the Jews had their own bankers, who gave and took loans without interest. They collected from each Jew the Temple tax or two denarii a year and deposited it in the Temple treasury.[22]

The Carpenter of Nazareth must have occasionally visited Lake Tiberias and the fishing towns on its northwestern shore, all of which were within a day's walk. He might have gone to these places with farming implements or household furniture and perhaps brought back home some fresh fish. The cities and towns on the southwestern shore of the lake would be nearest to Our Lord's home town. Tiberias, which became the residence of Herod Antipas during the hidden life, had a stadium for the amusement of its Greek population.[23] Near Tiberias were the warm springs of Hamman,[24] and a mile and half away was the town of Bethmaus.[25] About the middle of the western shore of the lake was situated Tarechias (Magdala) that got its name from a dried fish that was in popular demand. We learn that it had a hippodrome and a prayer hall.[26] At the extreme end of the lake was Homenoia,[27] and six miles to the southewest was Adamah.[28] Although the towns on the north-western shore were farther from Nazareth than the ones just mentioned, we may suppose that the Carpenter visited them during the hidden life as He did during the public ministry; for they were Jewish towns with a small minority of Gentiles, and the great caravan route led toward them. Since there were no Jewish cities on the

---

[21] The Syrian stater was accepted as equivalent to the Jewish shekel, about sixty-four cents in our money; and the Roman denarius was considered equal to the Greek drachma, about seventeen cents, the usual day's pay for a laborer.

[22] See Heichelheim, op. cit., pp. 211–23.

[23] Cf. Josephus, Life, 67 (12), 91 (17); Jewish War, III, 409 (vii, 9). Coarse cloths and mats were made at Tiberias (Helchelhcim, op. cit., p. 191).

[24] Josephus, Jewish War, IV, 11 (i, 3).

[25] Josephus, Life, 64 (12).

[26] Josephus, Life, 132 (27), 277 (54). He mentions the second floor of a house there, 146 (30). He says the town was four and a half miles from Tiberias, 156 (32), and says it had 40,000 inhabitants (Jewish War, II, 608 (xxi, 4) and a fishing fleet of 230 boats (ibid., II, 635 (xxi, 8). Cf. Dalman, Sacred Sites and Ways, p. 126. Some hold that Tarechias was situated toward the southern end of the lake.

[27] Josephus, Life, 281 (54).

[28] Ibid., 321 (62).

southwestern shore of the lake,[29] perhaps this section was not visited during either the public ministry or the hidden life.

The Carpenter of Nazareth must have been often in the Jewish town of Japhia, on the neighboring hills only a mile and a half away and on a main road that led southeast to the great plain.[30] In the following generation at the beginning of the Jewish War A.D. 67, doubtless many of the people of Nazareth took refuge in this near-by city that was favored by its position and its double wall. At any rate, our Savior must have known, as boys and girls, even as young men and young women, many of the victims of the Romans whom God brought "to punish the Galileans," according to Josephus.[31] In another place this historian speaks about the multitude of men of Japhia with their wives and children loudly voicing their loyalty to himself,[32] and also states that once he made his headquarters there.[33] Typical of the daring bordering on foolhardiness that characterized Our Lord's neighbors, was their sallying forth to attack the Roman forces on the plain. The latter, however, followed the retreating patriots so closely that they were able to penetrate the first rampart of the town. Upon perceiving their plight, the defenders of the second wall closed the inner gates against their own men, with the sad result that twelve thousand (according to Josephus' exaggerated figures) were caught between their own walls and easily slain. Soon afterward the city itself fell to the young Titus. Did the Carpenter of Nazareth weep over Japhia as He later wept over Jerusalem?

Josephus [34] indicates with some exaggeration, how populous the province of Galilee was, when he says that he was able to raise there

---

[29] Josephus says there was no Jewish city in the vicinity of Tiberias; *Life,* 349 (65). As Dalman (*op. cit.,* p. 181) states, Tiberias must have been predominantly Jewish in A.D. 66. See Mark 8:10; Matt. 15:39.

[30] Josephus says it was the largest village in Galilee, was strongly fortified, and contained a dense population, *Life,* 230 (45). According to a late tradition, Japhia was the birthplace of the two apostles, St. James and St. John. Cf. Meistermann, *Guide to the Holy Land,* p. 477.

[31] *Jewish War,* III, 293 (vii, 31).

[32] *Life,* 230 f. (45).

[33] *Ibid.,* 270 (52).

[34] *Jewish War,* II, 576 (xx, 6).

an army of a hundred thousand young men. He also testifies to many deeds of bravery and heroism. We learn that the Jewish and Gentile inhabitants of Galilee and the surrounding territories, seemingly living in harmony in Our Lord's day, were even then nursing mutual suspicions and hatreds; for when the Jews rose in rebellion, the Gentiles in the Greek and Phoenician cities, excepting Sidon,[35] immediately turned on them. Everywhere there were two armed camps, the Jews fighting not only the Roman army but also their Greek and Syrian neighbors; consequently "the most dreadful calamities befell the Jews," so that it was common to see cities "filled with dead bodies lying unburied." [36]

A Greek city, Scythopolis (Beth Shean), at the edge of the Jordan valley, a day's journey from Nazareth by a good road, in the valley of Jezreel, would be passed by anyone going to Jerusalem by the Jordan route. This city was predominantly Gentile, with a large Jewish population. In the Jewish War, the Jewish residents were first compelled to fight against their own brethren and then were treacherously massacred.[37] The historian Josephus mentions the city's amphitheater which, he says, "was foreign to the Jews." Scythopolis was one of the cities, the largest of them, that formed the district of Decapolis or Federation of Ten Cities, the others lying to the east of the Jordan.

Samaria, the district south of the plain of Esdraelon, was occupied by a people of mixed race, who were perpetually in contention with the Jews. Its capital, to which the whole province was subordinate, had been enlarged by Herod the Great, who had also settled there six thousand colonists of disbanded soldiers. During Our Lord's life Samaria supplied a great part of the Roman army in Judea. Indeed the police work for the whole of Palestine was done to a great extent by Samaritans.[38] This fact added to the mutual distrust

[35] *Ibid.*, II, 479 (xviii, 5).
[36] *Ibid.*, II, 461–65 (xviii, 2).
[37] As told by Josephus the story of one Simon, son of Saul, is most pathetic. *Jewish War*, II, 469–76 (xviii, 4); see also III, 466 (ix, 7).
[38] Samaria was rebuilt and refounded as Sabaste by Herod the Great. Troops raised here were called Sebasteonians. Josephus, *Jewish War*, II, 52 (iii, 4), etc.

and opposition. The Carpenter of Nazareth would pass through this territory on His yearly pilgrimages to Jerusalem.

The city of Gaba (Geba), situated as it was on the northern declivity of Mount Carmel, could be easily seen from the heights of Nazareth. It was called the "city of horsemen," [39] for Herod the Great had settled there a colony of retired cavalrymen. On the Phoenician border were the Syrian villages of Besara and Kedasa, and the Jewish Cabul.[40] North of Gaba was the plain of Acre (Ptolemais) that bordered on Galilee. The Phoenician city of this name had a large Jewish element, since we learn that many Jews were massacred there in the beginning of the Jewish war.[41] It was so closely associated with Galilee that it was called by Josephus "a maritime city of Galilee." [42] Ptolemias would be the town on the Mediterranean nearest to Nazareth that could be reached in an easy day's journey. In Our Lord's day Tyre [43] was famous for its textiles, its purple dyes, its sandals, and its slave market. Sidon produced philosophers, rhetoricians, and adepts in astronomy, mathematics, and medicine; and it could well boast of its cutlery and bronze works; furthermore, from its glass-blowing industry, which may have had its original home there, went forth glassware to countries far and near. On the Mediterranean, ships could be seen that brought goods and passengers from foreign lands to the Palestinian ports; just as below the hills of Nazareth could be observed caravans from Egypt and Damascus conducted by men with strange dress

[39] Josephus, Jewish War, III, 35 (iii, 1). In Our Lord's day Carmel was in the territory of the city of Tyre.

[40] Josephus, Jewish War, II, 459 (xviii, 1); also II, 520 (xviii, 9); IV, 105 (ii, 3); Life, 213 (43). Kedasa was perpetually at strife with the Galileans; and Cabul within the territory of Galilee had beautiful homes in Phoenician style.

[41] Josephus, Jewish War, II, 477 (xviii, 5). Herod built a gymnasium there; Jewish War, I, 422 (xxi, ii).

[42] Jewish War, II, 188 (x, 2). He says the town was built at the entrance to the Great Plain and was encompassed with mountains. It had a glass-blowing industry.

[43] For the industries of the Phoenician cities, see Heichelheim "Roman Syria," in Economic Survey of Ancient Rome, IV, 192, 198–207. Herod the Great built a theater for Sidon, and halls, porticoes, temples, and market places for Tyre and Beyruth; Josephus, Jewish War, I, 422 (xxi, 11). Prat thinks it doubtful whether Our Lord ever entered Tyre or Sidon, Jésus-Christ, I, 476.

and speech. Even from the hill of Nazareth looking beyond Thabor one might catch a glimpse of the country of the Decapolis. Indeed with the chief cities of Galilee predominantly Gentile, how could a resident of Nazareth avoid all contact with the Graeco-Roman world around him or not be influenced by it?

The Gentiles of Galilee at that time had various deities according to the races from which they sprang; yet it may be said they were never averse to adopting new ones. Their religious views were in a transitional stage. Dissatisfied with the old religions, the pagans throughout the Roman Empire were seeking new faiths in Greek philosophy. This explains their drifting toward the idealism of Platonism, or the pleasure-seeking of Epicureanism, or the discipline of Stoicism, or the Orphic mystery cults of Neo-Pythagoreanism, or the cynicism of skepticism. We are not surprised that the prevailing mood was one of pessimism, bordering on despair, from which many sought escape in the mystery initiation of Osiris and Mithras. The Jews both at home and in the Dispersion attracted converts, who were known as "proselytes of the gate."

That Gentiles controlled the business as well as the government of the country brought home to the Galileans the sad truth that their Holy Land of promise was in subjection to foreign rule. This grievance was aggravated by the fact that, because of God's special dealings with their race, they associated patriotism with religion. Galileans, being impetuous and brave to a fault, must have found the foreign yoke almost unbearable. Rome sought to teach them a severe lesson after the revolt of Judas the Galilean; yet later we hear of Galileans whose blood was mixed with the sacrifices of the Temple, because of their fiery outburst of patriot zeal (Luke 13:1). It was not much of a comfort to them that Rome left the governing of Galilee and Perea to Herod Antipas, for this ruler's shameful marriage to his brother's wife was a great source of scandal, and his armies and fortresses were an impregnable barrier against the return of national freedom and the assertion of national sovereignty.

A persistent reminder of foreign domination and an ever-recurring cause of irritation were the great number and variety of taxes.[44] Julius Caesar had granted a concession from a greater burden of taxation, inherited, it seems, from the Persian era, when he fixed the land tax at 12½ per cent; each seventh or Jubilee year to be excepted. In addition there was an annual poll tax of one denarius, and there seems to have been an additional land tax of one per cent in connection with the regular census. Besides there were numerous other taxes, such as taxes on goods bought or sold, taxes on goods in transit, municipal taxes, and pasturing taxes. The poll taxes and the land taxes were collected by Roman officials; the collecting of customs duties and the like was let out to tax farmers. No wonder the merchants of Jerusalem complained to Archelaus about the market duty on fruits bought or sold; [45] and no wonder, on the accession of Tiberius, when Our Lord was about twenty years of age, that people openly expressed their grievance, saying they were exhausted by the burden of taxation.[46] Added to these burdens were the Temple tax of half a shekel, or two denarii, and the expenses of Temple sacrifices.

The 100,000 inhabitants of the seven hundred square miles of Jewish Galilee [47] had another difficulty that beset the whole of Palestine, namely, that the country was not able to supply enough food and clothing to meet the needs of its own people. Despite the healthful climate, the fertility of the soil, and the industry of the natives, there was of necessity ceaseless emigration,[48] with its anguish of heart at separation of relatives and friends.

The neighbors of Christ, like the rest of the Jews of Palestine, did not engage notably in trade or commerce, being entirely shut off from the sea.[49] They were sober, industrious farming folk as a

[44] Cf. Heichelheim, op. cit., 231–45. Rostovtzeff, op. cit., II, 979–1007.

[45] Josephus, Jewish War, II, 4 (i, 2).

[46] Cf. Tacitus, Annals, II, 42.

[47] About 150 persons to the square mile. Cf. McCown, "The Density of Population in Ancient Palestine," Journal of Bib. Lit., LXVII (1947), 436.

[48] Ibid., p. 430.

[49] Josephus, Against Apion, I, 60 (12).

rule, who lived happy family lives. They were pugnacious by nature, willing to fight for their rights and to make sacrifices for principle. Loyal and devoted to their country, they always resisted an invader,[50] not reckoning the cost. They were ever ready to make vows and were more zealous for their religion than any other Jews of the time.[51] Josephus [52] praises their loyalty and constancy, but it is in the Gospel narrative of the call of the apostles and of the devotion of the disciples that we find illustrations of that sublime faith in God that has conquered the world. "Galilee of the Gentiles" (Isa. 9:1) was the soil selected by the Great Sower. In the proving, it was found to have enough good ground to nurture the good seed that was to multiply and to furnish the supply for the needs of the world.[53] There was a proximate preparing of this ground for the sowing, which was the work of the thirty years of good example of the Carpenter of Nazareth.

BIBLIOGRAPHY

Carpenter, J. E. Life in Palestine when Jesus Lived.

Dalman, G. Arbeit und Sitte in Palästina.

Furfey, P. H. " 'Plousios' and Cognates in the New Testament," Catholic Bib. Quart., V (1943), 243–63.

Grant, F. C. Economic Background of the Gospels.

Heichelheim, F. M. An Economic Survey of Ancient Rome, edited by T. Frank, IV, 123–257.

Masterman, E. W. Studies in Galilee.

[50] This is the testimony of Josephus. He says that Galileans were numerous and industrious. In tribute to them he writes: "Never did the men lack courage nor the country men." *Jewish War*, III, 41 f. (iii, 2). The Talmud says that they placed honor above wealth. Cf. Dalman, *Sacred Sites and Ways*, p. 6.

[51] Cf. *Mishnah*, Nedarim (Vows), 5, 5; Danby, p. 271. For their observances in which they surpassed the Judeans, see Dalman, *Sacred Sites and Ways*, p. 7.

[52] For example, *Life*, 84 (16); 102 (21).

[53] Lower Galilee, honored by the long years of the hidden life, received special care and attention during the public ministry; for during the early part of this ministry Our Lord made at least three tours of the towns of Lower Galilee; some say four, with two visits to Nazareth. Then, besides, He sent the twelve apostles through the towns of Galilee (Luke 9:6). These twelve apostles, who became the pillars of the Church, were from Galilee with the possible exception of Judas the traitor.

Merrill, S. Galilee in the Time of Christ.

Morrison, W. The Jews under Roman Rule.

Tarn, W. W. Hellenistic Civilization.

Rostovtzeff, M. The Social and Economic History of the Roman Empire.

————. The Social and Economic History of the Hellenistic World, 3 vols.

CHAPTER XXV

Conversation at Nazareth

THE people of Nazareth conversed a great deal while working in groups in the fields or while resting during the midday meal hour. There was also much interchange of views across roof tops in the summer evenings or within doors in the winter. After the mutual wishing of peace, the opening remarks would likely be on the weather. In the dry season any shower would be mentioned with gratitude and, what was much more infrequent, a fall of snow in the wet season would merit a comment.[1] The growing of crops and fruits and the raising of poultry and domestic animals would occupy a great deal of mutual talk. Praise and thanksgiving would be offered to God for the bountiful harvests followed no doubt by a little boasting that the yield per acre excelled that of other lands. To keep up appearances, exaggerations would naturally be indulged in: the number of trees in an olive grove was equal to that of a legion,[2] a neighboring community had so many figs that they were supplied to the poor,[3] a turnip-rooted cabbage was thirty pounds in weight, millet grew as tall as a man, or a mustard shrub covered a hut.[4]

---

[1] On weather conditions of the Nazareth district, see Abel, *Geographie de la Palestine*, I, p. 125–29. As there really were only two seasons, people would say, "before the rains," or "before the second shower." Cf. *Mishnah*, Nedarim (Vows), 8, 5; Danby, p. 274.

[2] This was an old proverb. See Dalman, *Sacred Sites and Ways*, p. 70.

[3] Ruma; see Dalman, *op. cit.*, p. 104.

[4] For the last three statements, see Dalman, *op. cit.*, p. 71.

Mention would be made of the comparative poverty of the people despite the fact that the land was so productive, and the causes for it would be discussed. High cost of living, profiteering and overtaxation would be subjects of complaint. That prices were higher in Palestine than in either Egypt or Babylonia would be a true statement.[5] Officials who garnered in immense profits from olive oil bought in Lower Galilee and sold in Caesarea Philippi,[6] would be named and censured. It would be told around that balsam cuttings obtained at Jericho for three hundred denarii apiece brought a thousand apiece in foreign lands.[7] Was there any conversation where resentment was not openly voiced over the frequent abuses on the part of money changers and tax collectors?

The chief priests at Jerusalem would receive a large share of blame. Remarks would be passed on their overbearing exercise of power, on their accumulation of wealth through exchange manipulations and transactions in Temple offerings, on their compromising dealings with Roman authorities, and on the lack of faith of so many of those who were Sadducees. Instances would be cited of the servants of the high priest beating the people with rods and visiting threshing floors to seize a large amount of the harvest that should have been divided among the priests of lower rank.[8] Some good townspeople of Nazareth would declare that they had no scruple in avoiding the payment of the yearly half-shekel assessment.[9] "The high authorities at Jerusalem," one would say, "do not conceal their contempt for us, Galileans, because we are not so well versed in the sacred laws, and because we do not pronounce so well the Aramaic gutturals. Why is it that they do not praise us for our great devotion to God and country?" He would go on to give some evident proofs of the fact that religion was really more genuine in Galilee than in Judea; namely, that in Galilee alone work was not

[5] On certain things, see Heichelheim, "Roman Syria," Economic Survey of Ancient Rome, IV, 149, 154, 163, 178, 181, 182, 209.

[6] Josephus, Life, 75 (14).

[7] Cf. Josephus, Antiquities, XV, iv, 2; Heichelheim, op. cit., p. 229.

[8] Cf. Josephus, op. cit., XX, ix, 4; Jewish War, IV, 155–59 (iii, 8).

[9] Cf. Mishnah, Nedarim (Vows), 2, 4; Danby, p. 265.

permitted on the eve of Passover,[10] the Day of Atonement was kept as a solemn fast, and a special service marked the New Year.[11] A word of praise would be given the general body of the priests, and it would be told with pride that some of them when taken to Rome ate only figs during the entire journey so that they would not break their own ceremonial regulations.[12]

A resident of Nazareth would impart to his neighbors information he had gathered from drivers of one of the caravans that could be seen almost every day winding along the great highway which from the southeast descended to the great plain of Esdraelon. The caravan, consisting of fifty camels, had come from Seluceia on the Tigris River, where there was a large Jewish population,[13] and had passed through Damascus and Capharnaum. It was going to Jerusalem and from there it would make a fifteen days' trip to Alexandria. On the return journey the coastal road would be followed all the way to Antioch, which would be reached in about thirty days; and then in about twice that time the desert would be recrossed and Seluceia would be reached. In the cities thus connected, with the exception of Rome they were the greatest in the world, the roads were paved; but once the open country was reached, there were only dirt roads hardened by traffic and the sun. Bridges over streams and rivers were kept in repair by the Roman government, and squadrons of Roman soldiers along the way were the best protection against robbers. Camp was pitched each night at a special inn near a fort or a town. An interesting detail was that both camels and their cargo were insured against loss.[14]

A large assortment of merchandise was being transported; carpets, and embroideries from Babylonia, furs and hides from Iran, carved

---

[10] Cf. *Mishnah*, Pesahim, 4, 5; Danby, p. 140.
[11] Cf. Dalman, *op. cit.*, p. 7.
[12] Josephus, *Life*, 14 (3).
[13] Fifty thousand. See Heichelheim, *op. cit.*, IV, 159.
[14] Cf. Heichelheim, *op. cit.*, 209. The Holy Land was a "land bridge" between Asia, Europe, and Africa. The main currents of traffic led north and south. See Charlesworth, *Trade Routes and Commerce of the Roman Empire*. He says a caravan took about 70 days to travel from Babylon to Antioch (*op. cit.*, p. 47). Camels, mules, and asses were employed.

ivory work and pottery from Persia, silk cloths from China, and pearls, drugs, and perfumes from India. From India also two tigers were being brought to Egypt. The return cargo from Alexandria would include dried fish, papyrus, parchments and copies of the Scriptures. The caravan was conveying more than a hundred letters, business and personal. Traveling with the caravan were business men, tourists, and students. The broker who handled the arrangements of the caravan was not with it. He was a wealthy man of Antioch, who, besides managing several caravans, owned a thousand vineyards, a thousand slaves, a thousand soldiers, and eight hundred horses.[15]

Hearing about this great wealth, the townspeople of Nazareth would express much surprise. One of them would state that riches is the cause of much evil, for he knew a neighbor who previously when poor had been a good God-fearing man, but since he became wealthy he had besides the wife and family here, a wife and family in Perea, and another wife and family in Judea.[16] Another townsman would assert that the Gentiles sometimes made use of their money for good purposes, while he related the case of a man in nearby Sephoris who had lost his fortune, but was able to maintain his high standard of living, because of charitable rich friends who supplied him the rest of his life with a pound of meat a day.[17] Another of those willing to express themselves would remark that he must, however, condemn the Gentiles for their evil practices, especially the heartless parents who cast their newly-born unwanted babes on the hillsides to be exposed to certain death.

Letters received from relatives or friends in far-off places of the Empire would be mentioned. Remarks would be passed on the great number of books being written, some of them, "outside books," containing most edifying reading matter; and comments would be

---

[15] Cf. Josephus, *Antiquities*, XVII, ii, 1; Heichelheim, *op. cit.*, IV, 180 f.

[16] Josephus says it was a custom permitted the Jews to have several wives. *Jewish War*, I, 477 (xxiv, 2); *Antiquities*, XVII (i, 2). Herod had nine wives; Josephus himself freely divorced his wife and remarried, *Life*, 426 (76). Cf. Dalman, *op. cit.*, p. 8; Neufeld, *Ancient Hebrew Marriage Laws*, pp. 118 ff.

[17] Cf. Dalman, *op. cit.*, p. 73.

made about certain Jews who became versed in Greek literature.[18] The comparison of their religion with that of the Gentiles would be a frequent matter of discussion and would bring out the superior elements in the belief of Israel and the inconsistencies in the religious ideas of their pagan neighbors. A word of warning would be given that it was forbidden to laugh at what others considered gods,[19] while it would be brought out that it was ridiculous to profess beliefs in gods and goddesses who were begotten by one another, some of whom were supposed to be under the earth, some in the sea, some in heaven, and some even bound in hell. It would be pointed out that it was utterly foolish and silly for pagans to distinguish their gods like animals, to mark them off according to trades, to call some servants and others tyrants, and to think them subject to the passions of jealousy, anger, or lust. A smile would be provoked by the question about who on earth has greater power than sculptors or painters who fix the proper shape of gods and goddesses. As information it would be said that for the pagans there were two ranks of deities, the oldest belonging to the first class and the newst to the second.[20] Perhaps the fickleness of Gentile belief would be illustrated by the all too empty temples at Sephoris. In the rebuilt city the temples were erected to the newcomers among the deities, but after the popularity of these divinities had declined, the temples were again deserted. Final remarks might be made to the effect that Gentiles did not believe the accounts of the pagan poets and that it was a good sign that here in Galilee and in all countries where the Jews had settled a number of sincere Gentiles were adopting the faith of Israel.

Glassware, that for the first time was being used in every home,

[18] Josephus records that Herod's son Alexander wrote four volumes attempting to clear himself of the conspiracy of his half brother Antipater. Cf. *Jewish War*, I, 498 (xxv, 1). Letters from abroad would sometimes complain about race prejudice; see Josephus, *Antiquities*, XVI, ii, 4. Philo complained that the Jewish nation was an orphan among races, *De specialibus legibus*, IV, xxxiv, 179; *Loeb Classical Library* (translation by Colson), VIII, 119.

[19] Cf. Josephus, *Against Apion*, II, 237 (xxiii).

[20] Cf. Josephus, *ibid.*, 239–53; Philo says a stranger would die with laughter at the Egyptians giving divine honors to irrational animals, birds, and fishes. *Decalogue*, XVI, 70–80; edition by Colson, VII, 45–47. Cf. *De specialibus legibus*, I, 13–31.

would be a topic of conversation. Perhaps a townsman would tell his neighbors of a visit he had made to the scene of the glass-blowing industry at Ptolemais, a town that could be seen from the northwestern hill of Nazareth. He would tell a strange tale of a bottomless mine of sand from which glass was made. He would describe how a little distance from the river Belus near Memnon's monument there was a round hole about two hundred feet in width that was continually being emptied of sand, and yet the supply was inexhaustible,[21] for the wind and waves brought in sand that soon became the proper kind from which to make glass. An odd piece of news would be that at Gamala there was a woman physician whose little son's name was Joseph.[22] There was a supposition that an underground river connected the Nile with a well at Capharnaum because a rare eel-like fish was found in the latter.[23]

A widespread notion was that the pool at Panion from which the Jordan took its source was bottomless.[24] A popular tradition reported that absolutely no rain fell in the daytime during the whole eighteen months while the priests were constructing the holy house of the Temple.[25] The Essenes and their strange manner of living would give rise to many a comment, especially the fact that they did not marry, and yet that there was an order among them that did enter the marriage state while preserving a remarkable modesty.[26] A discussion would arise on the reason why Egyptian Jews were permitted to have a temple at Leontopolis; which seemed to be contrary to the order of Moses (Deut. 12: 14).[27] The drying and salting of fish at Magdala (Tarechias) [28] would be described as well as the catch-

---

21 See Josephus, *Jewish War*, II, 189–91 (x, 2). Tacitus, (*Histories*, V, 7) also mentions the inexhaustible supply.

22 Josephus, *Life*, 185 (37); it could be son of a midwife.

23 Josephus, *Jewish War*, III, 419 f. (x, 8).

24 *Ibid.*, I, 405 (xxi, 3). Cf. Legendre, *Cradle of the Bible*, pp. 114–16.

25 *Antiquities*, XV, xi, 7.

26 *Jewish War*, II, 160 (viii, 13). Cf. Philo, *Quod omnis probus liber est*, XX, 75–87; *Loeb*, IX, 53–61.

27 According to both Philo (*De specialibus legibus*, I, xii, 67, ed. Colson, VII, 139) and Josephus (*Antiquities*, IV, 200 [viii, 5]), Moses gave orders that since God is one there should be only one temple.

28 Cf. Dalman, *Sacred Sites and Ways*, p. 126.

ing of the various kinds of fish in Lake Tiberias. Tales of the types of witchcraft practiced by wizards would reach Nazareth and be passed around; so also would the account of an amazing sight in near-by Gubbatha, where a juggler sent into the air a large ball which came down a calf.[29]

"Is it witchcraft that helps the Romans to be superior to all other races and nations?" some might ask.[30] Whereupon another would express the wish that the Jews could get possession of some wizard's power so as to destroy their enemies. The political situation would thus eventually find a place in nearly all conversation; and almost everybody would have something to say on the subject. On all sides they would condemn both the Romans and the Herods; and they would censure the Gentile citizens of Sephoris and Tiberias for their loyalty to Rome.[31] Words of scorn and hatred would be aimed at their civil governor, Herod Antipas, for certain representations of animals which he had installed in his palace at Tiberias.[32] Nevertheless the strongest words of contempt and enmity were reserved for Herod the Great, to whom all their woes could be attributed. Some might say it was a misfortune that he did not die at the beginning of his reign when on two occasions his life was greatly endangered.[33] Mariamne, Herod's wife, would be mentioned with pride for going to her death with noble bravery. Her heroism would be attributed to the fact that she was a descendant of the Machabees. Although for seventy years before the coming of Herod, members of the Hasmonean family brought disgrace as well as disunion on the Jews, this would not detract from the great glory which all would attribute to the great men, Judas Machabeus, Jonathan, Simon, and John Hyrcanus, names indeed on everyone's lips, for parents gave them as names to their children.

---

[29] Cf. *ibid.*, p. 111.
[30] Josephus, *Life*, 149 (31). Cf. Dalman, *op. cit.*, pp. 9, 12.
[31] Josephus, *Jewish War*, II, 461 (xviii, 2); *Life*, 30 (8), 104 (22), 384 (68). The pro-Roman towns in the vicinity of Tiberias are mentioned by Josephus, *Life*, 349 (65). Every city was divided into two camps. Cf. *Life*, 24 (6).
[32] *Ibid.*, 65 (12).
[33] Josephus, *Jewish War*, I, 340 ff. (xvii, 7); *Antiquities*, XIV, 455 (xvi, 11).

An old resident of Nazareth could relate an account heard from an eyewitness, of a battle sixty years previous (38 B.C.), the last fought under an Hasmonean, Antigonus.[34] The battlefield, the Plain of Arbeel, would be passed on the way to Lake Tiberias. The patriot soldiers took refuge in high caves of the steep cliffs of Arbeel that seemed impregnable. But they were smoked out by the crafty Herod who used baskets to lower his soldiers to the mouths of the caves. One brave Galilean refused the outstretched hand of Herod. Moreover, he publicy poured ridicule on him for his lowliness of birth. Then rather than submit he slew his wife and seven children and threw himself from the high cliff. Herod ever afterward had shown his sensitiveness about his humble origin by seizing every opportunity that presented itself to burn the genealogical lists of the Jews.[35]

A young enthusiast of the party of Zealots [36] would have his say in the conversation, insisting that his party had the key to the national problem. "Are not the Jews," he would ask passionately, "the chosen people of God who should have none but God for their

[34] Josephus, Jewish War, I, 305–13 (xvi, 2–4); Antiquities, XIV, 421–30 (xv, 5).

[35] Herod was called a low-born, an upstart, a commoner, a half-Jew. Cf. Josephus, Jewish War, I, 522 (xxvi, 2); Antiquities, XIV, 491 (xvi, 4). We would expect the Jews of Our Lord's time to speak about Augustus' long reign of fifty-seven years and a half, and of the thirty-seven years of Herod the Great's reign. They would say that Herod's family troubles began when he tried to desecrate the tomb of King David, and they would boast that he was prevented by a flame that burst forth. (Antiquities, XVI, vii, 1.) They would laugh at Herod's dyeing his hair in his old age (Jewish War, I, 490 [xxv, 7]) and at his striving to appear young and vigorous (Jewish War, I, 462, xxii, 5); and they would refer to monuments he built to Caesar over the whole land, and would lament over the great hurt and havoc he did to their religion and race. They would regret that the rise of Herod and his father was due to the quarrel of two brothers (Antiquities, XIV, 77 [iv, 5]); and that it was civil strife that brought about the end of the Hasmonaean rule. Yet Josephus like other Jews of his time applauded the Macchabees, Antiquities, XIV, 491 (xvi, 4).

[36] In Our Lord's time the Zealots were a religious party. Its origin may be traced back to the slogan of the Macchabean leader, Mathathias: "Everyone that hath zeal for the law (Books of Moses) and maintaineth the testament, let him follow me" (I Mach. 2:27). In the following generation they got out of control and became the desperadoes known as the sicarii, dagger men; see Herford, Judaism in the New Testament Period, p. 66; Oesterley, History of Israel, II, 366 f. There were some Pharisaic quietists, as is seen from the Apocalyptic writing, The Assumption of Moses, but there would be very few of them in Galilee. Cf. Oesterley, op. cit., p. 383.

Lord and Master? Why should they submit to the Romans who neither know nor care for the one true God? Is it not utterly wrong to pay taxes or show any loyalty to the foreign oppressor or his tools, the Herods? (Deut. 17:15.) Is it not better to go into a cave and there die of starvation than to compromise where God was concerned? [37] Did not Judas Machabeus declare it is better for us to die in battle than to see the evils of our nation? (I Mach. 3:59.) Is it not true that Wisdom itself and Power itself always intervened to help the Jews and promised that great things would be done through them? Can we not trust God that, when we fearlessly raise the standard of revolt, He will at once send the great Messianic King to lead us to victory and worldly success?"

Nearly all discussions and almost all prolonged conversations would lead to the all-important subject, the coming of the Messiah. Here gloom would disappear from the faces of the listeners and speakers while glowing accounts would be given of the person of the Messiah, the revolution He would bring about, and the signs of His coming. The most roseate language would be used as speakers, giving full rein to their imaginations, drew alluring pictures of the Messianic era to come. Inspired by the mounting enthusiasm, nearly everyone present would have something to add to the great expectation of a materialistic kingdom of great prosperity and glory that would be such a contrast to their present condition of oppression and slavery. Here are some of the predictions they would utter about the Messiah.[38]

[37] Cf. *Assumption of Moses*, IX (Charles, *The Apocrypha and Pseudegerapha*, II, 421).

[38] For the popular Messianic views, see the Old Testament Apocrypha, such as, Psalms of Solomon, Enoch, Assumption of Moses, The Sibylline Books, etc. Cf. Lagrange, *Le Messiasme chez les juifs*; Bonsirven, *On the Ruins of the Temple*, pp. 24–140; *Le Judaisme Palestinien au temps de Jésus-Christ*, I, 340–467. Moore, *Judaism in the First Centuries of the Christian Era*, II, 321, 76. The elements of the Messianic age, according to Philo, were: (1) reunion of the exiled, (2) national prosperity in the homeland, (3) reign of peace between men and men, and between men and beasts, and (4) punishment of unrepentant enemies. The Messiah was to have dauntless courage of soul and all-powerful might of body. Judaism was to become the universal religion, and there was to be a universal state for all poeples. Cf. Wolfson, *Philo*, II, 408–26.

The great Anointed One will be a king sent by God but will be descended from King David and perhaps also from the priestly line of Levi. First of all, beginning His victories on the plain of Arbeel,[39] He will destroy the enemies of Israel and put to death faithless Jews. When He comes hills will be rent in twain as if by mighty giants at work; strong walls will crumble like the very dust; heathens will be washed clean in their own blood, which will saturate the earth; and Rome will go down in defeat as Greece had been humbled in the past. The Israelites will rise to glorious supremacy, for the world was made for them.[40] Their exiles will return to the homeland and around the temple of God they will live in peace and joy, protected from their enemies by a high wall of flaming fire. Good Gentiles, friendly to the Jews, will be given light to recognize the one true God. After smashing their man-made images, they will form a procession hundreds of miles long as they come to worship God in His temple. Yes, from the isles of the Mediterranean and from all parts of the earth they will come to Jerusalem to exclaim how the Eternal One loves the people of Israel. Then through the power of the great champion, God, both Jew and Gentile will live forever secure from the dreadful horrors of war.

On that great day, the day of election, the greatest kind of blessings will crown the joys of the Jewish people. Cities will be filled with good things, land will yield corn, wine, and oil in superabundance, fruits in plenty will appear on the trees, flocks of kine, sheep, and goats will roam the fields to supply fountains of milk, and the heavens will rain down a luscious draught of honey. There will be most sumptuous banquets, and the most joyous entertainments here on earth, after which the Israelites will be translated into heaven. While they are being carried there on the necks and wings of eagles, they will look down on their enemies suffering punishments in Gehenna. The signs of the approach of the great day of glad change and glory will be the return of Elias, the breaking-up

[39] Cf. Dalman, *Sacred Sites and Ways*, p. 117.
[40] Tacitus (*Histories*, V, 13) witnesses the Jewish belief that they would possess the world.

of the sun, the moon turning into blood, swords appearing in the sky, a battle royal raging in the clouds, and the great voice of God shaking the foundations of the earth.

Besides the Messiah and the great prospects for the future, the past history of their race and the long list of religious and national heroes would be dwelt on in conversation by the people of Nazareth. To guide them through their pressing difficulties, perhaps the following advice would be given by an old man steeped in the wisdom of the Scriptures.

The Jews should consider themselves the most fortunate people in the world, for possessing the knowledge of the one true God, for God's special dealings with them and for their sacred books which contain God's revealed will.[41] Because of these privileges all the more have they the duty of ascertaining the will of the Creator and all the more have they the obligation of following it at all costs. Everything being under God's complete control, the loss of national independence and the dire consequences to them are permitted by Him and must be endured in the proper spirit in the way He wishes. How trials are to be borne may be learned from the Book of Job, which therefore contains the correct lesson for all to learn. Instead of seeking in vain the reasons for evils, man must remember he is sinful from his birth and that his life here is a spiritual warfare. When troubles come he should meet them with fortitude and confidence, even the trials that bring destruction and death; for there is the certainty that on the shores of eternity the Redeemer will be met and God's ruling of the world will be vindicated. Resorting to foolhardy methods to escape one's share of trial is sinful; for there is another text which warns: "Thou shalt not tempt the Lord thy God" (Deut. 6: 16).

Here the old man would propose pointed questions to which he would himself give the answers. "What happened to the young man from Cana who slew a Gentile for burning one of the sacred books? He was crucified. We are proud of him that he died on the cross

[41] Cf. Josephus, *Against Apion*, II, 184 (21).

with a smile.[42] What happened to the pilgrim to the Passover last year whose zeal brought him into conflict with the Samaritans? [43] In the riot that resulted he was slain and several others of our race were killed or wounded. What befell the Galilean who took it on himself to pound to death the Roman soldier who was acting disgracefully in the Temple? He and several of his companions were ruthlessly massacred.[44] You all know that Judas, son of Ezechias, twenty-five years ago bravely took to the field in armed uprising; with what result? From our hills here we could see Sephoris burning for days. Shall we ever forget the sight of hundreds of patriots hanging on their crosses? As you may have heard through a favor granted by Varus, three of the crucified were taken down alive, yet only one survived under treatment by physicians, and he is alive today.[45] I should like to ask our young friends among the Zealots, do they not think that the same fate that befell the followers of Judas the Galilean would be ours if today we resorted to arms against Rome? Within a few weeks the Roman legions now stationed at Antioch would be here on the soil of Palestine to crush us and surround the Holy City. As to Galilee, here the Gentiles in our midst and on our borders would be more than a match for us, and in all the large cities where we are in the minority we would be caught as in a death-trap." [46]

Encouraged by the general agreement on the part of his listeners, the old man would go on to deliver further advice, summarized as follows: Desperate means that would bring more calamities to the people are not to be resorted to until the Lord indicates clearly that there is a well-grounded hope for success. In the meantime, the patient bearing of our trials and the confident hope for God's day of deliverance are the proper preparations for the coming of the Messi-

[42] Cf. Josephus, *Jewish War*, III, 321 (vi, 33); also II, 152 (viii, 9); *Against Apion*, II, 233 (32).
[43] *Jewish War*, II, 232 ff. (xii, 3).
[44] Josephus, *Jewish War*, II, 224–27 (xii, 1).
[45] Josephus, *Life*, 421 (75).
[46] Such was the case in the beginning of the Jewish War, A.D. 66, 67. Cf. Josephus, *Jewish War*, II, 585 ff. (xxi, ff.).

Mount of Precipitation, Nazareth

anic King and His reign of peace and joy. In leading us out of the valley of woe and distress, the Messiah Himself will not use arms, but will conquer "with the breath of His mouth" (Isa. 11:4; cf. II Thess. 2:8). That He will share our sorrows and sufferings, is foretold in the Psalms and by the prophet Isaias. Also Jeremias' long suffering is prophetic in significance. Indeed, all may read in a new booklet, *The Assumption of Moses*,[47] which can be bought at a store in Japhia for ten denarii, that by suffering and death on the part of the Anointed One our liberation and happiness will be brought. Voluntary suffering and expiation for sin are pleasing to God, as all our sacred writings bear witness (I Mach. 2:37, 50). How much more efficacious then must be the voluntary sufferings of the great Messiah! He may be at hand, for the present national indignities may be his pangs or his footmarks. In the meantime, like the good Carpenter in our midst, let us lead a life of work and prayer and wait on the word of the Lord.

BIBLIOGRAPHY

Angus, S. The Environment of Early Christianity.

Baron, S. W. A Social and Religious History of the Jews.

Bevan, E. Jerusalem under the High Priests.

Bindley, H. Religious Thought in Palestine in the Time of Christ.

Booth, Henry K. The World of Jesus. A Survey of the Background of the Gospels.

Edersheim, A. In the Days of Christ; Sketches of Jewish Social Life.

Ganss, G. "The Messianic Ideas of Jesus' Contemporaries," Catholic Bib. Quart., VI (1944), 37–52.

Glover, T. R. The World of the New Testament.

Lagrange, J. M. Messianisme chez les Juifs.

Lattey, C. "Messianic Expectations in 'The Assumption of Moses,'" Catholic Bib. Quart., IV (1942) 9–21.

Radin, M. The Jews among the Greeks and Romans.

---

[47] Its date is given as soon after A.D. 6 by Torrey, *Apocryphal Literature*, p. 116. About that time appeared also the Hebrew Testament of the Twelve Patriarchs.

CHAPTER XXVI

The Nazarene and His Relatives

TOWARD the end of the fourth century a certain Helvidius, who has had successors down to our day, sought to gain notoriety by maintaining that our Blessed Lord had four brothers and several sisters. In answer, St. Jerome about the year 383 wrote *The Perpetual Virginity of Blessed Mary*, a treatise masterly in style and argumentation, which remains the classic work on the subject. Helvidius' errors and inconsistencies and "darkness and raging madness working to its own destruction" are vigorously condemned by St. Jerome. He holds the heretic up for ridicule by comparing him to a certain man who won notoriety by the crime of burning down the temple of Diana. He presents a clear exposition of the texts involved and gives an explanation of such words in the Gospel as "until" and "firstborn." [1] He discusses the knotty question about "the brethren of the Lord." The view put forth by some commentators that these "brethren" were children of St. Joseph by a former marriage, he calls an audacious invention. He sets forth the Catholic position, that he who was thought worthy to be called the father of the Lord remained a virgin and that "from a virgin wedlock a virgin was born." [2]

In the Aramaic language in use in Our Lord's day there was no term for "cousin." We must remember, too, that the word "brother"

[1] Cf. §§ 5–13; NPN, 2nd ser., VI, 326–34.
[2] *Ibid.*, §§ 16, 341.

at that time was employed to designate a nephew or a cousin, a usage that may have arisen in nomadic times when distant relatives had to live together. Further, against the view that Our Lord had true brothers are the words of the Blessed Mother to the archangel, and the statement of the Evangelist that she annually made the Passover pilgrimage to Jerusalem (Luke 2:40). Indeed the narrative of the episode of the boy Jesus in the Temple as well as the accounts of the nativity, the adoration of the Magi, and the flight into Egypt, all point to there being only three members of the holy family. One Gospel text (Luke 2:44) merely mentions "relatives," but there is no word about brothers or sisters. Furthermore, the name given the Savior of the public ministry by His own townspeople, "Son of Mary" (Mark 6:3), would be most appropriate for the only son of a widow. This condition would also explain why from the cross Jesus committed His Mother to the care of the apostle St. John. Accordingly from the earliest days we find in the wording of the Creeds and in the writings of the Fathers that the Blessed Mother is always called the Virgin. So much so that St. Jerome could use strong language to castigate Helvidius and could call his view an innovation worthless as well as sacrilegious. It was most becoming that the only-begotten of the Father in assuming human nature should be the only-begotten Son of His Mother.

In the Scriptural references to the "brethren of the Lord" do we find any information that would help us to form an opinion about their relationship to Christ? And do these inspired accounts throw any light on Our Lord's hidden life? St. John (2:12) relates that, after performing the miracle at the wedding feast at Cana, requested by His Mother, Jesus, accompanied by His Mother, His "brethren," and His apostles, went to Capharnaum. During the few days' stay in this lake city, the "brethren" must have been basking in the reflected fame and glory which the first great miracle brought to Christ. This brief visit to Capharnaum was the forerunner of His fixing His own headquarters there; yet it seems that the "brethren" with the Blessed Mother continued to reside at Nazareth.

According to the first three Evangelists, one day at Capharnaum Our Lord was in a house filled with people, and in the crowd outside were His brethren and His Mother, who had come from Nazareth to bring Him back home; for it had been reported that He had lost His common sense and had gone beyond the bounds of reason (Matt. 12: 46–50; Mark 3: 21, 31–35; Luke 8: 19–21; 11: 27 f.) . As they could not get near Him because of the crowd, they sent word to Him that they wished to see Him. In answer He said, pointing to His disciples: "Behold My Mother and My brethren." Here Our Lord was insisting on a fundamental point of doctrine, that our relationship with God is more binding and lasting than any human tie, and that accordingly those who do God's will He will hold dear and near to Him.

We might ask why the Blessed Mother accompanied the relatives on this strange mission. Would the reason be found in the fact that she had been living with these relatives for some years before the public ministry? The whole group is called "His own people" by St. Mark (3: 21) . The expression used by all three Evangelists, "His mother and His brethren," shows that these brethren are closely related to the Blessed Mother as well as to her divine Son. Their interest in Him and concern for Him, even if misguided, shown by their making a special journey of about twenty miles, would indicate a very close relationship, and might be a sign that He and they lived in the same house for some years. Mary's motherly heart, full of faith and confidence in Him as shown at Cana, would not be indifferent to rumors and accusations circulated among the townspeople. She would feel that it was her place to go with the others, just as afterward she felt that it was her place to stand at the foot of the cross.

On the occasion of Jesus' rejection at Nazareth, the townspeople referred not only to His Mother, whom they knew, but also to His brothers and sisters as there with them. Both St. Matthew (13: 55) and St. Mark (6: 3) give the names of these brethren: James, Joseph, Jude, and Simon. In regard to the sisters, St. Matthew using the words, "Are they not all with us," implies there were many, at least three in number. These sisters are not spoken of in the Gospels as accompanying their brothers to Capharnaum either after the miracle of Cana or when the latter went to bring Him home. Neither do we hear of any of them accompanying the women of Galilee who traveled with Our Lord and served Him and the apostles during the missionary journeys. The ready way the names of the brothers of Jesus are called off would show they were well known to the people of Nazareth; and it might also be an indication that they were present in the synagogue. St. Mark's expression of the "sisters" being "here with us" could refer to their living in the town, but also could refer to their being present in the synagogue. Powerless to prevent the angry mob from trying to cast Jesus from the precipice, these relatives probably stood beside the Blessed Mother, sharing her anxiety of heart and uniting with her in anguish and prayer for her Son's protection and safety. On the other hand, the lack of faith of some of these relatives may account for the extension of the proverb that a prophet is not accepted in his own country to his not being acclaimed "in his own house and among his own kindred" (Mark 6: 4) .

In the autumn before His death, knowing that His life was in danger, Jesus did not wish to go openly to Jerusalem to celebrate the feast of Tabernacles. It is related that his "brethren" urged Him to make the pilgrimage an occasion of publicly displaying His miracles in Judea, the very homeland of the rabbis, and thus of manifesting Himself to the world. This worldly point of view merited and received a sharp reprimand from our Savior, a rebuke that is parallel to that given to St. Peter when his remarks are concerned with the human point of view and not with the divine (Mark 8: 33) . In relating the incident St. John (7: 5) adds, "for neither did His brethren believe in Him." This must mean that as yet the majority [3] of His relatives had no faith in Him; for we know at least one faithful relative,

[3] There are two main views on St. John's assertion that Our Lord's cousins were without faith; either they were lacking in sufficient faith or some of them were without any faith in Christ's divine mission. Cf. Collins, "The Brethren of the Lord," and two recently published papyri, *Theological Studies*, V (1944), 490.

one of the women who had been ministering to Him and who was soon to prove her loyalty in the great hour of trial.

According to the Fourth Gospel (19:25) there stood at the cross of Christ the following: "His Mother, and His Mother's sister, Mary of Cleophas, and Mary Magdalen." It seems here that the persons are divided by the conjunction "and," and that it is best to take it that only three people are mentioned, Mary of Cleophas and the sister of the Blessed Mother being the same person. Through a fine sense of modesty, St. John did not state that his own mother was there. Neither do the other three Evangelists record that the Virgin Mother was present. However, in place of Mary of Cleophas, St. Matthew (27:56) mentions "Mary the Mother of James and Joseph," and St. Mark (15:40) speaks of "Mary the Mother of James the Less." In regard to the women who took notice of the burial of Christ and who on Easter morning went to the tomb, St. Matthew refers to "the other Mary," while St. Mark speaks of her at first as "Mary the mother of Joseph" (15:47), and then as Mary the mother of James (16:1). She is called by St. Luke "Mary of James" (24:10), perhaps for the reason that Joseph died within a few years, and his brother James assumed such prominence as the bishop of Jerusalem that the mother became known as "Mary of James." [4]

After Our Lord's resurrection and ascension, His "brethren" became staunch believers; more than that, they took a prominent part in the propagation of the Christian religion, while they themselves were treated with the greatest respect and endowed with the highest authority. We should notice that in the inspired accounts sometimes there is set forth a certain contrast between the brethren of the Lord and the apostles. After giving the name of the apostles, the Acts (1:14) states how with one mind they were giving themselves to

---

[4] St. Luke (24:18) also gives the name "Cleophas" to one of the two disciples to whom the risen Savior appeared on the way to Emmaus. Perhaps this was the brother of St. Joseph, as Hegesippus records that he bore this name; yet there is no definite information on the matter.

prayer "with the women, and Mary, Jesus' Mother, and His brethren." On the other hand, they are also coupled together without any resemblance of classification in such a text as I Cor. 9: 5, "the rest of the apostles and the brethren of the Lord and Cephas"; and Gal. 2: 9, where "James (the brother of the Lord) and Cephas and John" are mentioned together as "pillars" of the Church. St. Paul clearly includes among the apostles, St. James, the brother of Christ and bishop of Jerusalem, when he states that on his return to Jerusalem to see St. Peter he did not see any other apostle "except James, —the brother of the Lord" (Gal. 1: 19).

That St. James, the brother of Christ and the bishop of Jerusalem and author of the Epistle of St. James, is identical with the second James in the lists of the apostles whose father is given as Alpheus and whose mother was Mary of Cleophas, is commonly accepted by Catholic scholars today and is the tradition handed down by such prominent early writers as Clement of Alexandria [5] and St. Jerome.[6] It is also generally agreed that Jude, one of the four "brethren" of Christ, is the same as the author of the Catholic epistle and the apostle known as Thaddeus. For in the beginning of the Epistle he calls himself "the brother of James," and St. Luke in his list of the apostles styles him James' Jude, most probably as a way of distinguishing him. The Gospel text (John 14: 22) tells us that Jude the apostle showed his impatience and disappointment because Our Lord was not manifesting Himself to the world.[7] This is in harmony with the attitude of the brethren of Christ. Now in regard to the other brother of Christ, Simon is generally identified with the apostle of that name, called in the list of the apostles, the Cananean, the Aramaic equivalent of the "Zealot." [8] The obvious meaning of this title might indicate that he once belonged to the body of the

[5] *Hypotyposeis*, VII; as recorded in Eusebius, *Ecclesiastical History*, II, 1, 4; *PG*, 22, 136; translation by K. Lake (*Loeb*, I, 105). Here Clement states that, after His resurrection, Our Lord gave special instruction to "James the Just, John, and Peter."

[6] *The Perpetual Virginity of Blessed Mary*, 15; NPN, 2nd ser., VI, 326–34.

[7] How different is St. Jude in his Epistle (1:17–21)!

[8] Cf. Dalman, *Jesus-Jeshua*, p. 12.

extreme nationalists known as "Zealots," but the general meaning of the word is to be understood here.[9] The grouping together of the three names, James, Jude, and Simon in the lists of the apostles may be an indication of their relationship.

In trying to obtain more information about the four "brethren of Christ," it may be worth while to notice that both St. Matthew and St. Mark give the names of the four together, James, Joseph, Jude, and Simon; and yet later St. Matthew mentions Mary as the mother of only two, James and Joseph, whereas St. Mark writes of her separately, one time as the mother of James, and another time as the mother of Joseph. It may be also noticed that in the lists of the apostles James the Less has a father, Alpheus, who is not mentioned as father either of Jude or of Simon. Accordingly there does seem to be some basis for dividing the four brethren into two groups. Further support for such a demarcation may be found in Hegesippus,[10] who informs us that St. James, the bishop of Jerusalem, was of the tribe of Levi, and he was succeeded by "another cousin" of Our Lord, Simon, whose mother was Mary and whose father was Cleophas, the brother of St. Joseph. As it is certain that the foster father of Christ was of the tribe of Juda, the inference can be legitimately made that Alpheus, the father of St. James, was a different person from Cleophas, the father of Simon, and hence that, though all four "brothers" of Christ had the same mother, Mary, they had different fathers. This leads to the explanation suggested by Father Prat,[11] namely: the Virgin Mother had a stepsister, the daughter of her father by a previous marriage. This stepsister, whose name was also Mary, married at first Alpheus. Besides daughters they had two sons, James and Joseph. When Alpheus died, Cleophas, St. Joseph's brother, married the widow and besides daughters they had two sons, Jude and Simon. The latter two in the eyes of the people would be double first cousins of Our Lord. After the death of St. Joseph and

[9] As Lagrange points out, "we ought to understand it in its more general sense of fervent zeal for God" (Gospel of Jesus Christ, I, 148).

[10] Eusebius, op. cit., II, xxiii, 4–18; Loeb, I, 170–75.

[11] Jésus-Christ, I, 533–43.

Alpheus, all these cousins lived in the same house with Christ and His Blessed Mother. Because of this fact of their living together and of their close relationship, they were readily and naturally styled Jesus' brethren.

As Hegesippus is a reliable authority, for he wrote in Palestine a century and a half after Christ's death and could have known descendants of Christ's brethren, it may be worth while presenting a summary of the information he gives us about these "brothers." James, the first bishop of Jerusalem, a man of great holiness, who could enjoy the sacerdotal privilege of entering the sanctuary of the Temple, was put to death by the Jews in A.D. 62.[12] He was succeeded by another cousin of Our Lord, Simeon, or Simon, whose mother was Mary and whose father was Cleophas, a brother of St. Joseph, foster father of Christ. This Simeon was a cousin of James and was tortured and crucified about the year 107 at the age of 120.[13] Grandsons of Jude, the cousin of Christ, according to the flesh, were summoned to Rome by the Emperor Domitian.[14] As witnesses and as relatives descendants of the cousins of Our Lord took a leading part in the Church of the district in which they happened to live.

This account of St. James as given by Hegesippus fits in with the character of the "brother of the Lord" as portrayed in the Acts of the Apostles, and with the author of the epistle of St. James. Nourished on the word of God and animated with love of God, the first bishop of Jerusalem was able to define wisdom in its best sense, to act most prudently in several dangerous crises, and to give advice which was of far-reaching benefit to the whole Church. His pastoral zeal was displayed in his exhortations to "good works," in his solicitude and care of the poor and sick, and in his warnings against dangers from riches, ambition, and profane knowledge. His own personal life of self-imposed penances and privations was in strict accord with the Jewish regulations which he followed be-

---

[12] Eusebius, *op. cit.*, III, xxxii, 1–6; IV, xxii, 4; *Loeb*, I, 272–74, 374.

[13] *Ibid.*, III, xx; xxxii, 3; *Loeb*, I, 236–38, 274.

[14] *Ibid.*, III, ix, 1; xxxii, 5; *Loeb*, I, 236, 274. Jude, the brother of James, preached the Gospel in Edessa (*ibid.*, I, xiii; III, xix, xx; *Loeb*, I, 236).

cause of their ancient and national character, but which he did not impose on Gentile converts. Daily in the Temple praying for the salvation of his own people, he won from them the title of "Just," or virtuous. Yet he died at their hands,[15] giving testimony with his blood to Him with whom he had the privilege of being so closely associated as to be called His brother. St. James was rightly honored by St. Paul and the apostles because of his virtue and doctrine as well as on account of his close relationship to Jesus and "of their being brought up together." [16]

Besides the four "brothers" named in the Gospels and the several "sisters" mentioned there, our divine Lord must have had other relatives. Julius Africanus gives us the information that St. Joseph's grandmother had married twice and that his father Jacob had married the widow of his stepbrother, Heli.[17] From these intricate relationships there would be legal cousins and even distant cousins by blood, for Joseph was a kinsman of the Blessed Virgin. The latter was a blood relative of St. Elizabeth; and accordingly, our Savior was related by blood with the Precursor.

It is usual to visualize Our Lord in His hidden life as living alone with His blessed parents. Such was the situation undoubtedly for a certain number of years. It is probable that during the last part of His residence at Nazareth His home life became more complicated by the fact of His living in the same home with His cousins who became known as His brothers and sisters. That Christ's "brothers" profited by their long association with Him at Nazareth is clearly shown by their later lives of eminent holiness. As we have seen, the identity of some of them with apostles of the same name is highly probable if not certain; and their choice as members of the Twelve presupposes special gifts and graces. One of the brothers, James, was granted a special appearance by the risen Lord (I Cor. 15:7), and became one of the "pillars" of the Church. He reveals

[15] Josephus, Antiquities, XX, ix, 1.
[16] Origen, Against Celsus, I, 474; ANF, IV, 416.
[17] Cf. Eusebius, op. cit., I, vii, 1–11; Loeb, I, 54–60. Relatives of Our Lord were known as "Desposyni" (ibid., I, vii, 14; Loeb, I, 62).

lessons he learned in the school of the hidden life in his solicitude
for the poor (Gal. 2:10), in the instructions of his Epistle,[18] and
in his personal conduct.[19] So that we can say that the good example
in the home at Nazareth bore fruit a hundredfold in those who
saw Jesus almost daily for nearly three decades. Indeed, that Jesus
had relatives so close that they became known as His brothers is
itself a testimony of His true humanity. When these relatives professed their faith in His Messiahship, as they did within the first
year of His public ministry, then this was a genuine tribute to His
Messiahship; when later they openly proclaimed His divinity, we
would judge it also a tribute to the exalted life He had led with them
at Nazareth. The lack of faith of some of them in His divine mission
at the beginning of His ministry would be an indication that He

[18] As to vestiges of the hidden years to be found in St. James' Epistle, we can state
the following. The economic and social conditions reflected in the Epistle are such as
would be found in a country town like Nazareth. The class distinction between the rich
and the poor, with the rich exercising their power in having the poor dragged before
judges and in withholding the wages of harvesters, is an evil the Epistle sketches as be-
setting the farm laborer who lived from hand to mouth. It was also natural for the
author to refer to the opposite of this dependent God-fearing farm laborer; namely, the
city businessman, who boasted of the successful year of trade and the further money
he expected to make, without any thought of the uncertainties of life. Lastly, as we
would expect, he mentions the farmer's patience with the soil waiting for the early and
late rains.

[19] Was St. James influenced by Our Lord's hidden years at Nazareth, when he stated
that one of the chief essentials of true religion was for a person to keep himself unspotted from this world, and that whoever is a friend of the world is an enemy of God?
It may not be a mere accident that here St. James was accentuating the great lesson
from the hidden life. Then the praise for the poor and for those in lowly condition, and
on the other hand the condemnation of fawning respect and partiality toward the rich,
because of the gold ring on their finger or the fine clothes on their back, may well be
deductions from the lowly life of the God-man, who did not unduly respect the person
of men. Christ's thirty years of example could receive a reference in St. James' exhortations to be swift to hear, and to be doers of the word manifesting faith by good works.
A commentary on the hidden life is the description of wisdom as chaste, peaceful, moderate, docile, and meek. Then the strong insistence on control of the tongue, and on
the responsibility of teachers, and the assertion that covetousness and passion are the
causes of wars and quarrels; these could be illustrations from the silent, humble, and
peaceful years. There is a eulogy of these years in the text, "let the brother of lowly
condition glory in his high estate" (1:9); that is, in contrast to the poor man justly
taking pride in his lowly circumstances which elevate him, the rich man's pride in his
riches is founded on what really debases him. This doctrine perfectly harmonizes with
Christ's teaching both by word and by example. In a word, shun pretense and edify by
conduct, the motive of the hidden life, is the principal theme taught by St. James in his
Epistle, and exemplified in his life.

had not performed miraculous works during the hidden life; their later preaching His divinity, indeed sealing it with their life's blood, was a source of great assurance to the early Christians. To all who consulted them they could supply details of the hidden life as well as of the public ministry. This was an advantage they possessed, namely, that they could witness to and preach the whole life of Our Lord.[20]

BIBLIOGRAPHY

Collins, J. "The Brethren of the Lord" and two recently published papyri, Theological Studies, V (1944), 484–94.

Durand, A. The Childhood of Jesus Christ, pp. 259–316.

———. "Freres du Seigneur," Dictionnaire apologetique de la foi catholique, II, 1131.

Fillion, L. The Life of Christ, I, 411–21, 641–44.

Hetzenauer, M. De genealogia Jesu Christi, pp. 83–110.

Jerome, St. The Perpetual Virginity of Blessed Mary; NPN; 2nd ser., VI, 335–46.

Lagrange, J. M. Evangile selon S. Marc (5th ed.), Paris (1929), pp. 79–93.

———. The Gospel according to St. Mark, pp. 54 f.

Lebreton, J. The Life and Teaching of Jesus Christ, I, 32–37.

Lightfoot, J. B. Epistle to the Galatians (London, 1896), pp. 252–91.

Ollivier, M. The Friendships of Jesus, pp. 116–47.

Prat, F. Jésus-Christ, I, 137–45; 533–45.

Stoll, R. The Gospel according to St. Luke, pp. 409–13.

Vosté, J. M. De Conceptione Virginali Jesu Christi, pp. 111–29.

[20] The feast of St. James the Less comes with that of St. Philip on May 1st. St. Jude (Thaddeus) is celebrated on October 28th. St. Simeon's feast falls on February 28th. St. Elizabeth, probably Our Lord's grandaunt, has a feast on November 5th; and St. Mary of Cleophas, probably a half sister of the Blessed Mother, is commemorated on April 9th.

CHAPTER XXVII

Christ and St. John the Baptist

INTIMATE and frequent were the contacts between the Baptist and Our Lord. The accounts of their lives are interwoven in the Gospel narratives. To begin with, they were cousins, probably second cousins. A remarkable fact, the same archangel had brought the announcements of their coming. Again, a canticle was sung by the father of one and by the mother of the other, and extraordinary circumstances attended the birth of each. Their association began even before they were born, when the unborn Baptist manifested with joy the presence of the unborn Savior. Yet a great contrast must be acknowledged: the one was a mere voice heralding the approach of truth, the other was Truth itself; [1] the one was the messenger preparing the way for the King, the other was the King Himself; the one was a sinful creature needing a Savior, the other was the all-holy God bringing grace and salvation.

The scene of the two infants playing together painted by some of the great artists [2] may have had reality. The Gospels do not speak

[1] Origen writes: "that John is a voice, but that Jesus is the Word." *Commentary on the Gospel of John;* VI, 30: ANF, IX, 375. Origen goes on to claim that the unborn Baptist communicated to his mother some of his prophetic grace when she pronounced her salutation to Mary.

[2] Such as Botticelli, Boucher, Bouguereau, Credi, Da Vinci, Dürer, Luini, Murillo. See F. W. Farrar, "The Christ Child in Art," *McClure's Magazine,* II (1894–95), 75–82; H. Van Dyke, "The Childhood of Jesus," *Harper's New Monthly Magazine,* LXXXVII (1893), 723–30; *The Christ Child in Art,* New York, 1894; *The Childhood of Jesus Christ,* New York, 1905; J. J. Tissot, *The Life of Our Lord Jesus Christ.* New

of any meeting between the two, one of whom was only six months older than the other, yet it is likely that they were brought together as infants. By a mountainous path Ain Karem was only four miles distant from Bethlehem. The flight into Egypt did not take place for at least six weeks after Our Lord's birth and perhaps not until nearly a year after that event. When the Blessed Mother and St. Joseph brought their forty-days-old Infant to the Temple of Jerusalem, they could easily have continued on to the home of Zachary and Elizabeth. Or, we would expect a reunion at Bethlehem, since St. John, being older, would be considered better able to stand the journey, and his aged parents would be most anxious to see the divine Infant.

If St. John and Our Lord did not meet as infants while the holy family was at Bethlehem, it is unlikely that they ever met in their youth. The Gospel narrative tells us that on His return from Egypt our Savior was brought to Nazareth to live. About St. John it says: "And the child grew and was strengthened in spirit; and was in the deserts until the day of his manifestation to Israel" (Luke 1:80). The text mentions St. John's bodily growth and the strengthening of his character that grew as a mighty oak. Yet in the inspired words the only fact revealed about his life until he was thirty years of age is that it was passed in solitude. How old was he when he withdrew into the silent places of the desert? The Gospel text may imply that it was at an early age, or it may indicate that it was after a certain number of years of growth, but it does not specify the time. Origen, St. Jerome, and St. Chrysostom are of the opinion that St. John in his earliest years left his parental roof. There is a flat rock in the lower church of the Visitation which tradition designates as part of the miraculous hiding place into which St. John and his mother fled from King Herod.[3] A writer of the ninth century asserts that St. Elizabeth having retired into solitude with her son to save him

---

York, 1903; E. H. Broadus, A Book of the Christ Child, New York, 1910; E. Cammaerts, The Childhood of Jesus As Seen by the Primitive Masters.

[3] The story is found in the Apocryphal Gospel of James, 22.

from Herod, died there after forty days and that after her death an angel took care of the young Baptist.[4] However, it must be stated that this and other such late stories are mere fiction and cannot stand the scrutiny of history. John did not retire to the desert until he was physically able to sustain himself, that is, not before his seventh year or perhaps about his ninth or tenth year.[5]

Hard to decide is the question of what desert John retired to at such a tender age. A late tradition points to a place about two miles west of Ain Karem where in the twelfth century a church and monastery were consecrated to the first solitude of the Precursor. This site would be sufficiently near the home of the parents so that they could bring care and help when needed. It would be a desert only in the sense that it afforded retirement, for it is a picturesque fertile valley well protected by forest-covered hills. To support this claim it is pointed out that the bees and locusts mentioned in the Gospel could find food only in a place of vegetation; yet, on the other hand, the fact is that they abound more in uncultivated districts than in cultivated ones. St. John must have gone to other places during his life of seclusion. Deserts stretched all the way from Jerusalem to Jericho; and when he finally makes his appearance, it is in the neighborhood of the latter city that we find him. Origen said that the young John "fled from the din of cities, the tumult of crowds, and the vices of man to the desert where with purer air, a more open sky, and an easier familiarity with God he could give himself to prayer and to conversation with the angels.[6]

Thus the Baptist prepared himself for one of the greatest missions ever given to men, not by visiting cities and countries, not by attending great schools or universities, but by solitude and self-denial. By the simple way of walking alone with God in the silence of the desert and of preventing distractions by bodily privations, he became master over himself and built up the strongest character of all time. As to food, he denied himself even bread, living only on wild

[4] Cf. Meistermann, *Guide to the Holy Land*, p. 409.
[5] Cf. Buzy, *St. Jean-Baptist*, pp. 97–106.
[6] *Homilia*, XI, *In Lucam*; PG, 13, 1827.

honey and wild locusts.[7] His dress was that of an ascetic: a garment of camel's hair with a kilt of skin about the waist.[8] Think of him in such scant attire out in the elements, enduring the cold of winter and the heat of summer. Think of him frequently weak from hunger and thirst during the long years of his life, especially his growing years. Think of him emaciated and gaunt, but buoyed up by his dauntless spirit which seemed to peer out through his body. Think of him alone in the desert through the long hours of the day and the long watches of the night, the companion of wild beasts, avoiding the company of men yet living with nature, dead to all except the presence of God, truly alive to God's influences and responsive to the inspirations of the Holy Spirit. The recluse par excellence, the most perfect hermit, the greatest ascetic of all time, his life was one continuous prayer. By prodigious, continuous, and persevering efforts through twenty years he hammered out all the flaws from his character and made it into a structure of steel that could meet the greatest test. No one else has ever submitted to such austerities; no one else succeeded so well with self-discipline. No one else ever built up so sterling a character. How could he have endured these extreme, self-imposed penances?

Holy Scripture makes answer by saying, "the hand of God was with him," as indeed it was from the beginning. He was a wonder-child, foretold by an archangel and sanctified before his birth by the three months' visit of the unborn Savior. Was he not given the most sublime mission requiring the greatest courage and zeal? Did he not prove that he was sterling to the core with no clay in his composition? He fulfilled all expectations, avoiding all worldly intercourse and, by his extraordinarily severe ascetical life, winning praise from God.

Consider the contrast between the hidden life of John and that of Jesus. John is the recluse, alone in the desert all of his hidden years;

[7] Locusts are found mostly in uncultivated districts and even today are used for food by Bedouins. Cf. Dalman, *Sacred Sites and Ways*, p. 84.

[8] St. John's dress somewhat resembled that of a prophet. Cf. Joüon, "Le costume d'Elie et celui de Jean Baptist," *Biblica*, XVI (1935), 74–81.

Jesus passes these years living in a small town. John has no company except birds and other animals; Jesus lives on a little street as a member of a family group. John lives on the scantiest and hardest diet, refusing bread and wine; Jesus eats ordinary food and partakes of ordinary drink. John is sanctifying himself by the hard way, preparing himself for his exalted mission; Jesus does not need to prepare Himself nor to sanctify Himself, He is living the life of labor as an artisan to give salutary example. John keeps away from people so as to learn human nature and to avoid sin; Jesus lives among people to sanctify them and their everyday work. Jesus scandalized some by His ordinary manner of life whereas John attracted many by his extraordinary asceticism. Jesus ended His hidden life on a God-given sign. So, too, John began his public mission when "the word of the Lord" came to him in the desert.

Centuries had rolled by without the voice of a prophet having been heard. Then in A.D. 27, the Baptist's words rang out in the desert with a voice that could not be silenced. The very desert was vibrant with his stirring words. It was no longer a desert, for crowds were being attracted there from all parts of the Holy Land. At first he may have addressed scattered travelers, or festive bands of pilgrims; but soon greater numbers came from Jerusalem and other cities of populous Judea to see and hear the great ascetic, the hermit of the wilderness, prophetlike in voice and appearance. His fame traveled through all Palestine and even aroused hopes that he might be the Messiah or at least Elias returned to usher in the Messianic reign.

John's message was the same as that with which Jesus began: Repent, for the kingdom of God is at hand. He gave much the same advice as Jesus could give. He made the same enemies, men of power and influence; and he spoke to them in the same stern tones. He used a rite of baptizing with water which Jesus took up and to which He gave vivifying efficacy. John insisted that His missionary work was only a preparation for the coming of one who was yet unknown, though living, the strap of whose shoes he was unworthy to unfasten.

What an extraordinary tribute to pay to Jesus, who perhaps at that very time was working at a carpenter's bench (Mark 1:7; John 1:27)! So far Our Lord had been leading an ordinary life, so to speak, among the people as one of them. Yet the great Baptist who had led an extraordinarily ascetical life from his boyhood declared that he was unworthy to be the slave of the Carpenter of Nazareth, asserting that Jesus was mightier than he and was set above him. This was a great tribute to the Savior as He was closing the hidden life. There was a tradition among the Jews which St. Justin Martyr [9] declared to be groundless, that the Messiah would remain hidden and unknown until he was pointed out by Elias. St. John flatly denied he was the Messiah or that he was Elias; yet, when forced to speak about himself, he asserted that both his mission and his baptismal rite were preparatory to the coming of the Messiah who would baptize with the Holy Spirit.

Respect and deference toward the person of Christ as well as humility on his own part are shown in the Baptist's words: "It is I who ought to be baptized by Thee" (Matt. 3:14). This tribute to the personal holiness and dignity of the Carpenter of Nazareth was paid at the close of the hidden life. As a response our Savior uttered His second recorded saying: "Suffer it to be so now. For so it becometh us to fulfill all justice" (Matt. 3:15). This saying at the very close of the hidden life is an appropriate heading to characterize the whole of the hidden life. For the humility, the obedience, and the other family virtues practiced at Nazareth for our edification were the carrying out of sublime righteousness. Also as it was necessary for the Son of God to give a Gospel prelude in the visit to the Temple in His twelfth year; so it was highly becoming the God-man to give good example of goodness and virtue both at Nazareth and at the Jordan.

Then when that scene occurred in which John poured the water of baptism on the head of Jesus it called forth recognition from God the Father and God the Holy Ghost, which, in turn, effected a

[9] *Dialogue*, 8; ANF, I, 199.

great change. Jesus, who had come to obey and submit, now receives the homage of John, and this homage is joined to the God-sent signals in the ceremony which marks the public investiture of the Messianic King.

The first act of the Ruler of this new era was to hallow by example John's life of solitude and penance, to teach us that it is the safest and best way for men to prepare for God's work. Here was Our Lord for forty days of fasting and temptation in the same desert where St. John had passed so many years. When the fast was over, He returned to John to receive his testimony in regard to His own exceeding greatness and to the divine efficacy of His own rite of baptism. Pointing Him out to his followers, John used one of the most touching metaphors, "Lamb of God," suggested both by the Passover lamb (Apoc. 5:6) and by the prophecy of Isaias (53:6 f.), and thus designated Jesus' holiness, meekness, and sacerdotal character.

It was appropriate that Christ's first disciples were followers of the Forerunner. It was, however, prophetic when the disciples under Our Lord's direction baptizing near where John was performing this rite, attracted greater crowds than he who was known by the name of Baptist. The latter generously silenced the jealous complaints of his followers by pointing out that his function was to share in the joy and the glory of the Bridegroom, Jesus. John showed his humility by declaring that he received everything from Our Lord and by referring to himself as an impersonal thing, a mere "voice in the wilderness." Yet he claimed an exalted mission in preparing the way for the Lord, Like our blessed Redeemer, John upheld the dignity and indissolubility of marriage, and, like Him, too, he died a martyr for truth and holiness.

On His part, although He did not visit John in his prison dungeon, Jesus performed miracles to confirm his faith and to convince his disciples. Then Our Lord praised the Baptist in the highest terms, holding up for admiration the fortitude of his sterling character, the austerity of his ascetical life, and the shining example of his

zeal and virtue (John 5:35). In Our Lord's laudatory remarks there
was brought out the strong contrast that existed between the weak-
ling occupying one of the "houses of kings" (Matt. 11:8) on the
one hand, and on the other the unflinching hero languishing in
prison chains. In one, clothed "in soft garments" on the throne
above, weakness held sway to the shame and disgrace of our
whole human nature; in the other, strength shone forth through
the gloom of the dismal dungeon to supply us with one of our
noblest boasts. The utter lack of discipline of one led him from
one sin to another until he capped it all by the murder of the Lord's
own well-beloved herald; while in the sheer severity of his manner
of living, in his fearless assaults on the corrupt high and mighty,
and in his brave endurance of imprisonment and martyrdom, the
other is a strong beacon light to guide us in the dark waters of conflict and to inspire us to battle manfully in the storms and perils of
life. The Savior had previously referred to the contrast between
His manner of living and that of the Baptist. "For John the Baptist
came neither eating bread nor drinking wine; and you say, He hath
a devil. The Son of man came eating and drinking; and you say,
Behold a man who is a glutton and a wine drinker, a friend of pub-
licans and sinners" (Luke 7:33–35).

In contradistinction to these enemies to whom the preceding
words were addressed, and in contradistinction to John himself,
who would not say that he was "Elias," Jesus twice called the Baptist
"Elias," in the figurative sense (Matt. 11:14; 17:11–13); for in
a figurative sense the expectation of the Jews for the return of Elias
to earth just before the appearance of the Messiah was fulfilled in
John, who came "in the spirit and power of Elias" (Luke 1:17),
to be the forerunner of the true Messiah. He fulfilled all that the
prophet Malachias (4:5, 6) had foretold Elias would do. Although
John would not admit that he was a prophet, Our Lord said that
He was, and much more. He said that John was the extraordinary
herald foretold by the Prophet (Isa. 40:3; Mal. 3:1), and that there

was no greater prophet than he ever born: "I say to you: among those that are born of women, there is not a greater prophet than John the Baptist" (Luke 7: 28).

The incestuous Herod gladly heard the Baptist as the latter was weighted down with chains. So, too, he would have liked to see miracles from the Savior when He too was bound and chained, a prisoner. At the same time neither the eloquence of the one nor the silence of the other converted "the Fox." Yet what a testimony to John's character, that this shrewd politician, hearing of the great deeds of Jesus, thought it was the Baptist returned from the dead! The evidence of the enduring power of his missionary efforts is to be found in the fact that thirty years afterward at Ephesus, John's rite of baptism was given side by side with that of Jesus (Acts 19: 3 f.); and another thirty years later St. John the Evangelist was insisting that the Baptist was not the true Light, for his function was merely to give testimony to the true Light (John 1:8). The mission of the Precursor had lasted only seven months, and he had languished in prison about another ten. Besides being more limited in time, his public ministry, when compared with that of Christ, was also more limited in territory and was not accompanied by miracles (John 10: 41). There was, however, a conpensation for his lack of miraculous powers. He merited the open assertion that he had borne true testimony to the Savior. Toward the end of the public ministry, when Jesus returned to the place of His baptism, He was accepted by many because they realized that all John had said of Him was true (John 10: 42). He had been a true light that led the way to the source of light.

St. John's infancy was a counterpart of that of Jesus, for they had parallel annunciations, were associated for three months in their prenatal condition, and they were probably together as children. Their public lives blend to make one whole, in their preaching, in their rites of baptism, in their enemies, and in their deaths. Indeed, John's annunciation, birth, preaching, and death marked preludes in Our Lord's life.[10] Although showing forth a harmonious design, their hidden lives form a striking contrast. John's was different because the purpose of his life was different; he merely was to be an adjunct or complementary part with the principal function of bringing Jesus' hidden life to a close, and at the same time of laying down the preparatory work for the public ministry of the King of kings. He fulfilled this great mission not only by his preaching and baptizing, but also by his life of penance and by his death.

Our Lord, so far as we know, never referred to the fact that the Baptist was a cousin; but He did extol him for his strength of character and ascetical life. John was dear to Jesus since he excelled in doing God's will, keeping on the direct course of right and truth whatever the cost to himself. John was like an arrow in God's hand that went straight to its mark even though it was destroyed in so doing. He teaches that true asceticism consists in eradicating our evil inclinations and sanctifying our souls through the hard way of penance and mortification, removing the obstacles that prevent the coming of the Bridegroom of the human soul. "Make ready the way of the Lord, make straight His paths" (Luke 3:4), by blasting the hills of sin and by bridging over the valleys of defects.

BIBLIOGRAPHY

Barton, J. M. The Voice of One Crying . . . Scripture, IV (1949) 6–11

Blackiston, A. John the Baptist and His Relation to Jesus.

Buzy, D. St. Jean-Baptiste, pp. 64–106.

Fillion, L. The Life of Christ, I, 22–42.

Grandmaison, L. Jésus-Christ, I, 297 ff.

Lagrange, J. M. The Gospel of Jesus Christ, I, 56–107.

Lebreton, J. The Life and Teaching of Jesus Christ, I, 38–53.

Ollivier, M. The Friendships of Christ, pp. 169–99.

[10] A certain interdependence of action seemed to continue: Our Lord had His followers baptize near where St. John was baptizing (John 3:22); and when St. John was cast into prison, the Savior openly took over the public ministry (Matt. 4:12).

CHAPTER XXVIII

The Hidden Life

VERILY, Thou art a hidden God, the God of Israel, the Savior," are words addressed to God by the prophet Isaias (45: 15). In the beauty and harmony of created things we can detect and even demonstrate the existence of the great Designer and Conserver; yet, as God is essentially a spirit, He always remains hidden to bodily senses and imperceptible by them. Truly He dwells "in light inaccessible whom no man has seen or can see" (I Tim. 6: 16). The noonday sun dazzles by its brilliance although it is 93,000,000 miles away; yet the Creator of our sun and millions of other suns, who is around us and within us keeping us in existence, withholds from us the rays of His Godhead, and our eyes and senses remain opaque to the glare of the splendor, majesty, and beauty of Him who is "clothed with light as with a mantle" (Ps. 103: 2). Rightly, therefore, Isaias calls Him a hidden God, for we can see only a dim reflection of Him in the world around us.[1]

When the Word of God assumed human nature to bring man salvation and grace and to make God better known and loved, God continued to veil His splendor and glory, for He emptied Himself

---

[1] St. Bernard could say that since God's entrance into his soul the divine presence has not made itself felt there by voice or by appearance. Yet St. Bernard was able, as he says, to recognize the workings of God's grace in his soul. (*Sermons on the Canticle of Canticles*, Sermon 31; PL, 183, 940 ff. This progress of God's grace must be what holy Job meant when he was addressing God who had spoken from a whirlwind: "my eyes seeth Thee" (Job 42:5).

of them in taking the form of man. The fullness of the Godhead dwelt in Jesus corporeally but could not be seen by bodily eyes. All the divine treasures of wisdom and knowledge were hidden in Him but could not be grasped by man. He preached the kingdom of God, revealed the knowledge of the Father, proclaimed the function of the Holy Spirit, and confirmed by miraculous works the central teaching that He Himself was the Son. While He illumined minds and hearts with the light of faith to penetrate the secrets of heaven, only once, at the Transfiguration, did He permit flashes of His dazzling brilliance to shine through the veil of His human appearance. He could say to St. Philip at the end of the public life, "Have I been so long a time with you and have you not known Me?" (John 14:9.) There is the further fact that He became "a worm and no man" when "He was bruised for our offenses" in His sufferings and crucifixion. It was only after the ignominious death that He manifested His glory in His resurrection and ascension. Christ's divinity could neither be seen by human eye nor detected by mere human reason.[2]

Both His sacred humanity and divinity Our Lord has left us in the Holy Eucharist, yet here both are again hidden under the sacramental appearances of bread and wine. In the tabernacles of our chapels and churches throughout the world He assumes an even humbler appearance than was His when He was a preacher on the hillsides of Galilee, and His Godhead is even more deeply hidden than it was in the Carpenter of Nazareth.

Again, our great union with Christ, and through Him with all the faithful, that began in our rebirth at baptism cannot be either seen or felt by us. It is "a hidden mystery" beyond our power of

---

[2] Scheeben rightly points out that Our Lord's public miracles alone did not reveal His divine dignity. To those who saw Him He looked like other men; and they could not conjecture that within He was infinitely more than a mere man. Neither His divine glory nor the fullness of divinity dwelling within Him could be seen by any earthly eye or detected by any human intellect. No matter how dazzlingly the flashes of Jesus' divine nature shone forth on a few isolated occasions, His divinity remained concealed in an obscurity impenetrable to mere reason. It remained "a true mystery." *The Mysteries of Christianity*, pp. 336 f.

comprehension. Even when the divine Redeemer adds the greatest intensity and vigor to His union with us in the reception of Holy Communion, even then the dazzling brilliance that fills every part of our soul and body remains imperceptible to us. The greatest reality in life, our life of grace, is hidden in Christ (Col. 3: 3) . While we are being tried in the battle for salvation, God continues to be a hidden God. The eternal Son, who came out from the Father's bosom to take up our human nature, He alone has revealed the Father to us. By His life and death, by His words and example, He has marked out the way to the Father and has supplied us with the means of following along that way. "No one hath seen God at any time. The only-begotten Son who is in the bosom of the Father, He has declared Him" (John 1: 18; 6: 46) .

The public life, it is true, was the time of preaching the doctrines of Christianity and confirming everything by signs and wonders; yet it was a hidden one inasmuch as the glare of the divine Majesty was dimmed. Only a few rays were manifested, and even these few were revealed gradually according to plan. After a slow and cautious opening of the public ministry there was a gradual development in His teaching down to the last week. Yet despite His miracles His sublime doctrines proved unpopular whether at Nazareth or at Capharnaum or at Jerusalem. He fled alone to the mountains to escape being proclaimed king, and only at the end of His missionary campaign did He accept, as the official Messiah, the public reception and procession in the city of David. This was followed by His condemnation and death; and then His crucified body lay in a tomb for three days.

On the other hand, the hidden life was not altogether a hidden one, for it had occasional divine manifestations. There were the visions of the angel to Zachary, to St. Joseph, and to the Virgin Mary. Angels also appeared to the shepherds when the glory of God shone in the midnight sky at Bethlehem. As the Son of God was being presented in the Temple His presence was made known to Simeon and to Anna. Representatives of the Gentile world were led by a star to prostrate themselves before the divine Child. A prelude to the public ministry was given by Christ Himself in His teaching amid the doctors of Jerusalem, and in His words mentioning His divine sonship and His mission to carry out His Father's will. The incident of the twelfth year was, however, only a brief flash that flared up momentarily during the obscure life at Nazareth. Even during these three days out of the thirty years, moderation characterized the boy Jesus.

This preserving of great reserve and economy was His Father's will which He joyfully carried out; and He returned to His obscure home town for eighteen years of ordinary, everyday routine life of obedience, labor, and prayer. It is true that He reached the highest point of His teaching when He employed the words "My Father" in His earliest recorded saying. It is also true that the manifestation to the Magi had no parallel in the public life; yet the hidden life had no voice from heaven nor any appearance of the Holy Ghost in the form of a dove. The divine manifestations during these years were few and at long intervals. For many years the Messiah had the helpless appearance of a child, requiring care like other children. He showed, seemingly, great weakness in fleeing from Herod to a foreign country; yet did He not seem to display even greater weakness when He submitted to crucifixion and death from Pontius Pilate? He obeyed even unto death in the public life; yet He had already obeyed His "parents" and the civil and religious laws during the hidden years. Both the public life and the hidden life were for the purpose of founding a spiritual kingdom. In a way, the hidden life was the preparation for the public life and the public life was a preparation for the death on the cross, and the whole life of Christ was the necessary way for Him to enter into His glory, as He has done.

Our hidden God has revealed Himself to us as a Father full of mercy and of love. So infinitely great is His love that St. John could write, "God is charity" (I John 4:16). It was love that made God create the spiritual and material worlds. We live in an atmosphere of God's love. Especially the fact that man was elevated to be a partaker of the divine nature in grace with the destiny of seeing and enjoying His Creator in the heavenly home, is an astounding, deep mystery of God's eternal love.[3] The sequel, the companion mystery, more striking to us is man's restoration to grace through the Incarnation and Redemption. The whole purpose of the earthly life of the God-man was to illustrate God's infinite love. We know that love is shown when a person shares our life, its routine and its vicissitudes, and when one suffers and dies for us. The more Our Lord endured humiliations and sufferings in His sacred passion, the more He gave evidence of God's love; and the more of economy He employed in veiling His divinity and glory in the public life and especially in the hidden life, the more did He bring home to our reason the enormous dimensions of the immense ocean of His infinite love.[4]

We may ask, why only three years for preaching and miracles; why the thirty long years of inactivity in an obscure town; why should not every minute of the divine life be given the greatest publicity? The Savior strongly condemned the hiding of the talent; then why should any part of His precious life be hidden? The answer is simple. It was an illustration of God's love that surpasseth understanding. Which of us can give advice to God about how He is to show His love for us? Is He not great enough to be a law and standard to Himself? Is it not the part of wisdom to admire what God does and with grateful hearts humbly to seek the reasons? As God is a hidden God, it was right for the God-man to have a hidden life. That life was according to foreordained decrees of the Father made known by the Scriptures and by God's providence. Indeed, in the birth, infancy, and early life of Our Lord many prophecies of the Old Testament were fulfilled.

As to human nature, the fact is that the years of infancy, childhood, and young manhood are not given to public life. So that if

[3] St. Peter Chrysologus held that God's raising man to divine sonship was a more impressive mystery than His lowering Himself to our level. Sermon 67; PL, 52, 391. Cf. Scheeben, *Mysteries of Christianity*, p. 317.
[4] Cf. Thibaut, *Le sense de l'Homme-Dieu*, p. 78.

our divine Lord had performed His miracles and preached His doctrines as a child, people would have "deemed the thing a delusion"
and His enemies "would have hurried Him off" before His time
to an early death, as St. John Chrysostom [5] long ago pointed out.
Indeed, as St. Augustine [6] teaches, Jesus passed through all the
different stages of life to show He was truly human and to give us
salutary lessons. It was precisely to inculcate a wholesome fear in
the hasty and impetuous, says St. Gregory the Great,[7] that "even
He who could not slip did not preach the grace of a perfect life until
He was of a perfect age." St. Irenaeus [8] had early given the following
explanation of the reason why Our Lord was born as a babe and
subjected Himself to the ordinary law of growth: as a master He
did not wish to despise or evade any condition of humanity, nor
did He wish to set aside any law He had appointed for the human
race; but rather, on the contrary, by going through the various stages
of life He sanctified "every age by that period corresponding to it
which belonged to Himself." By becoming an infant, a child, a boy,
a youth, and a man, God sanctified and ennobled beyond measure
every condition of human life and demonstrated in no uncertain way
that He stands behind the rights of every human being, no matter
how seemingly insignificant.

The nine-tenths of Our Lord's life that was given over to teaching
by example should not, from this point of view, be called hidden.
Yet its chief characteristic is that it was not lived in the limelight
of publicity, and from this viewpoint it is rightly called hidden. But
why should anyone demand that the whole of the divine life be
lived in the glare of the public stage? Some of the features of the
perfect life that have a special attraction for us are those that are
classified under the hidden life. The obscure home town, the ordi-

[5] *Homily*, XXI, 2, *On St. John*; NPN, 1st ser., XIV, 73 f.

[6] Some of the salutary lessons from the model example of the early life of our Blessed
Lord are given by St. Augustine in his *Sermon on the Circumcision of Our Lord*; PL, 47,
1138. Cf. Epistle 137, 519, *to Volusianus*, III, 9; PL, 33, 519.

[7] *Pastoral Rule*, III, 25; NPN, 2nd ser., XII, 54.

[8] *Against Heresies*, II, xxii, 4; ANF, I, 391. Irenaeus had previously said that Christ
"passed through every stage of life, restoring to all communion with God" (III, xviii,
7; ANF, I, 448).

nary occupation, the poor surroundings, and the simple family circle, were deliberately chosen; for the Son of God became man to win our love as well as to bring us grace. Publicity-seeking wins neither our respect nor our love. Surely the thought of God seeking publicity among men would be more abhorrent than that of a man looking for fame among insects. By living a hidden life Our Lord taught the value of a hidden life and the danger of a life for mere vulgar publicity. Indeed, publicity-seeking is such a disorder that, if it infected the vast majority, it would completely disrupt the human race. Man is made for God, and thus the quiet life lived for God is ennobled and hallowed by the hidden life of the Son of God.

The second characteristic of the first thirty years of Our Lord's life is that it was, to all appearances, an ordinary one. While a child, He looked and acted as a child; during His boyhood His conduct was much like that of other boys. For many years He lived the routine life of a carpenter. He was like His brethren in all things. Of course, He was exceptional in His freedom from sin and in His supereminent perfection; but in outward appearances His manner of living conformed to His time and generation. Ordinariness in the hidden life is at first a matter of surprise to us because we would not expect the God-man to become so much like us. Yet, here too, He teaches us the salutary lesson of the importance of the everyday routine life and also the lesson that perfection consists in doing ordinary things extraordinarily well. For the Son of God to accommodate Himself to the ordinary was most extraordinary for Him; and hence the justice of St. Bonaventure's remark: "His doing nothing wonderful was a kind of miraculous action." [9]

A third remarkable feature of the hidden life is that it was social. It was lived in a family circle of a house on a street in a little town. There were daily contacts with human beings, daily salutations, and daily business and social relationships. The Carpenter of Nazareth was a familiar figure to His fellow citizens. He was in His carpenter shop to fill orders for His customers or He was with the farming folk

[9] *Life of Our Lord and Savior Jesus Christ,* p. 103.

who worked on the near-by plain of Esdraelon. Thus in His social life lived among men Our Savior stands out in strong contrast to the Baptist, whose early life was passed entirely in the desert to prepare himself for his mission of pointing out the Messiah. Since it was necessary for the latter to be pointed out, He must, therefore, first be hidden, as is asserted by St. John Chrysostom in the passage already cited. We also know that, according to a popular opinion of the time of Christ, the Messiah's origin was to be unknown. Our Lord satisfied this expectation, for His Virgin birth as well as the place of His nativity was unknown except to a few. He was personally known only within a narrow circle of relatives and acquaintances; especially His divine sonship was unknown outside the members of the holy family.

The long, silent, golden years of the hidden life point to the great lesson that silence is golden. In the second century St. Ignatius of Antioch [10] insisted on the great truth, "it is better to keep silence and to be, than to talk and not to be," and expected the followers of Christ "to hearken unto His silence." If St. James, the "brother" of the Lord, was the author of the Epistle of St. James, and probably he was, then it is most significant that one who was so closely associated with Our Lord during the hidden years at Nazareth should write so scathingly about the world of iniquity, that forest fire ignited, as he says, by hell, the evil tongue (3: 1–12) . Here St. James was echoing the teaching of the inspired books, Psalms, Proverbs, and Ecclesiasticus.

This same St. James asserts that whoever lays claim to be wise at all should give good example by living peacefully (3: 13) . He further teaches that a truly wise man is peaceful, moderate, and docile, and that, far from being given to dissimulation or affectation, he is one

[10] *To the Ephesians*, 15; Lightfoot, *Apostolic Fathers*, p. 141. Neither the vegetable world in its growth nor the spheres in their rush through space make sounds that are audible to us. Silence reigns among the spirits of our departed dead; and we are deaf to the mighty angelic choral hymn of praise. Strangest of all is the silence of the Creator and Preserver and the silence with which God has enveloped the Church and its head, Jesus Christ. We learn His will through the Scriptures and the Church. His silence is a powerful sermon on moderation of speech.

that is ready to be convinced in any good cause and is in harmony with all good projects. According to these wise maxims our blessed Lord passed His years at Nazareth winning the approval of God and man (Luke 2: 52). He did not employ engines of war or take part in any kind of strife, but lived in accord with all men. His whole life preached peace and the things of peace. This should be the ambition of every Christian, to pattern his life after Jesus' peaceful and industrious life. St. Paul preached this hard lesson that we should strive to live peacefully, minding our own affairs, working with our own hands; so that we may be becomingly honest toward outsiders, and may need nothing ourselves. (I Thess. 4:11 f.).

What Our Lord has done for us in the hidden life, who can reckon it? Benefits immeasurable come from the Christmas crib with its Babe of Bethlehem. Results beyond description accrue to us from Our Lord's living a life of obedience to His parents. Advantages inestimable flow to us from the example of His peaceful, useful trade as carpenter. How profoundly we have been influenced by the fundamental virtues displayed by the hidden Christ! The most sublime humility of the God-man shines out all through the obscure years at Nazareth. A continual source of edification is His implicit obedience to parents and to civil and religious authorities. The Carpenter is the personification of simplicity, meekness, and gentleness. Purity radiates from Him as the central figure of the holy family where all three members are the exalted examples for all times of modesty and chastity. Charity like a queen reigns supreme in that happy home where words and deeds are in accord with the highest standards of perfection. This charity of the God-man and His living unrecognized among His neighbors makes us recognize Him in every neighbor. The hidden life as a part of a family group exerts a profound, beneficial influence on the family unit. The important family virtues were illustrated and inculcated by the holy family.

Prayer dominated the whole hidden life; the perfect prayer of one who was God as well as man. His life began with the prayer of consecration (Heb. 10:7), and prayer dedicated all his golden acts and words, which were entirely for the honor and in the interests of His Father. His thoughts, words, and actions were thus of supreme value to us, bringing us untold graces and blessings, for He worked out our salvation not only by dying for us on the cross but also by continually praying and consecrating Himself.[11] There is, therefore, in the hidden life a mine of priceless treasures and a power house of divine energy.[12] All that the Nazarene did won the favor of God and men, for all that He did was according to the highest standards of perfection and was ennobled with God's grace. Although hidden, His private life was perfect; although obscure, it shines as the sun to illumine our ways. After an ideal life, the ideal man came to the baptism of John to hear the words of approval when the Father expressed His great pleasure in Him. After the life at Nazareth, Christ could be and "was heard for His reverence," because His devout, holy life lived among men, was one of the highest wisdom and of the richest grace.

Blessings were to be poured on the heads of those who would not be scandalized in the Lord God when He would come to save us. (Matt. 11:16; Isa. 35:4). A more direct way of expressing this matter is that they are blessed who would benefit by the good example of the God-man; namely, take notice of it and follow it.

Considered in itself, the hidden life is that part of the divine life that was devoted to teaching by example. Herein lies not the least of its values. That example is more effective than words, we know from experience. The elocutionist or the orator may move an audience to laughter or to tears, but neither has been known to bring about the conversion of a sinner. Indeed many who are ready to give advice and to instruct others are warned by St. James (3:1) of their responsibility and accountability, while he points out that the truly wise man is he who, genuine and honest with himself, living by principle

[11] Encyclical letter, *On the Sacred Liturgy*, 1.

[12] We were all the object of His knowledge and love from the first moment of the Incarnation when enjoying the vision of the blessed "all the members of His mystical body were continually and unceasingly present, and He embraced them with His redeeming love"; encyclical, *On the Mystical Body of Christ*, 75. See also Becker, *The Hidden Life of Christ*, pp. 136–43.

as well as by faith, "by his behavior shows his work in the meekness of wisdom" (3:13). This same truth is echoed by Shakespeare, when Portia says: "I can easier teach twenty what were good to be done, than be one of the twenty to follow mine own teaching." What is noted here as the result of experience is not at all to discourage preachers who preach what they practice. Indeed the Savior gave the highest place to those who follow the requirements of the Scriptures and teach others to follow them (Matt. 5:19). As Jesus practiced first and then preached, He could point to the hidden life and say: I have set you the example. The great martyr of Antioch points out that the things that Our Lord "had done in silence are worthy of the Father" [13] and are for our imitation. The very silence and seclusion have their own lesson. It is true that queen perfection is found to reign in silence and seclusion,[14] for the reason that in obscurity, purer motives can be reached and greater union with God can be attained. How can any life lived in the glare of the sunshine of God's grace be considered obscure? Did not the Savior extoll the obscure life in His teaching that the last shall be first and the first last, that those who serve are the greatest among us and that the highest ideal is childlike simplicity? In striving after perfection, it is our duty and privilege to walk as Jesus walked (John 2:6). Here for us the hidden life is most luminous, lighting up the way to truth and eternal life.

BIBLIOGRAPHY

Becker, T. The Hidden Life of Christ.
Faber, Frederick W. Bethlehem.
Husslein, J. (co-author and editor), The Golden Years.
Leen, E. In the Likeness of Christ.
Onofri, T. La Franciullezza di Gesu nei Vangeli.

[13] Loc. cit.
[14] "Whoever wishes to lead an interior life and to become spiritual, must with Jesus keep aloof from the crowd." The Following of Christ (transl. by J. Malaise, New York, 1940), I, xx, 10.

O'Shea, D. The Holy Family.
Scheeben, M. The Mysteries of Christianity.
Thibaut, R. Le Sens de l' Homme-Dieu.
Thomas à Kempis, The Following of Christ.

Nazareth from the road to Cana

The Early Chapters of St. Matthew and St. Luke

DURING the public life, in the realm of Herod Antipas, at a shore town on Lake Tiberias, a Jew named Levi, son of Alpheus, also called Matthew, collected customs duties on fish and other taxes for the hated foreign government. He gave a sympathetic hearing to the great preacher and wonder-worker from Nazareth; and further, he responded promptly to the call to the apostolate. Afterward, while preaching to his own people, being able to write both Aramaic and Greek, he felt called upon as first among the apostles to set forth in writing the great discourses of Our Lord in Galilee and Jerusalem with such narrative as would give them their proper setting.[1] He wrote in Palestine in the language of the Jews of that country (namely, Aramaic), striving to convince them that Jesus was the long expected Messiah foretold in the Scriptures and sent by God to establish God's reign on earth. Thus chiefly he showed in his work that Our Lord freed His followers from the narrow traditions of the scribes, that He sternly censured the often hypocritical externalism of the Pharisees, and that He condemned the worldly materialism of the Sadducees.

[1] Living at Capharnaum and first becoming acquainted with Our Lord in that city, Matthew naturally began his account of the public life with Our Lord taking up His headquarters in Capharnaum. Cf. Chapman, *Matthew, Mark and Luke*, p. 257.

According to his purpose, St. Matthew devotes two chapters to selections from Christ's hidden life. For Jews the first important step was to demonstrate that the person he sets forth as Messiah was descended from David; the title, son of David, was one of the most popular for the expected Anointed of the Lord. Therefore, the Evangelist begins by giving the genealogical list that traced the legal father of Our Savior back to David, arranging the members in three groups of fourteen because the Hebrew letters of the name, David, were equivalent to that number. As he is writing for Jews, St. Matthew presents the angel's communication to the legal father, regarding the way the virginal conception of Christ took place. He points out that the Virgin birth was in accordance with the great prophecy of Isaias and that this prophet's name for the Messiah, "Immanuel," applied precisely to Jesus born through the Holy Ghost. He selects two incidents from the sacred infancy, one the sequel of the other; Gentiles of distinction did homage to the divine Child as the "King of the Jews," being led to Him by a star, which was foreshadowed by Balaam's famous prophecy. Like the Jews of old the infant Savior was exiled in Egypt, and words used of Israel could be appropriately adapted to Him as He returned to His own land. Herod's seeking the life of the divine Child would be easily understood by Jews of the first century among whom his cruel deeds were handed down and mentioned with horror. They would understand the general application of several scriptural texts of Christ's being called a Nazarene because of His long sojourn in Nazareth. Thus the early chapters of the First Gospel are along the lines of the rest of a work by a Jew seeking to convert Jews. It may be noticed, moreover, that they contain more characteristic words and expressions than any other part. They are a perfect introduction to this carefully written and well arranged record.

In the Third Gospel a different author with a very different background, writing with a different aim for a different class of readers, gives us naturally a different selection of events from Christ's hidden life. St. Luke, according to tradition, was a Syrian from Antioch, who may have been a Jewish proselyte before his conversion to Christianity. He was a physician and was not merely a companion of St. Paul imbued with the latter's universal ideas; but more than that, he did his share in preaching and spreading those ideas. He had before him written accounts of Our Lord's life and preaching; and he could have interviewed not only the apostles and the blood relatives of Christ, but even the Blessed Mother herself during visits he made to Palestine. He controlled his sources so well that in his own language he gave us what he considered the best of what he found in an orderly way, that is, sometimes presenting events in groups and not in strict chronological sequence. It is instructive to examine how he treated the Gospel of St. Mark; he could have met this Evangelist at Rome in A.D. 61 and 62. St. Luke incorporated in his inspired narrative about two-thirds of the Second Gospel, faithfully employing the material with regard to both order and contents, and the parts he did not use were those that seemed to him to be accounts that were either duplicate or superfluous or unsuitable for Gentile readers.

St. Luke, being a Syrian, could have read the First Gospel in the original Aramaic or could have seen translations of it or of parts of it, for he reproduced accounts amounting to about one-fourth of his work that are parallel to various sections of St. Matthew. Yet before his work was completed, we can safely say that St. Luke saw our Greek text of St. Matthew and corrected his manuscript according to it. But why is his Infancy narrative so different from and so independent of St. Matthew? St. Luke had to keep his work to a convenient size. It is the longest Gospel, with about one-fourth of it peculiar to itself. As he left out what he considered duplicate in St. Mark, so likewise he would be inclined to do the same in regard to the Gospel of St. Matthew. For economy of space he decided rather to set forth in his early chapters events that could be complementary to those already presented by the First Evangelist. That limitations of size was a chief factor in forcing selections may be seen from the fact that this author's two works, both Gospel and Acts, have about the maximum convenient size of an ancient papyrus roll.

To tell the history of Christ's life to Gentile readers, St. Luke used his own words but sought to effect a distinctly Christian biblical style. He succeeded so well in producing an Old Testament atmosphere in his first two chapters that sections of them throb in intense feelings of Jewish patriotism and devotion. Here he seems to have set before him as guide the Hebrew text of the early chapters of the First Book of Samuel. The inspired account of the birth and youth of the great "Asked-of-God" leader appealed to the literary susceptibilities of St. Luke and impressed him so much that it served him as a model, which explains omissions as well as selections, and summary statements as well as expressions and words. The Old Testament exerted an external or merely literary influence, for few and vague were the similarities between Samuel and St. John on the one hand, and Our Lord and Samuel on the other.

From his ample and abundant sources, the Third Evangelist selected events from the hidden life that seemed to him most important and appealing. He set down contrasts between Christ and St. John that showed the former as far outranking the greatest prophet of all time. Being a physician, he was interested in the mother's account of the Virgin birth and gave us the superb description of the annunciation to Mary. Familiarity with the early chapters of the First Book of Samuel led him to preserve for us the incomparable canticles of Mary, Zachary, and Simeon. In the pagan Roman world the claim of divine Savior was put forward for the Emperor. This prompted the Evangelist to hold forth Christ as Savior and Lord from His very birth. That this real and true Savior was the consecrated first-born and was ever dedicated to the service of His Father, St. Luke chose to show in giving us the accounts of the presentation and finding in the Temple. Then he thought best to summarize the long obscure life at Nazareth, lived in subjection and holiness, in words which with one exception were already used for the prophet Samuel. The result of St. Luke's literary effort is one of surpassing beauty.[2] This Infancy section excels in appeal and in effect, and more than any other section of the Bible has supplied subjects to artists for their paintings and to authors of religious hymns.

The order of the Childhood events followed in this book is generally accepted as most in accord with the two different Gospel accounts. The Third Evangelist starts his sacred history at an earlier point than the First Evangelist does, for he had collected information from those who had known Our Lord's life from the beginning (Luke 1: 3). St. Luke began with Gabriel's announcement to holy Zachary to serve as a prelude to prepare us, so to speak, for the greatest message of all time, God's becoming man. In the announcements, a certain balance on the one hand, and yet on the other a certain contrast appear. Balance and contrast are continued in the sequel to each angelic announcement; namely, the Visitation with Mary's song of faith, and St. John's circumcision with Zachary's hymn of victory.

With Jewish outlook, St. Matthew begins with a genealogy of our Savior as the Son of David and he evidences throughout the childhood account special interest in St. Joseph, the legal father. As we expect in the Gospel written by a Jew for the Jews of Palestine, after the resolving of St. Joseph's doubt by an angelic assurance, there is the pointing out of the literal fulfillment of the famous prophecy of Isaias. The birth of Our Lord at Bethlehem receives only passing references from St. Matthew, but fortunately for us the physician and fellow missionary of St. Paul was so impressed with some of the attending circumstances that he supplied us with our Christmas Gospel.

Contrary to what we would expect, it is the Gentile Evangelist

[2] About the beauty of the account of the annunciation to Mary, Vosté writes: "How much dignity as well as celestial purity, what rare simplicity of language along with singular aptness of words in this narrative where all is sublime; God, the heavenly angel, the news of the Incarnation, Christ the Son of the Most High to be born, the most pure Virgin Mother, the eternal salvation of the whole human race. And most exalted as all these are and accepted as they were in a humble heart by Mary, they are recorded in a simple style that is expressive of serene faith in a profound mystery." *De conceptione virginali Jesu Christi*, p. 17.

who records the fulfilling of the prescriptions of the sacred law by the child Jesus, and it is Levi, son of Alpheus, who sets down the account of the adoration of the Gentile Magi. It is true that St. Matthew is here in line with contemporary Jewish traditions of Herod's cruelty, when he narrates the massacre of the Holy Innocents and the flight into Egypt; and he is in accord with Jewish usage of the time in his quotations of the ancient prophecies.

After narrating the presentation of the child Jesus in the Temple, St. Luke (2:39) states that the holy family returned to Nazareth. It has been asked how the Evangelist could make this statement if he was aware of St. Matthew's narrative of the coming of the Magi and the exile in Egypt.[3] We may answer first, that there is no explicit exclusion. Secondly, writing in imitation of the model of the early account of Samuel, St. Luke desired to couple the two somewhat similar Temple scenes. Thirdly, that the Lucan words imply that finally the holy family returned to Nazareth finds support in the style of writing throughout the Third Gospel. The Evangelist is fond of anticipating events and making summary statements that are to be understood in the light of further information. For example, it would be false to understand from Luke 1:80 that the Baptist retired to the desert as a mere infant; or from Luke 3:19 f. that St. John was cast into prison before Our Lord's baptism. The silence of the long years of hidden life at Nazareth is broken only once, and then only by St. Luke, in the episode of Our Savior's twelfth year. This Evangelist alone makes summary statements about Christ's growth and development, which he does in conscious imitation of the model of the inspired account of the young Samuel.

Although divergent subjects are treated in the first two chapters of St. Matthew and St. Luke, yet in important matters and doctrines there is perfect agreement in the accounts. In the two narratives the chief characters are Jesus, Mary, and Joseph. Both Gospel records are concerned with the chief event or doctrine, the Virgin birth of Our

---

[3] Cf. Lagrange, *Evangile selon S. Luc*, pp. 91–92; Vosté, *De synopticorum mutua relatione et dependentia*, p. 75; Schmid, *Mathaüs und Lukas*, p. 194.

Lord who was conceived of the Holy Ghost. Both assert that the birthplace was Bethlehem and the time was the reign of Herod. Both Evangelists narrate appearances of angels; both say that when the miraculous conception of Our Lord took place, the Virgin Mary was betrothed to St. Joseph; and both preserve a remarkable silence about the hidden years at Nazareth. Likewise both narratives are discreet and reserved in contrast with the Apocryphal Gospels. A genealogy is found in both Gospels. It is not the same in both; but if St. Luke's is that of Mary, it would be in harmony with the fact that he was furnishing us with Mary's memoirs. Not only in the genealogies but also throughout the two childhood narratives, there prevail a Hebraistic spirit and an Old Testament atmosphere.

When St. Luke wrote the Infancy section of his Gospel, most likely he had before him as chief sources, St. Matthew's account and probably also another written document in the Hebrew language. Differently from the First Evangelist St. Luke concerned himself with Annunciation accounts, the narrative of the birth of Our Lord and the temple episodes; and in so doing he treated St. Matthew's Gospel somewhat as St. John treated the Synoptic Gospels that he had before him when he wrote the Fourth Gospel. St. John supplemented the three earlier Gospels. He avoided duplications and left out the Infancy section to keep his volume to a convenient size. St. John thus indicated that in the life of Our Lord there was an inexhaustible supply of rich material. To a certain extent St. Luke also indicated that the hidden life was a rich mine of knowledge and edification, when he supplemented St. Matthew's account, when he avoided duplications, and when he presented episodes that were so different from the Matthew events yet so harmonious with them. By supplementing St. Matthew's childhood narrative, through his investigation of first-hand evidence, St. Luke gave his approval to the contents of this parallel account of the early life of Christ.

BIBLIOGRAPHY

Arendzen, J. The Gospels, Fact, Myth, or Legend? pp. 110–54.
Burrows, E. The Gospels of the Infancy and Other Biblical Essays,
    pp. 50–52.
Durand, A. The Childhood of Jesus Christ, pp. 172–258.
Fillion, L. The Life of Christ, I, 517–49.
Lagrange, M. J. Evangile selon S. Matthieu, pp. 39–44.
Lebreton, J. The Life and Teaching of Jesus Christ, I, 1–16.
Lepin, M. Christ and the Gospel, pp. 107–27.
Orr, J. The Virgin Birth of Christ, pp. 30–90.
Machen, G. The Virgin Birth of Christ, pp. 119–87.
Prat, F. Jésus-Christ, I, 114–16.
Ruffini, E. Introductio in S. Scripturam, I, 118–39.
Schmid, J. Matthäus und Lukas, pp. 14–21 and 192–98.
Sweet, L. M. The Birth and Infancy of Jesus, pp. 287–332.
Vosté, J. M. De Conceptione Virginali Jesu Christi, pp. 26–80.

The Childhood Account of Samuel and the Early Chapters of St. Luke

W E have no scriptural authority to warrant the saying that Samuel was a type of Our Lord; nor do we find sufficient foundation in tradition for this assertion.[1] There are, however, resemblances between the prophet who witnessed a climax in Jewish history and the divine Messiah who was the climax to all Jewish history. Christ's childhood account as given us in the Third Gospel contains several striking resemblances to the inspired account of the young Samuel.

In both accounts hill country is mentioned (I Sam. 1:1; Luke 1:39) and references are made to yearly pilgrimages to the house of God (I Sam. 1:3; Luke 2:41). In one account the mother of Samuel is childless; in the other the mother of the Baptist is childless and the mother of Our Lord is a virgin. Samuel's mother consecrated her son to God with a vow (I Sam. 1:11); in announcing the birth of the Baptist, Gabriel foretold that his life would be entirely given over to his holy calling. The Virgin Mother chanted a canticle in joyous thanksgiving; so did the father of St. John and the mother of Samuel.

[1] Cf. Sutcliffe, "Were Anna and Samuel Types of Our Lord, and Our Lady?" *Scripture*, I (1946), 57 f.

327

Especially in the canticle of Anna and that of Mary, and in the statements about growth and development, resemblances are so great that they show there must have been a dependence of some kind. (1) The Magnificat begins with the same ideas as those found in the opening verse of Anna's canticle: My soul doth magnify the Lord, and my spirit hath rejoiced in God my Savior (Luke 1:46 f.); My heart hath rejoiced in the Lord, and my horn is exalted in my God . . . because I have joyed in thy salvation (I Sam. 2:1). (2) Mary sang: He hath put down the mighty from their seat and hath exalted the humble. He hath filled the hungry with good things, and the rich He hath sent empty away (Luke 1:53 f.). Anna had laid emphasis on the same idea; for example: The Lord maketh poor and maketh rich; He humbleth and He exalteth (I Sam. 2:7). (3) Referring to herself, the Virgin Mother said: Because He hath regarded the humility of His handmaid (Luke 1:48). Previous to her canticle Anna had prayed: O Lord of hosts, if Thou wilt look down on the affliction of Thy servant, and wilt be mindful of me, and not forget Thy handmaid (I Sam. 1:11).

Concerning the growth of Samuel it is written: And Samuel grew and the Lord was with him (I Sam. 3:19); of John it is written: For the hand of the Lord was with him . . . and the child grew and was strengthened in spirit (Luke 1:66, 80); and of Our Lord: And the Child grew and waxed strong, full of wisdom, and the grace of God was in Him (Luke 2:40). Lastly, St. Luke's famous words about Our Savior: And Jesus advanced in wisdom and age, and grace with God and man (2:52), are said to be "an implicit quotation" [2] from I Sam. 2:26; but the child Samuel advanced and grew on, and pleased both the Lord and men.

Burrows finds forty-one more or less probable influences of the eighty-five verses at the beginning of I Samuel upon the text of the early chapters of St. Luke, some of them affecting more than one verse.[3] Above all, he points out that the Evangelist followed the

[2] Burrows, *The Gospel of the Infancy*, p. 27. Elsewhere (*ibid.*, p. 2), he calls it "an almost verbal counterpart."
[3] *The Gospel of the Infancy*, p. 27.

general scheme of Samuel's account, namely, division into scenes and mysteries that closed with an expression of departure.[4] He concludes that there was an external, literary influence; and he even makes the assertion that the author of the first two chapters of St. Luke may have had the Samuel childhood account "open before him when he wrote." [5]

On the other hand, when comparing St. Luke's Infancy section with that of Samuel we find differences that are impressive. The chief figures and the chief events are of course quite different. Samuel was the asked-of-God prophet; St. John the Baptist the last and greatest of the prophets; and Christ the God of the prophets. Samuel was born as a favorable response to the tears and prayers of his mother. Both St. John's birth and that of Our Lord were announced by the archangel Gabriel. There are no angelic apparitions in the Samuel infancy section. Nor is there any reference in the Old Testament chapters corresponding to the Evangelist's account of Christ's virgin birth, or His title of Son of God (Luke 1:32, 35; 2:49), or His career as divine Savior (Luke 1:32 f.; 2:11, 30, 38).

The boy Samuel is left in the house of the Lord (I Sam. 1:24, 28); whereas St. John retired to the desert (Luke 1:80); and Jesus remained at home with His parents at Nazareth (Luke 2:38). In the Lord's house God speaks to Samuel (I Sam. 3:4–14); whereas the boy Christ stupifies the doctors by His "understanding and His answers" (Luke 2:47). As the Son of God by nature, the young Savior refers to God as "My Father," and to His own necessity to be engaged in His Father's affairs (Luke 2:49), whereas the prophet calls God, "Lord," and himself, "servant"; and expresses his attitude as that of respectfully waiting for commands (I Sam. 3:10). In the Gospel narrative there are no characters corresponding to Heli or his sons, nor to Elcana or Phenenna. In the early chapters of I Samuel there are no passages that would have parallel roles to Simeon, Anna, the shepherds, Augustus, or Quirinius; nor can we find

---

[4] *Ibid.*, pp. 3–6.
[5] *Ibid.*, p. 2.

there accounts parallel to the Visitation, circumcision of John the Baptist, birth of Christ, presentation and finding in the Temple.

The similarities in the Magnificat and in Anna's canticle are so striking that it appears that the Blessed Virgin Mary assimilated some of Anna's ideas and used them for her purpose in praising and blessing God for her own exalted privilege of being the Mother of the divine Messiah. No words were taken over verbatim, but the ideas were employed after being absorbed and becoming part of Mary's mind by prayer and meditation. She leaned on an inspired model and used it as a help to proclaim her own gratitude to God. The name of her own mother and the visiting in Samuel's country would both suggest Anna's great favor and victory. Certainly there was a similarity of theme and occasion; and indeed in the lives of all His saints God is continually winning victories over His enemies. Anna's rival was Phenenna; Mary's enemy the forces of evil; the world, the flesh, and the devil. Expressions of victory already inspired by the Holy Spirit suited the great occasion of the crushing of the serpent's head. It was natural, therefore, for Our Lady to make use of some of the ideas of Samuel's mother.

The Virgin Mary also made use of the ideas found in the Psalms (97: 3; 102: 17; 106: 9; 110: 9) and in other places of the Old Testament.[6] We would expect that members of a family related to the priestly line, such as Mary's family was, would commit to memory the lyrics of their sacred writings. Indeed, twice St. Luke makes mention of Mary's reflecting on events. Her canticle is the result of her meditations on the Scriptures. It was accordingly natural for her that, in pouring out her soul in a song of praise to God, there should come spontaneously to her lips, as well as other Old Testament phrases, expressions she culled from meditations on Anna's canticle that had a somewhat similar occasion and purpose as her own.

The expressions about growth and development are somewhat reflected in Prov. 3: 4 and Rom. 14: 18. The similarity here between

[6] Cf. Plummer, *The Gospel according to St. Luke*, p. 31.

the Evangelist and I Samuel is so striking that it could not be accidental; there was a dependence. It is to be explained by St. Luke's conscious imitation of Old Testament biblical style which induced him especially to follow the model which he found in the account of the early career of Samuel.

The differences and the resemblances found in the first chapters of St. Luke and those of I Samuel point to extrinsic or literal dependence. There was no verbal dependence or borrowing of facts. Rather the influence the Old Testament narrative exerted on St. Luke was after a literary way. Namely, he was impressed by the account of Anna and her asked-of-God child, one of the most beautiful and most touching in the Old Testament, especially appealing to an artistic temperament by its simplicity and realism. When the Evangelist was writing the Infancy narrative of Christ he kept before him as a model the account of the young Samuel. The influence of the model showed itself in the omission of certain facts, in the recording of others, and in the emphasizing of certain points (Our Lord's growth). The result was that certain resemblances to the model were interwoven into the accounts of both St. John and Our Lord. In other words, the Evangelist, like the Blessed Virgin herself, was influenced by and made good use of the Scriptures already inspired by God.

Was St. Luke's ability as a literary artist responsible for the pronounced Hebrew coloring of the first two chapters of his Gospel? In striving to find a solution of this difficult question, we must closely examine the facts of the case. (1) St. Luke's characteristic words are found in sufficient number; in fact, more than the average proportion of them are in his first chapters; so that the wording of these chapters is evidently his. (2) There is a distinct biblical style throughout St. Luke's first two chapters. This is attributed by Dalman [7] to the Evangelist's affecting a "liturgical frame of mind" and, therefore, to a conscious effort to develop an Old Testament atmosphere. (3) Furthermore, the frequent use of Hebraisms

[7] *The Words of Jesus*, p. 40.

gives St. Luke's first chapters a Hebrew coloring, not an Aramaic one, nor a Greek one. (4) As Burrows shows, as indicated above, St. Luke, in writing the early chapters of his Gospel held before him, as a model, the early chapters of I Samuel.[8] (5) Much of St. Luke's two chapters can be rendered into Hebrew meter, as is done by Aytoun,[9] which might be evidence that it originally existed in the form of a Hebrew poem. If so, it is certain that St. Luke in translating it into Greek kept close to the original.[10]

This is certain: no writer could have composed St. Luke's childhood account without its being based on historic truth, "any more than an architect of that age could have produced the Milan cathedral." [11] The account came originally from the lips of the Blessed Virgin. When it reached the Evangelist it was a written document composed in Hebrew, as is suggested by Burrows.[12] As to the author of this written document, the hypothesis of Burrows seems the most plausible of the many advanced; namely, that St. John the Evangelist was the author of St. Luke's written source for the Infancy section of his Gospel.[13] First, what an excellent introduction to St. John's Gospel the Lucan childhood account would make! Everything in the early chapters of St. Luke fits so harmoniously with the Fourth Gospel that both could have been by the same author. Secondly, St. Luke's early section contains the memoirs of Mary of Nazareth. How appropriate they would be for the guardian of Jesus' mother after Our Lord's death: St. John's Cana scene is the sequel of the episode of Christ's twelfth year; and holy Simeon's

[8] Only in a few cases the Lucan text agrees with the Greek Septuagint text. In all other cases the parallels are more easily related to the Hebrew text. Cf. Burrows, *Gospel of the Infancy*, p. 34.

[9] This Hebrew rendering is based mostly on the Hebrew New Testament of Franz Delitzsch. "The Ten Lucan Hymns of the Nativity in Their Original Language," *Journal of Theological Studies*, XVIII (1917), 274–88.

[10] Cf. McLachlan, *St. Luke, the Man and His Work*, p. 84.

[11] Plummer, *The Gospel according to St. Luke*, p. 35.

[12] *Gospel of the Infancy and Other Biblical Essays*, p. 36.

[13] *Gospel of the Infancy*, pp. 39–58. Besides the reasons that we outline, Burrows gives others: chronological notices in Luke 1–2 the same as in John's Gospel, symbolism of numbers, etc. It seems that the intermediary between St. Luke and the Blessed Mother was a woman; and the one most favored in the surmises of scholars is Joanna, the wife of Chusa.

prophecy of the sword of sorrow is fulfilled at the foot of the cross, in the Joannine account. Thirdly, holy Simeon's pointing to the child Christ as "light" and "glory" is reminiscent of the Fourth Gospel. The child Jesus' consecration in the Temple and the boy Jesus' words of identification of His will with that of the eternal Father, both are Joannine. The beginning of St. John is an appropriate commentary of the Annunciation scene. Both St. Luke and St. John give special prominence to the Baptist. Both follow this order: testimony, signs, and faith.

Burrows well says that in the Infancy section St. Luke, like St. John, subordinates his authoritative story to that of no Evangelist, and both authenticate their work in the same way.[14] They both are fond of Temple episodes, St. John's Gospel giving us so much of the ministry of Our Lord at the Temple of Jerusalem. That St. John was a versatile writer is evidenced not only in his Gospel and in his Epistles, but also in his Apocalypse. Having considered all these factors, we may well conclude that, if St. Luke followed a written source in the Infancy section, and if that source was written in Hebrew along Old Testament lines, a plausible theory that may well be advanced is that St. John was its author. This hypothesis gives us another reason why the Fourth Gospel is without an Infancy section, for it supplies an additional reason why St. John was satisfied with the two Infancy accounts already in circulation [15] when he wrote his Gospel. Certainly, if he was the author of one of them, he would feel that he did not have to write another. In any case, by altogether omitting the narration of the incidents of the early life of Our Lord, the beloved disciple tacitly approved the early chapters of both St. Matthew and St. Luke.

[14] *Ibid.*, p. 54.
[15] Was St. Mark satisfied with St. Matthew's childhood account that he did not supply an Infancy section to his Gospel? St. Mark gives us the Gospel of St. Peter, who testified to the public life of Christ that he personally knew.

BIBLIOGRAPHY

Aytoun, R. "The Ten Lucan Hymns of the Nativity in Their Original Language," Journal of Theological Studies, XVIII (1917), 274–88.

Burrows, E. The Gospel of the Infancy and Other Biblical Essays.

Joüon, P. L'Evangile de notre-Seigneur Jésus-Christ, pp. 280 ff.

Lagrange, J. M. Evangile selon S. Luc, pp. 46–53.

Plummer, A. The Gospel according to St. Luke, pp. 30–35.

Strater, P. "De Probabile Origine Historiae Infantiae Christi," Verbum Domini. XXV (1947), 321–27.

Sutcliffe, E. "The Magnificat and the Canticle of Anna," Scripture, I (1946), 56–58.

The Date of Our Lord's Birth

PROBABLE LIMITS OF DATE

FOR the beginning of the Christian era we have been following the date that was set by Dionysius Exiguus, a monk of the sixth century. From the expression in St. Luke (3:23), that Jesus was about thirty years of age (the meaning of the text is rather that He was in His thirties), Dionysius figured thirty years from the fifteenth year of Tiberius (Luke 3:1); and thus fixed the birth of Christ as December 25 of the year 754 from the foundation of Rome. That this is incorrect we know from the fact that King Herod the Great, who was living after the birth of Our Lord (Luke 1:5; Matt. 2:1), died in the spring of the year 750 from the foundation of Rome. Josephus expressly tells us that this king died shortly before the Passover and sets the year of his death as the thirty-seventh after his appointment and the thirty-fourth after his conquest of Jerusalem.[1]

---

[1] *The Jewish War*, I, 665 (xxxiii, 8); *Antiquities*, XVII, viii, 1. Josephus also says that there was an eclipse of the moon shortly before Herod's death. This has been dated March 12–13, 750 from the foundation of Rome. Also from the number of years assigned to the reigns of the two sons of Herod, Archelaus ten years and Herod Antipas forty-three years, it is computed that the year of Herod's death was 750, A.U.C. See Maas, *Gospel according to St. Matthew*, p. 16; also Holzmeister, *Chronologia vitae Christi*, pp. 18–24. According to Holzmeister (*op. cit.*, pp. 25–28) at least six months must be allowed for Herod's illness and another six months for the confirmation of Herod's will after his death.

It is certain, therefore, that Our Lord was born at least four years before the date fixed by Dionysius. When we allow sufficient time for Herod's last illness, for the exile of the holy family in Egypt, and for the coming of the Magi, we arrive at 6 B.C. as the latest probable date for Christ's birth. That it was not many years before 6 B.C., we know from St. Luke's statement that Our Savior was in His thirties when He began His public ministry. The exact year in which He was born continues to be a matter of controversy. Considerable light has been shed on the question by the study of the evidence for the census of Quirinius which occurred the year of Christ's birth (Luke 2: 2).

THE GOSPEL TEXT

The registration during which Our Lord was born, according to St. Luke, took place while Quirinius was in charge of, or presided over Syria; the Greek word employed is quite general and need not be restricted to the meaning of legate.[2] We do know that Quirinius was legate of Syria in A.D. 6, when a census in that province occasioned the revolt of Judas the Galilean. St. Luke himself is aware of this fact for he mentions it in the Acts (5: 37). One explanation of the Lucan passage (2: 2) is that the word "first" found there is an adverb with the meaning "prior to." This view is held by Lagrange[3] and others, but has not been widely accepted. A second explanation is suggested by the fact that Tertullian[4] states that the census during which Christ was born was carried out by Sentius Saturninus. Judging from the references in Josephus, the governors of Syria about the time of Our Lord's birth were M. Titius, Sentius Saturninus, and Varus. Holding that these references are misleading and that there is room in this period for Quirinius, between Titius

[2] It is used for the ranking superior. See Lagrange, *Evangile selon S. Luc.*, pp. 67 f. O'Rourke, "Census Quirinii," *Verbum Domini*, I (1921), 206 note. For Josephus' use of this Greek word, see *Jewish War*, I, 20 (ii, 8); II, 358 (xvi, 4); I, 537 (xxviii, 1).

[3] *Evangile selon S. Luc.*, p. 67. Prat (*Jésus-Christ*, I, 315), says about this view that it must not be said to be impossible.

[4] *Adv. Marcion*, IV, 9; PL, II, 434.

and Saturninus, Corbishley [5] and others maintain that the census of Our Lord's birth was begun by Quirinius, but was completed by Saturninus. A third solution that appears to have most probability is that there were two legates at the same time in Syria at Christ's birth, Saturninus the civil one and Quirinius the military one. Because the more important, the military one, would have charge of the taking of a census, and because Quirinius had a remarkable military career, it was natural for St. Luke to write that this illustrious commander presided over Syria, without mentioning the civil legate, Saturninus.

QUIRINIUS' FIRST TIME AS GOVERNOR

Ramsay [6] must be given the credit for presenting the evidence which creates a strong probability that Quirinius was military commander of Syria about five years before Herod's death. Because of the discovery in Egypt of certain papyri [7] that tell of enrollments by household there between the years A.D. 61 and A.D. 237–38, and probably for the years A.D. 47–48 and A.D. 19–20, it is now accepted as a historical fact that there were periodical censuses every fourteen years. Also as Cobern [8] states, it is now "fairly certain" that Augustus began this system of periodical censuses. Arguing from the constructive genius of the Princeps,[9] Ramsay concluded that he inaugurated the series of fourteen-year censuses and that they may be dated from the first year of his principate, 23 B.C. The end of the first fourteen years would fall in 9 B.C., the next in A.D. 5, the next in

[5] *Journal of Roman Studies*, XXIV (1934), 43 ff.; also *Scripture*, I (1946), 77–80. In favor of this view is the fact that the taking of a census especially in the outlying provinces of the Empire was often prolonged a few years.

[6] *The Bearing of Recent Discovery on the Trustworthiness of the New Testament*, pp. 222–300. Also "Luke's Narrative of the Birth of Christ," *Expositor*, IV (1912), 385–407, 481–507.

[7] For the text, see Deissman, *Light from the Ancient East*, plate V, p. 271.

[8] *New Archeological Discoveries*, p. 46.

[9] *The Bearing of Recent Discoveries on Trustworthiness of the New Testament*, pp. 255–256. In "Luke's Narrative of the Birth of Christ," *Expositor*, IV (1912), 389, Ramsay writes that Augustus' bureaucratic system of administration fixed the general type for all modern methods.

A.D. 19, the next in A.D. 33, and so on. In each case, the counting would take place the following year. Accordingly the year 9 B.C. would mark the first series of fourteen-year periods, but the counting would be held in 8 B.C.

We know that Quirinius was legate of Syria when the census was taken up in Palestine in A.D. 6 during which there was the revolt of Judas the Galilean, as mentioned in the Acts and in Josephus. We have evidence that Quirinius was military commander in Syria previously. From Tacitus [10] and Strabo [11] we learn that Quirinius fought a successful war against the Homonadenses in Cilicia, an appendage of Syria. This must have been sometime after 12 B.C., when Quirinius was consul, and before A.D. 1–3, when as counselor he accompanied Gaius Caesar to Armenia. There is more definite evidence. Among the inscriptions that refer to Quirinius, the most important one was discovered by Ramsay in Pisidian Antioch.[12] This inscription on the base of a statue bears witness to the fact that a member of the family of Caristanii was the representative of Quirinius and filled his place so well that a statue was erected to him at the public expense. The date for this fact commemorated in the inscription, namely, that Quirinius was elected magistrate (duumvir) and nominated Caristanius to act for him, is given by Ramsay as between 10 B.C. and 7 B.C. Ramsay came to the conclusion that at the time mentioned there were two legates in Syria, Saturninus the civil one, and Quirinius the military one conducting the war against the Homonadenses.

JOSEPHUS AND HEROD

To have two legates in a province at the same time was not unheard of. But why is it that Josephus does not mention this first

[10] *Annals*, III, 48. He states here that Quirinius received a triumph for his victory, in capturing "the Homonadensian strongholds beyond the Cilician frontier."

[11] In *Geography*, XXII, VI, 5; he mentions the Homonadenses in the Taurus mountains (*Loeb*, V, 479).

[12] For the text, see Ramsay, *The Bearing of Recent Discoveries on the Trustworthiness of the New Testament*, p. 285; and plate I, opposite for the picture of the stone. Cf. Ruffini, *Introductio in S. Scripturam*, II, 217.

census? Moreover, would Herod permit a Roman census to be
taken in his semi-independent kingdom? As in the case of the Holy
Innocents so also here the silence of Josephus is no valid argument.
About more than one event of the last years of Herod the language
of Josephus is vague and confusing. Perhaps the account about
Quirinius first conducting a census was not in his source, the work
of Nicholas of Damascus. The latter, bent on glorifying Herod,
might have left out the application of the universal census to Palestine as an event that was derogatory to the monarch. Josephus only
indirectly and briefly mentions once Quirinius and once the second
census in his first work, the *Jewish War* (II, 433 and VII, 253);
and if he had not written the *Antiquities* a quarter of a century later,
it would be argued that he did not know much about this second
census either. In this later work the reference to the census is also
a brief one; here the emphasis is on the fact that the main body of
the Jews were dissuaded by the high priest Joazar from any open
acts of hostility, but that Judas the Galilean [13] and Sadduc the
Pharisee were bent on revolt. No details about the revolt are given
nor is it even mentioned that this Judas was put to death, a fact
which we know from Acts (5: 37). It is evidently an embarrassing
matter for Josephus. His calling Judas a Gaulanite pointed out that
he was not from the part of the Holy Land affected by the census,
and he goes on to outline the views of this founder of this "system
of philosophy" of the Zealots, that brought on robberies, murders,
tumults, and the destruction of the nation.

Josephus does mention that the Roman legate, Varus, twice interfered in Judea while that province was under Archelaus, as yet not
annexed to Roman Syria.[14] Josephus [15] also gives a brief mention of
the fact that Herod the Great toward the end of his life made the
Jewish people swear assurance of their good will to the emperor and

---

[13] *Antiquities*, XVIII, i, 1; ii, 1. Here Judas is called a Gaulanite from Gamala. There
were two cities of that name, one in Galilee, and one on the east of Lake Tiberias. In
Jewish War, II, 117 f. (viii, 1), the references to Judas are even more brief. Here he is
called a "sophist" to give him respectability.

[14] *Jewish War*, II, 40 (iii, 1); II, 72 (v, 2); *Antiquities*, XVII, x, 9.

[15] *Antiquities*, XVII, ii, 4.

to his government. The 6,000 Pharisees alone refused to take this oath and were fined. This occasion could well have been that of the registration of Our Lord's birth. It certainly showed that the Jews would submit to a census under Herod. It is to be noted that the Gospel text merely refers to a registration (Luke 2:2), without any reference to taxation.[16] We can conclude, therefore, that Josephus gives instances somewhat parallel to the Gospel account of the registration; and secondly, to the objection from the historian's silence, it may be replied that he does mention the second census only because it occasioned the rise of a sect that had an evil influence on his people. We may also safely state that Herod the Great would cooperate with the Emperor in the carrying out of a census, especially toward the end of his life, when he had fallen into disfavor with Augustus. He would employ his police force and indeed all his cruel methods in seeing to it that the Emperor's edict was complied with. He would join with Quirinius in suppressing ruthlessly any acts of violence or opposition.

Quirinius according to Josephus [17] went into Judea in A.D. 6 to take a valuation of the property of the country and to dispose of the wealth of Archelaus. He must have brought a considerable army with him, and was able to take care of the minor revolt of Judas the Galilean. There would be less likelihood of any revolt on the occasion of the registration of Christ's birth, for at that time the Jews were thoroughly subdued under the unparalleled suppressive methods of Herod. Perhaps this first registration was not accompanied by valuation of property for taxation. Perhaps it was merely a registration joined to the oath of allegiance mentioned by Josephus. The presence of this "able, energetic, hard and unlovable" general,[18] Quirinius, guaranteed a peaceful registration. It was the first time the Romans had imposed a registration. The word "first" is used by St. Luke either because it was the first of the series of Roman regis-

---

[16] Cf. Manson, *Gospel of Luke*, p. 18.
[17] *Antiquities*, XVII, i, 1.
[18] Ramsay, "Luke's Narrative of the birth of Christ," *Expositor*, IV (1912), 403.

trations, or because it was the first one under Quirinius. His importance as a military commander and his standing with the imperial family marked this Quirinius as a man "of great merit," [19] and an outstanding historical figure. It was natural for St. Luke to mention him rather than Saturninus, especially on account of the fact that the registration in Palestine and its pacification would come under his jurisdiction. There is positive evidence that he was in charge of military operations in Syria from about 11 B.C. to 8 B.C.

SUMMARY

In relation to the enrollment at Christ's birth, the following years may be assigned as dates for Quirinius as military prefect of Syria and for Saturninus as civil legate.

1. Quirinius in charge of the Homonadensian wars; 10–6 B.C.[20]
2. Saturninus legate of Syria: 9–6 B.C.[21]
3. From the series of censuses every fourteen years: 8 B.C. Concluding that the year October, 9 B.C. to October, 8 B.C. was the year of enrollment during which Our Lord was born, Ramsay calls the evidence for this year though scant, yet "coherent and unequivocal." [22] On the other hand Prat is not much impressed by the evidence; for he writes that Ramsay's arguments for 8 B.C. are "only probable," holding that the year 6 B.C. would be more suitable.[23] There are many scholars, however, who accept Ramsay's date for Christ's birth, such as Ruffini [24] (9–8 B.C.), Manson [25] (8 B.C.),

---

[19] Josephus, loc. cit.

[20] Corbishley, "The Date of Our Lord's Birth," Scripture, I (1946), 79. Ramsay gives 11–8 B.C. (op. cit., p. 406). Inscriptions that showed extensive road making in 6 B.C. induced Ramsay to conclude the war was over before that time. Prat gives 7–5 B.C.; Jésus-Christ, I, p. 314. Rees gives 11–7 B.C.; "Cyrinius the Governor of Syria," Scripture, III (1948), 78.

[21] This is Ramsay's figure (op. cit., p. 406). Corbishley says, not later than 8 B.C., Scripture, I (1946), 80; Prat says, 8–6 B.C.; loc. cit.

[22] Op. cit., p. 386.

[23] Jésus-Christ, I, 316.

[24] Chronologia Veteris et Novi Testamenti, pp. 119–28.

[25] Gospel of Luke, p. 17.

Lebreton [26] (8 or 7 B.C.), Holzmeister [27] (9–7 B.C.), Power [28] (9–8 B.C.), Corbishley [29] (8 B.C.), and Gaechter [30] (8–7 B.C.). In our work we have accepted the year 8 B.C. for the birth of Christ.

In regard to the day and month of the year, it may be said with Ruffini [31] that the Eastern and Western Churches are in agreement in holding that Our Lord was born in the winter season. It may also be said that there is no agreement among the Fathers as to the exact date.

If 8 B.C. for the year of Christ's birth is correct, than He was three years and some months old at Herod's death, March, 4 B.C. In this view the sojourn of the holy family in Egypt could not be more than four years nor less than two.[32] Again, if Christ's baptism occurred in January, A.D. 28, the hidden life of Our Lord lasted more than thirty-five years, and His residence at Nazareth continued for more than thirty-two years.

BIBLIOGRAPHY

Cobern, C. M. The New Archeological Discoveries, pp. 46 f., 538.

Corbishley, T. "The Date of Our Lord's Birth" Scripture, I (1946), 77–80.

Fillion, L. C. The Life of Christ, I, pp. 579–90.

Fonck, L. "Quandonam Christus Natus est?" Verbum Dominii, VII (1927) 363–72.

Holmeister, U. Chronologia vitae Christi, pp. 15–49.

[26] Life and Teaching of Jesus Christ, I, xiv.

[27] Chronologia vitae Christi, p. 29.

[28] "John 2:20 and the Date of the Crucifixion," Biblica, IX (1928), 288. This date also is given by Merk, Compendium, 1043. Delitzsch holds 9 B.C. or later; Jewish Artizan Life in the Time of Jesus, p. 54.

[29] "The Date of Our Lord's Birth," Scripture, I (1946), 77–80.

[30] This writer holds that Mary and Joseph went to Bethlehem for the enrollment in October–November 8 B.C., but that Christ was born in March–April, 7 B.C. "The Chronology from Mary's betrothal to the birth of Christ," Theological Studies, II (1941), 368. He shows that enrollments took place as a rule in the months from June to August. Op. cit., p. 361.

[31] Op. cit., p. 128. See also Holzmeister, Chronologia vitae Christi, pp. 36–49.

[32] Ruffini, op. cit., p. 125.

Johnston, T. A. "The Census of Quirinius," Irish Eccles. Record, XXXVIII (1939), 225–43.

Lagrange, M. J. Evangile selon S. Luc, pp. 65–69.

Luce, H. K. The Gospel according to S. Luke, pp. 14–17.

Manson, W. The Gospel of Luke, pp. 16–18.

O'Rourke, J. J. "Census Quirinii," Verbum Domini, I (1921), 206–11.

Ramsay, W. The Bearing of Recent Discovery on the Trustworthiness of the New Testament, pp. 222–300.

————. "Luke's Narrative of the Birth of Christ," The Expositor, IV (1912), 385–407, 481–507.

Rees, W. "Cyrinus the Governor of Syria," Scripture, III (1948), 76–83.

Ruffini, E. Chronologia Veteris et Novi Testamenti, pp. 119–28. Introductio in S. Scripturan, II, 206–22.

Valensin and Huby, Evangile selon S. Luc, pp. 31–34.

For other works, see Ruffini, (Chronologia V. et. N. Testamenti).

Herod's Temple

SOURCES

THE first primary source, superior to all others, is the Sacred Scriptures: III Kings 6–7; II Par. 3–4; Ezech. 40–42; I Esd. 3; I Mach. 4; Matt. 4:5; 21:12; 24:12; 27:51; Mark 11:11, 15 f.; 13:3; 14:49; Luke 1:8 ff.; 2:22 ff., 41 ff.; 19:45–47; 21:5; John 2:14–21; 7:14 ff.; 8:1 ff.; 10:23; 18:20; Acts 2:46; 3:1–10; 4:1; 5:20–25; 21:26–35; 24:6–18; Apoc. 11:2; 15:5–8, etc.

Secondly, a description of the Temple is given us by Josephus, *Wars*, V. 184–247 (v, 1–8); *Antiquities*, XV, xi, 1–7; *Against Apion*, I, 198–200 (22). His language is sometimes vague and at other times exaggerated; yet as he had been a priest and must have been frequently in the Temple, his accounts of it must receive careful consideration. There is also the brief statement by Philo, who saw the Temple, *De Specialibus Legibus*, I, XIII–XIV, 71–78 (Loeb, edited by Colson, VII, 140–45).

Another primary source is the *Mishnah*, especially the tractate Middoth (Measurements). This tractate does not mention either the inner or outer court, but concerns itself with the inner Temple. Its purpose is religious, namely, to put on record the lines of a future temple. We have every reason to expect, therefore, that the data set down have been carefully preserved.[1] It supplies a supplement to the general plan of the Temple given by Josephus.[2] Its date is given by Hollis as about A.D. 150.[3]

There remains as a genuine source and court of final appeal, the scientific survey of the site and ancient ruins of the Temple. Here we are fortunate in

---

[1] Cf. Hollis, *Archaeology of Herod's Temple*, p. 20. The cubit is now generally taken as 18 inches. *Ibid.*, p. 349.

[2] Cf. Oesterley, *History of Israel*, II, 376.

[3] *Op. cit.*, p. 358.

having the work of a mathematician and engineer, in which he presents the results of scientific measurements and calculations. The most valuable part of Mr. Hollis's book (*The Archaeology of Herod's Temple*) is undoubtedly the thirty full page plates. He has made use of the reconstruction efforts of the past and is most convincing in his scientific method of treatment. In his excellent commentary on the tractate Middoth, he has assembled information from many sources. We are following him in his conclusions, which we feel will stand until further exploration work has been done. An extensive literature has grown up on Herod's Temple. Besides that of Hollis, the following works in English may be consulted with profit.

Lightfoot, John. The Temple Service and the Prospect of the Temple, translated from the Latin by J. R. Pitman (London: J. F. Dove, 1825).

Davies, T. W. "Herod's Temple," Hastings Dictionary of the Bible, IV, 711–16.

Barton, G. A. "Temple of Herod," Jewish Encyclopedia, XII, 85–89.

Sanday, William. Sacred Sites of the Gospels, pp. 60–67, 106–17. The latter section is written by P. Waterhouse who also collaborated on the reconstruction plan and on the valuable large-sized sectional views.

Kennedy, A. R. "Temple of Herod," Hastings Dictionary of the Bible (single volume), pp. 901–905.

Meistermann, B. "Temple of Jerusalem," Catholic Encyclopedia, XIV, 499–504.

———. New Guide to the Holy Land, pp. 188–213.

Dalman, G. Sacred Sites and Ways, pp. 284–307.

Oesterley, W. O. E. History of Israel, II, 376–78.

Bailey and Kent. History of the Hebrew Commonwealth, pp. 338–42.

Ricciotti, G. The Life of Christ, pp. 44–52.

Finegan, J. Light from the Ancient Past, pp. 243–48.

GENERAL SUMMARY

Herod's Temple was built on Mt. Moriah, the site of Solomon's Temple of 966 B.C. After the Exile, Zorobabel's Temple was built on the same site in 537 B.C. Because this Temple was not destroyed but was replaced by Herod's Temple, both of them are referred to as the Second Temple. At the present time on Mt. Moriah there are two Mohammedan mosques, the Dome of the Rock, built A.D. 698, and the mosque of Aksa, built in 1236. The area known as Haram es Sharif (the Noble Sanctuary) is given as south 929 feet, north 1,041 feet, east 1,556 feet, and west 1,596 feet.[4] As was noted by Sanday,[5] this Haram area is about one-fifth greater than that occupied by Herod's Temple. Herod's northern wall was a little beyond the Platform of the Rock, so that seven acres were added on this side. The other three walls were those of Herod's Temple. The eastern one had been there previous to his time; it did not encroach on the Kedron ravine and extended only as far north as the golden gate, a later addition.[6] The axis of both Herod's temple and that of Zorobabel was due east and west, a five degree change having been made. It may be said that all the courts were rectangular, and especially the places used for ceremonial purposes were regularly square in shape. The length in feet on the outward walls was about as follows: 929 on the south, 990 on the north, 1,186 on the east, and 1,226 on the west. The irregular oblong enclosure veered a little toward the west and sloped from north to south as well as from west to east. More than half of this space was occupied by the sanctified area from which the Gentiles were excluded. This sanctuary was a 750 feet square set due north and south, leaving most space on the south for the Gentiles' Court. Less than half of this sanctuary was enclosed by the Chel (sacred platform) that went round the almost

---

[4] Finegan, *Light from the Ancient Past*, p. 244 note.

[5] *Sacred Sites of the Gospels*, p. 58.

[6] See Hollis, *op. cit.*, plate V, p. 119, where are indicated the later extensions to the north and to the west. See also plate VI, p. 121.

square shaped Court of Israel, which enclosed the Court of the Priests, the altar, and the holy house.

The Court of Israel was situated even with the platform of the Rock on the east side, went beyond it to the south, but did not reach as far as its western or northern boundary.[7] Thus the Nicanor gate was at the east edge of the Platform of the Rock, and it was west of the Women's Court. This latter extended almost to Solomon's Court and may have been a later addition.[8] The Sacred Rock was probably under the holy house and not under the altar.[9] The holy house was built on the highest part of the solid rock, and its foundations did not require much digging.[10] It towered above all the other structures, and behind it to the west was the parapet for defense. Indeed a definite plan for the protection of the holy of holies was followed in the construction of one court within another until the inner sanctum was reached. The series of strong courts constituted a great fortress, and the style of the whole may be said to be "eclectic with the predominance of a quasi classical spirit." [11]

OUTER COURTS AND GATES

The porticoes on three sides of the outer wall were double ones forty-five feet wide. The Royal Porch was much greater in proportion and more magnificent in design than the others, and extended without interruption along the entire length of the southern wall. It was a triple portico, 900 feet long and 105 feet wide. The statement of Josephus that there were 162 columns in this Stoa Basilica has been verified by the calculations of Hollis.[12] Solomon's Porch along the eastern wall received its name because it occupied the site

[7] See Hollis, *op. cit.*, plate XI, p. 165; and plate XXIII, p. 283.

[8] *Ibid.*, plate XIV, p. 183. Cf. A. Buechler, "The Fore Court of Women and the Brass Gate in the Temple," *Jewish Quarterly Review*, X (1897–98), 678–711.

[9] See Hollis, *op. cit.*, pp. 96–99, 104 f.

[10] See sectional elevation of rock in Hollis, *op. cit.*, plate XV, p. 187.

[11] Sanday, *Sacred Sites of the Gospels*, p. 63. "Roman, dignified and solemn, yet certainly not gloomy," is Dalman's characterization, *Sacred Sites and Ways*, p. 277.

[12] *Archaeology of Herod's Temple*, pp. 106 f.

of a porch erected by that king. This eastern porch did not extend
north of the Golden Gate, which was added after Herod's time.[13]

The outer walls were 37 feet high on three sides. The eastern wall,
however, was ten feet lower, permitting a view of the holy house
from Mt. Olivet.[14] The twin gates (Chuldah) [15] were the Double
Gate and the Triple Gate that divided the southern wall into three
equal parts. The name "twin" was applied to them because they had
similar double gangways that went under the Royal Porch without
interrupting this Stoa Basilica. The tunnels emerged into open passages that sloped to the east and to the south and led up by a long
ascent of about 400 feet to the Temple plateau. On the east there
were the Shushan gate [16] near the northeastern corner. About the
middle of the northern wall there was the Todi gate,[17] an underground passage opening on the Kedron ravine; and also on the north,
two bridgelike passages led from the Castle Antonia. On the west
there were toward the north two suburban gates, that of Quiponos
(or Jeconiah) and an unnamed gate behind the holy house.[18] About
the center there was an unnamed gate, now Wilson's Arch; and
further south there was a Lofty gate, at Barclay's gate, that led into
the upper city.[19] Besides, at the southwestern corner there was an approach that led from a roadway over the Tyropoeon Valley by Robinson's Arch.[20]

THE TEMPLE PLATEAU

The size of the plateau on which Herod built the Temple is as
follows: 929 feet on the south, 990 on the north, 1,186 feet on the
east, and 1,226 feet on the west. Hollis reconciles these measure-

[13] Ibid., p. 107.
[14] Ibid., p. 186; see Middoth, II, 4.
[15] Middoth, I, 3; Hollis, op. cit., pp. 244–47.
[16] Probably a memorial to Cyrus or Darius.
[17] According to Middoth, I, 3, not used at all. The underground passage was used by
priests.
[18] See Hollis, op. cit., p. 141; also plates IX (p. 151) and X (p. 161).
[19] This led down across the valley to the upper city.
[20] Hollis, op. cit., pp. 71–76.

ments with the statement of Josephus [21] that the Temple plateau was a square stadium (607 feet), and also with the figure given in Middoth,[22] 750 feet square. He points out that, when allowances are made for the 400 feet of sloping ground on the south and for the width of the porches around the outer wall, the figures arrived at would be 770, 870, 770 and 845 feet. Thus we see that Josephus was trying to give only a rough idea of the size.[23] When he also said that a circuit of the Temple measured six stadia, he was near the truth; for a circuit of the inside of the outer wall including the castle Antonia would amount to six and a quarter or six and a half stadia.[24]

The plateau, we are told, was paved with variegated stones [25] and provided more space for the Gentiles on the south and east than on the north or west. Marking off the sanctified ground reserved for Jews, there was a stone wall in which at intervals there were placed stone slabs with the warning written in Greek and Latin that Gentiles must not enter, under the penalty of death.[26] This was a low stone wall two and a half feet high according to Middoth; [27] but according to Josephus it was a finely executed trellis wall.[28] The explanation of this divergence may lie in the fact that one may have been replaced by the other.

Around the whole court of Israel to which women were forbidden there was a sacred platform fifteen feet wide, called the Chel.[29] This was approached on the south by a continuous flight of steps, possibly fourteen on the eastern part and twelve on the western part. Although this platform touched the walls of the inner court on the east and on the west, yet it was some distance away from the northern wall and the southern wall, leaving room for five broad landing-like

[21] Antiquities, XV, xi, 4.
[22] II, 1; Hollis, op. cit., p. 260.
[23] See Hollis, op. cit., pp. 113–22; plate XV, p. 121.
[24] Jewish War, V, 192 (v, 2). See Hollis, op. cit., pp. 108–13.
[25] Josephus, loc. cit.
[26] One of these has been found. For illustration, see Finegan, Light from the Ancient Past, plate III, p. 229.
[27] Middoth, II, 3; Hollis, op. cit., p. 263.
[28] Jewish War, V, 193 (v, 2). Here the height is four and a half feet.
[29] Middoth, II, 3; Hollis, op. cit., p. 263.

steps and for gate buildings.[30] Animals for slaughter could be made to climb these broad steps. These animals were led in probably through the northern gate of the west wall or the western one of the two gates of the south wall.[31]

INNER COURTS

The Chel did not surround the Women's Court [32] which, as previously said, may have been a later addition. This court required five steps to reach it from the outer court, but was itself ten feet lower than the Court of Israel. The Women's Court was 203 feet square, but in addition on the four corners were roofless chambers sixty feet square.[33] The walls were only eight feet high, but there were balconies or galleries on three sides. There was a gate on the north and one on the south.[34] The eastern entrance was the Great Gate,[35] and on the west leading into the Court of Israel was the famous Nicanor gate of Corinthian brass.[36] This gate was thirty feet high and fifteen feet wide. It had two wickets [37] and had attached chambers, probably under the Chel, for storing musical instruments.

The approach to the Nicanor gate was by a curved flight of fifteen steps, the first ten of which led up to the Chel, the last five spreading across the platform.[38] For the inner court, known as the Court of Israel, there were, besides the Nicanor gate, six others: three equally spaced on the north and three equally spaced on the south. These

[30] See Hollis, *op. cit.*, p. 228.

[31] *Ibid.*, p. 227.

[32] *Ibid.*, pp. 167–92.

[33] Middoth, II, 5; Hollis, *op. cit.*, p. 275 and plate XXIV, p. 291.

[34] Josephus, *Jewish War*, V, 190 (v, 2).

[35] It was seventy-five feet high and was overlaid with massive plates of silver and gold, according to Josephus, *Jewish War*, V, 204 f. (v, 3).

[36] Hollis, *op. cit.*, p. 184, points out that the statement of Middoth, I, 4, and II, 7, on the position of this gate is to be understood from the viewpoint of the Priests' Court; see Josephus, *Jewish War*, V, 240 (v, 3). All the other gates were gilded, but the Nicanor Gate was left in brass because it glittered like gold (Middoth, II, 3b). For the supposed miracle that happened in bringing this gate from Alexandria, see Hollis, *op. cit.*, p. 272.

[37] Middoth, II, 7; Hollis, *op. cit.*, p. 293.

[38] Hollis, *op. cit.*, plate XVII, p. 195.

were really gatehouses thirty-seven and a half feet high, whose names
have come down to us.[39] On the north from west to east there were
the House of the Burning Hearth,[40] the Gate of the Offering,[41] and
the Gate of Song. On the south were the Gate of Kindling, the
Gate of the First-born, and the Water Gate. These gate houses
had chambers, and there were other chambers for storing purposes.[42]
Between the gate houses there were porticoes with exceptionally
beautiful lofty columns.[43] The space allotted for men to worship was
350 feet square, but the ceremonial court was 300 feet square.[44]
There was a part on the north and on the south that seems to have
been considered unconsecrated. The Court of Priests was 264 feet
square, and was within the Court of Israel, a stone parapet two and
one quarter feet high separating the two. For the use of laymen
offering sacrifices, there was a sixteen and a half foot strip all around
the Court of Priests.[45]

Within the Priest's Court were the altar, the holy house, and the
laver between them toward the south.[46] On the north of the altar was
situated the slaughtering shed, thirty-six feet by twelve feet, with its
pillars, tables, and hooks.[47] The altar was forty-eight feet square and
thirteen and a half feet high. A red line marked the upper part from
the lower part, and on the southwest base were two openings for the
blood to flow. As it was not permitted to use steps in ascending the
altar, there was from the south an ascent forty-eight feet long by
by twenty-four feet wide.[48] Also around the altar there was the "surround," seven and a half feet high, with a path one and a half feet
wide which was used by the priest when sprinkling the blood.[49]

[39] Middoth, I, 47; Hollis, op. cit., pp. 247–60. See also Josephus, Jewish War, V, 198
(v, 2).

[40] Moqued, where priests on duty slept. From it an underground passage led out
under the northern gate. See plate XXI, p. 271, in Hollis, op. cit.

[41] Also called the Gate of Women since they came here to present sin offerings.

[42] Middoth, V, 3; Hollis, op. cit., p. 342.

[43] Josephus, Jewish War, V, 200 (v, 2).

[44] Middoth, V, 1 (Hollis, p. 335; also plate XV, p. 188).

[45] Ibid., II, 7 (Hollis, pp. 292, 196 f.).

[46] Ibid., III, 1–3 (Hollis, pp. 307–11).

[47] Ibid., III, 5 (Hollis, p. 312; see also plate XXX, p. 341).

[48] Ibid., III, 3 (Hollis, p. 308).

[49] Ibid., III, 2 (Hollis, pp. 214–16, 306).

THE HOLY HOUSE

Thirty-three feet west of the altar was situated the holy house, consisting of the holy place and the holy of holies, the building being ninety feet long, thirty feet wide, a hundred and fifty feet high.[50] In front of the building was the famous Porch, a development of the Pylon, that extended to form thirty feet wide shoulders. The Porch had an open entrance thirty feet wide and sixty feet high;[51] and twelve steps led up to this entrance.[52] The Porch was gilded, and over it hung the famous gold vine with golden "grape clusters as tall as a man."[53] The doorway leading from the Porch into the holy place was thirty feet high and fifteen feet wide, and it was supplied with two folding doors and two wickets.[54] Inside the holy place, which was sixty feet long by thirty feet wide, there were the altar of incense, the table of show bread on the north, and to the south the seven-branch candlestick.[55] There were no windows in either the holy place or the holy of holies, and the latter was entirely empty.[56] Before the holy of holies hung the two famous veils. The outside one was open only on the north, and the inside one only on the south; and they were a foot and a half apart. The high priest had to walk along the passage between these two veils to enter the holy of holies on the Day of Atonement.[57] The holy house was surrounded on north, south, and west by small apartments, thirty-eight in all, that arose in three tiers.[58] Also behind the holy house in the Western extension of the Court of Israel there was a parapet for defense with places for the

---

[50] *Ibid.*, IV, 6 (Hollis, p. 330; plate XVIII, p. 213).

[51] *Ibid.*, III, 7 (Hollis, p. 318).

[52] Josephus, *Jewish War*, V, 207 (v, 40).

[53] *Ibid.*, V, 210 (v, 4). See Middoth, III, 8 (Hollis, p. 319). According to Josephus (*Jewish War*, V, 212 [v, 4]) the many-colored, rich embroidered veil hung here.

[54] Middoth, IV, 1, 2; (Hollis, pp. 320–24; see plate XXVII, p. 323).

[55] Josephus, *Jewish War*, I, 152 (vii, 67); V, 217 (v, 5); *Antiquities*, XIV, iv, 5; *Against Apion*, II, 106 (8).

[56] *Jewish War*, V, 219 (v, 5).

[57] See Hollis, *op. cit.*, pp. 200–208.

[58] Middoth, IV, 3 (Hollis, p. 326).

storage of food and munitions of war. In this extension court there was a meeting place for the rabbis and their disciples.[59]

The holy house itself rose sixty feet above the surrounding apartments.[60] Thus being narrower on the top than on the lower part, and being broader in the front than at the back, it was considered to have the shape of a lion.[61] It dominated all the other Temple buildings and was seen from many miles, being the object of admiration especially from the upper city on one side and from Mt. Olivet on the other.

[59] Hollis, *op. cit.*, p. 230.
[60] Josephus, *Jewish War*, V, 221 (v, 5).
[61] Middoth, IV, 6 f. (Hollis, pp. 340–43).

The "Eighteen Benedictions"

THE "Eighteen Benedictions" [1] ("Shemoneh Esreh") are referred to as the Prayer (Tefillah). In the beginning these prayers were said apart from the Shema; [2] the Mishnah [3] has regulations for the recital of both. They became part of the daily synagogue service, to be recited morning and afternoon with an additional recitation for Sabbaths and festival days. In course of time they became the essential part of the daily prayers prescribed for every Israelite. The Shema was certainly in use at the time of Christ; but the "Eighteen Benedictions" as a collection must be dated after the destruction of Jerusalem. [4] Kohler [5] thinks they are a product of a gradual growth and development, the first three and the last three being of greater antiquity than the rest.

Following Finkelstein, Dugmore [6] assigns dates for these "Bene-

[1] There are now nineteen, as one was added against Christians and heretics, namely, Number XII. See Grandmaison, *Jésus-Christ*, II, 144 note.

[2] Kohler, *Origins of Synagogue and Church*, p. 65. See also Elbogen, *Der Jüdische Gottesdienst in seiner Geschichtelichen Entwicklung*, pp. 27–60.

[3] *Mishnah*, Berakoth (Benedictions), 1–5.

[4] Lagrange, *Evangile selon S. Luc.*, p. 15. Vincent (*Judaism*, p. 90) gives the date as "perhaps about 80." According to Schechter (*Lectures on Jewish Liturgy*, p. 14), Rabban Gamaliel II, revised number X after A.D. 80, and numbers XIV and XV were also revised. Dugmore says that the Benediction XII was composed by Samuel the Small who presided at Jabneh between A.D. 80 and 110. *The Influence of the Synagogue upon the Divine Office*, p. 3.

[5] *Origins of Synagogue and Church*, pp. 66 f.

[6] *The Influence of the Synagogue on the Divine Office*, pp. 114–27. In our present knowledge the dates assigned to the Benedictions must be considered tentative. Kohler

dictions": numbers I, XV, XVI, and XVII are considreed pre-Machabean; numbers XIV, IX, VIII, and II are assigned to the first and second centuries before Christ; shortly before A.D. 10 arose number VI; between that date and A.D. 40 numbers III, IV, and V were introduced; and after A.D. 40 came VII, X, XI, XVIII, XII, and XIII. Thus it appears that of the "Eighteen Benedictions" only twelve of them were in use in Our Lord's time. The translation of these twelve arranged chronologically is as follows:

1. IV. Grant us, our Father, knowledge from thee, and intelligence and comprehension of thy Law. Blessed be thou, I.H.V.H.,[7] who givest knowledge.

2. XV. Hear, I.H.V.H., our God, the voice of our prayer, and show unto us mercy, for thou art a God of clemency and mercy. Blessed be thou, I.H.V.H., who hearest our prayer.

3. XVI. Be pleased, I.H.V.H., our God, and dwell in Sion, and may thy servants see thee in Jerusalem. Blessed be thou, I.H.V.H., for we serve thee with fear.

4. XVII. We render thanks to thee; (thou art) I.H.V.H., our God and the God of our fathers, for all thy bounties, the favor and the mercies which thou hast accomplished and exercised toward us and toward our fathers before us; and if we say: "our foot is wavering," thy favor, I.H.V.H, strengthens us.
Blessed be thou, I.H.V.H., to whom it is good to render thanks.

5. XIV. Be merciful, I.H.V.H., our God, according to thy many mercies, on Israel, thy people, and on Jerusalem, the city, and on Sion, the dwelling place of thy glory, and on thy Temple and on thy dwelling and on the kingdom of the house of David, the anointed one of thy justice. Blessed be thou, I.H.V.H., God of David, founder of Jerusalem.

6. IX. Bless for us, I.H.V.H., this year, that it may be good in all the kinds of its fruits; and grant a speedy approach of the final year of our deliverance, and give dew and rain on the face of the earth, and fill the world with the treasures of thy bounty and bless the work of our hands. Blessed be thou, I.H.V.H., who blesseth the years.

7. II. Thou art a Hero, casting down those who are raised up, strong, and judging oppressors, living for ages, raising up the dead, bringing the wind

___

states that XIV and XV were originally a prayer for the Temple, but were reconstructed after its destruction A.D. 70. *Origins of the Synagogue and Church,* p. 74.
[7] This is the tetragrammaton for the ineffable name of God, namely, Yahweh.

and making the dew descend, maintaining life, vivifying the dead; with a glance thou makest salvation spring forth for us. Blessed be thou, I.H.V.H., vivifying the dead.

8. VII. Heal us, I.H.V.H., from the wound in our heart and banish from us sorrow and sighing; extend thy healing over all our wounds. Blessed be thou who healest the malady of thy people Israel.

9. VI. Forgive us, our Father, for against thee have we sinned; wash away our iniquities; banish them from thy sight, for thy mercies are many. Blessed be thou, I.H.V.H., always ready to pardon.

10. III. Thou art holy and thy name is fearful, there is no God apart from thee. Blessed art thou, Holy God.

11. I. Blessed be thou, I.H.V.H., our God and the God of our fathers, God of Abraham, God of Isaac, and God of Jacob; God great, heroic, and fearful, God most high, Creator of heaven and earth, our shield and the shield of our fathers, our hope forever and ever. Blessed be thou, I.H.V.H., shield of Abraham.

12. V. Bring us back to thee, I.H.V.H., and we will come; restore our days as of yore.

Blessed be thou, I.H.V.H., who art pleased with repentance.

In Luke 2:49, "House" or "Business"?

IN the only saying that has come down to us from Our Lord's hidden life there is a clear expression of His divine sonship. The same term "My Father" that afterward was made use of to express His unique relationship with God is heard in boyish accents, as His divine sonship is contrasted with the human relationship indicated in His mother's anxious words, "Thy father and I." Also during the public ministry our Savior employed the word "must" to express the necessity of His dedication to His mission. In the first recorded saying this word "must" is also found where it refers to the boy Jesus' necessity of taking part in the preparatory work of the establishment of God's kingdom. This saying is a dedication of the whole life of Our Lord, and it can be ranked alongside the great utterances of the public ministry.

We must regret that in the earliest recorded saying there is a problem which so far scholars have not been able to solve; namely, the interpretation of the ellipsis in the original Greek text. A literal translation of this text is, "I must be in these of My Father," [1] the word "these" being used to represent the plural of the definite article. The employment of ellipses, especially in popular expressions, is found

---

[1] Ἐν τοῖς τοῦ πατρός μου.

in all languages and is permissible when the word or words elided can be readily supplied. Yet it must be said that the meaning of the ellipsis in Luke 2:49 is not clear, as is evidenced by the history of the question.

Arguing against heretics who held that God the Father proclaimed by Our Lord was not the God of the Temple and of the Old Law, certain early Christian writers triumphantly pointed to Jesus' first words in which, according to their contention, He asserted that the Temple belonged to God.[2] These writers seem to have understood that the word "house" was behind the ellipsis in the Lucan text; and yet they could have held a wider view while making these same statements that they aimed against a heretical doctrine. In the early centuries the Syriac versions adopt "house," and the Latin ones imply the view of things or "affairs." In the period that followed that of the Fathers, while the view of "house" continued among certain writers, there grew up a wider view, namely, the Temple, and besides, all the things of the Father. St. Albert the Great in the thirteenth century mentions "temple and business." The European vernacular translations of the sixteenth century nearly all adopted "business." At the opening of the seventeenth century, the question became a subject of erudite controversy that has continued down to the present day. That no settlement has been reached is apparent from the fact that of the two recent English translations, the Revised Standard has "house," whereas the Berkeley version of Verkuyl has "affairs." [3] After the first hundred years of the controversy, two mon-

---

[2] This is done by Origen, St. Cyril of Jerusalem, and St. Epiphanius. Somewhat similar statements are made by St. Augustine and St. Leo. Definitely on the side of the view for "house" must be placed Origen and Didymus; in favor of the view for "business," can be placed St. Ambrose. See my article in *Irish Theol. Quart.*, XVII (1922), 261.

[3] I have attempted to compile a list of the scholars who have taken sides.
The following prefer "house": Fuller, Capellus, Price, Boys, Grotius, Pole, Lamy, Hammond, Fessellus, Vorst, Calmet, Estius, Bos, Keuchin, J. G. Michaelis, J. D. Michaelis, Hoffman, Wetstein, Mazochius, Kunioel, Paulus, Field, Trollope, Keim, Vincent, Bengel, Ebrard, Wendt, Sadler, Meyer, Olshausen, Ellicott, Keil, Hahn, H. Holtzmann, Zahn, B. Weiss, J. Weiss, Loisy, Burton, Box, Montefiori, Baljon, Hamyln, Plummer, Farrar, Walter Bauer, Thayer-Grimm, Moultin-Milligan, A. T. Robertson, Zorell, Lagrange, M. Power, Valensin-Huby, Schantz, Moffatt, Goodspeed, Torrey, Wade, Antoniadis, Spencer, Knox, Dausch, Storr, Easton, Burrows, Sutcliffe.
The following prefer "business": Cornelius a Lapide, Tirinus, Menochius, Buxtorf,

ographs on the question appeared of which we shall give a summary account.

In his congratulatory letter to Christian Schoettgen,[4] Kregel notes the existence of two choruses of scholars on the question of the meaning of the ellipsis in Luke 2:49. In the first were men of great name [5] who, he says, no doubt follow the lead of the Syriac paraphrase in adopting the view of "house." He goes on to give an answer to the four reasons assigned for this opinion.[6] (1) The prophetic utterances, especially that of Mal. 3:1–3, foretelling that the Messiah would come to the Temple. For the fulfillment of this prophecy it was not necessary that Our Lord should stay in the Temple as Samuel did or as the ordinary priest did; it was sufficient that He should come there occasionally as He did during His public life. (2) The genius of the Greek language and the mode of speech. Here are discussed some of the examples brought forward by such scholars as Keuchen, Schmid, and Bos. (3) The testimony of ancient writers such as Origen, Euthymius, and Theophylact. (4) The context and sense of the Lucan passage. Here it is pointed out that Keuchen begs the question by not proving that the boy Jesus must be in the Temple, and by not showing how the parents ought to know that He must be there. Rather, the paraphrase of Cartwright [7] is accepted, for it explains that Our Lord was carrying out the functions of His office when He was found after a diligent search on the part of the parents.

Kregel announces that he follows the second chorus of scholars, namely, these who hold that "business" is to be understood in Jesus'

Edzardo, Cartwright, Schottus, Valchenar, Loesnar, Natalis Alexander, Harduin, Wolf, Wouters, Bornemann, Morus, Ryle, Hofmeister, Patritius, Rosenmuller, Ewald, Oosterzee, Nebe, DeWette, Carr, Bond, Clarke, Stier, Alford, Briggs, O. Holtzmann, Nevin, Wallis, Edersheim, Wood, Nolloth, Bough, Fairbain, Green, Knabenbauer, Fouard, Fillion, Gigot, Seitz, Maas, Simon, Felder, Lebreton, Joüon, Preuschen ("belongings"), Dalman ("things"), V. Rose, Willam, Stoll, Lepin, Verkuyl, A. Power, Weymouth.

[4] M. J. Caspar Kregel, *Epistola Propemptike ad Christianum Schoettgenium*, Lipsiae, 1716.

[5] He mentions nine: Hammond, Grotius, Vorst, Fuller, Cappellus, Keuchen, Fesselius, Bos, and Scultetus, all of the previous century. *Op. cit.*, p. 6.

[6] *Kregal, op. cit.*, pp. 6–10.

[7] *Harmonia Evangeliorum*, p. 83.

saying. Setting forth his reasons,[8] he praised Buxtorf for pointing out that in the saying, place is not opposed to place, but rather business to business. He defends the example of I Tim. 4:15 from the charge of being non-Hellenic. As examples in favor of "business," he offers, I Cor. 7:32, 33, 34; and argues from several texts of St. John that Our Lord as the well-beloved Son always took delight in promptly carrying out the works assigned Him by the Father.

Twenty years after the publication of Kregel's monograph there appeared another on the same subject, taking the opposite side of the argument. This was from the pen of J. G. Michaelis.[9]

In the third chapter [10] of this monograph the author briefly sets forth and answers the three reasons given by those who favor the stand that "business" be understood in Luke 2:49. (1) Christ's sayings according to the Fourth Gospel that He was dedicated to the works of His Father. (2) The example from I Tim. 4:15. (3) The examples and reasons given by J. C. Wolf.[11]

In the fourth chapter,[12] Michaelis accepts and defends the view of the others, who assert that "place" or "house" is to be understood in the Lucan ellipsis. (1) This opinion is safeguarded by great antiquity; one cannot easily find an interpretation as old as the Syriac. (2) There are analogous Greek examples as given by Keuchen, Grotius, Causabon, Price, and Vorst.[13] (3) This interpretation better suits the context: Christ's parents should have known that as the Son set over His own house and as great high priest He should be in the Temple, where He stayed to give a specimen and prelude of His sacerdotal office. To give a further explanation of Our Lord's exercise of His priestly office in the Temple, Michaelis devotes the last two chapters of His work.[14] He concludes that as the high priest

[8] Kregel, *op. cit.*, pp. 10–13.

[9] J. G. Michaelis, *Exercitatio philologico-theologica de Christo onti en tois tou patros, ad Luc.*, 2:49, to be found in *Miscellanea Groningona* (Amstelodami, 1736), 1, fascil. II, 262–82.

[10] *Op. cit.*, pp. 269–71.

[11] *Curae Philolipicae et criticae in quot. S. Evangelia et Acta Apostolorum* (3rd ed., Hamburg, 1739), I, 594 f.

[12] *Op. cit.*, pp. 271–74.

[13] Later (p. 274) he cites Fuller, Hammond, and Calovius.

[14] *Op. cit.*, pp. 274–82.

it was right, proper, and necessary for Our Lord to be occupied in the Temple and in the carrying out of His eternal Father's business.[15]

In 1879 Frederick Field wrote a pamphlet [16] on the ellipsis in Luke 2:49. This learned work brought about the adoption of "house" in the text of the Revised Version, and has had a lasting influence on scholars. I venture to make the following observations, by way of strictures, on this work.

Field speaks of the child Jesus [17] and suggests that the reason for the ellipsis in Our Lord's first words is because St. Luke preferred an expression that was "more trivial and therefore more natural to a child." [18] An Oriental boy of twelve can hardly be considered a child. As to the boy Jesus, the Gospel text states that His understanding and His first saying were beyond the understanding of His parents. Does not this context rule out childish triviality?

When illustrating the usage of the expression "to be in," Field sets aside examples that relate to general pursuit or mode of life.[19] Here he is influenced by the approach from the childishness of Our Lord's saying, for this is the question at issue. That in the saying of the hidden years, the Savior laid down a principle that governed His whole life is what the proponents of the view of "business" maintain.

After examining the two ways of expressing in Greek the reading, "I must be about My Father's business," Field comes to this conclusion. The boy Jesus might have meant this idea while making use of the Gospel words; but if He did, "it is doubtful His hearers would have so understood Him." [20] It happens that it is expressly stated in the Gospel text that the parents did not understand the first recorded words. This failure to understand arose from the fact that Jesus' reply to them applied not only to the present situation of the twelfth-year episode but also to the future years, and indeed was to be fully under-

---

[15] *Op. cit.*, pp. 281 f.
[16] It was afterward incorporated in his work. *Notes on the Translation of the New Testament* (Cambridge University Press, 1899), pp. 50–56.
[17] *Op. cit.*, p. 52.
[18] *Op. cit.*, p. 55.
[19] *Ibid.*, p. 52.
[20] *Ibid.*, p. 53.

stood only in the unfolding of the public life. The fact that those
who knew the twelve-year-old Savior best did not understand His
saying, is a good reason for rejecting the view that it was simply a
childlike pointing to the place where He was to be found. The
parents' failure to understand the saying is also a strong support of
the opinion that it was a pithy saying, in a mysterious way outlining
a life's policy.

In his direct arguments for the view he prefers, Field says that the
plural article with the genitive of person came to be used specially for
a person's house. He cites examples from the classics and the Septuagint for this usage.[21] Of course he does not mean that the plural
article with the genitive of person did not continue to be used for
"affairs," "persons," etc.; in fact, we have evidence for such usages.[22]

Quoting the Syriac, Field contends that it is highly probable that
here we have "the identical sounds that fell from the lips of the
divine Child." [23] Yet Dalman assures us definitely that the Syriac
versions do not give us the certainty that in them can be found "a
first hand knowledge of the very words of our Lord." [24] The Syriac
versions are against the accepted text in other passages of the second
chapter of St. Luke.[25] In certain early Syriac churches it was customary that after the Gospel and sermon were delivered in Greek, a special minister presented the Syriac interpretation.[26] Such a custom
could easily give rise to popular interpretations and simplifications

[21] *Ibid.*, pp. 53 f.

[22] For example: Sophocles, *Trachiniae*, 498. τὰ μὲν θεῶν, "the things or tales of the
gods"; also in Oedipus, col., 351–352 there is an interesting example: τὰ τῆς ὀικοῖ δίαιτης,
"comforts of the house at home." The Papyri τὰ αὐτῶν, Par. 63, "their property" (Cf.
Mayser, *Grammatik der griesch.* Papyri, II, 1, p. 9). New Testament, Mark 8:30 τὰ τοῦ
θεοῦ . . . τὰ τῶν ἀνθρώπων, "matters of God . . . matters of men"; Rom. 16:10, 11,
ἐκ τῶν 'Αριστοβούλου . . . ἐκ τῶν Ναρκίσσου, "from the family of Aristobolus . . . from
from the family of Narcissus." Cf. Josephus, *Life*, 185 (37).

[23] *Ibid.*, p. 53. Field incorrectly claims St. Epiphanius and Theodoret for the side of
"house." St. Epiphanius is not definitely on this side. The quotation from Theodoret is
from a spurious work; see Bardenheuer, *Patrology*, p. 363.

[24] *Jesus-Jeshua*, p. 23.

[25] To cite a few important instances: The Curetonian, Peschitto, and Siniatic give
"age" before "wisdom" in 52. The Curetonian drops "thy father and I" in 48. The
Peschitto and Siniatic add "in spirit" in 40, and have "good hope to men" in 14. The
Sinaitic drops "in the inn" in 7; and in 21 and 22 its reading is a veritable targum.

[26] Cf. Dalman, *Jesus-Jeshua*, p. 10.

that might become stereotyped by usage. Is it possible that this custom occasioned the use of the word "house" in the Syriac versions?

Lastly, in regard to Field's assertion that "if any doubt should remain" an appeal to the context is "sufficient to turn the scale," [27] we shall refer to Kregel's answer to Keuchen given above.

Since no agreement among scholars has been reached about the meaning of the ellipsis in Luke 2:49, it seems that the correct procedure should be to give the second reading in a margin or a footnote. It is regrettable that a non-committal rendering cannot be found to give the proper meaning of the verse.[28]

BIBLIOGRAPHY

In favor of "house"

Bos, Lambert (1717). Greek Ellipses, translated by J. Seager (London, 1830), pp. 94–96, 115 f.

Field, Frederick. Notes on the Translation of the New Testament, (Cambridge University Press, 1899), pp. 50–56.

Fuller, Nicholas. Miscellania sacra (Londini, 1617), Bk. IV, pp. 383–85.

Keuchen, Peter. Annotations in N. T. (Amstelodami, 1689), Bk. I, pp. 119–22.

Lagrange, M. J. Evangile selon S. Luc (Paris, 1921), pp. 96 f.

Michaelis, J. G. Exercitatio philologico-theologica de Christo onti en tois tou patros, ad Luc. 2:49; to be found in Miscellanea Groningona (Amstelodami, 1736) 1, Fascil. II, pp. 262–82.

Price, John. Commentarii in varios N. T. libros (Londini, 1681), p. 218.

Vorst, John. Dissertationum sacrorum (Eliviae, 1662), Bk. III, pp. 150–55.

[27] Op. cit., p. 55.

[28] The difficulty of the ellipsis is increased by the fact that there is in the text another debatable question to be settled first: namely, the expression "to be in a thing." This is a separate problem from that of the meaning of the ellipsis. P. M. Barnard, "Business," Hastings Dict. of Christ and the Gospels, p. 243, says the equivalent of the Lucan text is our colloquialism, "I must be at my father's"; yet this is somewhat taking sides on the question at issue.

In favor of "business"

Bornemann, F. A. Scholia in Lucam (Lipsiae, 1830), pp. 307 f.

Buxtorf, John, (1664). Catalecta philologica-theologica (1707, Basileae), XXVIII, 29.

Joüon, Paul L. Evangile de N.S. Jésus-Christ (Paris, 1930), pp. 307 f.

Kregel, M. J. Epistola Prompemptice ad Chr. Schoettegnium (Lipsiae, 1830), pp. 27–30.

Temple, P. J. "What Is To Be Understood by En Tois?" Irish Theol. Quart., XXII (1922), 248–63.

————. " 'House' or 'Business' in Luke 2:49?" Catho. Bib. Quart., I (1939), 342–52.

Wolf, J. F. Curae Philogicae et Criticae in Quot. s. Evangelia et Acta Apostolorum (3rd ed., Hamburg, 1739), I, 594 f.

Bibliography

I. CHRIST AND THE GOSPELS

Arendzen, J. P. The Gospels, Fact, Myth, or Legend? Edinburgh, 1923.

Becker, Thomas J. The Hidden Life of Christ. New York, 1937.

Bonaventure, St. Life of Our Lord and Savior Jesus Christ. New York, 1881.

Burrows, Eric. The Gospel of the Infancy and Other Biblical Essays (Bellarmine series, VI). London, 1940.

Dausch, P. Die drei ältern Evangelien. Bonn, 1932.

Durand, A. The Childhood of Jesus Christ, according to the Canonical Gospels; translated by Joseph Bruneau. Philadelphia, 1910.

———. Evangile selon saint Matthieu, traduit et commenté, 3rd ed. Paris, 1939.

Fillion, L. C. The Life of Christ, a historical, critical and apologetical exposition; translated by Newton Thompson. St. Louis, 1928.

Graham, Dom Aelred. The Christ of Catholicism, a meditative study. London, 1947.

Grandmaison, Leonce de. Jésus-Christ, sa personne, son message, ses preuves, 11th ed. Paris, 1929.

Knabenbauer, Joseph. Commentarius in quatuor s. Evangelia. Paris, 1892.

———. Commentarius in Evangelium s. Matthaei. Paris, 1922.

Lagrange, M. J. Evangile selon S. Matthieu, 2nd ed. Paris, 1923.

———. The Gospel of Jesus Christ, 2 vols. English translation. London, 1938.

Lagrange, M. J. Evangile selon S. Marc. Paris, 1911. English translation. London, 1930.

———. Evangile selon S. Luc. Paris, 1921.

Lebreton, Jules. The Life and Teaching of Jesus Christ Our Lord, 2 vols. Milwaukee, 1935.

Leen, Edward. In the Likeness of Christ. New York, 1938.

Lepin, Marius. Christ and the Gospel, or Jesus the Messiah and Son of God. Philadelphia, 1910.

Maas, A. J. The Gospel according to St. Matthew, 2nd ed., St. Louis, 1916.

Maldonatus, John. A Commentary on the Holy Gospels. St. Matthew's Gospel, I–XIV; translated by G. Davie. London, 1888.

Prat, Ferdinand. Jésus Christ, sa vie, sa doctrine, son œuvre, 2nd ed., 2 vols. Paris, 1947.

Ricciotti, Guiseppe. The Life of Christ; translated by Alba I. Zizzamia. Milwaukee, 1947.

Schmid, Joseph. Matthäus und Lukas. Eine Untersuchung des Verhältnisses iherer Evangelien, Biblische Studien, v. 23, p. 1–4. Freiburg in Br., 1930.

———. Das Evangelium nach Lukas (Regensburger Neuen Testament) . Regensburg, 1940.

Simon, Hadriano. Praelectiones biblicae, Novum Testamentum, Vol. 1, Evangelia. Turin, 1924.

Stoll, Raymond F. The Gospel according to St. Luke, A study of the Third Gospel with a translation and commentary. New York, 1931.

Thibaut, Rene. Le Sens de l'Home-Dieu, l'Edition Universelle. Brussels, 1946.

Valensin, Albert, et Huby, Joseph. Evangile selon saint Luc, traduit et commenté, 2nd ed. Paris, 1927.

Vonier, Dom Anscar. The Personality of Christ. London, 1915.

The following non-Catholic works may be consulted with profit; their theological views, however, are sometimes incorrect.

Allen, Willoghby C. A Critical and Exegetical Commentary on the Gospel according to St. Matthew, 3rd ed. Edinburgh, 1922.

Cadbury, Henry J. The Making of Luke-Acts. New York, 1927.

Dalman, Gustav. Jesus-Jeshua, Studies in the Gospels. Translation by Paul P. Levertoff. New York, 1929.

————. The Words of Jesus Considered in the Light of Post-biblical Jewish Writings and the Aramaic Language; translated by D. M. Kay. Edinburgh, 1909.

Luce, H. K. The Gospel according to St. Luke. Cambridge, 1936.

MacLachlan, H. St. Luke the Man and His Work. Manchester, 1920.

McNeile, Alan Hugh. The Gospel according to St. Matthew, the Greek text with introduction, notes and indices. London, 1915.

Machen, J. Gresham. The Virgin Birth of Christ. London, 1930.

Manson, William. The Gospel of Luke. New York, 1930.

Orr, James. The Virgin Birth of Christ. New York, 1907.

Plummer, Alfred. An Exegetical Commentary on the Gospel according to Matthew. London, 1909.

————. The Gospel according to St. Luke, 9th ed. New York, 1910.

Robinson, Theodore. The Gospel of Matthew. New York, 1920.

Strack, H.-Billerbeck, P. Kommentar zum Neuen Testament aus Talmud und Midrasch, 2 vols. Munich, 1924.

Sweet, Louis M. The Birth and Infancy of Jesus Christ according to the Gospel Narrative. Philadelphia, 1907.

Thorburn, Thomas J. A Critical Examination of the Evidence of the Doctrine of the Virgin Birth. London, 1908.

Torrey, C. C. Our Translated Gospels, Some of the Evidence. New York, 1936.

Wade, G. W. New Testament History. London, 1922.

II. HISTORICAL AND RELIGIOUS BACKGROUND

Abel, F. M. Geographie de la Palestine, 2 vols., 2nd ed. Paris, 1933.

Allen, Bernard. Augustus Caesar. London, 1937.

Angus, S. The Environment of Early Christianity. New York, 1915.

The Apocrypha and Pseudepigrapha of the Old Testament in English, edited by R. H. Charles. Oxford, 1913.

The Apocryphal New Testament, being the Apocryphal Gospels, Acts, Epistles and Apocalypses; translated by Montague R. James. Oxford, 1945.

Arnold, W. T. The Roman System of Provincial Administration to the Ascension of Constantine the Great, 3rd ed Oxford, 1914.

Augustus, Res Gestae Divi, Monumentum Ancyranum, with translations by F. W. Shipley, Loeb Classical Library. London, 1924.

Bailey, Albert E. and Kent, Charles F. History of the Hebrew Commonwealth, Revised and enlarged edition. New York, 1935.

Bailey, Albert E. On Nazareth Hill. Boston, 1915.

Baker, G. P. Augustus, the Golden Age of Rome. London, 1937.

Bevan, Edwyn. Jerusalem under the High Priests, Five Lectures on the Period between Nehemiah and the New Testament. London, 1904.

Bindley, T. Herbert. Religious Thought in Palestine in the Time of Christ. London, 1931.

Bonsirven, Joseph. On the Ruins of the Temple (Judaism after Our Lord's Time), London, 1931.

———. Le Judaisme Palestinien au temps de Jésus-Christ, sa théologie, 2 vols. Paris, 1935.

Booth, Henry Kendall. The World of Jesus. A Survey of the Background of the Gospels. New York, 1939.

Boylan, Patrick. The Psalms. A Study of the Vulgate Psalter in the Light of the Hebrew Text. Dublin, 1926.

Buchan, John. Augustus. Boston, 1937.

Cablecott, W. Shaw. The Second Temple in Jerusalem. London, 1908.

Callan, C. J., and McHugh, J. A. The Psalms Explained for Priests and Students. New York, 1929.

Carpenter, J. Estlin. Life in Palestine when Jesus Lived. London, 1912.

Charlesworth, M. P. Trade Routes of the Roman Empire, 2nd ed. Cambridge, 1926.

Chapat, Victor. The Roman World, translated by E. A. Parker (History of Civilization). New York, 1928.

Dalman, Gustaf. Sacred Sites and Ways. Studies in the Topography of the Gospels; translated by P. Levertoff. New York, 1935.

———. Arbeit und Sitte in Palästina, Vols. I–VII. Guertersloh, 1928–41.

Delitzsch, Franz. Jewish Artisan Life in the Time of Christ according to the Oldest Sources; translated from the 3rd ed. New York, 1883.

Dio Cassius. Roman History (Loeb Classical Library). London, 1917.

Dugmore, G. W. The Influence of the Synagogue upon the Divine Office. Oxford, 1944.

Eaton, Robert. Sing ye to the Lord. Expositions of fifty Psalms. London, 1915.

Edersheim, Alfred. The Temple, Its Ministry and Services as They Were at the Time of Jesus Christ. New York, 1874.

———. In the Days of Christ; Sketches of Jewish Social Life. New York, 1876.

Elbogen, Ismar. Der Jüdische Gottesdienst in seine geschichtlichen Entwicklung. Leipzig, 1913.

Epstein, Louis M. Marriage Laws in the Bible and the Talmud. Cambridge, 1942.

Feldman, W. M. The Jewish Child, Its History, Folklore, Biology and Sociology. London, 1917.

Festugiere, A. J., and Fabre, P. Le monde Greco-Romain au temps de Notre Seigneur. Paris, 1935.

Firth, John B. Augustus Caesar and the Organization of the Empire. London, 1925.

Frank, Tenney. An Economic Survey of Ancient Rome, 4 vols. Baltimore, 1938.

Glover, T. R. The World of the New Testament. New York, 1931.

Gow, A. S. F. "The Ancient Plough," Journal of Hellenic Studies, XXXIV (1914), 249–75.

Grant, F. C. The Economic Background of the Gospels. Oxford, 1936.

Guignebert, C. The Jewish World in the Time of Jesus; translated from the French by S. H. Hooke. London, 1939.

Herford, Robert Travers. Judaism in the New Testament Period. London, 1928.

Herodotus. History; translated by A. D. Godloy, Loeb Classical Library. London, 1921–24.

Holmes, Thomas Rice. The Architect of the Roman Empire. Oxford, 1928–31.

Homo, Leon. Roman Political Institutions from City to State. History of Civilization. New York, 1929.

Jones, Henry Stuart. The Princeps (Cambridge Ancient History, X, 127–57. Cambridge, 1934).

Josephus. The Works of Josephus; Loeb Classical Library, London, 1926.

Kohler, Kaufman. The Origins of the Synagogue and the Church. Edited with a Biographical Essay. New York, 1929.

Krauss, Samuel. Talmüdische Archaeologie. Leipzig, 1910.

Kretzmann, Paul E. Education among the Jews, from the Earliest Times to the End of the Talmudic Period, 500 A.D. Boston, 1922.

Lagrange, M. J. Le Judaisme avant Jésus-Christ. Paris, 1931.

———. Le Messianisme chez les Juifs. Paris, 1909.

Legendre. The Cradle of the Bible; translated by Dominican Sisters of Portabella Rd. St. Louis, 1909.

Liber Psalmorum, cum canticis Breviarii Romani; new translation with critical and exegetical notes. Rome, 1945.

Lowrie, Walter. Art in the Early Church, with 500 Illustrations. New York, 1947.

Maas, A. J. A Day in the Temple. St. Louis, 1908.

Macgregor, G. H., and Purdy, A. C. Jew and Greek Tutors unto

Christ; the Jewish and Hellenistic Background of the New Testament. New York, 1936.

McClellan, William H. The Psalms, also the Canticles of the Roman Breviary; New English Translation. New York, 1946.

Masterman, Ernest W. G. Studies in Galilee. Chicago, 1909.

Meistermann, Barnabas. Guide to the Holy Land; translated from the new French edition. London, 1923.

Merrill, Selah. Galilee in the Time of Christ. London, 1891.

The Mishnah. Translated from the Hebrew with introduction and explanatory notes by Herbert Danby. Oxford, 1933.

Mommsen, Theodore. The Provinces of the Roman Empire from Caesar to Diocletian, 2 vols.; translated by W. Dickson. London, 1909.

Monigliano, A. Herod of Judaea (Cambridge Ancient History, X, 316–39).

Moore, G. F. Judaism in the First Centuries of the Christian Era, 2 vols. Cambridge, 1937.

Morrison, W. D. The Jews under Roman Rule. London, 1902.

Neil, James. Everyday Life in the Holy Land, with 32 pictures. London, 1912.

———. Palestine Life, Its Light on the Letter of Holy Scripture. London, 1916.

Neufeld, E. Ancient Hebrew Marriage Laws, with special references to general Semitic laws and customs. New York, 1944.

Oesterley, W. O. E. A History of Israel. Vol. II, from the fall of Jerusalem, 586 B.C. to the Bar-Kokhba Revolt, A.D. 135. Oxford, 1932.

———. A Fresh Approach to the Psalms. New York, 1937.

———. The Psalms translated with text, critical and exegetical notes. London, 1939.

Pliny. National History, 2 vols. Text and translation by H. Rockham, Loeb Classical Library. London, 1938.

Radin, Max. The Jews among the Greeks and Romans. Philadelphia, 1915.

Rostovtzeff, M. A History of the Ancient World; translated from the Russian by J. D. Duff, Vol. II. Oxford, 1928.

―――. The Social and Economic History of the Hellenistic World, 3 vols. Oxford, 1941.

Schauss, Hayyim. The Jewish Festivals from Their Beginnings to Our Own Day; translated by S. Jaffe. Cincinnati, 1938.

Schechter, Abraham. Lectures on Jewish Liturgy. Philadelphia, 1933.

Schürer, Emil. Geschichte des Jüdischen Volkes im Zeitalter Jesu Christi. Leipzig, 1901–1906. (English translation: A History of the Jewish People in the Time of Jesus Christ, 5 vols. New York, 1885.)

Smith, George Adam. Jerusalem, the Topography, Economics and History from Earliest Times to 70 A.D., 2 vols. London, 1908.

―――. The Historical Geography of the Holy Land with eight maps, 25th ed. London, 1931.

Smith, William W. The Student's Historical Geography of the Holy Land, revised edition. New York, 1924.

Strabo. Geography, Loeb Classical Library. London, 1918.

Suetonius. The Lives of the Caesars, Loeb Classical Library, Vol. I. London, 1915.

Tacitus. The Histories; text and translation by C. H. Moore, Loeb Classical Library. London, 1925.

―――. The Annals; translated by J. Jackson, Loeb Classical Library. London, 1931.

Tarn, W. W. Hellenistic Civilization, 2nd ed. London, 1936.

Van Dyke, Henry. Out-of-Doors in the Holy Land. New York, 1908.

Vincent, A. Judaism; translated by James D. Scanlon. London, 1934.

Winspear, Alban D. Augustus and the Reconstruction of the Roman Empire. Madison, 1935.

Wolfson, H. A. Philo, Foundations of Religious Philosophy in Judaism, Christianity and Islam, 2 vols. Harvard, 1947.

Zorell, Francisco. Psalterium ex Hebraeo Latinum. Rome, 1928.

III. SPECIAL WORKS

Albright, W. "The names 'Nazareth' and 'Nazoraean,' " Journal of Biblical Lit., LXV (1946), 397–401.

——. The Archaeology of Palestine. London, 1949.

Ambrose, St. Concerning Virgins. Nicene and Post Nicene Fathers (2nd ser.), X, 363–87.

Aytoun, R. A. "The Ten Lucan Hymns of the Nativity in Their Original Language," Journal of Theological Studies, XVIII (1917), 274–88.

Bagarri, B. Il Santuario della Visitazione ad Ain Karim (Montana Judaeae); with 40 plates. Jerusalem, 1948.

Bartmann, Bernhard. Christus ein Gegner des Marienkultust. Freiburg im Br., 1909.

Beckermann, C. "Et Nomen Virginis Mariae (Lk. 1:27)," Verbum Domini, I (1921), 130–36.

Blakiston, Alban. John Baptist and His Relation to Jesus. London, 1912.

Buzy, D. Saint Jean-Baptiste, études historiques et critiques. Paris, 1922.

Cobern, Camden M. The New Archeological Discoveries, 9th ed. New York, 1929.

Collins, John J. "Our Lady's Vow of Virginity (Lk. 1:34)," Catholic Biblical Quarterly, V (1943), 371–80.

Corbishley, T. "The Date of Our Lord's Birth," Scripture, I (1946), 77–80.

Deissmann, Adolf. Light from the Ancient East; translated by L. Strachan, London, 1927.

Eusebius, Pamphili. Ecclesiastical History; translated by Kirsopp Lake, Loeb Classical Library, 2 vols. London, 1926–32.

Faber, Frederick W. Bethlehem. Baltimore, 1860.

Feuillet, A. "Le signe proposé à Achaz et 'Emmanuel,' " Recherches de science religieuse, XXX (1940), 129–51.

Filas, F. L. The Man Nearest to Christ. Milwaukee, 1945.

Finegan, Jack. Light from the Ancient East, the Archaeological Background of the Hebrew-Christian Religion. Princeton, 1946.

Gaechter, Paul. "The Chronology from Mary's Betrothal to the Birth of Christ," Theological Studies, II (1941), 145–70, and 347–68.

Guyot, Gilmore H. "Balaam," Catholic Biblical Quarterly, II (1940), 330–40; III (1941), 235–42.

Hetzenauer, Michael. De genealogia Jesu Christi. Rome, 1922.

Hoepfl, Hildebrand. "Nonne, hic est Fabri Filius?" Biblica, IV (1923), 41–55.

Hollis, F. J. The Archaeology of Herod's Temple, with a commentary on the tractate "Middoth," with thirty plans. London, 1934.

Holzmeister, Urbanus. Chronologia vitae Christi. Rome, 1933.

Jerome, St. The Perpetual Virginity of Blessed Mary, against Helvidius; Nicene and Post-Nicene Fathers, 2nd ser., VI, 335–46.

———. Homilia de Nativitate, in Anecdota Maredsolama seu monumenta Ecclesiasticae Antiquitatis, III, 895. Maredsoli et Oxoniae, 1895.

Johnston, T. A. "The Census of Quirinius," Irish Ecclesiastical Record, XXXVIII (1931), 225–43.

Joüon, Paul. "Le costume d'Elie et celui de Jean Baptiste," Biblica, XVI (1935), 74–81.

———. "L'Annonciation," Luc. 1:26–38. Nouvelle Revue Theologique, LXVI (1939), 793–98.

Lessius, Ven. Leonard. The Names of God and Meditative Summaries of the Divine Perfections; translated by T. Campbell. New York, 1912.

Liddon, H. P. The Magnificat, Sermons in St. Paul's, 4th ed., 1895. London, 1889.

Lightfoot, John. The Temple Service and the Prospect of the Temple, edited by J. R. Pitman. London, 1825.

Lyonnet, S. "Quoniam Nazareaus Vocabitur" (Matt. 2:23); L' Interpretation de S. Jerome, Biblica, XXV (1944), 196–206.

Maas, A. J. "The Blessed Virgin Mary," Catholic Encyclopedia, XV, 464–72.

McClellan, William H. "El Gibbor," Catholic Biblical Quarterly, VI (1944), 276–88.

McCown, C. C. "The Destiny of Population in Ancient Palestine," Journal of Biblical Literature, LXVI (1947), 425–36.

McGarry, William J. "A Fundamental Principle in Mariology," Theological Studies, I (1940), 396–411; III (1941), 35–42.

Nolle, Lambert "Old Testament Laws of Inheritance and St. Luke's Genealogy of Christ," Scripture, II (1947), 38–42.

Ogg, George. The Chronology of the Public Ministry of Jesus. Cambridge, 1940.

O'Herlihy, Donal J. "The Year of the Crucifixion," Catholic Biblical Quarterly, VIII (1946), 298–305.

Olivier, M. J. The Friendships of Jesus; translated by M. C. Keogh, 4th ed. St. Louis, 1923.

O'Rourke, John Joseph. "Census Quirinii," Verbum Domini, I (1921), 206–11.

O'Shea, Denis. The Holy Family. Dublin, 1944.

Power, E. "The Emmanuel Prophecy of Isaias," Irish Ecclesiastical Record, LXX (1948), 289–304.

Power, M. "John, 2:20 and the Date of the Crucifixion," Biblica, XI (1928), 257–88.

Ramsay, William M. The Bearing of Recent Discovery on the Trustworthiness of the New Testament. London, 1915.

Ruffini, E. Chronologia Veteris et Novi Testamenti in aeram nostram collata. Rome, 1924.

———. Introductio in S. Scripturam. Rome, 1905.

Saller, S. J. Discoveries at St. John's, Ein Karim. Jerusalem, 1944.

Sanday, William. Sacred Sites of the Gospels, with illustrations, maps and plans. Oxford, 1908.

Schaefer, Aloys. The Mother of Jesus in Holy Scripture, Biblical-Theological Addresses; translated from German by F. Brossart. New York, 1913.

Scheeben, M. J. Mariology, 2 vols.; translated by T. Geuckers. St. Louis, 1946.

Sutcliffe, Edmund F. "St. Joseph's Trade, an Enquiry into the Evidence," Irish Theol. Quart., X (1915), 179–201.

———. "The Divine Carpenter," Irish Theological Quarterly, XI (1916), 147–63.

———. A Two Year Public Ministry Defended. London, 1938.

Temple, P. J. The Boyhood Consciousness of Christ, a critical examination of Luke 2: 49. New York, 1922.

Torrey, Charles C. The Apocryphal Literature, a Brief Introduction. New Haven, 1946.

Vaccari, A. "De signo Immanuelis, Isaias, VII," Verbum Domini, XVII (1937), 45–49; 75–81.

Vincent, H., and Abel, F. M. Bethlehem, Le Sanctuaire de la Nativité. Paris, 1914.

Vosté, J. M. De Synopticorum mutua Relatione et Dependentia. Rome, 1928.

———. De Conceptione Virginali Jesu Christi. Accedunt, I, De Duplici Genealogia; II, De Fratribus Domini. Rome, 1933.

———. De Baptismo, Tentatione et Transfiguratione Jesu. Rome, 1934.

Index